Applied Mathematics and Information Sciences

Applied Mathematics and Information Sciences

Editors

Cheng-Shian Lin
Chien-Chang Chen
Yi-Hsien Wang

Basel • Beijing • Wuhan • Barcelona • Belgrade • Novi Sad • Cluj • Manchester

Editors
Cheng-Shian Lin
Tamkang University
New Taipei City
Taiwan

Chien-Chang Chen
Tamkang University
New Taipei City
Taiwan

Yi-Hsien Wang
Chinese Culture University
Taipei
Taiwan

Editorial Office
MDPI
St. Alban-Anlage 66
4052 Basel, Switzerland

This is a reprint of articles from the Special Issue published online in the open access journal *Axioms* (ISSN 2075-1680) (available at: https://www.mdpi.com/journal/axioms/special_issues/applied_mathematics_and_information_sciences).

For citation purposes, cite each article independently as indicated on the article page online and as indicated below:

Lastname, A.A.; Lastname, B.B. Article Title. *Journal Name* **Year**, *Volume Number*, Page Range.

ISBN 978-3-7258-0125-1 (Hbk)
ISBN 978-3-7258-0126-8 (PDF)
doi.org/10.3390/books978-3-7258-0126-8

© 2024 by the authors. Articles in this book are Open Access and distributed under the Creative Commons Attribution (CC BY) license. The book as a whole is distributed by MDPI under the terms and conditions of the Creative Commons Attribution-NonCommercial-NoDerivs (CC BY-NC-ND) license.

Contents

About the Editors vii

Chien-Chih Lin, Yuan Chung Lee, Chien-Jen Su and Pei-Ling Lin
The Influence of Hedge, Arbitrage, and After-Hours Trading on the Holding Returns of TAIEX Futures
Reprinted from: *Axioms* 2023, 12, 71, doi:10.3390/axioms12010071 1

Radi Romansky
Mathematical Model Investigation of a Technological Structure for Personal Data Protection
Reprinted from: *Axioms* 2023, 12, 102, doi:10.3390/axioms12020102 14

José Alfredo Soto-Álvarez, Iván Cruz-Aceves, Arturo Hernández-Aguirre, Martha Alicia Hernández-González, Luis Miguel López-Montero and Sergio Eduardo Solorio-Meza
Numerical Modeling of the Major Temporal Arcade Using BUMDA and Jacobi Polynomials
Reprinted from: *Axioms* 2023, 12, 137, doi:10.3390/axioms12020137 25

Yeh-Cheng Yang, Wen-Sheng Shieh and Chun-Yueh Lin
Applying the Fuzzy BWM to Determine the Cryptocurrency Trading System under Uncertain Decision Process
Reprinted from: *Axioms* 2023, 12, 209, doi:10.3390/axioms12020209 37

Marcos dos Santos, Carlos Francisco Simões Gomes, Enderson Luiz Pereira Júnior, Miguel Ângelo Lellis Moreira, Igor Pinheiro de Araújo Costa and Luiz Paulo Fávero
Proposal for Mathematical and Parallel Computing Modeling as a Decision Support System for Actuarial Sciences
Reprinted from: *Axioms* 2023, 12, 251, doi:10.3390/axioms12030251 59

Marcin Pietrasik and Marek Z. Reformat
Probabilistic Coarsening for Knowledge Graph Embeddings
Reprinted from: *Axioms* 2023, 12, 275, doi:10.3390/axioms12030275 84

Pablo Dorta-González
A Multiple Linear Regression Analysis to Measure the Journal Contribution to the Social Attention of Research
Reprinted from: *Axioms* 2023, 12, 337, doi:10.3390/axioms12040337 97

Miguel-Angel Gil-Rios, Claire Chalopin, Ivan Cruz-Aceves, Juan-Manuel Lopez-Hernandez, Martha-Alicia Hernandez-Gonzalez and Sergio-Eduardo Solorio-Meza
Automatic Classification of Coronary Stenosis Using Feature Selection and a Hybrid Evolutionary Algorithm
Reprinted from: *Axioms* 2023, 12, 462, doi:10.3390/axioms12050462 110

Stelian Alaci, Ioan Doroftei, Florina-Carmen Ciornei, Ionut-Cristian Romanu, Toma-Marian Ciocirlan and Mariana-Catalina Ciornei
Proposed Shaft Coupling Based on RPRRR Mechanism: Positional Analysis and Consequences
Reprinted from: *Axioms* 2023, 12, 707, doi:10.3390/axioms12070707 128

Rakesh P. Badoni, Jayakrushna Sahoo, Shwetabh Srivastava, Mukesh Mann, D. K.Gupta, Swati Verma, et al.
An Exploration and Exploitation-Based Metaheuristic Approach for University Course Timetabling Problems
Reprinted from: *Axioms* 2023, 12, 720, doi:10.3390/axioms12080720 150

About the Editors

Cheng-Shian Lin

Cheng-Shian Lin received their Ph.D. degree from the Department of Computer Science at National Chung Cheng University, Taiwan, in 2015. He is currently an Assistant Professor at the Department of Computer Science and Information Engineering, Tamkang University, Taiwan. His research interests include secret image sharing, image/video forgery detection, and deep learning.

Chien-Chang Chen

Chien-Chang Chen received their B.S. degree from the Department of Computer and Information Science at Tunghai University, Taiwan, in 1991, and their Ph.D. degree from the Department of Computer Science at National Tsing Hua University, Taiwan, in 1999. He is currently a Professor at the Department of Computer Science and Information Engineering, Tamkang University, Taiwan. His research interests include secret image sharing, image watermarking, image forgery detection, and texture analysis.

Yi-Hsien Wang

Yi-Hsien Wang received their Ph.D. degree from the Graduate School of Management at Ming Chuan University, Taiwan, in 2006. He is currently a Professor at the Department of Department of Banking and Finance, Chinese Culture University, Taiwan. His research interests include applied economics, time series, financial management, and decision science.

Article

The Influence of Hedge, Arbitrage, and After-Hours Trading on the Holding Returns of TAIEX Futures

Chien-Chih Lin *, Yuan Chung Lee, Chien-Jen Su and Pei-Ling Lin

Department of Banking and Finance, Tamkang University, New Taipei City 25137, Taiwan
* Correspondence: 139714@mail.tku.edu.tw; Tel.: +886-22621-5656-2992; Fax: +886-22621-4755

Abstract: This study points out a new explanation of the non-trading effect of financial derivatives from the perspective of hedging demand. We examine the influence of hedging demand on the non-trading effect of TAIEX (Taiwan Stock Exchange Capitalization Weighted Stock Index) Futures. By dividing the sample period into trading period and non-trading period and testing the difference between the risk premiums in these two intervals, we find that there is a non-trading effect in TAIEX Futures, which means that the holding returns of TAIEX Futures in the non-trading period are higher than those in the trading period. By estimating a dummy-regression model, the evidence shows that when the VIX (Taiwan Index Option Volatility Index) indicator is relatively high, the non-trading effect will be more significant, indicating that the non-trading effect may come from investors' hedging needs. In addition, it is found that when the futures index is higher than the spot index, the non-trading effect becomes less obvious. The possible reason is that when there is a positive spread in index futures, investors will expect a bull market, thus reducing the hedging demand of index futures. In the end, we find that the liquidity in the after-hours trading session is poor, resulting in high hedging costs, and forcing investors to hedge during the regular trading period. Therefore, the after-hours trading of TAIEX Futures fails to reduce the non-trading effect.

Keywords: non-trading effect; hedging demand; arbitrage; after-hour trading

Citation: Lin, C.-C.; Lee, Y.C.; Su, C.-J.; Lin, P.-L. The Influence of Hedge, Arbitrage, and After-Hours Trading on the Holding Returns of TAIEX Futures. *Axioms* **2023**, *12*, 71. https://doi.org/10.3390/axioms12010071

Academic Editor: Boualem Djehiche

Received: 13 December 2022
Revised: 5 January 2023
Accepted: 6 January 2023
Published: 10 January 2023

Copyright: © 2023 by the authors. Licensee MDPI, Basel, Switzerland. This article is an open access article distributed under the terms and conditions of the Creative Commons Attribution (CC BY) license (https:// creativecommons.org/licenses/by/ 4.0/).

1. Introduction

The so-called non-trading effect generally refers to the considerable difference between the return rate of financial products during the regular trading period and the non-trading period. The relevant research on non-trading effects can be traced back to the 1930s when Ref. [1] first discovered that there were non-trading effects in the stock market, and many scholars began to seek answers and to try to explain the reasons for its occurrence. Some scholars, such as [2–4], showed that the difference in liquidity is the main reason for the difference in holding returns during trading and non-trading periods. In addition, some scholars show that the difference between investors' trading behavior before the weekend and other trading days may be the reason for the non-trading effect. For example, Ref. [5] found that investors' reactions to earnings announcements are related to the timing of the announcement. Investors' reaction to market information on Friday is significantly different from that of normal trading days (see [6,7]), resulting in significantly longer reaction times for the stock prices of companies that make announcements on Friday. On the other hand, Ref. [8] showed that investors are accustomed to shorting stocks on normal trading days and that choosing to close their positions before weekends becomes the main reason for the non-trading effect. In addition, some scholars indicate that the non-trading effect may be caused by the robustness of the measurement method. For example, Refs. [9,10] proved that the size of the sample or the difference of the regression model may affect the significance of the non-trading effect. However, Ref. [11] conducted research on international data and found that non-trading effects exist in many countries in the world and that there is no clear correlation between the causes and the size of the sample or the difference in regression models.

Most of the research on the trading period and non-trading period focuses on the difference of the return rate in these two periods; however, there is also some research on the difference in the volatility. For example, Ref. [12] found that the volatility is significantly greater than that during non-trading periods, the main reason being that the speed of information flow is not the same during trading periods and non-trading periods. Ref. [13] analyzed the influence of non-trading periods on the forecasting ability of volatility and found that volatility significantly declined on the first trading day after holidays and weekends.

The research objects of the above literature all focus the stock market, and we found that only a few studies discuss the non-trading effects of financial derivatives. Related literature, such as [14], took options as the research object and found that the difference in risk during trading and non-trading periods was the main reason for non-trading effects; Ref. [15] examined the influence of informed trades on options trading around holidays.

The trading purpose of stocks is mainly for investment or speculation, while derivatives can not only expand investment benefits, but also have hedging functions. Therefore, the differences in the price behavior of derivatives during trading and non-trading periods may not be the same as of stocks. Most of the previous literature focuses on the stock market, and only a few studies discuss the non-trading effect of financial derivatives. The trading purpose of financial derivatives is quite different from that of the stocks, especially for hedging, which makes it necessary for us to analyze how hedging demand influences the non-trading effect.

The main aim of this study is to get new knowledge about the non-trading effect of financial derivatives from the perspective of hedging demand. In fact, many studies have found that the hedging demand of futures has a significant impact on the futures holding return. For example, Ref. [16] found that hedging pressure has a significant effect on futures returns; Refs. [17,18] introduced hedging demand into the model and re-derived the equilibrium price of futures. In scientific research, the efficient market hypothesis holds that when new information comes into the market, it is immediately reflected in the prices in financial markets. However, the existence of the non-trading effect shows that the financial market is inefficient. The reason for the market inefficiency needs to be discovered, especially for the financial derivatives markets which have been receiving little attention. Since investors may sell futures due to hedging demand before long holidays or weekends, we reasonably suspect that hedging demand may be one of the reasons that causes the non-trading effect of financial derivatives. As far as the author understands, there is no literature to explain the non-trading effects through hedging demand. Therefore, in this study, we take TAIEX Futures as the research object to discuss the relationship between hedging demand and non-trading effects. We hypothesize that when the market risk is high, investors will have a greater incentive to sell futures for hedging before the long holiday, resulting in the low futures price and high holding rate of return in non-trading period and leading to the non-trading effects. In this study, we found that the holding rate of TAIEX Futures in the non-trading range is higher than that in the general trading range, and the gap between the two tends to become larger when the market volatility increases. The evidence suggests that non-trading effects of financial derivatives can be explained by hedging demand. In addition, we also found that when the positive spread widens, the non-trading effect will become less significant. The evidence shows that the non-trading effect is weaker in a bull market. A possible explanation is that when the positive spread widens, investors are optimistic about the future market trend, so the demand for hedging will be low, leading to non-trading effects being less pronounced. Moreover, we found that the after-hours trading of TAIEX Futures did not reduce the non-trading effect. The reason may be that the lack of liquidity in the after-hours trading session increased the cost of hedging, forcing the hedgers to hedge during the regular trading period. As a result, although TAIEX Futures has after-hours trading measures, it has not yet been able to reduce the non-trading effect. Finally, comparing with [14], which showed that option mispricing during periods of market closure causes the option returns to be lower over non-trading periods, we show in this study that, to the contrary, hedging demand has a positive impact on the returns of financial derivatives over non-trading periods. In other words, when the market risk rises, the returns of financial derivatives could be higher over non-trading periods. Our results point out that the non-trading effect in the financial derivatives markets should be analyzed according to the level of market risk.

This paper is divided into five sections, in addition to the introduction of this section. The following sections are arranged as follows. Section 2 presents the methodology and data, while Section 3 discusses the empirical results. Section 4 discusses the findings and their implications. The Section 5 is the conclusion of this paper.

2. Methodology and Data

This study applies TAIEX Futures as the research object. The sample is daily data for six futures contracts (including three consecutive months from the current month, plus three consecutive quarterly monthly contracts in March, June, September, and December) per day from 21 July 1998 to 14 January 2019. We refer to the definition of [14] to calculate the risk premium of hedging background index futures. First, we assume that the investor holds a long position in futures and shorts the spot for hedging, and thus the change in the value of the portfolio is

$$(F_t - F_{t-1}) - (S_t - S_{t-1}) \tag{1}$$

where F_t is the price of TAIEX Futures on t day, and S_t is the spot index on t day. In Equation (1), we assume that we can short the spot index. Although we cannot directly short the spot index in practice, theoretically, we can short the spot index by shorting the market portfolio or index ETF. In addition, the same as [14], we assume that the spot short position can generate cash inflow $S_t - S_{t-1}$, which can be reinvested in risk-free assets to earn a risk-free interest rate. Therefore, the return on investment (since shorting stocks in Taiwan does not generate immediate cash inflows, the definition of return in Equation (2) implies that investors hold market portfolios for a long time) can be expressed as

$$\frac{(F_t - F_{t-1}) - (S_t - S_{t-1}) + S_{t-1} r_{t-1} ND_{t-1,t}}{F_{t-1}/L} \tag{2}$$

where r_{t-1} represents the risk-free interest rate from day $t-1$ to day t (the frequency of interest calculation is calculated on a daily basis), $ND_{t-1,t}$ represents the number of days between day $t-1$ and day t. In addition, L represents the leverage multiple. Unlike the holding rate of return of options, which is calculated through the change of the premium, futures trading does not need to pay the premium, but trades through the margin. Investors can adjust the leverage ratio through margin. For example, on 19 August 2019, the closing price of the futures contract due to expire in August is 10,484 points, so its contract value is 10,484 × 200 = $2,096,800. If an investor deposits a margin equal to the contract value ($2,096,800) in the margin account, the investor's trading leverage is 1, which means that the risk of investing in the index futures with a margin equal to the contract value is actually the same as the risk of investing in spot indices. If the investor only deposits half of the contract value in the margin account ($1,048,400), then the trading leverage is 2, which means that the risk of investing in TAIEX Futures is twice that of investing in the spot index. The L in Equation (2) is used to measure the leverage ratio of futures trading. The higher the value of L, the higher the leverage ratio becomes.

Extending Equation (2), we define the risk premium of the hedged position in the index futures as follows:

$$\frac{(F_t - F_{t-1}) - (S_t - S_{t-1}) + S_{t-1} r_{t-1} ND_{t-1,t}}{F_{t-1}/L} - r_{t-1} ND_{t-1,t}$$
$$= \left[L \frac{F_t - F_{t-1}}{F_{t-1}} - r_{t-1} ND_{t-1,t} \right] - L \frac{S_{t-1}}{F_{t-1}} \left(\frac{S_t - S_{t-1}}{S_{t-1}} - r_{t-1} ND_{t-1,t} \right) \tag{3}$$

Equation (3) divides the risk premium of the hedged position in the index futures into two parts; the part in brackets is the risk premium of the unhedged position in the index futures, and the minus sign is the hedged position the impact caused. In addition, in Formula (3), $(S_t - S_{t-1})/S_{t-1}$ should be regarded as the actual rate of return of the spot index rather than the percentage change of the price. The spot index will deduct the value of the spot index to reflect the impact of the ex-dividend. Simply calculating the percentage of change will underestimate the risk aversion effect and overestimate the risk premium of the index futures hedging position. Therefore, in this study, we will regard $(S_t - S_{t-1})/S_{t-1}$ as the actual rate of return of the spot index from day $t-1$ to day t. Finally, the futures pricing theory proves that the futures price will be affected by the spot price and the risk-free interest rate, so Equation (3) can also be regarded as the TAIEX Futures rate of return after excluding the influence of the spot index and the risk-free interest rate (in this article, we use the one-year deposit rate as the risk-free rate). The descriptive statistics of the risk premium of the hedged position in the index futures are presented in Table 1. In order to compare the impact of the spot index on the index futures rate of return, Table 1 also presents the risk premium of the non-hedged positions. In addition, to understand whether the leverage ratio has an impact on our research results, four kinds of leverage ratios are considered in Table 1 and subsequent analyses: $L = 1, 5, 10$, and 20. The data in Table 1 show that the risk premiums of both the hedged and non-hedged positions of TAIEX Futures are positive. Since the spot index has a long-term positive return, the risk premium of the non-hedged position will be slightly higher than that of the hedged position, and the gap between the two will increase with the increase of the leverage ratio. For example, when the leverage ratio is 1, the position that has not been hedged is only 0.0051% higher than the position that has been hedged. As the leverage ratio increases, the gap between the hedged position and the non-hedged position also increases. When the leverage increases to 20, the gap between the two comes to 0.1033%.

Table 1. Descriptive statistics.

		Mean%	Std.%	Skewness	Kurtosis
$L = 1$	Non-hedged	0.0171	1.5400	−0.0729	4.1220
	Hedged	0.0120	0.5861	0.1684	15.3029
$L = 5$	Non-hedged	0.1186	7.6984	−0.0672	4.1224
	Hedged	0.0928	2.9296	0.1852	15.2911
$L = 10$	Non-hedged	0.2455	15.3965	−0.0665	4.1224
	Hedged	0.1938	5.8591	0.1873	15.2892
$L = 20$	Non-hedged	0.4992	30.7926	−0.0662	4.1225
	Hedged	0.3959	11.7182	0.1883	15.2882

Sample size: 25,515. Sample period: 21 July 1998~14 January 2019.

Next, we observe that adopting a hedging strategy will significantly reduce the risk of the TAIEX Futures. The data in Table 1 show that through hedging, the standard deviation falls by about 62%. These data are close to those of [14] for stock call options. The results of [14] show that through delta hedging, the standard deviation of call options risk premium decreases by about 63%. Then we observe that the skewness coefficients of the hedged positions are higher than those of the non-hedged positions. This result is also consistent with [14]. In addition, we also observe that the skewness of the non-hedged positions is all negative, while the skewness of the hedged positions is all positive, which is slightly different from [14]. Ref. [14] found that the skewness of both the hedged and non-hedged positions of options are positive, which shows that futures have a higher probability of falling sharply than options. Finally, in the part of the kurtosis, we observe that the risk premium of the index futures has a thick tail, and the thick tail of the hedged position is more obvious. Ref. [14] also have similar findings, but our data show that the kurtosis of the hedged position of the TAIEX Futures is about 15.3, while Ref. [14] show that the kurtosis of call options is as high as 51.3. The main reason is that since the options uses delta hedging, ignoring the convexity of the option price, the hedging effect is less effective when the stock price rises and falls sharply, and so it is prone to the thick tail phenomenon.

These observations illustrate that futures and options are still quite different in nature, which underscores the need for this study.

3. Empirical Results

In this section, we will analyze the difference between the holding rate of index futures during the trading period and the non-trading period after excluding the impact of the spot index and the risk-free interest rate. The non-trading period referred to in this study is the same as the definition in [14], which means the interval between two consecutive closing prices is more than one day. The most important non-trading period is weekends, and a small part of the data for non-trading periods comes from national holidays.

3.1. Non-Trading Effects

First, we divide the sample period into trading period and non-trading period and test the difference between the risk premiums in these two intervals. The results are presented in Table 2. First, we observe that the average risk premium of the spot index during the trading period is 0.0268%, which is significantly positive at the 90% confidence level, and −0.074% during the non-trading period, which is significantly negative at the 90% confidence level. Similar to [14], we define the difference between the two as the non-trading effect. The data in Table 2 show that the non-trading effect of the spot index is −0.101%, which is significantly negative at the 95% confidence level. Following on, we observe that when the leverage ratio is 1, the average risk premium of the non-hedged position of the TAIEX Futures during the trading period is 0.0355%, which is significantly positive at the 99% confidence level, and −0.049% during the non-trading period, which is significantly negative at the 95% confidence level, and the non-trading effect is −0.084%, which is significantly negative at the 99% confidence level. In addition, we found that the non-hedged position of the TAIEX Futures and the spot index have the same positive and negative values in the data during the trading period and the non-trading period, whether it is the risk premium or the non-trading effect. However, the risk premium and non-trading effect of the non-hedged positions of the TAIEX Futures are more significant than those of the spot index. Furthermore, when the leverage multiples are 5, 10, and 20, the same phenomenon is also observed. Next, we consider the hedged position, when the leverage ratio is 1 and the average risk premium is 0.0078% and 0.0268% during the trading period and non-trading period, respectively. The results of the t-test show that these two values are significantly greater than 0. Since the risk premium in the non-trading period is higher than that in the trading period, the non-trading effect is positive and significant by the t-test. The non-trading effects of the three portfolios with leverage ratios of 5, 10, and 20 are also significantly positive, and the higher the leverage ratio is, the higher the significance becomes.

Table 2. The difference between the risk premium in trading periods and non-trading periods.

		Trading Period %	Non-Trading Period %	Non-Trading Effect %
Spot index		0.0268 (1.300 *)	−0.074 (−1.588 *)	−0.101 (−1.978 **)
$L = 1$	Non-hedged	0.0355 (3.399 ***)	−0.049 (−2.083 **)	−0.084 (−3.289 ***)
	Hedged	0.0078 (1.883 **)	0.0268 (3.394 ***)	0.0190 (2.130 **)
$L = 5$	Non-hedged	0.2007 (3.838 ***)	−0.175 (−1.494 *)	−0.375 (−2.931 ***)
	Hedged	0.062 (2.992 ***)	0.2029 (5.147 ***)	0.1409 (3.164 ***)
$L = 10$	Non-hedged	0.4071 (3.894 ***)	−0.332 (−1.421 *)	−0.739 (−2.886 ***)
	Hedged	0.1297 (3.131 ***)	0.423 (5.367 ***)	0.2933 (3.294 ***)
$L = 20$	Non-hedged	0.8199 (3.921 ***)	−0.647 (-1.384 *)	−1.467 (−2.864 ***)
	Hedged	0.2652 (3.200 ***)	0.8632 (5.476 ***)	0.598 (3.358 ***)

Sample size of trading period: 19,939. Sample size of non-trading period: 5579. Sample period: 21 July 1998~14 January 2019. * 90% confidence level, ** 95% confidence level, *** 99% confidence level.

From Table 2, we observe that the non-trading effect of non-hedged positions is negative, due to the influence of the spot index. After excluding the influence of the spot index, we find that the hedged positions have a positive non-trading effect. In the following sections, we will focus on the hedged positions. The main reason is that the hedged positions have eliminated the influence of the spot; therefore, the reason for its non-trading effect comes from other factors than the spot index. We are curious about what causes such a significant non-trading effect after excluding the impact of the spot index. Furthermore, Ref. [14] found that the non-trading effect of stock options in the hedged position was negative, while we found in Table 2 that the non-trading effect of the hedged position in TAIEX Futures was positive. These differences also make it necessary for us to analyze the hedged positions.

3.2. Hedging and Non-Trading Effects

When the market risk is high, investors' demand for hedging also increases, so they hedge by selling futures. Especially before weekends or long holidays, investors will have stronger demand for hedging, causing futures to be oversold before weekends or long holidays, resulting in low futures prices and a high holding rate of return in the non-trading period and leading to the non-trading effects. Base on the above inference, we have the following hypothesis:

Hypothesis 1. *The higher the hedging demand, the higher the non-trading effect.*

Ref. [19] took the S&P500 index as the research object and found that when the implied volatility of the index is higher, investors will have higher hedging needs. To test the hypothesis, we use the Taiwan Index VIX to measure the market's hedging demand. The Taiwan Index VIX is the implied volatility derived from the market price of the Taiwan Index option to reflect market investors' expectations of the volatility of the stock market in the short term in the future. If the VIX of the Taiwan index decreases, it means that investors believe that the volatility of the Taiwan stock market will slow down in the future, so the demand for hedging will also decrease. On the contrary, if the VIX of the Taiwan index rises, it means that the investors believe that the volatility of the Taiwan stock market will increase significantly in the future, so the demand for hedging will also increase.

The Taiwan Futures Exchange has been compiling the Taiwan Index VIX since 2006. The largest sample collected in this study was 3000 daily data from 1 December 2006 to 14 January 2019. During our sample period, the average VIX was 19.74, the highest was 60.41, the lowest was 7.82, and the median was 17.08, slightly lower than the average; the skewness of 1.38 shows that the distribution of VIX is slightly skewed to the right. Please refer to Table 3 for relevant data.

Table 3. Descriptive statistics of VIX.

Mean	Median	Std.	Kurtosis	Skewness	Min.	Max.
19.74	17.08	8.55	1.85	1.38	7.82	60.41

Sample size: 3000. Sample period: 1 December 2006~14 January 2019.

We divide the sample into the following two sub-samples with Med (the median of the VIX) as the critical value:

Sub-sample I: {Risk premium of hedged positions in TAIEX Futures | VIX > Med}   (4)

Sub-sample II: {Risk premium of hedged positions in TAIEX Futures | VIX < Med}   (5)

Sub-sample I collects the data when the value of VIX is higher than the median, so the market has a high demand for hedging during the period covered by this sample. The relative sub-sample II is the sample that represents the market with low hedging demand. During the sample period from 1 December 2006 to 14 January 2019, we collected a total of 14,968 pieces of data, with 7484 pieces of data in each of the two sub-samples.

We test the differences between the two sub-samples during the trading period and the non-trading period, respectively, and the results are presented in Table 4. The result shows that when the leverage ratio is 1, the risk premium of sub-sample I is 0.0125% and 0.0547% during the trading period and non-trading period, respectively, and in sub-sample II it is 0.0164% and 0.0353%, respectively. These four values are significantly positive at the 99% confidence level. We observe significant non-trading effects for both sub-samples. When the VIX is higher than the median, the non-trading effect is 0.0422%, and when the VIX is lower than the median, the non-trading effect drops to 0.0189%. Since we define the difference between these two data as the effect gap, the effect gap is 0.0233% when the leverage is 1. A positive effect gap indicates that the VIX has a positive correlation with the non-trading effect, which means that the higher the VIX, the more obvious the non-trading effect. To test whether the effect gap is significant we consider the following regression model:

$$ER_t = \beta_1 D_{1,t} + \beta_2 D_{2,t} + \beta_3 D_{3,t} + \beta_4 D_{4,t} + \varepsilon_t \quad (6)$$

where ER_t is the risk premium of the hedged position in the TAIEX Futures on day t, and $D_{i,t}$ is the dummy variable defined as follows:

$$D_{1,t} = \begin{cases} 1, & t \in \text{trading period and } VIX_t > \text{Med} \\ 0, & \text{others} \end{cases} \quad (7)$$

$$D_{2,t} = \begin{cases} 1, & t \in \text{trading period and } VIX_t < \text{Med} \\ 0, & \text{others} \end{cases} \quad (8)$$

$$D_{3,t} = \begin{cases} 1, & t \in \text{nontrading period and } VIX_t > \text{Med} \\ 0, & \text{others} \end{cases} \quad (9)$$

$$D_{4,t} = \begin{cases} 1, & t \in \text{nontrading period and } VIX_t < \text{Med} \\ 0, & \text{others} \end{cases} \quad (10)$$

Table 4. The influence of volatility on non-trading effect.

		Trading Period %	Non-Trading Period %	Non-Trading Effect %	Effect Gap %
$L = 1$	VIX > Med	0.0125 (2.516 ***)	0.0547 (5.824 ***)	0.0422 (3.970 ***)	0.0233 (1.549 *)
	VIX < Med	0.0164 (3.294 ***)	0.0353 (3.756 ***)	0.0189 (1.779 **)	
$L = 5$	VIX > Med	0.0789 (3.146 ***)	0.3252 (6.867 ***)	0.2463 (4.597 ***)	0.1204 (1.590 *)
	VIX < Med	0.0958 (6.354 ***)	0.2217 (4.679 ***)	0.1259 (2.348 **)	
$L = 10$	VIX > Med	0.1618 (3.220 ***)	0.6634 (6.987 ***)	0.5015 (4.669 ***)	0.2420 (1.593 *)
	VIX < Med	0.1951 (3.883 ***)	0.4547 (4.787 ***)	0.2595 (2.416 ***)	
$L = 20$	VIX > Med	0.3278 (3.257 ***)	1.3397 (7.046 ***)	1.012 (4.704 ***)	0.4851 (1.594 *)
	VIX < Med	0.3937 (3.912 ***)	0.9207 (4.841 ***)	0.5269 (2.449 ***)	

Sample size of trading period: 11,694. Sample size of non-trading period: 3275. Sample period: 1 December 2006~14 January 2019. * 90% confidence level, ** 95% confidence level, *** 99% confidence level.

Let $\hat{\beta}_i$ be the estimator of the regression coefficient, then $\hat{\beta}_3 - \hat{\beta}_1$ represents the non-trading effect when the VIX is higher than the median, which is 0.0422% from Table 4, and $\hat{\beta}_4 - \hat{\beta}_2$ represents the non-trading effect when the VIX is lower than the median, which is 0.0189%. The effect gap is $(\hat{\beta}_3 - \hat{\beta}_1) - (\hat{\beta}_4 - \hat{\beta}_2)$ = 0.0233%. To confirm our hypothesis, we do the following hypothesis tests:

$$H_0 : (\beta_3 - \beta_1) - (\beta_4 - \beta_2) = 0$$

$$H_1 : (\beta_3 - \beta_1) - (\beta_4 - \beta_2) > 0$$

The t-statistic of the test results is 1.549, rejecting H_0 at the 90% confidence level. The results show that the non-trading effect when the VIX is higher than the median is significantly higher than the non-trading effect when the VIX is below the median. This phenomenon can also be seen when the leverage ratio is 5, 10, and 20, and when the leverage ratio is higher, the effect gap is larger.

From Table 4, we observe that the higher the market volatility, the more obvious the non-trading effect. The result supports our hypothesis, because when the market is more volatile, investors' demand for hedging also increases (refer to [19] for related literature), and hence the incentives for investors to sell futures for hedging are relatively high. Especially before weekends or long holidays, investors will have stronger hedging needs, causing the oversold phenomenon of TAIEX Futures before weekends or long holidays, resulting in TAIEX Futures having a higher holding return during non-trading periods and thereby bringing about more serious non-trading effects.

3.3. Arbitrage and Non-Trading Effects

In addition to hedging, the purpose of futures trading may also be arbitrage. In this section, we will analyze the impact of arbitrage on non-trading effects. First, we define the price spread between futures and spot as the settlement price of the futures minus the closing price of the spot. When the futures price is higher than the spot price, the spread is positive, which is the so-called positive spread. At this time, investors can make arbitrage by buying the spot and selling the futures. On the contrary, when the futures price is lower than the spot price, the spread is negative, which is the so-called backward spread. At this time, investors can make arbitrage by selling the spot and buying futures. In this section, we will only test whether the arbitrage behavior of investors by selling futures and buying spot is related to non-trading effects when the TAIEX Futures are in contango. The main reason is that the ex-dividend peak season for Taiwan stocks is in July, August, and September. At this time, the index will "evaporate" due to ex-dividend, resulting in a serious backwardation. Using the backwardation to measure the market's arbitrage demand may be distorted. On the other hand, since the closing time of the Taiwan index is 13:30 and the closing time of the futures index is 13:45, there is a 15-min time difference between the futures settlement price and the spot closing price. As a result, the spread we define is not the spread that investors can arbitrage but is only an indicator used to measure the demand for arbitrage.

During our sample period, there are 6926 transactions in the market with positive spreads, of which 5430 transactions belong to the trading period, accounting for 78%, and 1496 transactions belong to the non-trading period, accounting for 22%. The descriptive statistics for the positive spread are shown in Table 5. The data show that the average positive spread is 75.20, while the median is only 34.31, which was about half the average. The maximum value of 1015.39 occurred on 14 April 2000, when the settlement price of the TAIEX Futures expiring in December was 10,390 and the spot closing price was 9374.61. Since we exclude the data of negative spreads, the distribution of spreads tends to be skewed to the right, and the skewness coefficient of 2.79 shows a right-skewed characteristic. Finally, the kurtosis coefficient of 11.04 shows that the spread is prone to large changes.

Table 5. Descriptive statistics of positive spreads.

Mean	Median	Std.	Kurtosis	Skewness	Min.	Max.
75.20	34.31	102.08	11.04	2.79	0.01	1015.39

Sample size: 6926. Sample period: 21 July 1998~14 January 2019.

We divide the data when the market is in a contango into two sub-samples during the trading period and the non-trading period and test the difference between the two sub-samples of the TAIEX Futures risk premium. The results are presented in Table 6. When the index is in a contango, investors have incentives to sell futures and buy spot for arbitrage trading. Therefore, when the positive spread widens, theoretically, futures may be oversold due to arbitrage demand, resulting in low futures prices and high holding returns. Through the data in Table 6, we observe that when the market is in a contango, the risk premium of the hedged position in the TAIEX Futures is relatively high. For example, when the leverage ratio is 1, the average risk premium during the trading period is 0.1532%, which is only 0.0078% compared to the average risk premium of the hedged positions in Table 2. On the other hand, when the market is in a positive spread, the risk premium during the non-trading period is 0.1502%, which is also higher than the average risk premium of 0.0268% in the non-trading period for the hedged positions in Table 2. Next, we observe that there is no significant difference in the risk premium between trading and non-trading periods when the market is in a contango. For example, when the leverage ratio is 1, the risk premiums during the trading period and the non-trading period are 0.1532% and 0.1502%, respectively, and the non-trading effect is −0.003%. The difference between the two is found to be insignificant by the t-test. When the leverage multiples are 5, 10, and 20, although the non-trading effect turns positive, it is still insignificant. This result shows that the non-trading effect becomes less obvious when the TAIEX Futures is in a contango.

Table 6. The difference between the risk premium in trading periods and non-trading periods when the market is in a contango.

	Trading Period %	Non-Trading Period %	Non-Trading Effect %
$L = 1$	0.1532 (19.535 ***)	0.1502 (10.056 ***)	−0.003 (−0.134)
$L = 5$	0.8016 (20.248 ***)	0.8530 (11.308 ***)	0.0514 (0.470)
$L = 10$	1.6122 (20.305 ***)	1.7315 (11.445 ***)	0.1193 (0.546)
$L = 20$	3.2334 (20.331 ***)	3.4884 (11.512 ***)	0.2551 (0.584)

Sample size of trading period: 5430. Sample size of non-trading period: 1496. Sample period: 21 July 1998~14 January 2019. *** 99% confidence level.

To analyze whether the magnitude of the spread is related to the non-trading effect, we adopt the analysis method similar to Table 4 and use the median of the positive spread as the cut-off point to divide the data into the following two sub-samples:

Sub-sample III: {Risk Premium of Hedged Positions | Positive spread > Med} (11)

Sub-sample IV: {Risk Premium of Hedged Positions | Positive spread < Med} (12)

Both sub-sample III and sub-sample IV collect the risk premium of the hedged positions when the TAIEX Futures are in a contango. Among them, the positive spread of sub-sample III is higher than the median, so the arbitrage demand covered by this sample is relatively high. Sub-sample IV, on the other hand, has a positive spread lower than the median, so the need for arbitrage is relatively low. We test the differences between the two sub-samples during the trading period and the non-trading period, respectively, and the results are presented in Table 7. First of all, when the leverage is 1, the average risk premium of sub-sample III is 0.2041% and 0.1868% during the trading period and non-trading period, respectively, while the average risk premium of sub-sample IV is 0.1020% and 0.1144% during the trading period and non-trading period, respectively. These four values are all significantly positive at the 99% confidence level. Then we observe that the non-trading effects of sub-sample III and sub-sample IV are −0.0170% and 0.0124%, respectively. The t-test shows that the non-trading effects of these two sub-samples are not significant. These results are consistent with Table 6, showing that when the index is in a positive spread, the non-trading effect will become less obvious. The effect gap is negative, which means that the larger the positive spread, the lower the non-trading effect. Using the method in Table 4 for testing, it is found that the effect gap is not significant. Roughly, the data in Table 7 shows that the expansion of the positive spread will reduce the non-trading effect; however, the test results show that the effect is not significant. The same phenomenon can also be observed at leverages of 5, 10, and 20.

Table 7. The influence of contango on non-trading effect.

		Trading Period %	Non-Trading Period %	Non-Trading Effect %	Effect Gap %
$L = 1$	Contango > Med	0.2041 (18.440 ***)	0.1868 (8.8066 ***)	−0.0170 (−0.490)	−0.0290
	Contango < Med	0.1020 (9.197 ***)	0.1144 (5.444 ***)	0.0124 (0.479)	(−0.880)
$L = 5$	Contango > Med	1.0674 (19.102 ***)	1.0652 (9.948 ***)	−0.0020 (−0.0125)	−0.1120
	Contango < Med	0.5346 (9.545 ***)	0.6448 (6.078 ***)	0.1100 (0.855)	(−0.6604)
$L = 10$	Contango > Med	2.1465 (19.154 ***)	2.163 (10.073 ***)	0.0167 (0.0473)	−0.2159
	Contango < Med	1.0752 (9.574 ***)	1.3078 (6.147 ***)	0.2326 (0.903)	(−0.632)
$L = 20$	Contango > Med	4.3048 (19.178 ***)	4.3592 (10.134 ***)	0.0545 (0.0772)	0.4227 (0.618)
	Contango < Med	2.1566 (9.587 ***)	2.6338 (6.181 ***)	0.4772 (0.926)	

Sample size of trading period: 5430. Sample size of non-trading period: 1496. Sample period: 21 July 1998~14 January 2019. *** 99% confidence level.

In the previous section, we found that the non-trading effect may come from investors' hedging demand. Specifically, the higher (lower) investors' hedging demand, the more serious (moderate) the non-trading effect. On the other hand, Ref. [20] found that when the hedgers are extremely optimistic, they tend to simply hold spot positions instead of hedging. Combining the result of the previous section with the results of [20], we have the following inferences: When the index is in a contango, investors are optimistic about the future trend of the market and expect larger gains, resulting in relatively low demand for hedging. Since the need for hedging decreases, the non-trading effect will be moderated at this time based on the results of the previous section. The results in Table 7 (the widening of the positive spread has the effect of reducing the non-trading effect) support our inferences made above.

3.4. After-Hours Trading and Non-Trading Effects

In recent years, there have been frequent black swan events and frequent fluctuations in financial markets around the world. In order to provide market participants with better trading and hedging channels, the Futures Exchange, on considering the practices of major international markets, plans for the domestic futures market to conduct after-hours trading after the general trading hours. Starting from 15 May 2017, the trading hours of TAIEX Futures have been extended from the original 5 h to 19 h, and the after-hours trading hours will start from 15:00 to 5:00 am the next day. After-hours trading allows investors to hedge after hours. Therefore, the sell orders of TAIEX Futures generated by the demand for hedging before weekends or long holidays may be dispersed to after-hours, thus slowing down the non-trading effect. In this section, we will analyze the impact of after-hours trading measures on TAIEX Futures on non-trading effects.

We divide the data into two sub-samples with after-hours trading and no after-hours trading and test the differences in risk premiums between the two sub-samples during trading and non-trading periods. The results are presented in Table 8. It has been shown that the non-trading effect is greater when there is after-hours trading than when there is no after-hours trading, although the difference between the two is not significant. For example, when the leverage is 1, when there is after-hours trading, the risk premium during the regular trading period is 0.0146%, during the non-trading period is 0.0509%, and the non-trading effect is 0.0363%. On the other hand, when there is no after-hours trading, the risk premium is 0.0072% during the trading period, increases to 0.0245% during the non-trading period, and the non-trading effect is 0.0173%. The non-trading effect with after-hours trading is 0.0190% higher than that without after-hours trading, but the test results show that the difference is not significant.

Table 8. The influence of after-hours trading on non-trading effect.

	After-Hours Trading	Trading Period %	Non-Trading Period %	Non-Trading Effect %	Effect Gap %
$L = 1$	With	0.0146 (1.041)	0.0509 (1.933 *)	0.0363 (2.759 ***)	0.0190
	Without	0.0072 (1.657 *)	0.0245 (2.993 ***)	0.0173 (1.787 **)	(0.0001)
$L = 5$	With	0.0847 (1.191)	0.2904 (2.180 **)	0.2057 (3.134 ***)	0.0711
	Without	0.0598 (2.742 ***)	0.1945 (4.709 ***)	0.1346 (2.783 ***)	(0.0001)
$L = 10$	With	0.1722 (1.208)	0.5896 (2.207 **)	0.4174 (3.166 ***)	0.1362
	Without	0.1257 (2.872 ***)	0.407 (4.914 ***)	0.2813 (2.907 ***)	(0.0001)
$L = 20$	With	0.3472 (1.216)	1.1881 (2.220 **)	0.8409 (3.188 ***)	0.2663
	Without	0.2574 (2.936 ***)	0.832 (5.015 ***)	0.5746 (2.970 ***)	(0.0001)

Sample size with after-hours trading: 2207. Sample size without after-hours trading: 23,308. Sample period: 21 July 1998~14 January 2019. * 90% confidence level, ** 95% confidence level, *** 99% confidence level.

After the opening of after-hours trading, some of the hedging demand for TAIEX Futures before the weekend or long holiday should be scattered after the market. Intuitively, the oversold phenomenon of TAIEX Futures should be slowed down before weekends or long holidays, thus reducing the non-trading effect. However, our empirical results found that the non-trading effect did not decrease, but increased slightly, although the increase was not significant. We believe that such a phenomenon may be related to hedging costs. During our sample period, the after-hours trading volume of TAIEX Futures only accounted for 17.61% of the trading volume during normal trading hours. In addition, the after-hours trading time is as long as 14 h, while the general trading time is only 5 h. Calculated per unit hour, the hourly after-hours trading volume only accounts for 6.29% of the hourly trading volume during the regular trading period. The liquidity of post-trading is obviously not as good as during normal trading. Insufficient liquidity will increase the cost of hedging (for related literature refer to [21]), thus reducing the hedging demand of the hedgers (Ref. [22] show that insufficient liquidity will lead to an increase in the cost of hedging and thus reduce the hedging demand of investors) forcing the hedgers to conduct hedging transactions during the regular trading period. As a result, although there are after-hours trading measures in the TAIEX Futures, the measures have not been able to effectively reduce the non-trading effect.

4. Discussion

In this study we analyze the difference between the holding returns of index futures during the trading period and the non-trading period. First, excluding the influence of the spot index, we find that the futures index has a significant non-trading effect. In comparison to [14], who found that the non-trading effect of stock options was negative, we found a positive non-trading effect in TAIEX Futures.

Second, we hypothesize that the higher hedging demand leads to a higher non-trading effect. By testing a dummy-regression model, the evidence shows that the higher the value of the VIX indicator, the more significant the non-trading effect will be. The evidence indicates that the non-trading effect may come from investors' hedging needs and hence supports our hypothesis. On the other hand, Ref. [23] show that when the VIX is high, investors tend to reduce the volatility of their portfolios. In order to do so, investors sell high-risk stocks in favor of low-risk stocks, and as a result the return of low-risk stocks is increased. In this study, we have similar results: when the VIX is high, investors tend to sell futures before weekends or long holidays to reduce the market risk, which leads to the return of hedged positions being relatively high during the non-trading periods.

Third, using the price spread between futures and spot to measure the demand for arbitrage, we found that the larger the positive spread, the lower the non-trading effect. The possible reason is that when the index is in a contango, the market is usually in a bullish pattern. Therefore, the investors' hedging needs before weekends or long holidays will drop significantly, and thus, the non-trading effect is reduced. The result can also be interpreted from the perspective of [20], who shows that when the hedgers are extremely optimistic, they tend to simply hold spot positions instead of hedging.

Finally, dividing the data into two sub-samples with after-hours trading and no after-hours trading and testing the differences in risk premiums between the two sub-samples, we found that the non-trading effect with after-hours trading is higher than that without after-hours trading, although the evidence is not significant. Since the liquidity in after-hours session is worse, forcing the hedgers to hedge during the regular trading period, as a result the non-trading effects have no significant difference between the sub-samples with and without after-hours trading.

5. Conclusions

The main aim of this study is to get new knowledge about the non-trading effect of financial derivatives from the perspective of hedging demand. We hypothesize that when the market fluctuates more, investors' demand for hedging also increases, so they hedge by selling futures. Especially before weekends or long holidays, investors will have a stronger demand for hedging, causing futures to be oversold before weekends or long holidays, resulting in higher holding returns of futures during non-trading periods, leading to a positive non-trading effect. Our empirical results show that when the market volatility is higher, the non-trading effect is more obvious, which shows that the non-trading effect may come from investors' hedging demand and supports our hypothesis. The evidence also points out a new explanation of the non-trading effect of financial derivatives from the perspective of hedging demand and indicates that the non-trading effect in the financial derivatives markets should be analyzed according to the level of market risk.

Moreover, we found that the after-hours trading measures of the TAIEX Futures have not been able to reduce the non-trading effect. The possible reason is that the liquidity of the after-hours trading of the TAIEX Futures is not as good as that of the regular trading period, resulting in high after-hours hedging costs, forcing hedgers to hedge during normal trading periods, thus failing to effectively reduce non-trading effects. The result indicates the lack of liquidity of TAIEX Futures during the after-hours trading period. To increase the liquidity, we suggest the Futures Exchange should increase the incentive by, for example, decreasing the transaction cost for after-hours trading.

Theoretically, the persistently higher holding returns of the TAIEX Futures in the non-trading period appear to be evidence of market inefficiency. Practically, one simple trading strategy based on this information would be for an individual to long the index futures and short sell the spot index before weekends or long holidays when the VIX is relatively high, and then close out the strategy on the following trading day. In the future research, it is tempting to create trading strategies base on our findings and analyze the profitability of the strategies.

Finally, in this research we collect a large sample which covers a period over two decades. Even though the tested result is reliable base on the large sample size, reform of the trading system or an evolution of market structure may change the research results. These limitations are also suggested for future research. On the other hand, the result of the study is only confined to the index futures, and further research is needed to extend the scope of the study to other derivatives such as warrants and options.

Author Contributions: Conceptualization, C.-C.L.; methodology, Y.C.L.; software, C.-J.S.; validation, P.-L.L.; formal analysis, C.-C.L.; investigation, C.-C.L.; data curation, C.-C.L.; writing—original draft preparation, C.-C.L.; writing—review and editing, C.-C.L. All authors have read and agreed to the published version of the manuscript.

Funding: This research received no external funding.

Data Availability Statement: The data supporting reported results can be found from TEJ (Taiwan Economic Journal). For the link: http://schplus.tej.com.tw/ (accessed on 12 December 2022).

Conflicts of Interest: The authors declare no conflict of interest.

References

1. Fields, M.J. Stock Prices: A Problem in Verification. *J. Bus. Univ. Chic.* **1931**, *4*, 415. [CrossRef]
2. French, K.R. Stock returns and the weekend effect. *J. Financ. Econ.* **1980**, *8*, 55–69. [CrossRef]
3. Longstaff, F.A. How Much Can Market Ability Affect Security Values? *J. Financ.* **1995**, *50*, 1767–1774. [CrossRef]
4. Kelly, M.A.; Clark, S.P. Returns in trading versus non-trading hours: The difference is day and night. *J. Asset Manag.* **2011**, *12*, 132–145. [CrossRef]
5. Dellavigna, S.; Pollet, J.M. Investor Inattention and Friday Earnings Announcements. *J. Financ.* **2009**, *64*, 709–749. [CrossRef]
6. Singal, V.; Tayal, J. Risky Short Positions and investor sentiment: Evidence from the Weekend Effect in Futures Markets. *J. Futures Mark.* **2019**, *40*, 479–500. [CrossRef]
7. Kim, K.; Ryu, D. Sentiment changes and the Monday effect. *Financ. Res. Lett.* **2022**, *47*, 102709. [CrossRef]
8. Chen, H.; Singal, V. Role of Speculative Short Sales in Price Formation: The Case of the Weekend Effect. *J. Financ.* **2003**, *58*, 685–705. [CrossRef]
9. Connolly, R.A. An Examination of the Robustness of the Weekend Effect. *J. Financ. Quant. Anal.* **1989**, *24*, 133. [CrossRef]
10. Connolly, R.A. A posterior odds analysis of the weekend effect. *J. Econ.* **1991**, *49*, 51–104. [CrossRef]
11. Chang, E.C.; Pinegar, J.M.; Ravichandran, R. International Evidence on the Robustness of the Day-of-the-Week Effect. *J. Financ. Quant. Anal.* **1993**, *28*, 497. [CrossRef]
12. French, K.R.; Roll, R. Stock return variances: The arrival of information and the reaction of traders. *J. Financ. Econ.* **1986**, *17*, 5–26. [CrossRef]
13. Diaz-Mendoza, A.-C.; Pardo, A. Holidays, Weekends and Range-Based Volatility. *N. Am. J. Econ. Financ.* **2020**, *52*, 101124. [CrossRef]
14. Jones, C.S.; Shemesh, J. Option Mispricing around Nontrading Periods. *J. Financ.* **2018**, *73*, 861–900. [CrossRef]
15. Ryu, D.; Yu, J. Informed options trading around holidays. *J. Futures Mark.* **2021**, *41*, 658–685. [CrossRef]
16. De Roon, F.A.; Nijman, T.E.; Veld, C. Hedging Pressure Effects in Futures Markets. *J. Financ.* **2000**, *55*, 1437–1456. [CrossRef]
17. Stoll, H.R. Commodity Futures and Spot Price Determination and Hedging in Capital Market Equilibrium. *J. Financ. Quant. Anal.* **1979**, *14*, 873. [CrossRef]
18. Hirshleifer, D. Determinants of Hedging and Risk Premia in Commodity Futures Markets. *J. Financ. Quant. Anal.* **1989**, *24*, 313. [CrossRef]
19. Pan, M.-S.; Liu, Y.A.; Roth, H.J. Volatility and trading demands in stock index futures. *J. Futures Mark.* **2003**, *23*, 399–414. [CrossRef]
20. Wang, C. Investor Sentiment and Return Predictability in Agricultural Futures Markets. *J. Futures Mark.* **2001**, *21*, 929–952. [CrossRef]
21. Barclay, M.J.; Hendershott, T. Price Discovery and Trading After Hours. *Rev. Financ. Stud.* **2003**, *16*, 1041–1073. [CrossRef]
22. Arias, J.; Brorsen, B.; Harri, A. Optimal Hedging under Nonlinear Borrowing cost, Progressive Tax Rates, and Liquidity Constraints. *J. Futures Mark.* **2000**, *20*, 375–396. [CrossRef]
23. Qadan, M.; Kliger, D.; Chen, N. Idiosyncratic Volatility, the VIX and Stock Returns. *Am. J. Econ. Financ.* **2019**, *47*, 431–441. [CrossRef]

Disclaimer/Publisher's Note: The statements, opinions and data contained in all publications are solely those of the individual author(s) and contributor(s) and not of MDPI and/or the editor(s). MDPI and/or the editor(s) disclaim responsibility for any injury to people or property resulting from any ideas, methods, instructions or products referred to in the content.

Article

Mathematical Model Investigation of a Technological Structure for Personal Data Protection

Radi Romansky

Department of Informatics, Faculty of Applied Mathematics and Informatics, Technical University of Sofia, 1000 Sofia, Bulgaria; rrom@tu-sofia.bg

Abstract: The contemporary digital age is characterized by the massive use of different information technologies and services in the cloud. This raises the following question: "Are personal data processed correctly in global environments?" It is known that there are many requirements that the Data Controller must perform. For this reason, this article presents a point of view for transferring some activities for personal data processing from a traditional system to a cloud environment. The main goal is to investigate the differences between the two versions of data processing. To achieve this goal, a preliminary deterministic formalization of the two cases using a Data Flow Diagram is made. The second phase is the organization of a mathematical (stochastic) model investigation on the basis of a Markov chain apparatus. Analytical models are designed, and their solutions are determined. The final probabilities for important states are determined based on an analytical calculation, and the higher values for the traditional version are defined for data processing in registers ("2": access for write/read −0.353; "3": personal data updating −0.212). The investigation of the situations based on cloud computing determines the increasing probability to be "2". Discussion of the obtained assessment based on a graphical presentation of the analytical results is presented, which permits us to show the differences between the final probabilities for the states in the two versions of personal data processing.

Keywords: personal data protection; cloud; formalization; data flow diagram; Markov chain; stochastic investigation; analytical assessments

MSC: 37M21

Citation: Romansky, R. Mathematical Model Investigation of a Technological Structure for Personal Data Protection. *Axioms* **2023**, *12*, 102. https://doi.org/10.3390/axioms12020102

Academic Editors: Cheng-Shian Lin, Chien-Chang Chen and Yi-Hsien Wang

Received: 31 December 2022
Revised: 13 January 2023
Accepted: 13 January 2023
Published: 18 January 2023

Copyright: © 2023 by the author. Licensee MDPI, Basel, Switzerland. This article is an open access article distributed under the terms and conditions of the Creative Commons Attribution (CC BY) license (https://creativecommons.org/licenses/by/4.0/).

1. Introduction

The contemporary Information Society (InSoc) is characterized by the massive informatization and penetration of digital technologies in all areas. This is described in [1] as *"the most recent long wave of humanity's socioeconomic evolution"*, with an emphasis on the fact that the current digital age *"focuses on algorithms that automate the conversion of data into actionable knowledge"*. The massive globalization of processes leads to increased activity in the Internet space, which has a reflection on the efficiency of the data network [2] due to the increased access to remote resources and use of cloud data centers [3], data sharing in virtual environments [4], Internet of Things (IoT), including the sensor collection of personal data [5], and others. For example, the previously cited article confirms that today's advanced sensor technologies *"generate a large amount of valuable data"* for different applications, such as *"health care, elderly protection, human activity abnormal detection, and surveillance"*. One result of technologies in the digital space is the dissemination of personal data (freely or unknowingly), which raises a serious question concerning the privacy of users and the reliable protection of their personal data. This requires that, when developing environments for remote multiple access, organizational and technical measures to protect the data provided to users are adopted. A basic requirement should be countermeasures against the illegal distribution of user data and their use for purposes other than those announced, including the introduction of strict rules for authorization and authentication [6].

One direction for regulating the access to and use of objects and data is discussed in [7], where it is emphasized that building systems with multiple services increases the security impact when compared with the monolithic style. In order to answer important security questions in complex environments, a systematic review of the main challenges when using mechanisms and technologies for authentication and authorization in micro-services is performed.

The purpose of this article is to present a point of view on the technological organization of personal data protection processes in an example environment (administrative system) that uses cloud services and data centers and applies the requirements of the CIA (Confidentiality, Integrity, Availability) triad. The requirements of this triad and their implementation in various technological solutions are well discussed. For example, a holistic study of the shortcomings of existing technological solutions for the IoT and cyber physical systems (CPS) is presented in [8], and a solution involving blockchain technology is proposed with an analysis of the similarities and differences. Another study *"on the improvement of CIA triad to reduce the risk on online banking system"* is presented in [9].

Cloud computing allows us to take advantage of the leasing of infrastructure, software, and platforms offered as cloud services (IaaS, SaaS, PaaS). In this way, the costs of maintaining and administering one's own assets are reduced. For the user, the "cloud" is a virtual environment for data processing and storage. The services offered provide various cloud capabilities, requiring the proper pre-allocation of resources to overcome congestion, resource loss, load balancing, Quality of Service (QoS) violation, migration of virtual machines (VM), etc. A primary goal of the cloud is to correctly map VM to physical machines (PM) so that the PM can be effectively used. In this respect, an extensive survey of cloud resource management schemes is presented in [10] in order to identify the main challenges and point out possible future research directions. Another study [11] discusses how cloud service reliability should be further evaluated in specific conditions and proposes an approach based on combining cloud service reliability indicators to obtain an effective evaluation and improve data security. Despite cloud service providers' claims of good information security at the platform level, doubts have been expressed about the protection of personal data. To overcome possible problems, a patent has been registered to define a "Data Protection as a Service" (DPaaS) paradigm for generating dynamic updates of data protection policy using the machine-learning model and comparisons with previous instructions [12].

When researching processes developing in a computer environment, as well as for organizing structures, various possibilities are applied, such as benchmark and synthetic workload; monitoring through hardware, software, and combined means; computer modeling (abstract, functional, analytical, simulation, empirical); as well as statistical analysis of empirical data. Each of these approaches has its advantages and peculiarities, and the use of each of them depends on the researched object and the set tasks.

One of the applied approaches when researching processes in various systems and applications is modeling based on an appropriate apparatus and instrumentation. For example, simulation modeling is applied in [13] to study the probabilistic behavior and timing characteristics of interdependent tasks of arbitrary durations. The goal is to estimate the duration of the project and the possible risks of untimely completion. Another approach is the development of a mathematical description of processes, as is done in [14] to study the possibilities of minimizing power losses in a distribution transformer and evaluating energy efficiency. The proposed mathematical model describes the relationship between all the parameters of the transformer using the direct global iterative algorithm technique.

It is known that processes developing in systems most often have a probabilistic nature, which determines the effectiveness of the stochastic approach to research and indicates Markov processes and, in particular, Markov chains (MC) to be a suitable apparatus. An example of this is the application of MC to study technological limitations in stochastic normalizing flows presented in [15]. Another application of MC is discussed in [16], where the approach is combined with the Monte Carlo method for assessing the characteristics of probability distributions and a review of the *"methods for assessing the reliability of the simulation effort, with an emphasis on those most useful in practically relevant settings"* is performed. In addition, the strengths and weaknesses of these methods are discussed.

The main goal is to carry out a preliminary study of the constructed structural objects of the designed administrative system and the processes supported by them by applying the apparatus of Markov chains (MC). The choice of tool is determined by the stochastic nature of the processes in an essentially discrete hardware (computer) environment. To conduct the experiments, an author's programming environment, as developed in the APL2 language [17], is used and a graphic interpretation of the evaluations is additionally made. An approach using MC to conduct model research is applied in [11] to study the reliability of network services as well as in [18] to investigate basic performance and optimization measures in resource planning in the cloud and the IoT in order to improve performance and QoS. An efficient algorithm for infinite-time task scheduling in IaaS using MC with continuous parameters to search for an optimal solution is proposed, and a prototype is realized based on the designed model. A comparison of this prototype with a group of working models confirms the usefulness of the project.

This article is organized as follows. In the next section, an analytical representation of the researched object is presented using a Data Flow Diagram (DFD) and a mathematical description of the applied approach based on the Markov Chain (MC). The third section is devoted to the implementation of the model experiments, and a discussion of the experimental results is presented in Section 4.

2. Materials and Methods

The right to a private life and its inviolability ("right to privacy") are directly related to the procedures for Personal Data Protection (PDP), which is an internationally recognized right, based on the understanding that personal data are the property of the person (Data Subject). As stated, the expansion of network communications and the growing possibilities of remote access to distributed information resources impose increasingly strict requirements on the applied information security policies. The globalization of public processes, the socialization of communications, and the use of cloud services pose challenges to ensuring reliable PDP. Cloud service providers emphasize the advantages of the cloud, mainly those related to cost reduction, but the process of protecting information is not one of the main objects of discussion. Possible problems when providing personal data determine a high rate of distrust among users toward the digitalization of services (over 70%). In particular, for cloud services, this is associated with basic features such as multi-tenancy, storing copies of data in different places in the virtual environment, applying common and standard security approaches, etc. In addition, a study by the Computer Security Institute shows that a fairly high share (more than 55%) of compromised information security is due to accidental errors by staff, which necessitates paying attention to internal procedures for countering potential threats when processing personal data.

The classical organization of computer data processing takes place in an environment with a discrete structure, although the supported processes are probabilistic in nature. This allows both deterministic and probabilistic means to be used for the preliminary formalization of processes. One possibility for a deterministic description involves the State Transition Network (STN), which allows us to study the possible developments of the processes by analyzing the paths "from beginning to end". In this direction is also the application of a Data Flow Diagram (DFD) for the formal description of the movement of data flows in a given structure, with an indication of the important places for their communication with other processes and objects. This has been applied to formalize the structural organization when conducting research, taking into account the peculiarities and requirements of the PDP procedures.

The application of the probabilistic (stochastic) approach is often based on Markov processes, and when modeling computer data processing, the apparatus of Markov chains is suitable because they are used to describe the probabilistic transitions between discrete states in determinate moments of time. The preliminary formalization in this case requires the definition of a finite set of states $S = \{s_1, \ldots, s_n\}$ for the studied process and a matrix of transition probabilities between those states $p_{ij} = P(s_i \rightarrow s_j)$. Stochastic analysis examines the sequence of states $<S(0), S(1), \ldots, S(k)>$ in which the MC falls, for which it is necessary to define a vector of the initial probabilities for the formation of the initial state $S(0) = S(k = 0)$. It is usually assumed that the process starts from the first state $s_1 \in S$, i.e., $P_0 = \{1, 0, \ldots, 0\}$. Starting from the initial state, for each successive step $k = 1, 2, \ldots$ of the process development, the conditional probability of a transition from the current state s_i to the next state s_j can be determined by $p_{ij}(k) = P[S(k) = s_j / S(k-1) = s_i]$ based on the full probability Formula (1):

$$p_j(k) = \sum_{i=1}^{n} p_i(k-1) \cdot p_{ij}; j = 1 \div n \qquad (1)$$

which can also be used to calculate the final probabilities $P(k \rightarrow \infty)$ of falling into a certain state by

$$\lim_{k \to \infty} p_{ij}(k) = p_j.$$

To investigate the processes in the proposed technological environment, s stochastic Markov models are designed, and for their study, the developed author's program function "MARKOV" in the APL2 language environment [17] is used. This allows us to determine the vector of the probabilities for the states $P(k) = \{p_1(k), \ldots, p_n(k)\}$ for successive steps, the number of which is set by the user. After starting, it requires the definition of the main characteristics of the Markov chain: N—number of states; P[I,J]—the elements of the matrix of transition probabilities; and PO [1 ÷ N]—the elements of the vector of initial probabilities. A complete study can be organized through the additional program functions "PATHS' and "ESTIMATES" [19], which, together with "MARKOV", create a common program space for conducting analytical experiments in the APL2 environment.

3. Preliminary Formalization

The problems of data protection related to the growing threats of illegal access and incorrect use are the subject of different documents. A basic example here are the rules of conduct established in the USA to ensure the necessary protection of information and corporate resources, which are known as the SOX rules, as consolidated in the Sarbanes-Oxley Act of 2002. A study of the impact of these rules on the possible risk in resource management is done in [20], with an analysis of the situations before and after the adoption of these rules. Overall, the article highlights the positive impact of risk-reducing rules on resource management and increasing factor productivity and incentive compensation.

In reality, it should be noted that the security of information resources requires the provision of adequate and functional security policies, which place specific requirements on the Digital Rights Management System (DRMS). The main trends are related to the inclusion of important components aimed at protecting personal data, for example: ✓ cryptographic algorithms for information encryption; ✓ cryptographic key management strategies; ✓ access control methods; ✓ methods and means of user identification and authentication; and ✓ information content management with provenance verification and data copy control. At the heart of any DRMS are two processes, authentication and authorization, which are used to prove that the specific information is used by the individual who has pre-set rights to access it, allows all his actions to be tracked and checked, and controls what means of access is used. In this regard, all the currently used technologies for authentication, especially biometrics, are important for the reliable management of access to information resources.

According to regulatory documents, PDP refers to any action related to them—collection, storage, updating, correction, provision to a third party, transfer to another country, archiving, destruction, etc. All these processes must be carried out under strict organizational and technological measures to protect the means of storing personal data (Personal Data Registers [PDR]). The formalization of the classical version of personal data processing in a centralized corporate system is presented in Figure 1 by using a DFD with five external entities (source/receiver), nine basic information procedures, and three storage units. Part of the Information Security System (ISS) is the maintenance of a log (audit) file for access and activities carried out with the PDR.

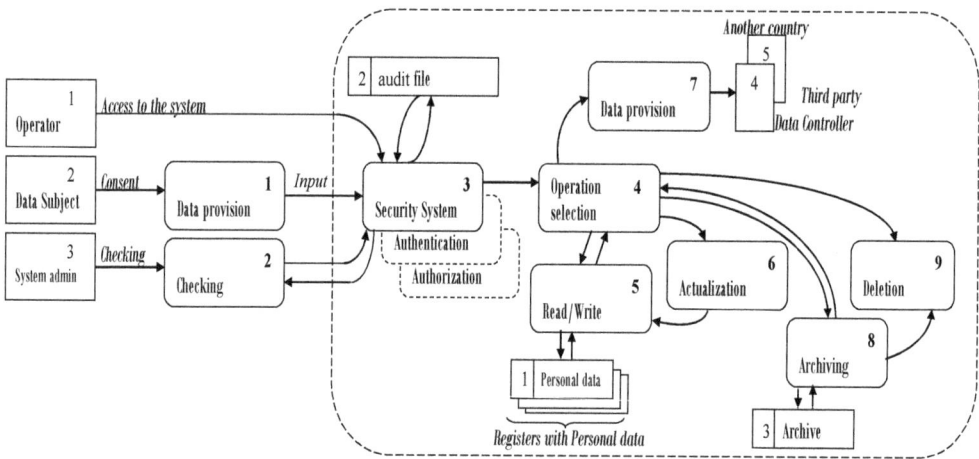

Figure 1. Formalization of personal data processing using a Data Flow Diagram (DFD).

A modification to a centralized environment can be made by transferring certain activities, including the storage of personal profiles with personal data, to the cloud. This leads to the modification of the formalized description as well, introducing a generalized process "5C", thereby uniting the undertaking of the activities of archiving, updating, and deleting personal data with the maintenance of the stored arrays and profiles in data centers. The modified DFD model of the decentralized structure is shown in Figure 2. The introduction of the new general process requires actualizing the role of the processes that are transferred to the cloud, which this is marked in the DFD by "*" (6 *, 8 *, 9 *). In addition, the new version requires the duplication of procedures for ensuring information protection (identification, registration, authentication, authorization) with partial transfer to the cloud.

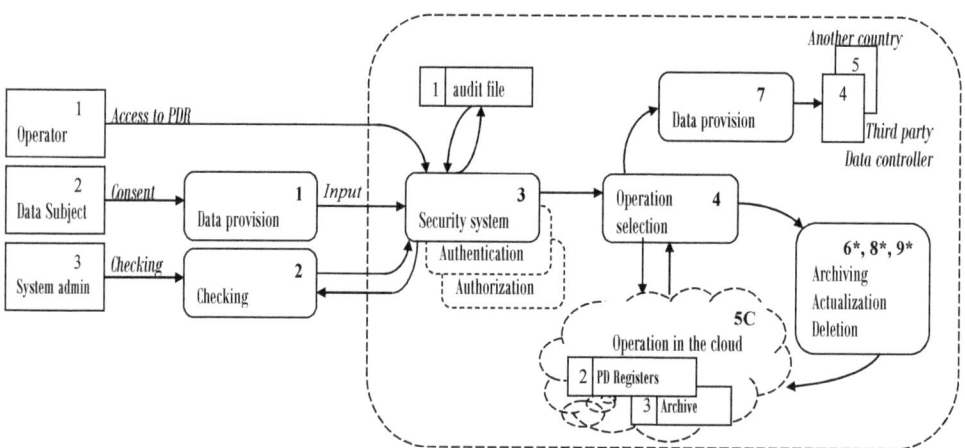

Figure 2. Modified DFD presenting the processing of personal data in the cloud.

4. Stochastic Model Investigation

To conduct the model investigation, two models are defined and solved using MC for the two formal DFD descriptions presented in the previous section: traditional and "cloud" PDP. It is assumed that any random process, regardless of the source of a submitted request, begins with access to internal ISS funds. The basis for this assumption is the nature of the PD provisioning procedures by the individual.

4.1. Analytical Investigation of Traditional PDP

The Markov model of traditional PDP presented in Table 1 is defined on the basis of the assumptions made regarding the start of processes and selection of typical values for the real traditional PDP values for the transition probabilities. The visual presentation of the MC graph of the states is shown in Figure 3 with the following states:

Table 1. Definition of the designed Markov model.

Set of States: Vector of Initial Probabilities						$S = \{s_1, s_2, s_3, s_4, s_5, s_6, s_7\}$ $P_0 = \{1,0,0,0,0,0,0\}$		
$\{p_{ij}\}$	s_1	s_2	s_3	s_4	s_5	s_6	s_7
s_1	0.2	0.8	0	0	0	0	0
s_2	0	0	0.4	0.2	0.2	0.1	0.1
s_3	0	1	0	0	0	0	0
s_4	0	0	1	0	0	0	0
s_5	0	0	0	0	0	0	0
s_6	0	0.3	0	0	0	0	0.7
s_7	0	0	0	0	0	0	0

s_1—verification of the legitimacy of the request through authentication and authorization;
s_2—selection of operation when access is allowed from the internal ISS;
s_3—write/read to PDR;
s_4—PD update in registry;
s_5—provision of PD to a third party, another Data Controller, or sending abroad;
s_6—archiving of PD in the presence of a legal requirement for this;
s_7—destruction of PD after fulfilling the purpose for which they were collected.

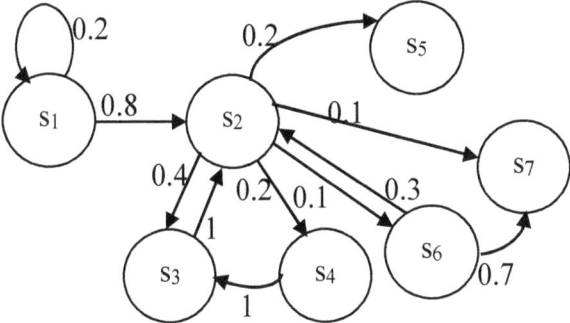

Figure 3. Markov model of traditional personal data processing (model "A").

The analytical definition of a model as a system of probabilities is as follows:

$$p_1 = 0.2p_1$$
$$p_2 = 0.8p_1 + p_3 + 0.3p_6$$
$$p_2 = 0.8p_1 + p_3 + 0.3p_6$$
$$p_3 = 0.4p_2 + p_4$$
$$p_4 = 0.2p_2$$
$$p_5 = 0.2p_2$$
$$p_6 = 0.1p_2$$
$$p_7 = 0.1p_2 + 0.7p_6$$
$$\sum_{i=1}^{7} p_i = 1$$

One possible solution to the presented system of probability permits us to calculate the values for all the final probabilities as follows:

$$p_1 = \tfrac{0.37}{0.8}p_2 = 0.4625p_2;\ p_3 = 0.6p_2;\ p_4 = p_5 = 0.2p_2;\ p_6 = 0.1p_2;$$
$$p_7 = 0.27p_2$$

This permits us to construct Equation (2) for the calculation of the value of the final probability p_2.

$$(0.4625 + 1 + 0.6 + 0.2 + 0.2 + 0.1 + 0.27)p_2 = 1 \qquad (2)$$

After solving Equation (2) and substituting it into the expressions, the following estimates are formed for the final probabilities of falling into each of the states:

$$p_1 = 0.165;\ p_2 = 0.353;\ p_3 = 0.212;\ p_4 = p_5 = 0.071;\ p_6 = 0.035;$$
$$p_7 = 0.095$$

4.2. Analytical Investigation of "Cloud" PDP

The Markov model for "cloud" PDP (Figure 4) is a modification of the previous one and corresponds to the processes from the DFD (Figure 2). A generalized state s_C is created, replacing states s_3, s_6, and s_7, whose activities are taken over by cloud services.

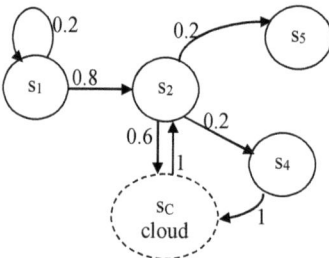

Figure 4. Markov model of "cloud" PDP (model "C").

As updating is a process involving incoming new (or corrected) PDs for an individual and receiving them from a Data Controller operator (employee), the s_4 state activity cannot be migrated to the cloud. The same applies to the process of providing PD, as it is related to certain regulatory requirements. The analytical Markov model notation for this situation is as follows:

$$p_1 = 0.2p_1$$
$$p_2 = 0.8p_1 + p_C$$
$$p_4 = 0.2p_2$$
$$p_4 = 0.2p_2$$
$$p_C = 0.6p_2 + p_4$$
$$p_1 + p_2 + p_4 + p_5 + p_C = 1$$

After solving the system of probabilistic equations, the following estimates for the final probabilities are determined: $p_1 = 0.102$; $p_2 = 0.408$; $p_4 = 0.082$; $p_5 = 0.082$; and $p_C = 0.326$.

4.3. Experimental Results Discussion

The diagram in Figure 5 presents a visual summarization of the obtained analytical results for model "A", allowing for easy comparison of the probabilities of falling into the separate states. It can be seen that the load of the states related to the selection operations of relevant data processing activities and operation with the registry system for their storage is the greatest.

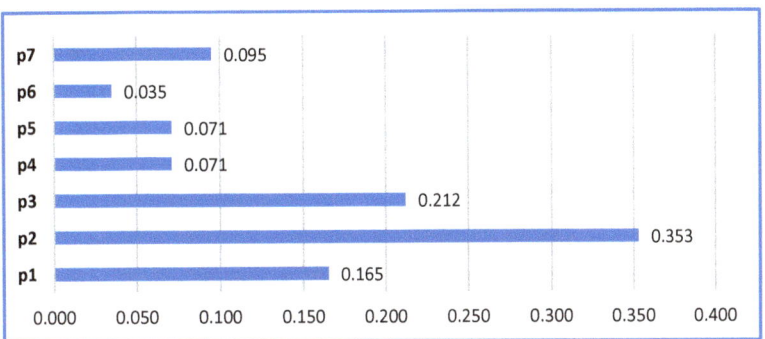

Figure 5. Graphical visualization of analytical assessments for the states of Model "A".

A joint visualization of the analytical results of the solutions for the two models is presented in Figure 6, where the probabilities of performing the corresponding activities in a steady state are presented. The comparative analysis shows non-significant differences in the marginal probability values for the two situations (the two models), although model "B" (the cloud option) has a certain advantage for the main PDP fulfillment activities related to the responsibilities of the Data Controller employees (Data Operators). This confirms the high importance of complying with legal requirements and ensuring strict internal rules in the relevant institution.

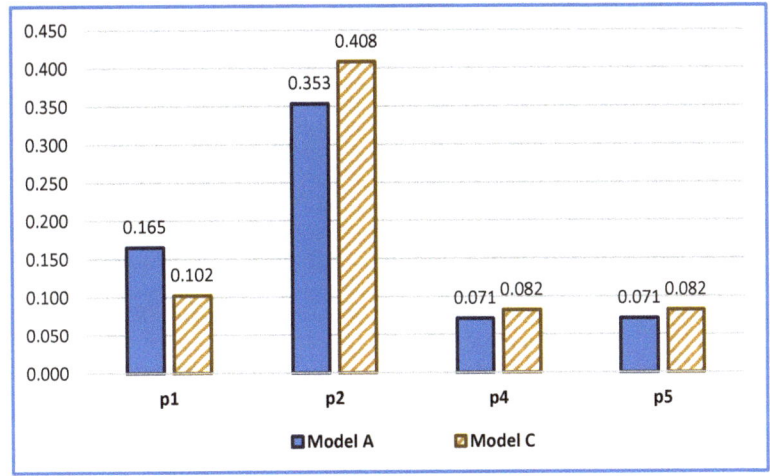

Figure 6. Comparison of basic activities for the two models.

On the other hand, it should be emphasized that moving some PDP activities to the cloud has a certain effect, leading to a certain reduction in the level of employment in certain states (DFD processes). This can be seen from the joint presentation of the transferred activities in the two models, "A" and "C", in Figure 7.

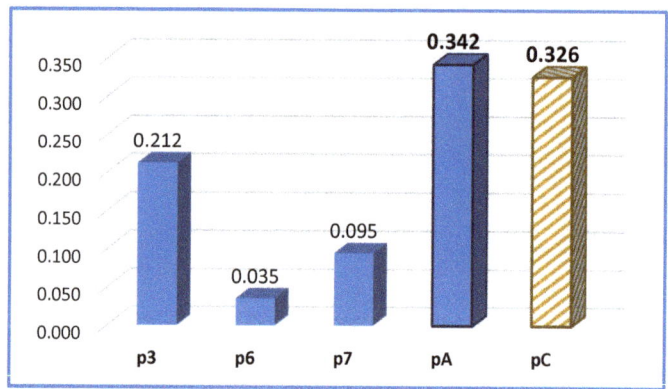

Figure 7. Equivalence of assessments before and after moving activities to the cloud ($p_A = p_3 + p_6 + p_7$ for model "A"; p_C for model "C").

Although moving certain process activities (6 *, 8 *, and 9 * of DFD [Figure 2]) to the cloud eases the workload of ISS service operators, it does not change the responsibility of the Data Controller or the requirement to ensure internal rules for identification and access management. Due to the fact that standard data protection mechanisms are traditionally applied in the cloud, the use of data centers and cloud services should only take place after providing serious guarantees for ensuring adequate data protection related to access management, authorization, authentication, maintenance of audit information, implementation of architectural requirements for the cloud platform, etc. In this sense, the patent from [12] can provide the necessary level of security when processing personal data in a distributed environment. One solution is to define authorization in depth and implement it at three levels: high level—for meta-level management of access to applications and resources; middle level—for data level access control; and low level—to control functions with specific data.

5. Conclusions

The main purpose of this article is to present a point of view for transferring certain personal data processing activities to a cloud environment using data centers (data warehouses) and the virtual environment of the cloud for multiple communication. The main problem for discussion is the implementation of adequate procedures for information security in the organization of a heterogeneous environment for maintaining information resources. This article specifically discusses the organization of a system for ensuring the reliable protection of profiles with personal data. The relevance of this problem is confirmed by the continuous development of digital technologies, which creates challenges for personal privacy [21]. In practice, this is one stage of the overall development and investigation of the heterogeneous environment, where a stochastic approach is applied to further validate the effectiveness of the planned PDP procedures.

The main contribution is the formalization of personal data processing using the DFD apparatus and the analytical development of the presented stochastic models, allowing us to make a comparison of the features of the processes supported in the traditional and cloud versions. From the conducted model investigation and analysis of the obtained estimates in the case of stationary processes, it can be seen that regarding the obligations of the Data Controller, there is no significant difference between the relative weights of the two options. At the same time, both models maintain the importance of authorization and authentication as information security processes. This confirms the need to build a serious ISS with specific measures to protect PDR, which must meet clearly defined rules and responsibilities when working with cloud resources. Such a cloud platform should provide the following capabilities: ✓ integrity of stored user data; ✓ preventing unauthorized access to personal data; ✓ maintaining complete information about every attempt to access personal data; ✓ possibility of easy verification by the user as to whether the PDP policy is followed; and ✓ possibility of efficient and secure processing of sensitive personal data.

The obtained results of this research provide an idea of the relevance of the processes in the two selected implementation options, and the goal is to determine the effectiveness of the application of cloud services. They can be used in the selection of specific techniques and means, mainly in the organization of the security of access to personal data, as well as in the implementation of heterogeneous systems, such as proposed in [22].

The research carried out allows for an extension in several directions defining future research, for example, an extension of the model study by applying deterministic means such as graph theory [23] and the Petri nets apparatus [22], as well as possibly simulation modeling of the main work processes with personal data, mainly in cloud services, with statistical analysis of the accumulated data from experiments [24].

Funding: This research received no external funding.

Institutional Review Board Statement: Not applicable.

Informed Consent Statement: Not applicable.

Data Availability Statement: Not applicable.

Conflicts of Interest: The author declares no conflict of interest.

Abbreviations

CIA	Confidentiality, Integrity, Availability
CPS	Cyber Physical Systems
DFD	Data Flow Diagram
DRMS	Digital Rights Management System
InSoc	Information Society
IoT	Internet of Things
ISS	Information Security System
PD	Personal Data
PDP	Personal Data Protection
PDR	Persona Data Register
MC	Markov Chain
PM	Physical Machines
STN	State Transition Network
VM	Virtual Machines

References

1. Hilbert, M. Digital technology and social change: The digital transformation of society from a historical perspective. *Dialogues Clin. Neurosci.* **2020**, *22*, 189–194. [CrossRef] [PubMed]
2. Gregory, R.W.; Henfridsson, O.; Kaganer, E.; Kyriakou, H. Data network effects: Key conditions, shared data, and the data value duality. *Acad. Manag. Rev.* **2022**, *47*, 189–192. [CrossRef]
3. Halili, M.K.; Cico, B. SLA management for comprehensive virtual machine migration considering scheduling and load balancing algorithm in cloud data centers. *Int. J. Inf. Technol. Secur.* **2020**, *12*, 23–34.
4. Williamson, J.R.; O'Hagan, J.; Guerra-Gomez, J.A.; Williamson, J.H.; Cesar, P.; Shamma, D.A. Digital Proxemics: Designing Social and Collaborative Interaction in Virtual Environments. In Proceedings of the CHI'22 Proceedings of the 2022 CHI Conference on Human Factors in Computing Systems, New Orleans, LA, USA, 29 April–2 May 2022; pp. 1–12. [CrossRef]
5. Qian, X.; Chen, H.; Cai, Y.; Chu, K.-C.; Xu, W.; Huang, M.-C. Transfer learning model knowledge across multi-sensors locations over body sensor network. *IEEE Sens. J.* **2022**, *22*, 10663–10670. [CrossRef]

6. Trnka, M.; Abdelfattah, A.S.; Shrestha, A.; Coffey, M.; Cerny, T. Systematic review of authentication and authorization advancements for the Internet of Things. *Sensors* **2022**, *22*, 1361. [CrossRef] [PubMed]
7. de Almeida, M.G.; Canedo, E.D. Authentication and authorization in microservices architecture: A systematic literature review. *Appl. Sci.* **2022**, *12*, 3023. [CrossRef]
8. Bhattacharjya, A. A holistic study on the use of blockchain technology in CPS and IoT architectures maintaining the CIA triad in data communication. *Int. J. Appl. Math. Comput. Sci.* **2022**, *32*, 403–413.
9. Alshathri, S.; Alrashidi, E.; Albawardi, N.; Almojel, H.; Jamail, N.S.M. Improvement of the CIA triad for Al-Rajhi Online Banking System. In Proceedings of the 5th International Conference of Women in Data Science at Prince Sultan University (WiDS PSU), Riyadh, Saudi Arabia, 28–29 March 2022; pp. 67–69. [CrossRef]
10. Swain, S.R.; Singh, A.K.; Lee, C.N. Efficient Resource Management in Cloud Environment. *arXiv* **2022**, arXiv:2207.12085. Distributed, Parallel, and Cluster Computing. [CrossRef]
11. Yang, M.; Gao, T.; Xie, W.; Jia, L.; Zhang, T. The assessment of cloud service trustworthiness state based on DS theory and Markov chain. *IEEE Access* **2022**, *10*, 68618–68632. [CrossRef]
12. Balasubramanian, V.A.; Kulasekaran, R.; Subramanian, V. Data Protection as a Service. U.S. Patent 17/077,571, 28 April 2022.
13. Oleinikova, S.A.; Selishchev, I.A.; Kravets, O.J.; Rahman, P.A.; Aksenov, I.A. Simulation model for calculating the probabilistic and temporal characteristics of the project and the risks of its untimely completion. *Int. J. Inf. Technol. Secur.* **2021**, *13*, 55–62.
14. Digalovski, M.; Rafajlovski, G. Distribution transformer mathematical model for power losses minimization. *Int. J. Inf. Technol. Secur.* **2020**, *12*, 57–68.
15. Hagemann, P.; Hertrich, J.; Steidl, G. Stochastic normalizing flows for inverse problems: A Markov Chains viewpoint. *SIAM/ASA J. Uncertain. Quantif.* **2022**, *10*, 1162–1190. [CrossRef]
16. Jones, G.L.; Qin, Q. Markov Chain Monte Carlo in Practice. *Annu. Rev. Stat. Its Appl.* **2022**, *9*, 557–578. [CrossRef]
17. Romansky, R. An approach for program investigation of computer processes presented by Markov models. *Int. J. Inf. Technol. Secur.* **2022**, *14*, 45–54.
18. Nithiyanandam, N.; Rajesh, M.; Sitharthan, R.; Shanmuga Sundar, D.; Vengatesan, K.; Madurakavi, K. Optimization of performance and scalability measures across cloud based IoT applications with efficient scheduling approach. *Int. J. Wirel. Inf. Netw.* **2022**, *29*, 442–453. [CrossRef]
19. Romansky, R. Mathematical Modelling and Study of Stochastic Parameters of Computer Data Processing. *Mathematics* **2021**, *9*, 2240. [CrossRef]
20. Hillier, D.; McColgan, P.; Tsekeris, A. How did the Sarbanes–Oxley Act affect managerial incentives? Evidence from corporate acquisitions. *Rev. Quant. Finance Account.* **2022**, *58*, 1395–1450. [CrossRef]
21. Romansky, R.; Noninska, I. Challenges of the Digital Age for privacy and personal data protection. *Math. Biosci. Eng.* **2020**, *17*, 5288–5303. [CrossRef] [PubMed]
22. Romansky, R.; Noninska, I. Deterministic Model Investigation of Processes in a Heterogeneous e-Learning Environment. *Int. J. Hum. Cap. Inf. Technol. Prof.* **2022**, *13*, 28. [CrossRef]
23. Romansky, R. Formalization and Discrete Modelling of Communication in the Digital Age by Using Graph Theory. In *Handbook of Research on Advanced Applications of Graph Theory in Modern Society*; Pal, M., Samanta, S., Pal, A., Eds.; IGI Global: Hershey, PA, USA, 2020; Chapter 13; pp. 320–353. [CrossRef]
24. Romansky, R. Investigation of Network Communications by Using Statistical Processing of Monitored Data. In Proceedings of the 2022 IEEE International Conference on Information Technologies (InfoTech-2022), Varna, Bulgaria, 15–16 September 2022; pp. 37–40. [CrossRef]

Disclaimer/Publisher's Note: The statements, opinions and data contained in all publications are solely those of the individual author(s) and contributor(s) and not of MDPI and/or the editor(s). MDPI and/or the editor(s) disclaim responsibility for any injury to people or property resulting from any ideas, methods, instructions or products referred to in the content.

Article

Numerical Modeling of the Major Temporal Arcade Using BUMDA and Jacobi Polynomials

José Alfredo Soto-Álvarez [1], Iván Cruz-Aceves [2,*], Arturo Hernández-Aguirre [1], Martha Alicia Hernández-González [3], Luis Miguel López-Montero [3] and Sergio Eduardo Solorio-Meza [4]

1. Centre for Research in Mathematics A.C., Jalisco S/N, Col. Valenciana, Guanajuato 36000, Mexico
2. CONACYT-Centre for Research in Mathematics A.C., Jalisco S/N, Col. Valenciana, Guanajuato 36000, Mexico
3. High Speciality Medical Unit (UMAE), Specialities Hospital No. 1, Mexican Social Security Institute (IMSS), Leon 37320, Mexico
4. Department of Health Sciences, Universidad Tecnológica de México (UNITEC) Campus León, Leon 37200, Mexico
* Correspondence: ivan.cruz@cimat.mx

Abstract: Within eye diseases, diabetic retinopathy and retinopathy of prematurity are considered one of the main causes of blindness in adults and children. In order to prevent the disease from reaching such an extreme, a timely diagnosis and effective treatment must be applied. Until now, the way to verify the state of the retina has been to make qualitative observations of fundus images, all carried out by an ophthalmological specialist; however, this is totally restricted to their experience, and some changes in the vascular structure of the retina could be omitted, in addition to the fact that very high resolution images would be needed to be able to detect significant changes. Accordingly, with the help of computational tools, this diagnostic/monitoring process can be improved. This paper presents a novel strategy for the modeling of the MTA by using an estimation of distribution algorithm (EDA) based on the probability density function in order to determine the coefficients and parameters (α, β) of a Jacobi polynomial series. A model using polynomials is the novel aspect of this work since in the literature there are no models of the MTA of this type, in addition to seeking to better cover the profile of the retinal vein. According to the experimental results, the proposed method presents the advantage to achieve superior performance in terms of the mean distance to the closest point (4.34 pixels), and the Hausdorff distance (14.43 pixels) with respect to different state-of-the-art methods of the numerical modeling of the retina, using the DRIVE database of retinal fundus images with a manual delineation of the MTA performed by an specialist.

Keywords: Boltzmann univariate marginal distribution algorithm; estimation of distribution algorithm; jacobi polynomials; major temporal arcade; retinal fundus images

1. Introduction

Blindness is a condition that can occur in a patient who, due to not having been treated promptly in the diagnosis of a disease such as diabetic retinopathy, experiences non-recoverable loss of vision. Specifically, this disease prevails mainly in industrialized countries, is prevalent in subjects between 20 and 64 years of age, and represents 10% of new cases of annual blindness [1–3]. In addition to diabetic retinopathy, which only adults present, there is also a very important type that affects infants: retinopathy of prematurity (ROP). This is the main cause of childhood blindness worldwide; the diagnosis and treatment must be timely because its evolution occurs in an accelerated manner within the first 8 to 12 weeks after the birth of the infant [4].

Both diseases are the result of damage of the blood vessels of the tissue located in the back of the eye, that is, in the retina. In order to carry out a diagnosis, it is necessary to obtain a set of fundus images, which must be examined by an physician expert in ophthalmology. However, this restricts the diagnosis to the experience acquired by the specialist, that is, it becomes qualitative. From fundus images, it is possible to carry out a quantitative analysis of the vascular structure of the retina, which is helpful to the specialist who can use the technique both for the diagnosis of the pathology and for its follow-up throughout the treatment.

A great challenge that arises next is that the detection of small changes in the structure of the retinal veins is a challenging task; for this, the images taken of the patient would be required to have a very high resolution. However, using computational tools that process medical images is a way to deal with this problem, which would result in a support tool for specialists when giving a diagnosis.

On the other hand, the major temporal arcade (MTA) is the thickest branch present in retinal fundus images. Structural changes in this vein have been identified by detailed analysis; these include tortuosity, change in thickness, and the angle of insertion, characteristics that have emerged as sequelae in both diabetic retinopathy and ROP [5–8]. Likewise, when there are changes in the opening of the MTA, this is understood as an important indicator of the structural integrity of the macular region [8,9].

A complementary technique that can be used to help both the diagnosis and the monitoring of the disease throughout its treatment is obtaining a simple mathematical expression that allows one to model the MTA. Currently in the literature, there are some works that have addressed modeling. Oloumi et al. [10,11] proposed two different methods based on a parabolic modeling of the MTA; one consists of a single parabola and the second of two parabolas, one for each branch extending from the optic nerve head. In both two works, the well-known strategy of the Hough transform was used for detecting the parabolic shape of the MTA. The objective of their work was to quantify changes in the opening of the MTA associated with diabetic retinopathy as well as to measure the angle of the arch, which showed significant differences when models obtained from images of healthy subjects were compared with patients diagnosed with diabetic retinopathy. As mentioned, one of the most used techniques for curve detection in images is the Hough transform [12]. Unfortunately, the computational time of the Hough transform makes it unfeasible to used in clinical practice. In this way, with the aim of reducing the analysis time, new techniques have been explored. Valdez et al. [13] proposed a method for the detection of MTA in fundus images. This consisted of hybridization by combining the UMDA algorithm with simulated annealing (SA), which allowed one to guide the search to promising regions. A segmented image was used as an objective function, being weighted with the pixel according to the distance to the parabola vertex.

More recently, Giacinti et al. [14] proposed parabolic modeling; however, this was done using the evolutionary univariate marginal distribution algorithm (UMDA). This model yielded an average accuracy value of 0.85 compared to the ground-truth of the trace performed by an ophthalmologist. Alvarado et al. [15] carried out a numerical modeling of the MTA using second-order spline curves. However, it has the disadvantage that in some images the modeling fails since the method is very sensitive to the automatic location of the control points of the spline, making this a characteristic to improve in the technique, in addition to the fact that only five control points are used to generate the second-order spline.

In this paper, a novel method based on Jacobi polynomials and the Boltzmann univariate marginal distribution algorithm (BUMDA) for the numerical modeling of the MTA is proposed. The method determines the optimal coefficients that build a linear combination of polynomials up to fourth order, in addition to determining the value of the parameters (α, β). The efficiency of the method was quantified using two measures: the mean distance to the closest point (MDCP) and the Hausdorff distance. The results obtained were contrasted with those presented in the works mentioned above.

In this paper, a robust method for the detection and modeling of the MTA in fundus images is presented. The algorithm follows a BUMDA strategy, building multiple MTA models from pixels data of the blood-vessel segmented retinal image. Implementing a model using polynomials is the novel aspect of this work since in the literature there are no models of the MTA of this type, in addition to seeking to better cover the profile of the retinal vein. Each model consists of a Jacobi polynomial curve with the ability to consider both symmetric and asymmetric scenarios. To choose the best MTA model, the method considers the two smallest measures of the MDCP and the Hausdorff distance.

The contributions of this work are summarized as follows:

1. A modeling strategy addressing both symmetric and asymmetric scenarios is presented to improve the MTA characterization.
2. A BUMDA scheme together with Jacobi polynomials with the purpose of improve the modeling of the MTA.
3. A set of MTA manual delineations for the benchmark DRIVE dataset has been released for scientific purposes

The rest of this paper is organized as follows. In Section 2, the database of the MTA images, a description of the Jacobi polynomials, and the BUMDA algorithm are detailed. In Section 3, the proposed method is presented in addition to the MTA segmentation and the evaluation metrics. Section 4 shows the experimental results and the discussion. Finally, in Section 5, the most relevant conclusions of the work are presented.

2. Materials and Methods

The DRIVE database [16] of 40 retinal fundus images was used in experiments. Since this database is used for blood vessel segmentation, the specific delineation of the MTA was performed by an ophthalmologist (Dr. Luis M. López-Montero).

2.1. Database of the MTA Images

Each image used is in RGB 8-bits format with size 565 × 584 pixels. The DRIVE database consists of 40 retinal fundus images, 20 images of training, and 20 images of testing; this database is publicly available and is used mainly for blood-vessel segmentation. In this paper, the database was only used for the detection of the MTA; the training and testing sets of retinal fundus images were specifically outlined to work with the major temporal arcade. This images were performed by an ophthalmological specialist (Dr. Luis M. López-Montero) from the highly specialized medical unit (UMAE) T1-León.

2.2. Jacobi Polynomials

The Jacobi polynomials [17], expressed as $J_n^{(\alpha,\beta)}(x)$, are an important class of orthogonal polynomials. They are orthogonal with respect to the weight $w(x) = (1-x)^\alpha (1+x)^\beta$ on $[-1,1]$, with the restriction $\alpha, \beta > -1$:

$$\int_{-1}^{1} J_n^{(\alpha,\beta)}(x) J_m^{(\alpha,\beta)}(x)(1-x)^\alpha (1+x)^\beta dx = \frac{2^{\alpha+\beta+1}}{2n+\alpha+\beta+1} \frac{\Gamma(n+\alpha+1)\Gamma(n+\beta+1)}{\Gamma(n+\alpha+\beta+1)} \delta_{n,m}, \quad (1)$$

being $\Gamma(x)$ the gamma function.

The Jacobi polynomials $J_n^{(\alpha,\beta)}(x)$ are the solution for the Sturm–Liouville equation:

$$\left(1-x^2\right) y''(x) + [\beta - \alpha - (\alpha + \beta + 2)x] y'(x) + n(n + \alpha + \beta + 1) y(x) = 0. \quad (2)$$

Each Jacobi polynomial can be obtained through the Rodrigues formula:

$$J_n^{\alpha,\beta}(x) = \frac{(-1)^n}{2^n n!} (1-x)^{-\alpha} (1+x)^{-\beta} \frac{d^n}{dx^n}\left[(1-x)^\alpha (1+x)^\beta \left(1-x^2\right)^n\right]. \quad (3)$$

For the calculation of the k-*th* derivative, it can be obtained by:

$$\frac{d^k}{dx^k}\left[J_n^{(\alpha,\beta)}(x)\right] = \frac{\Gamma(\alpha+\beta+n+1+k)}{2^k \Gamma(\alpha+\beta+n+1)} J_{n-k}^{(\alpha+k,\beta+k)}(x). \quad (4)$$

2.3. Boltzmann Univariate Marginal Distribution Algorithm (BUMDA)

In the search for the solution to an optimization problem, computational techniques emerge as immediate strategies to be implemented. In order for these solutions to be found in a reasonable amount of time, metaheuristic algorithms become the most appropriate. In particular, the estimation of distribution algorithms (EDAs) builds probabilistic models that are iteratively refined with the intention of obtaining better solutions for an objective problem. Let us bear in mind that maintaining probabilistic models is more complicated than simply applying evolutionary operators to a population; however, these models allow EDAs to adapt to the structure of the problem, giving them an advantage over other metaheuristics [18].

In the last decade, attention has been paid to the Boltzmann Probability Density Function (Boltzmann-PDF) [19] to the point of making it the probabilistic model of EDAs [20]. The Boltzmann-PDF emerged in the 19th century, in the area of physics for the field of statistical mechanics, as a way to model the distribution of particles in their energy states

$$P_x = P(x, \beta) = \frac{1}{Z} e^{\beta g(x)}, \tag{5}$$

where Z is a normalization parameter known as "partition function", and $g(x)$ is the energy of the states x and $\beta = \frac{1}{T}$, with T the temperature of the system. Equation (5) shows that there is a greater probability of the particles occupying the states of lower energy than those of higher energy, and that it is less probable that they occupy more energetic states. Thus, by coupling this Boltzmann-PDF to an EDA, the minimization of an "energy" function will be sought through stochastic optimizations.

So far it can be inferred that it is simply enough to use the said PDF to solve any optimization problem through an EDA. However, a significant problem arises: it is impossible to generate new possible solutions through the Boltzmann distribution since it lacks parameters such as the mean and standard deviation. However, this problem can be addressed by approximating the Boltzmann distribution to a Gaussian distribution, which is defined as

$$Q_x = Q(x; \mu, \nu) = \frac{1}{\sqrt{2\pi\nu}} \exp\left(-\frac{1}{2} \frac{(x-\mu)^2}{\nu}\right). \tag{6}$$

That approximation is carried out by minimizing a measure of divergence between the two PDFs with respect to the parameters of interest, which in this case would be those of the Gaussian $(\mu, \nu = \sigma^2)$. The divergence measure to be used is the Kullback–Liebler divergence (KL-divergence), which is given by the following equation:

$$D_{KL}(Q, P) = \int_x Q_x \log\left(\frac{Q_x}{P_x}\right) dx. \tag{7}$$

Then, a mathematical analysis associated with a minimization process and taking into account the considerations as in [20] must be carried out, and selection operators that are Boltzmann-based (μ, ν) can be obtained that will allow numerical calculations to be made for the mean and standard deviation ,

$$\mu \approx \frac{\sum_j g(x_j) x_j}{\sum_j g(x_j)}, \tag{8}$$

and

$$\nu \approx \frac{\sum_j g(x_j)(x_j - \mu)^2}{1 + \sum_j g(x_j)}. \tag{9}$$

Once the selection operators have been determined, it will be possible to estimate new individuals in subsequent generations during the evolutionary process. The steps to be followed by the BUMDA are shown in the following Algorithm 1.

Algorithm 1 MTA numerical modeling by BUMDA

Input: *Population Size, Generations*
Output: P_{best}
1: *Initialize Population (randomly real numbers)*
2: *Evaluate Population* ▷ Obtain fitness values
3: *Sort fitness values*
4: *Elite Selection* ▷ Best individual is extracted
5: **for** *gen 2 to Generations* **do**
6:     *Compute the approximations to μ and v*
7:     *Generate a New Population, (n − 1 individuals) keeping the elite value from the last generation*
8:     *Evaluate Population*
9:     *Sort fitness values* (Obtain New Best Fitness)
10:     **if** *New Best Fitness is better than Best Fitness* **then**
11:         *Upload Best Solution*
12:     **end if**
13: **end for**
14: **return** P_{best}

3. Proposed Method for the Numerical Modeling of the MTA

In order to improve the previous numerical modelings of the MTA, it is proposed to use a polynomial fit by means of a linear combination of Jacobi polynomials [21] because, throughout history, polynomials in general are considered adequate functions to carry out fit of data sets [22–24].

3.1. MTA Segmentation

To perform the numerical modeling of the MTA, a binary segmentation step is required in order to extract the thickest vessel from the background image. In this step, the multiscale Gaussian matched filter (MGMF) [25] was applied on the set of retinal fundus images since it presents suitable results in multiscale blood vessel segmentation. The method is governed by the four parameters σ, κ, L, T, and the neural network architecture. The main idea of the method is to approximate blood vessels by using a Gaussian profile as a matching template. This template is formed by a Gaussian curve, which can be defined as follows:

$$G(x,y) = exp\left(\frac{x^2 + y^2}{2\sigma^2}\right), \quad (10)$$

where σ controls the width of the vessel-like structures, L and T are the length and width of the template, and κ is the number of oriented filters. In the present work, the MGMF parameters were experimentally determined as $sigma = [1.8, 2.2]$, $L = 13$, $T = 15$, $\kappa = 12$, and the neural network was designed with 2 hidden layers with 3 and 8 hidden neurons, respectively.

3.2. BUMDA and Jacobi Polynomials

A linear combination of the first four Jacobi polynomials has been proposed to build the curve that models the MTA. The general expression for the fit function is given as

$$f(x;\alpha,\beta) = C_0 + C_1 J_1^{(\alpha,\beta)}(x) + C_2 J_2^{(\alpha,\beta)}(x) + C_3 J_3^{(\alpha,\beta)}(x) + C_4 J_4^{(\alpha,\beta)}(x) = C_0 + \sum_{i=1}^{4} C_i J_i^{(\alpha,\beta)}(x), \quad (11)$$

where $J_i^{(\alpha,\beta)}$ is the i-th Jacobi polynomial, C_i the coefficients associated with each of them, and $\alpha, \beta > -1$. The search space for the coefficients that accompany each polynomial in the general fit function was established in an interval of $[-200, 200]$. Likewise, the parameters (α, β) had a search space in the interval $(-1, 1]$.

The decision to take only the first four polynomials to generate the fit curve was based on the fact that in previous papers the fit was made using a second degree curve so that when performing several experiments it was observed that a good fit was obtained through curves generated by a fourth order function, that is, using only the first four polynomials.

Both, the set of coefficients C_i and the parameters (α, β) were determined using the BUMDA algorithm since it has fast convergence and its computational cost is low. A brief description of the operation of this type of algorithm is given below.

The BUMDA algorithm optimizes seven parameters: five coefficients corresponding to the polynomial series and the two parameters associated with the determination of the specific Jacobi polynomial.

The proposed method consists of the following steps: (1) the blood vessel segmentation of the retinal fundus image; (2) the skeletonization and extraction of the parameters of interest; (3) the construction of the numerical model of the MTA from the extracted parameter and the evolutionary algorithm; and (4) demonstrating the best solution. Figure 1 shows a general scheme of the methodology proposed in this work to obtain the adjustment function for the MTA.

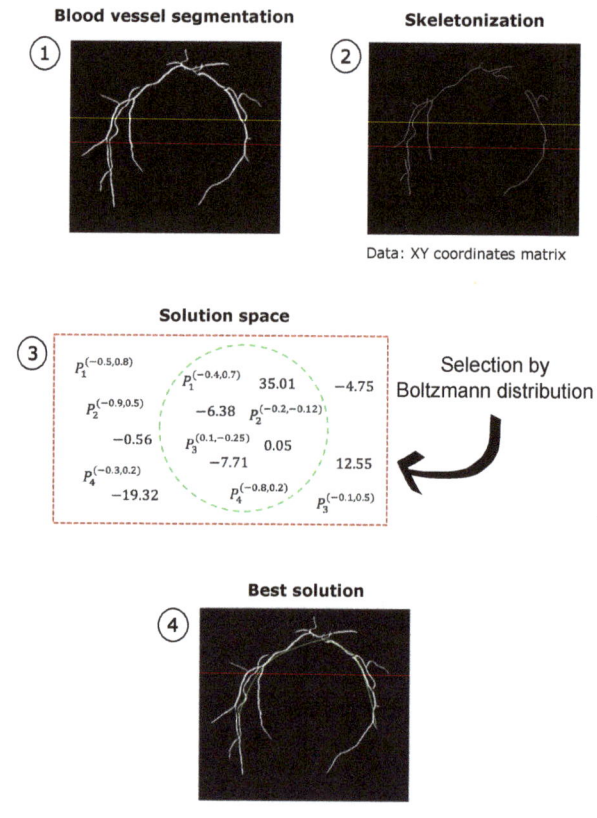

Figure 1. MTA-modeling schematic diagram. (1) Segmentation of the MTA; (2) skeletonization performance and data acquisition; (3) execution of the BUMDA algorithm with Boltzmann-based selection operators to sample new solutions; and (4) solutions that best fit the MTA.

3.3. Evaluation Measures

Once the stop criteria are achieved (i.e., an optimal solution has been found), it is necessary to analyze how close it is to the original data set; for this, two measures are used—the mean distance to the closest point (MDCP) and the Hausdorff distance—since they have been commonly used in literature to solve this problem.

MDCP calculates the average of the distances from each point (coordinate) of the set obtained by the algorithm with respect to the original data set; this is mathematically expressed as

$$MDCP(A,B) = \frac{1}{N}\sum_{i=1}^{N} DCP(a_i, B), \quad (12)$$

where N is the cardinality of the obtained set and DCP is the distance to the closest point, which is calculated as

$$DCP(a_i, B) = min||a_i - b_j||. \quad (13)$$

On the other hand, the Hausdorff distance performs a calculation very similar to the MDCP. The way in which the DCP is calculated is exactly the same; the change now occurs in the fact that an average is not calculated, but rather the maximum value of the DCP is taken.

$$H(A,B) = maxDCP(a_i, B). \quad (14)$$

Small values in both metrics ensure that the model generated by the algorithm at the end of the evolutionary process is good enough.

The proposed method can be seen in summary form in Algorithm 2.

Algorithm 2 Proposed Method

Input: *Fundus Image*
Output: *Best MTA fit*
1: *Load fundus image*
2: *Perform MTA segmentation*
3: *Skeletonization of the image to choose principal pixels*
4: *Execution of BUMDA-Jacobi Algorithm* ▷ Algorithm 1
5: *Calculation of evaluation measures* ▷ MDCP and Hausdorff Distance
6: **Return** *Best MTA fit*
---

4. Experimental Results and Discussion

The BUMDA-Jacobi algorithm was coded and executed in MATLAB® R2021b running on MacOS Catalina. The experiments were carried out with Intel®Core™i5-45706SM CPU @ 2.9–3.6 GHz, and 16 GB RAM. For each of the twenty testing images in the DRIVE database, thirty runs were performed with the intention of obtaining enough information for subsequent statistical analysis. Based on several experiments carried out, the starting configuration of the algorithm was set to 200 individuals in the population and 40 generations of evolution.

In Table 1, the mean, median, variance, and maximum and minimum values of the results obtained for the MDCP, the Hausdorff distance, and the execution time of the thirty executions of the best solution found by the BUMDA are reported.

Table 1. Statistical values obtained from 30 runs by the proposed method using the test set of 20 retinal fundus images.

	MDCP (px.)	Hausdorff (px.)	Time (s)
Mean	7.51	26.27	3.44
Median	6.17	21.29	3.43
Variance	16.30	190.91	0.001
Maximum	21.36	69.92	3.54
Minimum	4.34	14.43	3.4

Regarding convergence, Figure 2 shows the behavior of each of the 30 executions for the MTA modeling. It can be seen that the optimal result is reached below generation 40.

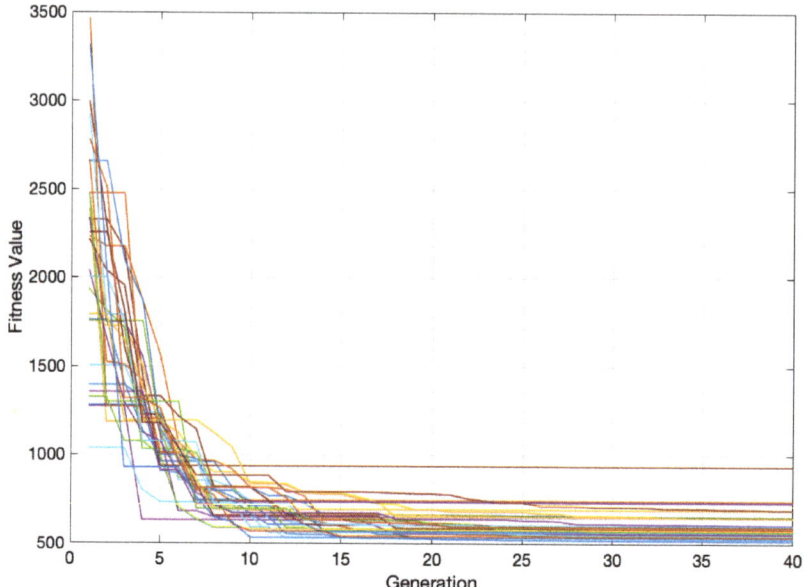

Figure 2. Convergence profile for the 30 runs by the proposed method using the test set of 20 retinal fundus images.

For the distance values, Table 2 shows the results obtained from the best fit for the MDCP and the Hausdorff distance together with the values reported in the literature.

Table 2. Mean Distance to the Closest Point and Hausdorff distance values for proposed method and the methods reported in the literature for several types of modeling approximation for MTA.

Method	MDCP (px.) Mean ± Std.	Hausdorff (px.) Mean ± Std.
General Hough	31.28 ± 0.00	64.49 ± 0.00
MIPAV	25.69 ± 0.00	59.91 ± 0.00
UMDA + SA	30.45 ± 12.94	105.8 ± 27.54
weigthed-RANSAC	7.40 ± 5.34	27.96 ± 17.66
Proposed Method	**7.51 ± 4.1**	**26.27 ± 14.05**

Table 3 shows the execution time used by each method; it is observed that the UMDA + SA method is the one that requires the least time during its execution; however, the BUMDA method is less than two seconds above it, unlike the two others where the time required is much longer.

Table 3. Execution time comparison of the MTA detection and numerical modeling.

Method	Execution Time (s)
General Hough	4.7641 (per pixel)
MIPAV	230
UMDA + SA	1.68
weighted-RANSAC	9.93
Proposed method	**3.4**

Table 4 shows a comparison of the evaluation measures results of the existing methods in the literature and the proposed method. The first column shows the compared method;

in the second and third column, values for differences between the existing method and the proposed method are calculated. The results for the weighted-RANSAC method are the closest to those of the proposed method, having a better result in the MDCP value, with 0.11 px less. However, there is 1.69 px more for the Hausdorff distance.

Table 4. Comparison table for MDCP and Hausdorff distance between the four methods in literature and proposed method.

Method Compared	MDCP (px.)	Hausdorff (px.)
General Hough	23.77	38.22
MIPAV	18.18	33.64
UMDA + SA	22.94	79.53
weigthed-RANSAC	−0.11	1.69

In Table 5, the difference in the execution time between the proposed method and the methods in the literature is presented. Regarding the general Hough method, since its execution time is calculated per pixel, the total time is high compared to the other methods. The negative value shown by the UMDA + SA method indicates this method is 1.72 s faster than the proposed method.

Table 5. Difference for the execution time between proposed method and literature methods.

Method Compared	Execution Time Difference (s)
General Hough	very high
MIPAV	226.6
UMDA + SA	−1.72
weighted-RANSAC	6.54

Figure 3 shows a subset of retinal fundus images overlapping the outline with the numerical modeling. In each image, the MTA appears in white, and its best fit is represented in green. Table 6 shows the polynomial series together with their coefficients for each image of Figure 3.

Table 6. Fourth-order polynomial series for each MTA fit from images of Figure 3 (in order, left to right and upper to bottom).

Image	(α, β)	Polynomial Serie
01_test	$(-0.6190, -0.6274)$	$154.37 - 203.8 J_1^{\alpha,\beta} + 139.89 J_2^{\alpha,\beta} - 22.28 J_3^{\alpha,\beta} + 36.52 J_4^{\alpha,\beta}$
03_test	$(-0.8510, -0.7823)$	$138.51 - 134.27 J_1^{\alpha,\beta} + 172.28 J_2^{\alpha,\beta} + 2.54 J_3^{\alpha,\beta} + 32.49 J_4^{\alpha,\beta}$
06_test	$(-0.5412, -0.9929)$	$148.23 - 6.32 J_1^{\alpha,\beta} + 165.49 J_2^{\alpha,\beta} - 16.78 J_3^{\alpha,\beta} + 16.07 J_4^{\alpha,\beta}$
07_test	$(-0.9687, -0.4990)$	$103.17 - 34.92 J_1^{\alpha,\beta} + 125.34 J_2^{\alpha,\beta} - 15.44 J_3^{\alpha,\beta} 3.98 J_4^{\alpha,\beta}$
09_test	$(-0.9713, -0.1148)$	$102.76 - 67.39 J_1^{\alpha,\beta} + 114.92 J_2^{\alpha,\beta} - 5.16 J_3^{\alpha,\beta} + 20.85 J_4^{\alpha,\beta}$
12_test	$(-0.5027, -0.4413)$	$139.96 + 5.90 J_1^{\alpha,\beta} + 137.52 J_2^{\alpha,\beta} + 32.75 J_3^{\alpha,\beta} + 14.43 J_4^{\alpha,\beta}$
14_test	$(-0.6905, -0.9758)$	$134.44 - 8.25 J_1^{\alpha,\beta} + 207.18 J_2^{\alpha,\beta} + 6.35 J_3^{\alpha,\beta} + 16.69 J_4^{\alpha,\beta}$
16_test	$(-0.7432, -0.6318)$	$141.09 - 11.64 J_1^{\alpha,\beta} + 195.86 J_2^{\alpha,\beta} - 1.14 J_3^{\alpha,\beta} + 8.98 J_4^{\alpha,\beta}$
17_test	$(-0.9920, -0.4718)$	$81.91 - 88.11 J_1^{\alpha,\beta} + 159.60 J_2^{\alpha,\beta} - 1.82 J_3^{\alpha,\beta} + 28.04 J_4^{\alpha,\beta}$

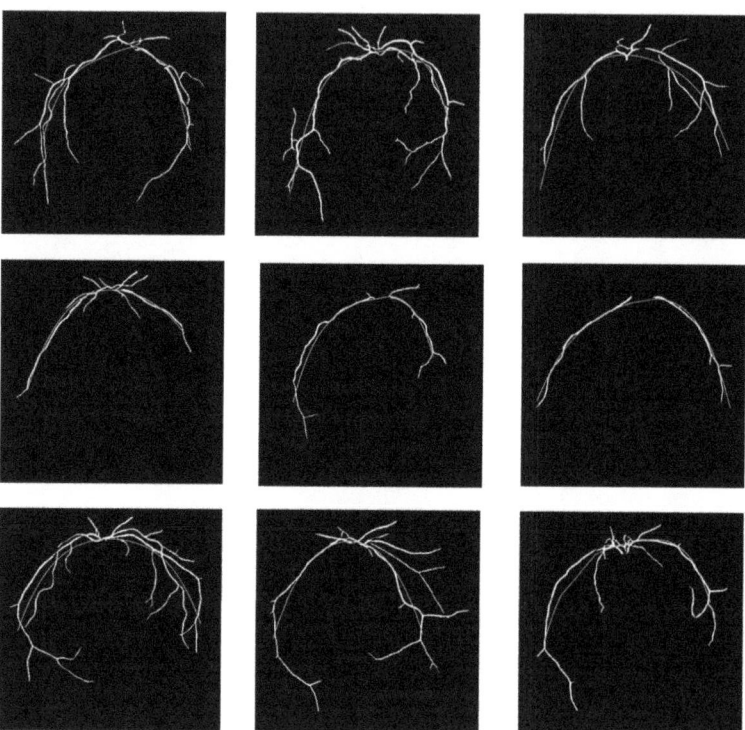

Figure 3. Numerical modeling on a subset of retinal fundus images.

The proposed method seeks to generate a numerical model that best fits the set of pixels that make up the major temporal arcade in fundus images. Using a BUMDA-type evolutionary algorithm, the coefficients and parameters associated with a linear combination of the first four Jacobi polynomials were optimized. From the previous works that have addressed this problem, the values of the MDCP and the Hausdorff distance have been used to verify how good the model obtained is. The results generated for the proposed method produce values of 22.94 and 79.53 pixels, respectively, below for the fastest state-of-the-art method. Although the results for the measures values between the proposed method and the weighted-RANSAC are very similar, the execution time is 6.53 s faster for the BUMDA proposed.

On the other hand, the proposed method reaches convergence quickly, and as can be seen in Figure 3, the model found is quite close to the MTA. Another important factor to consider is the time used to generate the model; the proposed method requires an average of 3.44 s, a particularly short time considering that one seeks to apply the method in the clinic to patients during a consultation.

Knowing the functional expression for adjustment allows some type of mathematical analysis to be carried out in such a way that more information can be extracted to help with the diagnosis and monitoring of the type of eye disease presented by the subject whose fundus images have been analyzed by the proposed method.

5. Conclusions

In this paper, the modeling of the Major Temporal Arcade in fundus images was carried out using an evolutionary algorithm strategy with a linear combination of the first four Jacobi polynomials. Here lies the novelty of this paper since the numerical modeling of the MTA using any kind of polynomial has not been addressed in the literature. The proposed method consists of using a BUMDA algorithm for the determination of the five coefficients of the polynomial series, in addition to the two parameters (α, β) associated with each polynomial. Once the parameters were determined, the fit function obtained was evaluated using two measures (the mean distance to the closest point (MDCP) and the Hausdorff distance) in order to verify how close the fit was to the delineation made by the expert. The results obtained were compared with four models from the literature. In the first instance, the proposed method generated numerical models for the MTA in a very short time, only 3.4 s. Although the UMDA + SA method remained the fastest, the difference with the proposed method was only 1.76 s; nevertheless the MDCP and Hausdorff distance values were 22.94 and 79.53 pixels, respectively, higher than the proposed method. Additionally, analyzing the results for the measurements of the MDCP and the Hausdorff distance allowed for the verification of the high closeness of the numerical model generated by the proposed method with respect to the original data set. With the proposed method, it was possible to generate a good numerical model to be able to describe in the best possible way the profile described by the MTA. For all of the above, the BUMDA method for polynomial adjustment by Jacobi polynomials can be considered as a support tool for the ophthalmologist for the diagnosis and treatment of diseases associated with diabetic retinopathy and ROP.

Author Contributions: Conceptualization, J.A.S.-Á., I.C.-A.; Formal Analysis, J.A.S.-Á., I.C.-A.; Investigation, I.C.-A., A.H.-A.; Supervision, M.A.H.-G., L.M.L.-M.; Validation, S.E.S.-M. All authors have read and agreed to the published version of the manuscript.

Funding: This research received no external funding.

Informed Consent Statement: Not applicable.

Data Availability Statement: Not applicable.

Acknowledgments: The authors thank CONACYT for the supporting granted for the post-doctoral stay carried out by the author José Alfredo Soto-Álvarez.

Conflicts of Interest: The authors declare no conflict of interest.

Abbreviations

The following abbreviations are used in this manuscript:

MTA	Major Temporal Arcade
EDA	Estimation of Distribution Algorithm
ROP	Retinopathy of Prematurity
MDCP	Mean Distance to the Closest Point
RGB	Red, Green, Blue
BUMDA	Boltzmann Univariate Marginal Distribution Algorithm
PDF	Probability Density Function
KL	Kullback - Liebler
DCP	Distance to the Closest Point

References

1. Rodríguez-Villalobos, Á.J.; Alvarado-Carrillo, D.E.; Cruz-Aceves, I.; Castellón-Lomelí, C.I.; López-Montero, L.M.; Hernández-González, M.A.; Giacinti, D.J. Estudio de la vida real sobre el modelado numérico de las arcadas temporales superiores e inferiores en imágenes de fondo de retina. *Nova Sci.* **2022**, *14*. [CrossRef]
2. Teus, M.A.; Arranz-Márquez, E.; López-Guajardo, L.; Jiménez-Parras, R. Fondo de ojo. *An. PediatrÍA Contin.* **2007**, *5*, 163–166.
3. Tenorio, G.; Ramírez-Sánchez, V. Retinopatía Diabética; conceptos actuales. *Rev. MÉdica Del Hosp. Gen. MÉxico* **2010**, *73*, 193–201.
4. Oloumi, F.; Rangayyan, R.M.; Ells, A.L. Quantification of the changes in the openness of the major temporal arcade in retinal fundus images of preterm infants with plus disease. *Investig. Ophthalmol. Vis. Sci.* **2014**, *55*, 6728–6735. [CrossRef] [PubMed]
5. Wilson, C.M.; Cocker, K.D.; Moseley, M.J.; Paterson, C.; Clay, S.T.; Schulenburg, W.E.; Mills, M.D.; Ells, A.L.; Parker, K.H.; Quinn, G.E.; et al. Computerized analysis of retinal vessel width and tortuosity in premature infants. *Investig. Ophthalmol. Vis. Sci.* **2008**, *49*, 3577–3585. [CrossRef] [PubMed]

6. Wong, K.; Ng, J.; Ells, A.; Fielder, A.R.; Wilson, C.M. The temporal and nasal retinal arteriolar and venular angles in preterm infants. *Br. J. Ophthalmol.* **2011**, *95*, 1723–1727. [CrossRef] [PubMed]
7. Oloumi, F.; Rangayyan, R.M.; Ells, A.L. Quantitative analysis of the major temporal arcade in retinal fundus images of preterm infants for detection of plus disease. In Proceedings of the IASTED International Conference on Signal and Image Processing, Wuxi, China, 8–10 July 2013; pp. 464–469.
8. Oloumi, F.; Rangayyan, R.M.; Ells, A.L. Tracking the major temporal arcade in retinal fundus images. In Proceedings of the 2014 IEEE 27th Canadian Conference on Electrical and Computer Engineering (CCECE), Toronto, ON, Canada, 4–7 May 2014; pp. 1–5.
9. Grewal, J.S.; Fielder, A.R. Sequelae of retinopathy of prematurity. *Paediatr. Child Health* **2012**, *22*, 19–24. [CrossRef]
10. Oloumi, F.; Rangayyan, R.M.; Ells, A.L. Parabolic modeling of the major temporal arcade in retinal fundus images. *IEEE Trans. Instrum. Meas.* **2012**, *61*, 1825–1838. [CrossRef]
11. Oloumi, F.; Rangayyan, R.M.; Ells, A.L. Computer-aided diagnosis of proliferative diabetic retinopathy via modeling of the major temporal arcade in retinal fundus images. *J. Digit. Imaging* **2013**, *26*, 1124–1130. [CrossRef] [PubMed]
12. Ballard, D.H. Generalizing the Hough transform to detect arbitrary shapes. *Pattern Recognit.* **1981**, *13*, 111–122. [CrossRef]
13. Valdez, S.I.; Espinoza-Perez, S.; Cervantes-Sanchez, F.; Cruz-Aceves, I. Hybridization of the Univariate Marginal Distribution Algorithm with Simulated Annealing for Parametric Parabola Detection. In *Hybrid Metaheuristics for Image Analysis*; Springer: Cham, Switzerland, 2018; pp. 163–186.
14. Giacinti, D.J.; Cervantes Sánchez, F.; Cruz Aceves, I.; Hernández González, M.A.; López Montero, L.M. Determinación de la parábola de la vasculatura de la retina mediante un algoritmo computacional de segmentación. *Nova Sci.* **2019**, *11*. [CrossRef]
15. Alvarado-Carrillo, D.E.; Cruz-Aceves, I.; Hernández-González, M.A.; López-Montero, L.M. Robust Detection and Modeling of the Major Temporal Arcade in Retinal Fundus Images. *Mathematics* **2022**, *10*, 1334. [CrossRef]
16. Staal, J.; Abràmoff, M.D.; Niemeijer, M.; Viergever, M.A.; Van Ginneken, B. Ridge-based vessel segmentation in color images of the retina. *IEEE Trans. Med. Imaging* **2004**, *23*, 501–509. [CrossRef]
17. Van Assche, W. Ordinary Special Functions. In *Encyclopedia of Mathematical Physics*; Springer: Berlin, Germany, 2006; pp. 637–645.
18. Pelikan, M.; Hauschild, M.W.; Lobo, F.G. Estimation of distribution algorithms. In *Springer Handbook of Computational Intelligence*; Springer: Berlin, Germany, 2015; pp. 899–928.
19. de Anda-Suárez, J.; Carpio-Valadez, J.M.; Puga-Soberanes, H.J.; Calzada-Ledesma, V.; Rojas-Domínguez, A.; Jeyakumar, S.; Espinal, A. Symmetric-approximation energy-based estimation of distribution (SEED): A continuous optimization algorithm. *IEEE Access* **2019**, *7*, 154859–154871. [CrossRef]
20. Valdez, S.I.; Hernández, A.; Botello, S. A Boltzmann based estimation of distribution algorithm. *Inf. Sci.* **2013**, *236*, 126–137. [CrossRef]
21. Szeg, G. *Orthogonal Polynomials*; American Mathematical Soc.: Washington, DC, USA, 1939; Volume 23.
22. Choksi, B.; Venkitaraman, A.; Mali, S. Finding best fit for hand-drawn curves using polynomial regression. *Int. J. Comput. Appl.* **2017**, *975*, 8887. [CrossRef]
23. Tong, Y.; Yu, L.; Li, S.; Liu, J.; Qin, H.; Li, W. Polynomial fitting algorithm based on neural network. *ASP Trans. Pattern Recognit. Intell. Syst.* **2021**, *1*, 32–39. [CrossRef]
24. Ameer, S. Investigating Polynomial Fitting Schemes for Image Compression. 2009. Available online: http://hdl.handle.net/10012/4255 (accessed on 1 December 2022).
25. Cruz-Aceves, I.; Cervantes-Sanchez, F.; Avila-Garcia, M. A Novel Multiscale Gaussian-Matched Filter Using Neural Networks for the Segmentation of X-Ray Coronary Angiograms. *J. Healthc. Eng.* **2018**, *11*, 5812059. [CrossRef] [PubMed]

Disclaimer/Publisher's Note: The statements, opinions and data contained in all publications are solely those of the individual author(s) and contributor(s) and not of MDPI and/or the editor(s). MDPI and/or the editor(s) disclaim responsibility for any injury to people or property resulting from any ideas, methods, instructions or products referred to in the content.

Article

Applying the Fuzzy BWM to Determine the Cryptocurrency Trading System under Uncertain Decision Process

Yeh-Cheng Yang, Wen-Sheng Shieh and Chun-Yueh Lin *

Department of Public Finance and Tax Administration, National Taipei University of Business, 321, Sec. 1, Jinan Rd., Zhongzheng Dist., Taipei City 100, Taiwan
* Correspondence: ljy898@ntub.edu.tw

Abstract: The crypto and digital assets ecosystems have attracted investment, regulators, and speculators to their environment. As the blockchain-based framework can reduce transaction costs, generate distributed trust, and enable decentralized platforms, it has become a potential new base for decentralized business models. Previous studies have highlighted the advantages and drawbacks of each platform, such as interest rates, cost concerns, transparency issues, hacking issues, and hazards. Consequently, it is challenging for investors to evaluate the cryptocurrency trading system which determines the optimum exchanges and crucial aspects. Therefore, in order to rank the optimal digital token trading system, this paper develops an evaluation architecture to determine the various token trading systems. The developed architecture integrates fuzzy theory and the best-worst method (BWM) into the decision-making process to assess decision behaviors regarding preference for digital token trading systems in investors in Taiwan. First, this work establishes the views and parameters by modifying the Delphi method based on a literature review and survey. Second, the fuzzy-BWM is applied to obtain the fuzzy weights of the views and parameters. Then, defuzzification and BWM are used to rank the optimal alternatives of the digital token trading systems for investors. The results indicate that the optimal digital token trading system is the decentralized platform, and the critical parameters are gas fees, interest rates, and the mechanism of savings under fuzzy uncertain scenarios. This means that when considering the uncertain and ambiguous characteristics of the expert decision process in digital token trading systems, the evaluation is decentralized and the gas fees are the most important parameter in the digital token investment platform. Academically, the fuzzy BWM-based decision-making architecture can provide corporations and investors with valuable guidance to rank the optimal digital token trading systems based on fuzzy uncertain scenarios. Commercially, the proposed architecture could provide corporations and investors with a useful model to measure the optimal digital token trading system.

Keywords: cryptocurrency trading system; fuzzy sets; modified Delphi method; best-worst method (BWM); fuzzy best-worst method (FBWM); blockchain

MSC: 90B50; 90C70; 91B06

Citation: Yang, Y.-C.; Shieh, W.-S.; Lin, C.-Y. Applying the Fuzzy BWM to Determine the Cryptocurrency Trading System under Uncertain Decision Process. *Axioms* **2023**, *12*, 209. https://doi.org/10.3390/axioms12020209

Academic Editor: Oscar Castillo

Received: 16 December 2022
Revised: 9 February 2023
Accepted: 13 February 2023
Published: 16 February 2023

Copyright: © 2023 by the authors. Licensee MDPI, Basel, Switzerland. This article is an open access article distributed under the terms and conditions of the Creative Commons Attribution (CC BY) license (https://creativecommons.org/licenses/by/4.0/).

1. Introduction

The crypto and digital assets ecosystems have attracted investment, regulators, and speculators to their environment. Chen and Bellavitis (2020) indicated that the blockchain-based framework can reduce transaction costs, generate distributed trust [1], and enable decentralized platforms, thus becoming a potential new base for decentralized business models. This means that they were interested in developing a new economic system and business models for trade and investment. From a financial point of view, the blockchain was initially developed as the technology behind cryptocurrencies such as Bitcoin. Tapscott and Tapscott (2017) stated that the worldwide distributed ledger runs on millions of devices and can record everything with value [2]. Zhang et al. (2020) suggested that the blockchain system can securely store transactions, such as digital cryptocurrencies, data/information regarding debt, copyrights, shares, and digital assets [3]. The CoinMarketCap website shows the rising market of the cryptocurrency field, where its total market capital in August of 2020 [4] was over 366 billion USD, and the ten main market shares and relevant cryptocurrency criteria were detailed in Table 1. The Libra association (2019) expressed that numerous companies have invested in digital tokens and accept them as major commercial instruments [5].

Table 1. The top 10 on market capitals of cryptocurrencies in 2020.

Rank	Name	Market Cap	Price	Volume	Circulating Supply
1	Bitcoin	$219,679,310,494	11,889.05	27,330,559,813	18,477,450 BTC
2	Ethereum	$53,740,791,220	477.99	19,321,812,596	112,431,030 ETH
3	XRP	$13,468,921,708	0.30	1,858,933,164	44,994,863,318 XRP
4	Tether	$13,459,127,857	1.00	50,455,204,000	13,430,692,319 USDT
5	Chainlink	$5,630,358,881	16.09	1,483,004,097	350,000,000 LINK
6	Bitcoin Cash	$5,362,817,506	289.78	1,825,084,351	18,506,269 BCH
7	Litecoin	$4,108,015,224	62.85	2,726,870,502	65,364,257 LTC
8	Bitcoin SV	$3,731,654,286	201.66	913,662,559	18,504,883 BSV
9	Binance Coin	$3,658,101,413	25.33	549,692,320	144,406,560 BNB
10	Crypto.com Coin	$3,578,866,307	0.18	82,320,135	19,733,333,333 CRO

Source: CoinMarketCap [4].

Chen and Bellavitis (2020) proposed that merchants can considerably reduce their costs and increase their profitability due to the low transaction fees of cryptocurrency [1]. For investors, initial coin offerings (ICOs) have emerged as an innovative funding mechanism for the early stage ventures of investors which allows startups and innovators to raise billions of dollars from global investors [6]. This indicates that different digital asset exchanges are available worldwide and can be accessed. The operational features of digital asset investment platforms (exchanges) are disassembled into three styles: (1) decentralized exchanges [7–14], (2) centralized exchanges [7–10,12], and (3) margin lending exchanges [7,8].

Ivaniuk (2020) indicated that the purpose of decentralized trading systems is to provide direct person-to-person trades for individuals without the need for a middleman, meaning that it is entirely administered and maintained by software [7]. Popular decentralized trading systems such as Compound and Dharma have some distinctions between them. Dharma has a set interest rate, while Compound has a fluctuating interest rate. The deposit restriction is a time deposit for Dharma and current in Compound, meaning that the Compound platform has a mechanism for compounding interest, whereas Dharma does not. Thus, the accompanying currencies on the two platforms are also different. According to the DeFi Market Cap website, the market for decentralized tokens is growing, with an overall market capitalization total of more than 170 billion USD [15]. Table 2 displays the top ten market capitalizations on decentralized exchanges, as well as their respective token requirements. Investors may benefit from decentralization trading platforms in several ways, including transparency, anonymity, peer-to-peer cryptocurrency networks, no inflation, and open-source cryptocurrency mining. Meanwhile, the downsides include the potential for money laundering, terrorist activities, illegal activity financing, and the lack of a central issuer, meaning that there is no legal formal body to guarantee in the event of bankruptcy [1,16,17]. Previous studies of the decentralized applications ecosystem focused on analyzing possible problems and providing solutions for the decentralized applications ecosystem [1,18], blockchain technology applications [19–22], the examination of business models, and their implementation on the decentralized trading platform [1,14,23–25].

Table 2. The top 10 on market capitals of decentralized trading systems in 2020.

Rank	Name	Market Cap	Price	Circulating Supply
1	UMA Voting Token v1	$1,463,396,629	$26.86	54,475,686 UMA
2	Compound Dai	$1,016,510,374	$0.02	48,829,509,452 cDAI
3	Yearn.finance	$1,014,590,443	$33,860.99	29,963 YFI
4	EthLend Token	$941,993,746	$0.75	1,256,361,932 LEND
5	Synthetix Network Token	$871,275,367	$7.45	116,890,573 SNX
6	Compound	$773,709,650	$240.09	3,222,544 COMP
7	Curve Y Pool	$686,504,604	$1.05	655,355,323 yCrv
8	Maker	$643,939,815	$713.89	902,021 MKR
9	Ampleforth	$505,359,342	$2.40	210,465,977 AMPL
10	Compound Ether	$472,244,935	$9.55	49,443,723 cETH

Source: DeFi Market Cap [15].

Centralized exchanges, which are online marketplaces for purchasing and selling bitcoins, are one of the most crucial means of trading for most cryptocurrency investors. In order to ease trade, the centralized trading system contains middlemen, such as businesses, that function as proxies [26]. This concept relates to the employment of an intermediary or third party to facilitate transactions, wherein buyers and sellers alike entrust their possessions to middlemen that perform fiat-to-cryptocurrency and crypto-to-crypto exchanges through the centralized exchange ecosystem [27]. According to Arslanian and Fischer (2019), a user may deposit fiat money into their e-wallet (e.g., USD, EUR, and JPY) and convert it to the selected crypto-asset via a fiat-to-cryptocurrency converter [27]. The crypto-to-crypto exchange does not include fiat currencies and solely allows the exchange of one crypto-asset for another. The members of the centralized trading ecosystem, such as NEXO and Celsius, also have certain differences between them. Celsius has a fluctuating interest rate, whereas NEXO has a fixed interest rate. The interest is paid daily in NEXO, whereas in Celsius, the interest is paid weekly. According to the CoinGecko website, there are more than 70 million USD market capitals in the NEXO system [28], while the Celsius network has over 174 million USD in market capitalization [29]. As a result, the centralized trading ecosystem is an essential vehicle for digital currency transactions. Shapiro (2018) demonstrated that the centralized approach benefits both market participants and regulators, as traders and investors need not be concerned with execution details or counterparty default risk [30]. This means that they can obtain the benefits from liquidity, as provided by market makers on the centralized trading exchange, and custodians can be relied on by regulators for rule enforcement, accountability, and information reporting [30]. Nevertheless, centralized trading exchanges have several drawbacks, such as costs [30], hacking activities and financial mismanagement by custodians, that lead to insolvency, employee operational failures, and sudden account freezes [12]. Furthermore, because centralized financial organizations must safeguard their centralized ledgers by limiting access, centralized finance cannot have complete transparency [1]. Prior research on centralized finance mostly emphasized price discovery [31,32], examination of risk exposure [33,34], and the volatility of digital tokens [35–37].

In light of the literature on the most recent token trading ecosystem, the hybrid trading system, we can conclude the following. The EtherDelta system is more akin to a hybrid architecture [13]. The benefits of the centralization and decentralization ecosystem are combined in the hybrid trading ecosystem. While all transactions were always carried out through calling operations in smart contracts, hybrid systems address the problem of trade discovery by keeping a centralized order management database. Nevertheless, the high price of gas fees and confirmation of transactions delay brought on by such frequent on-chain transactions is not resolved by hybrid exchanges. This would be particularly pertinent for cryptocurrency dealers who trade frequently, since more cryptocurrency transactions cause higher gas prices and longer transaction confirmation times. Therefore, hybrid trading systems do not address the possible transaction congestion issue created by too many simultaneous transactions [13].

With the emergence of blockchain technology in cryptocurrency, an increasing number of investors are paying attention to crypto concerns, such as Bitcoin, Ethereum, and Ripple. According to the above literature review, this study summarized three different types of exchanges in the digital token trading ecosystem: a centralized system, a decentralized system, and a hybrid system. Based on the foregoing arguments, several studies have highlighted the advantages and drawbacks of each platform, such as interest rates, cost concerns, transparency issues, hacking issues, and hazards. Consequently, evaluating a cryptocurrency trading system for investors is challenging, as is determining the optimum exchanges and crucial aspects. Moreover, numerous traders in digital assets do not evaluate the cryptocurrency trading system before adding cryptocurrencies to their portfolios, which entails significant financial risks. Previous works on cryptocurrencies focused on price forecasting [21–31,38], examination of risk exposure [33,34], the volatility of digital tokens [35–37,39], and risk problems in tokens [40–42]. Even though there is an increasing amount of material available regarding the cryptocurrency field, solutions to the issue of the optimal cryptocurrency trading platform and important assessment criteria for token traders have not been found. To date, no research has produced a comprehensive framework for investors during decision-making processes when evaluating the optimal cryptocurrency trading platform, the critical critera, or the digital asset traders in Taiwan. This means that they frequently lack objective scientific decision-making procedures when assessing the ideal cryptocurrency trading platform; thus, the risks of using an inappropriate token exchange are quite significant. Therefore, the goal of this investigation is to establish an evaluation framework based on a scientific decision-making process for obtaining the optimal cryptocurrency trading platform and critical criterion.

In order to establish a framework and obtain the optimal solution, the multi-criteria decision-making (MCDM) process was adopted to evaluate the optimal cryptocurrency trading platform and critical criterion [43–47]. The literature has demonstrated that the analytic hierarchy process (AHP) approach can solve optimization problems [48–50]. While AHP is quite popular in various industries, it requires the use of a pairwise comparison matrix, which requires additional indications, meaning the evaluation process would be more complicated. Therefore, Rezaei (2015) and Rezaei (2016) presented a novel MCDM methodology, known as the best-worst method (BWM) [51,52], which may simplify the complicated process of the AHP method and provide the ideal alternative and criterion weights through MCDM planning. Furthermore, one of the benefits of the BWM method is that it is a powerful way to identify the parameter weights of MCDM problems [53–56]. Omrani et al. (2020) integrated data envelopment analysis (DEA) with a BWM model to analyze the efficiency of road safety [57], while Malek and Desai (2019) proposed a BWM model to evaluate sustainable manufacturing hurdles [58]. Kheybari et al. (2019) implemented the BWM process to evaluate a bioethanol factory site [55]. However, despite its advantages, the BWM model cannot fully address the inherent uncertainties and imprecisions associated with translating decision makers' impressions into accurate figures [59].

According to Ayhan (2013) and Khan et al. (2019), unclear and ambiguous specialist judgments lead to greater complexities, which implies that numerical prediction is much more difficult for humans than qualitative prediction [60,61]. Thus, Güngör et al. (2009) proposed that fuzzy features could aid in translating human qualitative expressions into meaningful numerical forecasts [62]. Akram and Niaz (2022) determined an attribute group decision-making method that combines compromise solutions (COCOSO) with criteria importance through inter-criteria correlation (CRITIC) into Fermatean fuzzy numbers, which can solve uncertain issues in valve selections [63]. Mahmood and Ali (2022) indicated that decision-making involves erratic conditions and uncertainties [64]. They developed the complex single-valued neutrosophic with a prioritized Muirhead mean (PMM) (CSVNPMM) operator and a CSVN prioritized dual Muirhead mean (PDMM) operator based on a fuzzy environment to deal with MADM problems. Therefore, to reduce the uncertainties and imprecisions in this paper, this study integrated a fuzzy model and the BWM process to provide an assessment architecture for prioritizing, in which expert comparison judgments were represented by fuzzy triangular numbers. The evaluation architecture in this study is a fuzzy variation of BWM, and its usefulness is demonstrated by numerical examples. Based on previous reports and interviews with financial specialists, including investors and financial academics, this study employed the modified Delphi technique and fuzzy-BWM to establish an assessment architecture capable of determining the optimal cryptocurrency trading system and critical parameters in Taiwan for investors.

Consequently, this work integrated the fuzzy concept with the BWM process to calculate the weights of the perspectives and elements in the digital asset market for investors or businesses, and then assigned an appropriate relative weight to each view and parameter within the fuzzy-BWM architecture in order to obtain suitable alternatives. Regarding academic works, the fuzzy-BWM decision-making architecture may provide significant recommendations to investors or companies to determine the optimal cryptocurrency trading system for their investment projects in cryptocurrency areas. Regarding commercial works, the proposed architecture can provide administrators with a valuable instrument to determine the optimal cryptocurrency trading system and critical parameters for investors or corporations in Taiwan.

This work is constructed in three sections. Section 1 explains the evaluation architecture, including the modified Delphi method, BWM, and fuzzy-BWM. Section 2 presents the findings of the empirical investigation. Finally, Section 3 offers our remarks and conclusions.

2. Evaluation Architecture

Expert opinions were produced using the modified Delphi technique, which highlights the procedure determinants, examines the weighted parameters, and ranks opinions using the fuzzy-BWM framework. The modified Delphi technique, fuzzy ideas, and BWM assessment processes are as follows (see Figure 1).

2.1. Modified Delphi Method

According to Wu et al. (2007), the Delphi technique proceeds as follows [65]: (I) determine the anonymous professionals; (II) present the questionnaire survey with the first round; (III) present the questionnaire survey with the second round; (IV) present the questionnaire survey after the third round; and (V) collect suggestions from professionals to reach an agreement. Steps (III) and (IV) are typically performed when a specific issue is resolved [66]. All the survey's common perspectives were determined according to the literature review and expert interviews. The modified Delphi approach was used to replace the regularly utilized open-style inquiry in step (II) [66]. Additionally, Hasson and Keeney (2011) recommended the number of professional practitioners to be between five and nine [67].

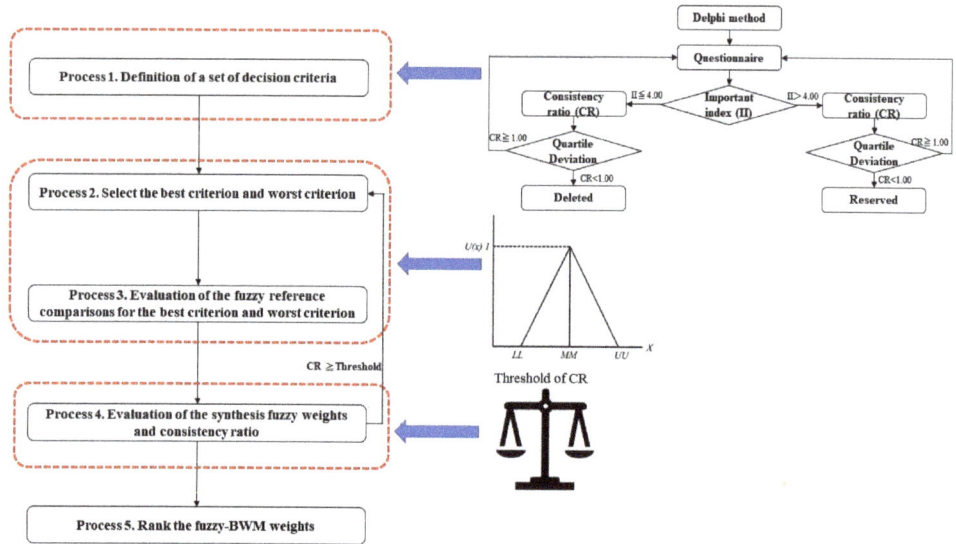

Figure 1. The evaluation processes.

2.2. Best-Worst Method (BWM)

Rezaei (2015) and Rezaei (2016) presented the BWM, which has five phases for evaluating weights in a decision issue [51,52]. The BWM method has been effectively used in various research topics, such as measuring an optimal location [55], quantifying the hurdles to sustainable manufacturing [58], and evaluating logistics performance indicators [54]. The BWM's five phases are presented as follows [51,52]:

Phase 1. Definition of a set of decision parameters

In the first phase, the decision variables $\{C_1, C_2, C_3, \ldots C_n\}$ must be determined to arrive at a conclusion, and the parameters that should be utilized to assess the alternatives are evaluated. The modified Delphi approach was used in this study to obtain the assessment parameters for rating the optimal cryptocurrency trading system for Taiwanese traders, and can be presented at distinct levels.

Phase 2. Best parameter and worst parameter

The second phase selects the best parameter (the most important parameter) and the worst parameter according to the experts, but does not evaluate the values of the parameters and alternatives.

Phase 3. Confirmation of the preference in best-to-others (BO)

In Phase 3, participants ranked their preferences on a scale of 1 to 9, with 1 representing equal importance and 9 indicating that the best parameter is more essential than the remaining parameters. The resulting BO vector is as follows.

$$A_b = (a_{b1}, a_{b2}, \ldots a_{bn}) \quad (1)$$

where a_{bj} represents that the preference of b over j and $a_{bb} = 1$.

Phase 4. Confirmation of the preference in others-to-worst (OW)

In Phase 4, participants chose a number between 1 to 9 that denotes their preference for all other factors over the criterion chosen as the least important, with 1 representing equal importance and 9 denoting that the parameter in the issue is significantly more essential than the least important parameter. The resulting OW vector is as follows.

$$A_w = (a_{1w}, a_{2w}, \ldots a_{nw})^T \qquad (2)$$

where a_{jw} denotes that the preference of j over w and $a_{ww} = 1$.

Phase 5. Determine the synthesis weights

In phase 5, the synthesis values $(w_1^*, w_2^*, w_3^*, \ldots, w_n^*)$ were determined. The synthesized value for such linear system is one that minimizes the largest absolute difference for the set ($\left|\frac{W_b}{W_j} - a_{bj}\right|$, $\left|\frac{W_j}{W_w} - a_{jw}\right|$). The sum of all the weights should equal one, and no value may be negative, thus prompting the subjects to decide on the best answer.

$$\min \max_j \left\{ \left|\frac{W_b}{W_j} - a_{bj}\right|, \left|\frac{W_b}{W_j} - a_{bj}\right| \right\} \qquad (3)$$

Subject to
$$\sum_j w_j = 1$$
$$w_j \geq 0, \text{ for all } j.$$

This problem is solvable by converting it to a linear programming problem (4).

$$\min \zeta^L \qquad (4)$$

Subject to
$$\left|w_b - a_{bj}w_j\right| \leq \zeta^L, \text{ for all } j$$
$$\left|w_j - a_{jw}w_w\right| \leq \zeta^L, \text{ for all } j$$
$$\sum_j w_j = 1$$
$$w_j \geq 0, \text{ for all } j$$

Through the outcome of this linear programming issue (4), the optimal weight and ζ^L are obtained. The consistency rate of the comparison system is denoted by ζ^L, and a consistency rate value close to 0 indicates that the participants' pairwise comparisons are consistent.

We use the following formula to ensure the consistency ratio of the comparisons:

$$\text{Consistency Ratio} = \frac{\zeta^L}{\text{Consistency index}} \qquad (5)$$

Table 3 shows the consistency index.

Table 3. The consistency index (CI).

a_{bw}	1	2	3	4	5	6	7	8	9
CI (max ζ)	0.00	0.44	1.00	1.63	2.30	3.00	3.73	4.47	5.23

Source: Rezaei [51].

2.3. Fuzzy-BWM

The BWM model, as proposed by Rezaei in 2015 [51], can improve the complexity problem of an AHP model based on a multi-objective programming concept to analyze the optimal solution and critical factors. While BWM can improve decision-making efficiency, it is unable to effectively address the inherent uncertainties and imprecisions involved with translating decision makers' views into exact numbers [59]. In order to describe the uncertainties generated by imprecise and confusing human cognitive processes, Zadeh (1965) created the fuzzy set theory [68]. Negoita (1985) and Zimmermann (1985) proposed that the theory's fundamental concept of fuzzy logic in each parameter includes a membership degree in a fuzzy system, meaning it has the advantage of quantitatively capturing uncertainty and ambiguity. Therefore, this study integrated the fuzzy theory in the BWM model to solve the uncertainty field [69,70].

This study adopted triangular fuzzy numbers (TFNs) to indicate preferences for one criterion over another. Figure 2 depicts the structure of TFNs, while Table 4 depicts the membership function. The fuzzy-BWM assessment phases are as follows.

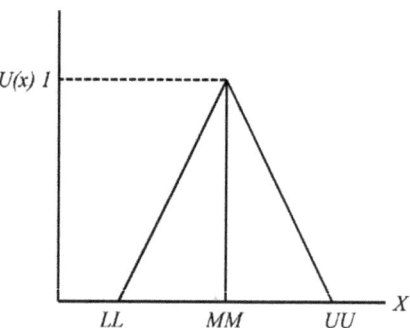

Figure 2. Triangular fuzzy numbers.

Phase 1. Definition of a set of decision parameters

In the first phase, the decision parameters $\{C_1, C_2, C_3, \ldots C_n\}$ must be determined in order to arrive at a conclusion, and the parameters that assess the alternatives are evaluated.

Phase 2. Confirm the best parameter and worst parameter

The second phase confirms the best parameter (the critical important parameter) and worst parameter according to experts, where C_B is the definition of the best parameter and C_W is the worst parameter.

Phase 3. Evaluating fuzzy reference comparisons for the best and worst parameters

Table 4 illustrates the linguistic scale of the fuzzy system, which makes it possible to confirm the fuzzy preferences of the best parameter over all other parameters. The final fuzzy best-to-others (FBO) vector obtained is:

$$\widetilde{A}_B = (\widetilde{\alpha}_{B1}, \widetilde{\alpha}_{B2}, \ldots, \widetilde{\alpha}_{Bn})$$

$\widetilde{A}_B$ indicates the FBO vector; $\widetilde{\alpha}_{Bj}$ indicates the best parameter in fuzzy C_B over parameter $j, j = 1, 2, \ldots, n$. Therefore, the fuzzy preference of $\widetilde{\alpha}_{BB}$ is (1, 1, 1).

Table 4 presents the fuzzy inference scale, where all parameters above the worst parameter of fuzzy preferences were examined. The resulting fuzzy others-to-worst (FOW) vector is:

$$\widetilde{A}_W = (\widetilde{\alpha}_{1W}, \widetilde{\alpha}_{2W}, \ldots, \widetilde{\alpha}_{nW})$$

$\widetilde{A}_W$ indicates the FOW vector; $\widetilde{\alpha}_{iW}$ indicates parameter i in the fuzzy preference over the worst parameter C_W, $i = 1, 2, \ldots, n$. Therefore, the fuzzy preference of $\widetilde{\alpha}_{WW}$ is (1, 1, 1).

Phase 4. Evaluation of the synthesis fuzzy weights and consistency ratio

This process was applied to evaluate the synthesis fuzzy weights, where Equation (6) was applied to obtain the fuzzy weights.

$$min\ max_j \left\{ \left| \frac{\widetilde{W}_B}{\widetilde{W}_j} - \widetilde{\alpha}_{Bj} \right|, \left| \frac{\widetilde{W}_j}{\widetilde{W}_w} - \widetilde{a}_{jw} \right| \right\} \qquad (6)$$

Subject to
$$\sum_{j=1}^{n} R(\widetilde{w}_j) = 1$$
$$ll_j^w \leq mm_j^w \leq uu_j^w$$
$$ll_j^w \geq 0$$
$$j = 1, 2, \ldots, n$$

where $\widetilde{W}_B = (ll_B^w, mm_B^w, uu_B^w)$, $\widetilde{W}_j = (ll_j^w, mm_j^w, uu_j^w)$, $\widetilde{W}_w = (ll_w^w, mm_w^w, uu_w^w)$, $\widetilde{\alpha}_{Bj} = (ll_{Bj}, mm_{Bj}, uu_{Bj})$, $\widetilde{\alpha}_{jw} = (ll_{jw}, mm_{jw}, uu_{jw})$.

Equation (6) can transfer to the following nonlinearly optimization model.

$$\min \widetilde{\zeta} \tag{7}$$

Subject to
$$\left| \frac{\widetilde{W}_B}{\widetilde{W}_j} - \widetilde{a}_{Bj} \right| \leq \widetilde{\zeta}$$
$$\left| \frac{\widetilde{W}_j}{\widetilde{W}_w} - \widetilde{a}_{jw} \right| \leq \widetilde{\zeta}$$
$$\sum_{j=1}^{n} R(\widetilde{w}_j) = 1$$
$$ll_j^w \leq mm_j^w \leq uu_j^w$$
$$ll_j^w \geq 0$$
$$j = 1, 2, \ldots, n$$

where $\widetilde{\zeta} = (ll^{\zeta}, mm^{\zeta}, uu^{\zeta})$; suppose $\widetilde{\zeta}^* = (k^*, k^*, k^*)$, $k^* \leq ll^{\zeta}$, then Equation (7) can transfer as:

$$\min \widetilde{\zeta}^* \tag{8}$$

Subject to
$$\left| \frac{ll_B^w mm_B^w uu_B^w}{ll_j^w mm_j^w uu_j^w} - (ll_{Bj}, mm_{Bj}, uu_{Bj}) \right| \leq (k^*, k^*, k^*)$$
$$\left| \frac{ll_j^w mm_j^w uu_j^w}{ll_W^w mm_W^w uu_W^w} - (ll_{jW}, mm_{jW}, u_{ujW}) \right| \leq (k^*, k^*, k^*)$$
$$\sum_{j=1}^{n} R(\widetilde{w}_j) = 1$$
$$ll_j^w \leq mm_j^w \leq uu_j^w$$
$$ll_j^w \geq 0$$
$$j = 1, 2, \ldots, n$$

This work employed the defuzzification process of Chen and Hsieh (2000), meaning the graded mean integration representation (GMIR) model, to identify the fuzzy synthesis results of TFN and obtain the crisp weight [71].

$$R_{(\widetilde{a_i})} = \frac{ll_i + 4mm_i + uu_i}{6} \tag{9}$$

$R_{(\widetilde{a_i})}$ represents the ranking of TFN. The crisp weights of the fuzzy preference results were obtained through Equation (9).

Finally, as the sum of the defuzzification weights of each criterion is not equal to 1, the defuzzification weights must be normalized to a new weight (NW).

The formula of NW is:
$$NW_i = \frac{R_{(\widetilde{a_i})}}{\sum_{i=1}^{n} R_{(\widetilde{a})}} \tag{10}$$

where NWi is the weight of fuzzy-BWM in each criterion.

The consistency ratio (C.R.) for fuzzy-BWM is a significant measure for determining the degree of consistency in pairwise comparisons (see Equation (5)). Guo and Zhao (2017) presented the fuzzy-BWM's consistency index (CI), as shown in Table 5 [72]. This study integrated the C.R. ratio in [72,73] to examine the obtained C.R.

Table 4. Transformation rules of linguistic scale.

Linguistic Terms	Membership Function
Equally importance (EI)	(1, 1, 1)
Weakly important (WI)	(2/3, 1, 3/2)
Fairly Important (FI)	(3/2, 2, 5/2)
Very important (VI)	(5/2, 3, 7/2)
Absolutely important (AI)	(7/2, 4, 9/2)

Source: Guo and Zhao [72].

Table 5. Consistency index for fuzzy-BWM.

Linguistic Terms	Equally Importance (EI)	Weakly Important (WI)	Fairly Important (FI)	Very Important (VI)	Absolutely Important (AI)
$\tilde{a}_{BW}$	(1, 1, 1)	(2/3, 1, 3/2)	(3/2, 2, 5/2)	(5/2, 3, 7/2)	(7/2, 4, 9/2)
Consistency index	3.00	3.80	5.29	6.69	8.04

Source: Guo & Zhao [72] and Liang et al., [73].

Phase 5. Rank the fuzzy-BWM weights

A selection of solutions can be shown in a preference list in the descending order of NW_i.

3. Case Study

This study developed parameters for evaluating the optimal cryptocurrency trading systems and crucial parameters for investors in Taiwan, and then determined a suitable relative weight for each criterion according to the fuzzy-BWM architecture. By doing so, the optimal cryptocurrency trading systems were ranked and the research architecture was constructed, as shown in Figure 3. Based on the fuzzy-BWM algorithm, the modified Delphi technique was applied to create an assessment architecture for analyzing the ideal cryptocurrency trading systems and criteria in Taiwan. The following are the phases of the proposed model:

Phase 1. Definition of a set of decision parameters

When constructing a research model, a broad agreement in line with the literature review should be obtained among specialists [74,75]. Hasson and Keeney (2011) recommended the number of practitioners to be between five and nine [67]. This phase was intended to collect the parameters through a literature review, and the seven specialists enrolled in this study included two investors of digital tokens in the commercial field, three scholars in the financial technology field, and two government experts. The goal of this study is to obtain the optimal cryptocurrency trading system and essential parameters for Taiwan, followed by four assessment views that include the cost perspective (CP), benefit perspective (BP), technology perspective (TP), and risk perspective (RP). Meanwhile, the 15 parameters in this study are gas fees (GF), withdrawal costs (WC), time costs of transaction (TCT), mechanism of savings (MS), interest rate (IR), returns of stablecoins (RST), mechanism of withdrawal (MW), regulated exchanges and providers (REP), the number of support coins (NSC), degree of difficulty in operation (DDO), risk of smart contract execution (RSCE), risk of operational security (ROS), risk of legal and regulatory issues (RLR), risk of volatility in token price (RVTP), and risk of collapse (ROC). The final cryptocurrency trading system is illustrated in Figure 3, and the data sources are shown as follows.

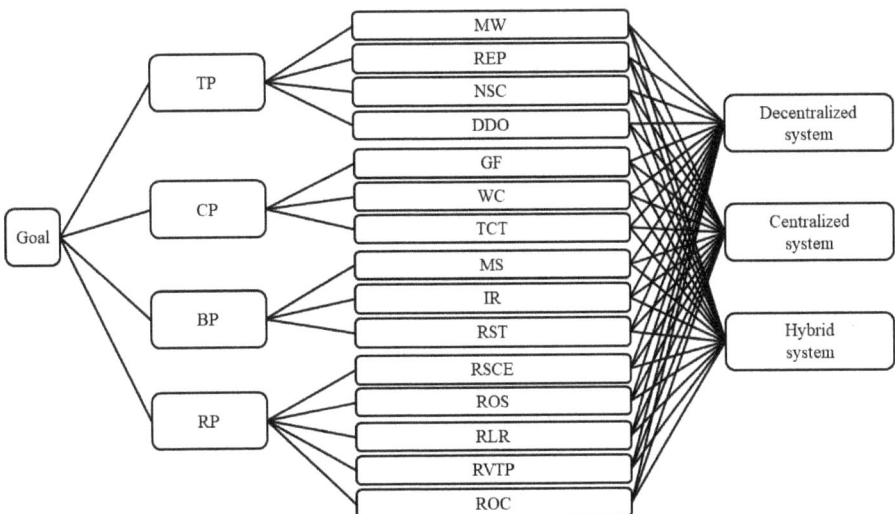

Figure 3. The research framework to evaluate the optimal cryptocurrency trading systems and critical parameters.

The assessment factors and parameters were implemented to determine the optimal cryptocurrency trading system and essential parameters in Taiwan as follows.

1. CP:
   1.1 GF [1,76,77]: the maker and taker's commissions on the cryptocurrency trading system.
   1.2 WC [78]: the trading system's withdrawal costs for digital tokens.
   1.3 TCT [76,79]: the trading system's deposit/withdrawal speed and efficiency for digital tokens.
2. BP:
   2.1 MS: various saving mechanisms, including current deposit and timed deposit, within the cryptocurrency trading system.
   2.2 IR: the various levels of interest rates, such as fixed and variable rates, within the cryptocurrency trading system.
   2.3 RST [80]: the internal rate of return of a pegged token within a system for digital token trading.
3. TP:
   3.1 MW: the many withdrawal mechanisms in cryptocurrency trading systems, such as slowly, promptly, and immediately, by trader payback.
   3.2 REP [81]: the many types of regulated trading systems and service providers in cryptocurrency trading systems, such as smart contracts, Bitgo, and Gemini.
   3.3 NSC [80]: each cryptocurrency trading system has a distinct scale of tokens.
   3.4 DDO [76,82]: the user experience and user interface of many trading systems, such as operation speed and transaction process complexity.
4. RP:
   4.1 RSCE [83]: the security concerns associated with smart contracts, including code flaws and hacking.
   4.2 ROS [83,84]: The admin keys enable a specific set of people to update contracts and undertake emergency actions. If keyholders do not create or preserve their keys securely, malevolent third parties may gain access to them.
   4.3 RLR [76,85]: the uncertainty of regulations in the digital assets market.

4.4 RVTP [76,84]: the level of volatility in token prices within the trading systems.
4.5 ROC [76]: the threat that the trading system for digital currencies may collapse due to a low transaction volume, liquidity issues, and exit fraud.
5. Cryptocurrency trading system:
  5.1 Decentralization of the trading system [7–12,14]: This trading system was designed to provide direct person-to-person trades for individuals without the need for a middleman, and it is administered and maintained entirely by smart contracts, which reduces the possibility of exit fraud. However, the fundamentals are fraught with ambiguity.
  5.2 Centralization of the trading system [7–10,12]: This trading system denotes the employment of a middleman or third party to facilitate transactions, meaning both buyers and sellers alike entrust their possessions to this middleman. While the volume and liquidity of transactions are steady, the hazards of security and fraud concerns are greater for investors.
  5.3 Hybrid trading system [7,8,12]: The hybrid trading system integrates the benefits of decentralized and centralized ecosystems. However, hybrid trading systems do not address the issues of high gas fees or transaction confirmation delays, as caused by frequent on-chain transactions.

Phase 2. Confirm the best parameter and worst parameter

This phase confirms the best and worst parameters via seven experts. These experts include two investors of digital tokens in the commercial field, three scholars in the financial technology field, and two government experts. The best and worst parameters could be different according to the perceptions of experts. Table 6 shows the best and worst parameters based on the opinions of each expert.

Table 6. The best and worst parameters.

Specialties	Views		Parameters							
			TP		CP		BP		RP	
	Worst	Best	Worst	Best	Worst	Best	Worst	Best	Worst	Best
A	TP	BP	REP	NSC	GF	TCT	ROS	IR	RLR	ROC
B	TP	RP	NSC	DDO	GF	TCT	ROS	IR	RLR	ROC
C	CP	RP	MW	REP	WC	TCT	ROS	IR	RSCE	ROC
D	TP	BP	MW	NSC	TCT	GF	MS	ROS	ROC	RLR
E	TP	CP	REP	MW	WC	GF	MS	ROS	RVTP	ROS
F	CP	BP	REP	MW	WC	GF	MS	IR	RLR	ROC
G	TP	BP	REP	DDO	WC	GF	MS	IR	RLR	ROC

Source: expert results of this study.

Phase 3. Evaluating fuzzy reference comparisons for the best and worst parameters

In line with the linguistic scale of the fuzzy system, as shown in Table 4, it is feasible to validate the best parameter's fuzzy preferences over all other parameters. Then, the fuzzy best-to-others (FBO) and fuzzy others-to-worst (FOW) values were computed. Table 7 displays the FBO and FOW results, meaning that it is possible to obtain the outcomes of fuzzy preferences of all parameters over the worst parameter. The FOW vectors were then validated, and Table 8 displays the FOW results.

Table 7. The FBO vectors.

Specialties	Fuzzy Preferences of the Best Parameter over All the Views			
	TP	CP	BP	RP
A	(7/2, 4, 9/2)	(2/3, 1, 3/2)	(3/2, 2, 5/2)	(1, 1, 1)
B	(1, 1, 1)	(5/2, 3, 7/2)	(3/2, 2, 5/2)	(1, 1, 1)
C	(7/2, 4, 9/2)	(3/2, 2, 5/2)	(1, 1, 1)	(3/2, 2, 5/2)
D	(7/2, 4, 9/2)	(3/2, 2, 5/2)	(1, 1, 1)	(2/3, 1, 3/2)
E	(7/2, 4, 9/2)	(1, 1, 1)	(3/2, 2, 5/2)	(2/3, 1, 3/2)
F	(3/2, 2, 5/2)	(7/2, 4, 9/2)	(1, 1, 1)	(3/2, 2, 5/2)
G	(5/2, 3, 7/2)	(2/3, 1, 3/2)	(1, 1, 1)	(3/2, 2, 5/2)

Source: expert results of this study.

Table 8. The FOW vectors.

Specialties	Fuzzy Preferences of All Views over the Worst Parameter			
	TP	CP	BP	RP
A	(1, 1, 1)	(5/2, 3, 7/2)	(2/3, 1, 3/2)	(7/2, 4, 9/2)
B	(7/2, 4, 9/2)	(1, 1, 1)	(3/2, 2, 5/2)	(5/2, 3, 7/2)
C	(1, 1, 1)	(3/2, 2, 5/2)	(5/2, 3, 7/2)	(2/3, 1, 3/2)
D	(1, 1, 1)	(3/2, 2, 5/2)	(7/2, 4, 9/2)	(2/3, 1, 3/2)
E	(1, 1, 1)	(7/2, 4, 9/2)	(2/3, 1, 3/2)	(3/2, 2, 5/2)
F	(3/2, 2, 5/2)	(1, 1, 1)	(7/2, 4, 9/2)	(3/2, 2, 5/2)
G	(1, 1, 1)	(5/2, 3, 7/2)	(7/2, 4, 9/2)	(3/2, 2, 5/2)

Source: expert results of this study.

Phase 4. Evaluation of the synthesis fuzzy weights and consistency ratio

This phase evaluates the synthesis fuzzy weights based on the TFNs. Equation (5) was employed to obtain the fuzzy weights, and the results are as follows. To reduce the complexity of the case study, Expert 1 was taken as an example to illustrate this phase, where Equation (11) is the fuzzified results of Expert 1's opinion.

$$\min k^* \tag{11}$$

$$s.t. \begin{cases} -k * uu_3 \leq ll_4 - 3.5 * uu_3 \leq k * uu_3 \\ -k * mm_3 \leq mm_4 - 4 * mm_3 \leq k * mm_3 \\ -k * ll_3 \leq uu_4 - 4.5 * ll_3 \leq k * ll_3 \\ -k * uu_1 \leq ll_4 - 0.67 * uu_3 \leq k * uu_1 \\ -k * mm_1 \leq mm_4 - 1 * mm_3 \leq k * mm_1 \\ -k * ll_1 \leq uu_4 - 1.5 * ll_3 \leq k * ll_1 \\ -k * uu_2 \leq ll_4 - 1.5 * uu_3 \leq k * uu_2 \\ -k * mm_2 \leq mm_4 - 2 * mm_3 \leq k * mm_2 \\ -k * ll_2 \leq uu_4 - 2.5 * ll_3 \leq k * ll_2 \\ -k * uu_3 \leq ll_1 - 2.5 * uu_3 \leq k * uu_3 \\ -k * mm_3 \leq mm_1 - 3 * mm_3 \leq k * mm_3 \\ -k * ll_3 \leq uu_1 - 3.5 * ll_3 \leq k * ll_3 \\ -k * uu_3 \leq ll_2 - 2.5 * uu_3 \leq k * uu_3 \\ -k * mm_3 \leq mm_2 - 3 * mm_3 \leq k * mm_3 \\ -k * ll_3 \leq uu_2 - 3.5 * ll_3 \leq k * ll_3 \\ \frac{1}{6} * ll_1 + \frac{1}{6} * 4 * mm_1 \frac{1}{6} * uu_1 + \frac{1}{6} * ll_2 + \frac{1}{6} * 4 * mm_2 \frac{1}{6} * uu_2 + \\ \frac{1}{6} * ll_3 + \frac{1}{6} * 4 * mm_3 \frac{1}{6} * uu_3 + \frac{1}{6} * ll_4 + \frac{1}{6} * 4 * mm_4 \frac{1}{6} * uu_4 = 1 \\ ll_1 \leq mm_1 \leq uu_1; ll_2 \leq mm_2 \leq uu_2; ll_3 \leq mm_3 \leq uu_3; ll_4 \leq mm_4 \leq uu_4 \\ ll_1 \geq 0; ll_2 \geq 0; ll_3 \geq 0; ll_4 \geq 0; k \geq 0 \end{cases}$$

This study integrated the C.R. ratios of Guo and Zhao (2017), and Liang et al. (2020) to examine the C.R. of this case study (see Tables 5 and 9) [72,73]. The fuzzy weights of all experts' opinions in views, parameters, and C.R. are shown in Table 10. The fuzzy weights of the cryptocurrency trading systems and C.R. are shown in Table 11.

Table 9. The threshold of C.R. in BWM.

Scales	No. Parameter	3	4	5	6	7	8	9
	3	0.168	0.168	0.168	0.168	0.168	0.168	0.168
	4	0.112	0.153	0.190	0.221	0.253	0.258	0.268
	5	0.135	0.199	0.231	0.255	0.272	0.284	0.296
	6	0.133	0.199	0.264	0.304	0.314	0.322	0.326
	7	0.129	0.246	0.282	0.303	0.314	0.325	0.340
	8	0.131	0.252	0.296	0.315	0.341	0.362	0.366
	9	0.136	0.268	0.306	0.334	0.352	0.362	0.366

Source: Guo & Zhao [72] and Liang et al., [73].

Table 10. The fuzzy weights of views, parameters, and C.R.

Views	ll	mm	uu	C.R.	Parameters	ll	mm	uu	C.R.
TP	0.06	0.071	0.08		MW	0.24	0.257	0.279	
					REP	0.098	0.106	0.117	0.056
					NSC	0.159	0.174	0.204	
					DDO	0.181	0.207	0.241	
CP	0.208	0.221	0.231		GF	0.343	0.349	0.408	
					WC	0.18	0.194	0.226	0.07
				0.059	TCT	0.21	0.25	0.262	
BP	0.195	0.204	0.222		MS	0.087	0.102	0.126	
					IR	0.24	0.25	0.265	0.053
					RST	0.27	0.276	0.289	
RP	0.141	0.175	0.186		RSCE	0.142	0.146	0.151	
					ROS	0.147	0.165	0.173	
					RLR	0.088	0.094	0.12	0.084
					RVTP	0.11	0.14	0.154	
					ROC	0.157	0.164	0.172	

Source: expert results of this study.

Table 11. The fuzzy weights of cryptocurrency trading systems and C.R.

Views	Systems	ll	mm	uu	C.R.
MW	Decentralized	0.291	0.316	0.378	
	Centralized	0.163	0.166	0.174	0.069
	Hybrid	0.178	0.204	0.258	
REP	Decentralized	0.301	0.313	0.327	
	Centralized	0.163	0.163	0.163	0.082
	Hybrid	0.149	0.229	0.261	
NSC	Decentralized	0.327	0.344	0.408	
	Centralized	0.119	0.119	0.13	0.051
	Hybrid	0.233	0.262	0.28	

Table 11. Cont.

Views	Systems	ll	mm	uu	C.R.
DDO	Decentralized	0.322	0.339	0.377	0.061
	Centralized	0.146	0.156	0.178	
	Hybrid	0.17	0.213	0.246	
GF	Decentralized	0.269	0.31	0.379	0.053
	Centralized	0.127	0.136	0.153	
	Hybrid	0.259	0.273	0.298	
WC	Decentralized	0.305	0.344	0.425	0.047
	Centralized	0.148	0.157	0.17	
	Hybrid	0.173	0.2	0.237	
TCT	Decentralized	0.292	0.304	0.316	0.081
	Centralized	0.177	0.183	0.188	
	Hybrid	0.135	0.203	0.251	
MS	Decentralized	0.285	0.315	0.379	0.067
	Centralized	0.164	0.173	0.186	
	Hybrid	0.17	0.201	0.237	
IR	Decentralized	0.278	0.325	0.437	0.063
	Centralized	0.138	0.147	0.159	
	Hybrid	0.208	0.237	0.252	
RST	Decentralized	0.287	0.322	0.406	0.053
	Centralized	0.14	0.149	0.164	
	Hybrid	0.22	0.238	0.243	
RSCE	Decentralized	0.307	0.318	0.327	0.081
	Centralized	0.171	0.171	0.171	
	Hybrid	0.147	0.201	0.257	
ROS	Decentralized	0.285	0.347	0.454	0.058
	Centralized	0.134	0.134	0.136	
	Hybrid	0.206	0.234	0.254	
RLR	Decentralized	0.31	0.317	0.339	0.079
	Centralized	0.31	0.317	0.339	
	Hybrid	0.16	0.231	0.25	
RVTP	Decentralized	0.279	0.309	0.385	0.047
	Centralized	0.146	0.149	0.162	
	Hybrid	0.183	0.253	0.272	
ROC	Decentralized	0.281	0.314	0.366	0.065
	Centralized	0.154	0.16	0.166	
	Hybrid	0.185	0.232	0.258	

Source: expert results of this study.

The graded mean integration representation (GMIR) model was implemented in this study to defuzzify the synthesized fuzzy weights of TFN in order to acquire the crisp weights. Finally, as the sum of the defuzzification weights of each criterion was not equal to 1, the defuzzification weights were normalized to new weights (Equations (8) and (9)). Table 12 shows the results of defuzzification, normalization, and synthesis weights in views and parameters (each view to each parameter), while Table 13 shows the results of defuzzification, normalization and synthesis weights in three cryptocurrency trading systems (each parameter to alternatives).

Table 12. The results of defuzzification, normalization and synthesis weights in views and parameters.

Views	DF	NF	PA	DF	NF	SW
TP	0.072	0.108	MW	0.258	0.344	0.037
			REP	0.107	0.143	0.015
			NSC	0.177	0.235	0.025
			DDO	0.209	0.278	0.03
CP	0.22	0.329	GF	0.358	0.447	0.147
			WC	0.198	0.247	0.081
			TCT	0.246	0.307	0.101
BP	0.205	0.307	MS	0.104	0.165	0.051
			IR	0.251	0.397	0.122
			RST	0.277	0.438	0.135
RP	0.171	0.256	RSCE	0.146	0.206	0.053
			ROS	0.164	0.231	0.059
			RLR	0.098	0.137	0.035
			RVTP	0.138	0.194	0.05
			ROC	0.164	0.231	0.059

Note: defuzzification (DF), normalization (NF), synthesis weight (SW), parameters (PA).

Table 13. The results of defuzzification, normalization and synthesis weights in cryptocurrency trading systems.

Views	Systems	DF	NF	SW
MW	Decentralized	0.322	0.449	0.017
	Centralized	0.167	0.234	0.009
	Hybrid	0.208	0.317	0.012
REP	Decentralized	0.313	0.492	0.008
	Centralized	0.163	0.186	0.003
	Hybrid	0.221	0.322	0.005
NSC	Decentralized	0.352	0.443	0.011
	Centralized	0.121	0.266	0.007
	Hybrid	0.26	0.291	0.007
DDO	Decentralized	0.342	0.461	0.014
	Centralized	0.158	0.209	0.006
	Hybrid	0.212	0.329	0.010
GF	Decentralized	0.315	0.433	0.064
	Centralized	0.138	0.189	0.028
	Hybrid	0.275	0.378	0.056
WC	Decentralized	0.351	0.46	0.037
	Centralized	0.158	0.25	0.020
	Hybrid	0.202	0.29	0.024

Table 13. Cont.

Views	Systems	DF	NF	SW
TCT	Decentralized	0.304	0.462	0.047
	Centralized	0.183	0.239	0.024
	Hybrid	0.200	0.299	0.030
MS	Decentralized	0.321	0.46	0.023
	Centralized	0.174	0.248	0.013
	Hybrid	0.202	0.292	0.015
IR	Decentralized	0.336	0.494	0.060
	Centralized	0.148	0.222	0.027
	Hybrid	0.235	0.284	0.035
RST	Decentralized	0.33	0.468	0.063
	Centralized	0.150	0.205	0.028
	Hybrid	0.236	0.327	0.044
RSCE	Decentralized	0.317	0.48	0.025
	Centralized	0.171	0.165	0.009
	Hybrid	0.202	0.355	0.019
ROS	Decentralized	0.355	0.371	0.022
	Centralized	0.134	0.371	0.022
	Hybrid	0.233	0.258	0.015
RLR	Decentralized	0.32	0.481	0.017
	Centralized	0.32	0.222	0.008
	Hybrid	0.222	0.297	0.01
RVTP	Decentralized	0.317	0.445	0.022
	Centralized	0.151	0.212	0.011
	Hybrid	0.244	0.343	0.017
ROC	Decentralized	0.317	0.45	0.027
	Centralized	0.160	0.227	0.013
	Hybrid	0.228	0.323	0.019

Note: defuzzification (DF), normalization (NF), synthesis weight (SW).

Phase 5. Rank the fuzzy-BWM weights

The new weights were evaluated with fuzzy-BWM in order to determine the optimal cryptocurrency trading system, as based on Tables 12 and 13. The NWs of each view, parameter, and system are the SW results from Tables 12 and 13, and the comprehensive results and ranking of the systems, views, and parameters are shown in Table 14.

Table 14 shows the fuzzy-BWM synthesis results regarding the determination of the optimal cryptocurrency trading system for investors in Taiwan's crypto-token fields: decentralized (0.030), centralized (0.015), and hybrid (0.021). Therefore, the sequential weights of the three cryptocurrency trading systems are decentralized > hybrid > centralized. The sequential weights of the four perspectives are costs (0.329) > benefit (0.307) > risks (0.256) > technologies (0.108), and the sequential weights of the 15 parameters are gas fees (0.147) > returns of stablecoins (0.135) > interest rate (0.122) > time costs of transaction (0.101).

Thus, the optimum cryptocurrency trading system was decentralized, which implies that when businesses or investors in Taiwan wanted to include the commodity of crypto-tokens into their portfolio, the decentralized trading system would be the focus of their investment strategy based on the fuzzy concept. Additionally, the critical views for determining the optimal cryptocurrency trading system in Taiwan were CP and GF, and some critical parameters were ROS, IR, and TCT. This result indicates that when investors utilized crypto-tokens in their financial plan, GF, ROS, IR, and TCT were the important factors to consider. As digital tokens are a virtual commodity for businesses and investors, the cost of gas fees and returns (interest rates) are very important to their financial portfolio. Moreover, investors must also be concerned with the transaction time and operational risks, meaning the transaction times of some trading systems are longer and lack security; thus, hacks may occur in the token field. Even though digital assets become more popular, high returns imply high risks. Overall, investors in Taiwan should concentrate on the costs field and GF when they implement cryptocurrency in an investment project.

Table 14. The synthesis results of fuzzy-BWM weights.

Views	NW	Rank	PA	NW	Rank	Systems	NW	Rank
TP	0.108	4	MW	0.037	11	Decentralized	0.03	1
			REP	0.015	15	Centralized	0.015	3
			NSC	0.025	14	Hybrid	0.021	2
			DDO	0.03	13			
CP	0.329	1	GF	0.147	1			
			WC	0.081	5			
			TCT	0.101	4			
BP	0.307	2	MS	0.051	9			
			IR	0.122	3			
			RST	0.135	2			
RP	0.256	3	RSCE	0.053	8			
			ROS	0.059	6			
			RLR	0.035	12			
			RVTP	0.05	10			
			ROC	0.059	7			

Note: new weight (NW), parameters (PA).

4. Conclusions

Blockchain technology can decrease the costs of transactions, build distributed trust and empower decentralized networks, which can create a new basis for decentralized business models. Crypto-tokens have been implemented by numerous corporations and investors for their financial portfolios. The cryptocurrency trading system comprises three types: decentralized, centralized, and hybrid; the benefits and drawbacks of these systems differ for different firms and investors. However, as investors and corporations in Taiwan lack the ability to assess the optimal alternatives for a crypto trading system based on the decision support concept, the evaluation and selection of the optimal cryptocurrency trading system is a complex problem for corporations and investors in Taiwan.

Hence, this study integrated the fuzzy theory and BWM to construct an evaluation architecture for prioritization, where TFNs were used to illustrate expert comparison assessments. As the evaluation architecture, the fuzzy modification of BWM could be used, and its usefulness was demonstrated with numerical examples. According to previous research and surveying specialists in economic and financial fields, such as investors and financial scholars, this study applied the modified Delphi method and fuzzy-BWM to develop an evaluation architecture that can evaluate the optimal cryptocurrency trading system and critical parameters for investors in Taiwan. The results show that the optimal cryptocurrency trading system was decentralized and the critical criterion was GF, which can facilitate investors and corporations to assess the suitable systems and key factors in crypto investment projects. The presented model and the corresponding findings can provide academic and commercial support for firms and investors in Taiwan. In the academic field, the fuzzy-BWM decision-making architecture can provide investors and corporations with valuable guidance for measuring the optimal cryptocurrency trading system for investment projects in crypto-token fields in Taiwan. In the commercial field, the proposed architecture can provide administrators with a valuable method to assess the optimal cryptocurrency trading system for investors and corporations in Taiwan. In addition, as the model integrates fuzzy-BWM, it can address other areas of uncertain decision problems, such as performance evaluation, location selection issues, strategic planning, optimal alternative evaluations, and determining the key factors.

This study has three limitations as follows:

1. In order to reduce the complexity of the evaluation process, we implemented triangular fuzzy numbers in the BWM algorithm. Future studies can apply and compare the results of trapezoidal fuzzy numbers and Gaussian fuzzy numbers in this field.
2. This study did not consider the α-cut or λ in triangular fuzzy numbers. We suggest that future studies implement these two concepts in fuzzy numbers to obtain a degree of fuzzy sensitivity.
3. The BWM algorithm cannot deal with the internal and external dependent relationships of perspectives and parameters. Future studies can also utilize the network concept to solve these relationships, for example, through the analytic network process.

Author Contributions: Conceptualization, Y.-C.Y. and C.-Y.L.; methodology, C.-Y.L. and W.-S.S.; software, C.-Y.L. and W.-S.S.; validation, Y.-C.Y., W.-S.S. and C.-Y.L.; formal analysis, Y.-C.Y.; investigation, C.-Y.L. and W.-S.S.; resources, Y.-C.Y.; data curation, C.-Y.L.; writing—original draft preparation, C.-Y.L.; writing—review and editing, Y.-C.Y. ; visualization, W.-S.S.; supervision, C.-Y.L.; project administration, Y.-C.Y., W.-S.S. and C.-Y.L.; funding acquisition, Y.-C.Y. All authors have read and agreed to the published version of the manuscript.

Funding: This research received no external funding.

Institutional Review Board Statement: Not applicable.

Informed Consent Statement: Not applicable.

Data Availability Statement: Data sharing is not applicable to this article.

Conflicts of Interest: The authors declare no conflict of interest.

References

1. Chen, Y.; Bellavitis, C. Blockchain disruption and decentralized finance: The rise of decentralized business models. *J. Bus. Ventur. Insights* **2020**, *13*, e00151. [CrossRef]
2. Tapscott, A.; Tapscott, D. How blockchain is changing finance. *Harv. Bus. Rev.* **2017**, *1*, 2–5.
3. Zhang, L.; Xie, Y.; Zheng, Y.; Xue, W.; Zheng, X.; Xu, X. The challenges and countermeasures of blockchain in finance and economics. *Syst. Res. Behav. Sci.* **2020**, *37*, 691–698. [CrossRef]
4. Coin Market Cap. Cryptocurrencies by Market Capitalization. 2020. Available online: https://coinmarketcap.com/ (accessed on 25 August 2020).
5. Libra Association. Libra White Paper. 2019. Available online: https://libra.org/en-US/white-paper/ (accessed on 26 August 2020).
6. Martino, P.; Wang, K.J.; Bellavitis, C.; DaSilva, C.M. An introduction to blockchain, cryptocurrency and initial coin offerings. *New Front. Entrep. Financ. Res.* **2019**, 181–206. [CrossRef]
7. Ivaniuk, V. Cryptocurrency exchange regulation–An international review. *Stud. Prawnoustr.* **2020**, *48*, 67–77.
8. Xia, P.; Wang, H.; Zhang, B.; Ji, R.; Gao, B.; Wu, L.; Luo, X.; Xu, G. Characterizing cryptocurrency exchange scams. *Comput. Secur.* **2020**, *98*, 101993. [CrossRef]
9. Tian, H.; Xue, K.; Luo, X.; Li, S.; Xu, J.; Liu, J.; Zhao, J.; Wei, D.S.L. Enabling Cross-Chain Transactions: A Decentralized Cryptocurrency Exchange Protocol. *IEEE Trans. Inf. Forensics Secur.* **2021**, *16*, 3928–3941. [CrossRef]
10. Bentov, I.; Ji, Y.; Zhang, F.; Breidenbach, L.; Daian, P.; Juels, A. Tesseract: Real-time cryptocurrency exchange using trusted hardware. In Proceedings of the 2019 ACM SIGSAC Conference on Computer and Communications Security, London, UK, 11–15 November 2019; pp. 1521–1538.

11. Nabilou, H. How to regulate bitcoin? Decentralized regulation for a decentralized cryptocurrency. *Int. J. Law Inf. Technol.* **2019**, *27*, 266–291. [CrossRef]
12. Luo, X.; Cai, W.; Wang, Z.; Li, X.; Leung, C.V. A payment channel based hybrid decentralized ethereum token exchange. In Proceedings of the 2019 IEEE International Conference on Blockchain and Cryptocurrency (ICBC), Seoul, Republic of Korea, 14–17 May 2019; pp. 48–49.
13. Luo, X. Application and Evaluation of Payment Channel in Hybrid Decentralized Ethereum Token Exchange. Doctoral Dissertation, University of British Columbia, Vancouver, BC, Canada, 2019.
14. Lee, J.Y. A decentralized token economy: How blockchain and cryptocurrency can revolutionize business. *Bus. Horiz.* **2019**, *62*, 773–784. [CrossRef]
15. DeFi Market Cap. Top 100 Defi Tokens by Market Capitalization. 2020. Available online: https://defimarketcap.io/ (accessed on 1 September 2020).
16. Bunjaku, F.; Gorgieva-Trajkovska, O.; Miteva-Kacarski, E. Cryptocurrencies–advantages and disadvantages. *J. Econ.* **2017**, *2*, 31–39.
17. Vora, G. Cryptocurrencies: Are Disruptive Financial Innovations Here? *Mod. Econ.* **2015**, *06*, 816–832. [CrossRef]
18. Ghosh, A.; Gupta, S.; Dua, A.; Kumar, N. Security of Cryptocurrencies in blockchain technology: State-of-art, challenges and future prospects. *J. Netw. Comput. Appl.* **2020**, *163*, 102635. [CrossRef]
19. Singh, A.; Click, K.; Parizi, R.M.; Zhang, Q.; Dehghantanha, A.; Choo, K.-K.R. Sidechain technologies in blockchain networks: An examination and state-of-the-art review. *J. Netw. Comput. Appl.* **2020**, *149*, 102471. [CrossRef]
20. Pereira, J.; Tavalaei, M.M.; Ozalp, H. Blockchain-based platforms: Decentralized infrastructures and its boundary conditions. *Technol. Forecast. Soc. Chang.* **2019**, *146*, 94–102. [CrossRef]
21. Nizamuddin, N.; Salah, K.; Azad, M.A.; Arshad, J.; Rehman, M. Decentralized document version control using ethereum blockchain and IPFS. *Comput. Electr. Eng.* **2019**, *76*, 183–197. [CrossRef]
22. Issaoui, Y.; Khiat, A.; Bahnasse, A.; Ouajji, H. Smart logistics: Study of the application of blockchain technology. *Procedia Comput. Sci.* **2019**, *160*, 266–271. [CrossRef]
23. Kimani, D.; Adams, K.; Attah-Boakye, R.; Ullah, S.; Frecknall-Hughes, J.; Kim, J. Blockchain, business and the fourth industrial revolution: Whence, whither, wherefore and how? *Technol. Forecast. Soc. Chang.* **2020**, *161*, 120254. [CrossRef]
24. Ahluwalia, S.; Mahto, R.V.; Guerrero, M. Blockchain technology and startup financing: A transaction cost economics perspective. *Technol. Forecast. Soc. Chang.* **2020**, *151*, 119854. [CrossRef]
25. Kumar, G.; Saha, R.; Buchanan, W.J.; Geetha, G.; Thomas, R.; Rai, M.K.; Kim, T.-H.; Alazab, M. Decentralized accessibility of e-commerce products through blockchain technology. *Sustain. Cities Soc.* **2020**, *62*, 102361. [CrossRef]
26. Matkovskyy, R. Centralized and decentralized bitcoin markets: Euro vs USD vs GBP. *Q. Rev. Econ. Financ.* **2019**, *71*, 270–279. [CrossRef]
27. Arslanian, H.; Fischer, F. The Crypto-asset Ecosystem. In *The Future of Finance*; Palgrave Macmillan: Cham, Switzerland, 2019; pp. 157–163.
28. CoinGecko. Celsius Network Market Capitals. 2020. Available online: https://www.coingecko.com/en/coins/celsius-network-token (accessed on 7 September 2020).
29. CoinGecko. NEXO Market Capitals. 2020. Available online: https://www.coingecko.com/en/coins/nexo#markets (accessed on 7 September 2020).
30. Shapiro, D.C. Taxation and Regulation in Decentralized Exchanges. *J. Tax. Investig.* **2018**, *36*, 3–13.
31. Patel, M.M.; Tanwar, S.; Gupta, R.; Kumar, N. A Deep Learning-based Cryptocurrency Price Prediction Scheme for Financial Institutions. *J. Inf. Secur. Appl.* **2020**, *55*, 102583. [CrossRef]
32. Alexander, C.; Choi, J.; Massie, H.R.; Sohn, S. Price discovery and microstructure in ether spot and derivative markets. *Int. Rev. Financ. Anal.* **2020**, *71*, 101506. [CrossRef]
33. Corbet, S.; Larkin, C.; Lucey, B.; Meegan, A.; Yarovaya, L. Cryptocurrency reaction to fomc announcements: Evi-dence of heterogeneity based on blockchain stack position. *J. Financ. Stab.* **2020**, *46*, 100706. [CrossRef]
34. Brauneis, A.; Mestel, R. Cryptocurrency-portfolios in a mean-variance framework. *Financ. Res. Lett.* **2019**, *28*, 259–264. [CrossRef]
35. Conrad, C.; Custovic, A.; Ghysels, E. Long- and Short-Term Cryptocurrency Volatility Components: A GARCH-MIDAS Analysis. *J. Risk Financ. Manag.* **2018**, *11*, 23. [CrossRef]
36. Walther, T.; Klein, T.; Bouri, E. Exogenous drivers of Bitcoin and Cryptocurrency volatility—A mixed data sampling approach to forecasting. *J. Int. Financ. Mark. Inst. Money* **2019**, *63*, 101133. [CrossRef]
37. Ma, F.; Liang, C.; Ma, Y.; Wahab, M. Cryptocurrency volatility forecasting: A Markov regime-switching MIDAS approach. *J. Forecast.* **2020**, *39*, 1277–1290. [CrossRef]
38. Poongodi, M.; Sharma, A.; Vijayakumar, V.; Bhardwaj, V.; Sharma, A.P.; Iqbal, R.; Kumar, R. Prediction of the price of Ethereum blockchain cryptocurrency in an industrial finance system. *Comput. Electr. Eng.* **2020**, *81*, 106527.
39. Andrada-Félix, J.; Fernandez-Perez, A.; Sosvilla-Rivero, S. Distant or close cousins: Connectedness between cryp-tocurrencies and traditional currencies volatilities. *J. Int. Financ. Mark. Inst. Money* **2020**, *67*, 101219. [CrossRef]
40. Xu, Q.; Zhang, Y.; Zhang, Z. Tail-risk spillovers in cryptocurrency markets. *Financ. Res. Lett.* **2020**, *38*, 101453. [CrossRef]
41. Enoksen, F.; Landsnes, C.; Lučivjanská, K.; Molnár, P. Understanding risk of bubbles in cryptocurrencies. *J. Econ. Behav. Organ.* **2020**, *176*, 129–144. [CrossRef]

42. Liu, W.; Semeyutin, A.; Lau, C.K.M.; Gozgor, G. Forecasting Value-at-Risk of Cryptocurrencies with RiskMetrics type models. *Res. Int. Bus. Financ.* **2020**, *54*, 101259. [CrossRef]
43. Ahmad, Q.S.; Khan, M.F.; Ahmad, N. Multi-Criteria Group Decision-Making Models in a Multi-Choice Environ-ment. *Axioms* **2022**, *11*, 659. [CrossRef]
44. Wang, W.-Y.; Yang, Y.-C.; Lin, C.-Y. Integrating the BWM And Topsis Algorithm to Evaluate the Optimal Token Exchanges Platform in Taiwan. *Technol. Econ. Dev. Econ.* **2022**, *28*, 358–380. [CrossRef]
45. Lin, C.Y. Optimal Core Operation in Supply Chain Finance Ecosystem by Integrating the Fuzzy Algorithm and Hier-archical Framework. *Int. J. Comput. Intell. Syst.* **2020**, *13*, 259–274. [CrossRef]
46. Hamdan, S.; Cheaitou, A. Supplier selection and order allocation with green criteria: An MCDM and multi-objective optimization approach. *Comput. Oper. Res.* **2017**, *81*, 282–304. [CrossRef]
47. Lin, S.-W. Identifying the Critical Success Factors and an Optimal Solution for Mobile Technology Adoption in Travel Agencies. *Int. J. Tour. Res.* **2017**, *19*, 127–144. [CrossRef]
48. Baidya, R.; Dey, P.K.; Ghosh, S.K.; Petridis, K. Strategic maintenance technique selection using combined quality function deployment, the analytic hierarchy process and the benefit of doubt approach. *Int. J. Adv. Manuf. Technol.* **2018**, *94*, 31–44. [CrossRef]
49. Kamaruzzaman, S.N.; Lou EC, W.; Wong, P.F.; Wood, R.; Che-Ani, A.I. Developing weighting system for re-furbishment building assessment scheme in Malaysia through analytic hierarchy process (AHP) approach. *Energy Policy* **2018**, *112*, 280–290. [CrossRef]
50. Ho, W.; Ma, X. The state-of-the-art integrations and applications of the analytic hierarchy process. *Eur. J. Oper. Res.* **2018**, *267*, 399–414. [CrossRef]
51. Rezaei, J. Best-worst multi-criteria decision-making method. *Omega* **2015**, *53*, 49–57. [CrossRef]
52. Rezaei, J. Best-worst multi-criteria decision-making method: Some properties and a linear model. *Omega* **2016**, *64*, 126–130. [CrossRef]
53. van de Kaa, G.; Kamp, L.; Rezaei, J. Selection of biomass thermochemical conversion technology in the Netherlands: A best worst method approach. *J. Clean. Prod.* **2017**, *166*, 32–39. [CrossRef]
54. Rezaei, J.; van Roekel, W.S.; Tavasszy, L. Measuring the relative importance of the logistics performance index indicators using Best Worst Method. *Transp. Policy* **2018**, *68*, 158–169. [CrossRef]
55. Kheybari, S.; Kazemi, M.; Rezaei, J. Bioethanol facility location selection using best-worst method. *Appl. Energy* **2019**, *242*, 612–623. [CrossRef]
56. Pamučar, D.; Ecer, F.; Cirovic, G.; Arlasheedi, M.A. Application of Improved Best Worst Method (BWM) in Re-al-World Problems. *Mathematics* **2020**, *8*, 1342. [CrossRef]
57. Omrani, H.; Amini, M.; Alizadeh, A. An integrated group best-worst method—Data envelopment analysis approach for evaluating road safety: A case of Iran. *Measurement* **2020**, *152*, 107330. [CrossRef]
58. Malek, J.; Desai, T.N. Prioritization of sustainable manufacturing barriers using Best Worst Method. *J. Clean. Prod.* **2019**, *226*, 589–600. [CrossRef]
59. Tsai, H.-Y.; Chang, C.-W.; Lin, H.-L. Fuzzy hierarchy sensitive with Delphi method to evaluate hospital organization performance. *Expert Syst. Appl.* **2010**, *37*, 5533–5541. [CrossRef]
60. Ayhan, M.B. A fuzzy AHP approach for supplier selection problem: A case study in a Gear motor company. *Int. J. Manag. Value Supply Chain.* **2013**, *4*, 11–23. [CrossRef]
61. Khan, A.A.; Shameem, M.; Kumar, R.R.; Hussain, S.; Yan, X. Fuzzy AHP based prioritization and taxonomy of software process improvement success factors in global software development. *Appl. Soft Comput.* **2019**, *83*, 105648. [CrossRef]
62. Güngör, Z.; Serhadlıoğlu, G.; Kesen, S.E. A fuzzy AHP approach to personnel selection problem. *Appl. Soft Comput.* **2009**, *9*, 641–646. [CrossRef]
63. Akram, M.; Niaz, Z. 2-Tuple linguistic Fermatean fuzzy decision-making method based on COCOSO with CRITIC for drip irrigation system analysis. *J. Comput. Cogn. Eng.* **2022**, *forthcoming*.
64. Mahmood, T.; Ali, Z. Prioritized muirhead mean aggregation operators under the complex single-valued neutro-sophic settings and their application in multi-attribute decision-making. *J. Comput. Cogn. Eng.* **2022**, *1*, 56–73.
65. Wu, C.-R.; Lin, C.-T.; Chen, H.-C. Evaluating competitive advantage of the location for Taiwanese hospitals. *J. Inf. Optim. Sci.* **2007**, *28*, 841–868. [CrossRef]
66. Sung, W.C. Application of Delphi Method, a Qualitative and Quantitative Analysis, to the Healthcare Management. *J. Healthc. Manag.* **2001**, *2*, 11–19.
67. Hasson, F.; Keeney, S. Enhancing rigour in the Delphi technique research. *Technol. Forecast. Soc. Chang.* **2011**, *78*, 1695–1704. [CrossRef]
68. Zadeh, L. Fuzzy Sets. *Inf. Control.* **1965**, *8*, 338–353. [CrossRef]
69. Negoita, C.V. *Expert Systems and Fuzzy Systems*; Benjamin/Cummings: Menlo Park, CA, USA, 1985.
70. Zimmermann, H.J. *Fuzzy Set Theory and Its Applications*; Kluwer: Boston, MA, USA, 1985.
71. Chen, S.H.; Hsieh, C.H. Representation, ranking, distance, and similarity of LR type fuzzy number and application. *Aust. J. Intell. Process. Syst.* **2000**, *6*, 217–229.
72. Guo, S.; Zhao, H. Fuzzy best-worst multi-criteria decision-making method and its applications. *Knowl.-Based Syst.* **2017**, *121*, 23–31. [CrossRef]

73. Liang, F.; Brunelli, M.; Rezaei, J. Consistency issues in the best worst method: Measurements and thresholds. *Omega* **2020**, *96*, 102175. [CrossRef]
74. Linden, G.; Kraemer, K.L.; Dedrick, J. Who Captures Value in a Global Innovation Network? The Case of Apple's iPod. *Commun. ACM* **2009**, *52*, 140–144. [CrossRef]
75. Ali-Yrkkö, J.; Rouvinen, P.; Seppälä, T.; Ylä-Anttila, P. Who Captures Value in Global Supply Chains? Case Nokia N95 Smartphone. *J. Ind. Compet. Trade* **2011**, *11*, 263–278. [CrossRef]
76. Rehman, M.H.U.; Salah, K.; Damiani, E.; Svetinovic, D. Trust in Blockchain Cryptocurrency Ecosystem. *IEEE Trans. Eng. Manag.* **2019**, *67*, 1196–1212. [CrossRef]
77. Easley, D.; O'Hara, M.; Basu, S. From mining to markets: The evolution of bitcoin transaction fees. *J. Financ. Econ.* **2019**, *134*, 91–109. [CrossRef]
78. Chuen, D.L.K.; Guo, L.; Wang, Y. Cryptocurrency: A New Investment Opportunity? *J. Altern. Invest.* **2017**, *20*, 16–40. [CrossRef]
79. Ricci, S.; Ferreira, E.; Menasche, D.S.; Ziviani, A.; Souza, J.E.; Vieira, A.B. Learning blockchain delays: A queueing theory approach. *ACM SIGMETRICS Perform. Eval. Rev.* **2019**, *46*, 122–125. [CrossRef]
80. Moin, A.; Sekniqi, K.; Sirer, E.G. SoK: A Classification Framework for Stablecoin Designs. In Proceedings of the 24th International Conference on Financial Cryptography and Data Security, Kota Kinabalu, Malaysia, 10–14 February 2020; pp. 174–197. [CrossRef]
81. Silfversten, E.; Favaro, M.; Slapakova, L.; Ishikawa, S.; Liu, J.; Salas, A. *Exploring the Use of Zcash Cryptocurrency for Illicit or Criminal Purposes*; RAND: Santa Monica, CA, USA, 2020. [CrossRef]
82. Peters, G.W.; Chapelle, A.; Panayi, E. Opening discussion on banking sector risk exposures and vulnerabilities from Virtual currencies: An Operational Risk perspective. *J. Bank. Regul.* **2016**, *17*, 239–272. [CrossRef]
83. Schär, F. Decentralized Finance: On Blockchain- and Smart Contract-Based Financial Markets. *Fed. Reserve Bank St. Louis Rev.* **2021**, *103*. [CrossRef]
84. Aziz, A.T.I.F. Cryptocurrency: Evolution & Legal Dimension. *Int. J. Bus. Econ. Law* **2019**, *18*, 31–33.
85. Söylemez, Y. Cryptocurrency Derivatives: The Case of Bitcoin. In *Blockchain Economics and Financial Market Innovation*; Springer: Cham, Switzerland, 2019; pp. 515–530.

Disclaimer/Publisher's Note: The statements, opinions and data contained in all publications are solely those of the individual author(s) and contributor(s) and not of MDPI and/or the editor(s). MDPI and/or the editor(s) disclaim responsibility for any injury to people or property resulting from any ideas, methods, instructions or products referred to in the content.

Article

Proposal for Mathematical and Parallel Computing Modeling as a Decision Support System for Actuarial Sciences

Marcos dos Santos [1,2], Carlos Francisco Simões Gomes [3], Enderson Luiz Pereira Júnior [3], Miguel Ângelo Lellis Moreira [2,3,*], Igor Pinheiro de Araújo Costa [2,3] and Luiz Paulo Fávero [4]

[1] Systems and Computing Department, Military Institute of Engineering, Rio de Janeiro 22290-270, Brazil
[2] Operational Research Department, Naval Systems Analysis Centre, Rio de Janeiro 20091-000, Brazil
[3] Production Engineering Department, Federal Fluminense University, Rio de Janeiro 24210-240, Brazil
[4] School of Economics, Business, and Accounting, University of São Paulo, São Paulo 05508-010, Brazil
* Correspondence: miguellellis@hotmail.com

Abstract: This paper aims to find the actuarial tables that best represent the occurrences of mortality and disability in the Brazilian Armed Forces, thus providing a better dimensioning of the costs of military pensions to be paid by the pension system. To achieve this goal, an optimization software was developed that tests 53 actuarial tables for the death of valid military personnel, 21 boards for entry into the disability of assets, and 21 boards for mortality of invalids. The software performs 199 distinct adherence tests for each table analyzed through linear aggravations and de-escalations in the probabilities of death and disability. The statistical–mathematical method used was the chi-square adherence test in which the selected table is the one with the null hypothesis "observed data" equal to the "expected data" with the highest degree of accuracy. It is expected to bring a significant contribution to society, as a model of greater accuracy reduces the risk of a large difference between the projected cost and the cost observed on the date of the year, thus contributing to the maintenance of public governance. Additionally, the unprecedented and dual nature of the methodology presented here stands out. As a practical contribution, we emphasize that the results presented streamline the calculation of actuarial projections, reducing by more than 90% the processing times of calculations referring to actuarial projections of retirees from the armed forces. As a limitation of the study, we emphasize that, although possibly replicable, the database was restricted only to the Brazilian Armed Forces.

Keywords: operational research; actuarial science; parallel computing; computer science; decision-making process

1. Introduction

The decision-making process in political environments involves different areas, interconnecting strategic, tactical, and operational levels in favor of a direction aligned with the objectives in a given problematic situation [1–9]. The high-level decision-making sphere is complex, where the given form of solution can generate influences not only in the political sphere but also impacts other areas of society [10,11]. In this context, the decision analysis in complex environments, integrating multiple stakeholders analyzing aspects relevant to the problem is common [12,13], enabling, from multiple perspectives, a consensus in the process [14,15].

With the involvement of multiple scenarios and circumstances, the increase in complexity in a given analysis becomes noticeable [16,17], with different points of view as to the importance or influence of a decision variable, although, it is necessary to consider it in favor of a substantial evaluation and greater assertiveness in the final decision [18–20].

It is usual to apply operational research (OR) techniques and methods, to provide the optimization of the resource environment [21], enabling the cost reduction and, consequently, a better understanding, analysis, and solution of complex problems [22,23]. In this context, the decision concerning public pension is one of the most important economic decisions [24], if we consider that it defines, at an aggregate level, the performance of the economy investments [25,26].

In this scenario, the social security schemes are generally very relevant to the well-being of large numbers of beneficiaries [27]. Thus, one sought to create an unprecedented methodology capable of providing the best possible accuracy in the projection of revenues and costs of the military pension system over a 75-year time horizon in the context of actuarial science.

This analysis is restricted to the military pensions defined by Law No. 3765, dated May 4, 1960, of Brazil. With regard to social security, it emphasizes that, besides the legal and social aspect, there is also the economic aspect [28]. It cannot be neglected that rights generate costs, especially the rights that demand a "doing" of the public administration [29,30].

It should be noted that the military of the armed forces are not part of the social security system, published in Brazil, since in the military pension system, there is no accumulated equity to bear the future costs, and it is therefore financed by regime without capital accumulation [31,32]. Corroborating this statement, it points out that, legally, the federal military does not have a social security system, and its proceeds are fully funded by the National Treasury [33]. Hence the importance of keeping track of the projected values and values effectively contributed by the Union, year by year [34].

Thus, extensive research was conducted in the social security system (SSS) and in the general social security system (GSSS) [35]. It was verified that the methodology, parameters, and biometric assumptions adopted by these regimes could not be used for the social protection of military personnel (SPMP), in view of the peculiarities of the military career [36,37].

The armed forces have a considerable mass of financial and biometric data of their pensioners that needs to be submitted to its own actuarial mathematical model [38] to obtain the result of the actuarial projection of 75 years, which is a legal requirement that must be met annually [39]. In this context, the objective of the present study is to reduce the computational times necessary to obtain the results of the referred projection, through the application of operations research, parallel computing, and software engineering techniques.

This paper is divided into six sections. The first presents a brief introduction on the problem. The second describes the problem and the proposed methodology. The third is the implementation of the proposed methodology. The fourth presents the results of the proposed heuristic called the adhesion cube. The fifth brings some details of the armed forces actuarial software (AFAS) and the sixth makes some final considerations with their respective conclusions.

2. Background

There is the regular compulsory contribution of active and inactive military, whose rate is 7.5% in the social security system [40]. The projection of the collection and the constitutional cost with proceeds aims to confer transparency and predictability on the obligations of the armed forces, in order to guide the formulation of policies to maintain the long-term fiscal sustainability [41].

The theme of social security became important for Brazilian society since the year 1995 (the year of the establishment of the real as the Brazilian currency). The deficit has billions of shares that grow systematically year by year [42]. Analyzing a historical series, since 1995, this deficit was around one billion reals in 1997, and in 2017 it surpassed two hundred and sixty billion reals (USD 250,000.00) according to the Secretariat of Social Security of the Ministry of Finance [42]. The parameters for the calculation of the pension deficit in the referred historical series remained unchanged, and such numbers were confirmed and validated by the Federal Court of Accounts (TCU) [43]. In order to maintain the solvency of the Brazilian State, the Federal Government presented a series of proposals aimed at reducing the medium to long-term welfare deficit, or at least interrupting its growth trend [44].

To conduct the application of actuarial science to the costs of pensioners of the armed forces, it is necessary to study and design the constitutional costs of the current assets, inactive, and pensioners [45]. However, it is known that demographic–actuarial projections cannot be absolutely accurate. However, long-term projections are carried out by the Brazilian government and constitute a set of decisions of strategic relevance for the country; its limits have to be more clearly stated and the use of more recent projection and scenario construction techniques should be the basis of a more robust and reliable decision support system [46].

Indemnity pensions or special pensions of the group of ex-combatants (soldiers who fought in wars) and political amnesties (after democratization in 1985) are not included in this study, because if they were considered, they would cause unnecessary distortions, given the specificity of each one. The work is restricted to the military pensions defined by Law No. 3765. The proposed model was initially tested with data from the Strategic and Management Information Bank (SMIB) for the month of October/2015 and the actuarial projections were made for the period from 2017 to 2091. The article proposes a methodology capable of evaluating, with the best possible accuracy, the income and costs of pensioners of the armed forces over a 75-year horizon, based on existing data, using actuarial science and operational research [47].

2.1. Actuarial Tables

Actuarial tables are tables that include the social and biometric characteristics of a given sample for analysis of expectations and risk in actuarial science. The tables selected in an actuarial study must effectively represent the biometric events (such as death, disability, and illness) that affect the analyzed population. They should be chosen based on the historical experience and perspectives of the sample. Most studies of seasonal variation in mortality rely on aggregated counts of deaths at the population level. The use of actuarial tables that are out of step with reality can result in cumulative actuarial losses or gains over time, generating structural imbalances in the system [48].

According to [49], the actuarial table is the basic tool for analyzing population evolution, representing the oldest demographic model in use, historically used to measure the longevity of a population [50]. The earliest known tables date back to the 3rd century, but modern actuarial ones were developed from the 17th century [51]. Since then, its practical applications were diversified, with new relationships developed and functions improved [52]. The actuarial tables are the foundation for any product in the social security area and may come from data from a demographic censuses or the insurance companies' experience [53].

2.2. Goodness-of-Fit (GoF) Tests

GoF tests are statistical methods that allow you to examine how well a data sample matches a given distribution [54,55]. The purpose of these tests is to assess whether two frequency distributions are approximately identical or whether they can be considered heterogeneous [56]. It is considered as a statistical test of probability distribution model, in which the observed proportions are adjusted to the expected proportions [57], mathematically deduced, or established according to some [58].

GoF tests consist of verifying the suitability of a probabilistic model to a data set. In the GoF tests, there is a null hypothesis H_0 that X, a random variable, follows a declared probability law $F(x)$. The techniques of these tests consist of mathematical models to measure the conformity of the data of a sample, that is, set of values of x with the hypothetical distribution; or, equivalently, with its discrepancy about it [59]. In other words, the basic concept is that, given a random sample of size n, observed from a random variable X, it is desired to test the null hypothesis H_0 that the sample follows a certain distribution function $F(x)$, confronting it with the alternative hypothesis H_1, that the sample does not follow the distribution function $F(x)$:

H_0. *X has distribution $F(x)$* vs. **H_1.** *X has no distribution $F(x)$.*

In the formal structure of the adherence test, the null hypothesis H_0 can be a simple hypothesis when $F(x)$ is specified completely or H_0 can provide an incomplete specification and then it will be a compound hypothesis.

Among the most used GoF tests in actuarial studies and the social security market, the chi-square test was applied in this paper [48].

2.3. Chi-Square Adherence Test

The performance of the adherence tests has the objective of evaluating if two frequency distributions are approximately identical or if they are considered heterogeneous [60]. The test consists of analyzing whether the distribution of decrements (death and disability) given by the analyzed actuarial tables represent or not the distribution of decreases in the databases of the Brazilian Armed Forces, that is, Brazilian Navy (BN), Brazilian Army (BA), and Brazilian Air Force (BAF).

The objective of the test is to compare the differences between the (E) and the observed (O) frequencies, considering as observed the deaths, or inflows, occurring in a specific time horizon for each age group, inactive and pensioners [61].

The estimation of average death or disability is performed by multiplying the probabilities associated with each age, according to the tables, by the number of individuals exposed to the risk of this same population [62].

Approaches are useful to improve accuracy [63]. In order to test whether the calculated discrepancies are statistically significant, the x^2 compares with the same factor ($x^2_{critical}$) obtained from the chi-square distribution table [64]. In order to obtain the results, a 5% significance level was adopted, that is, a 5% probability of rejection of the null hypothesis, which considers that the observed frequency is equal to the mean frequency [65], that is, the distribution of deaths or entry into invalidity of the Brazilian Armed Forces identical to the distribution of a certain actuarial table. According to [66], the index, x^2 is calculated by the formula expressed in (1).

$$X^2 = \sum_{i=1}^{n} \frac{(O_i - E_i)^2}{E_i} \quad (1)$$

where:
- X^2 = chi-square test statistics;
- n = maximum age in the actuarial tables;
- O_i = observed frequency of deaths/disability with age i;
- E = average death/disability frequency with age i.

The lower the divergence between the observed frequency and the mean frequency, the lower the statistic X^2 and the probability of not rejecting the hypothesis of adherence between the actual mortality/disability experience and the board adopted as the premise is greater. After calculating the X^2, the critical X^2, is verified, taking into account the level of significance adopted and the degrees of freedom considered in the test. In the study, each age group represents an independent observation of the sample. Thus, the number of degrees of freedom of the statistic X^2 is represented by the number of age ranges used subtracted from one, due to the intrinsic characteristic of the test model used.

3. Methodology

Considering the Brazilian political–economic scenario, it became mandatory to generate the results of actuarial projections as quickly as possible in order to support the decision of the armed forces high command [67]. Thus, the research in hand proposes the methodology explained in Figure 1.

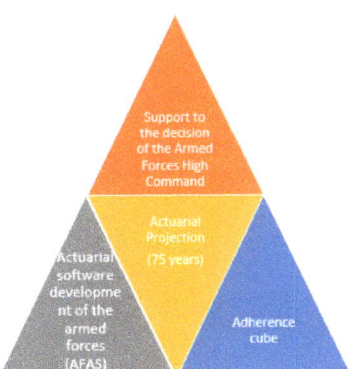

Figure 1. Methodology for the actuarial projection of the costs with pensioners of the armed forces.

In the central part of Figure 1, the armed forces have the need to carry out the actuarial projection of the pensioners by determination of the TCU. This projection must have the best accuracy possible, which motivated the creation of the conceptual model of the adherence cube. With the computational effort imposed by the adherence cube, it was necessary to use parallel computing in order that the projections were calculated quickly [68].

In addition, it was necessary to create an application that allowed the entry of the data of the armed forces and generated the results of the projections. This application was called the actuarial software of the armed forces (AFAS). This technical–methodological procedure, formed by the adherence cube, the use of parallel computing, and the development of AFAS [69], aims to support the high command of the armed forces through precise results generated in time to support the decision.

Several researchers already developed and published studies related to the estimation of actuarial tables using adhesion tests, such as chi-square, mean square deviation and Kolmogorov–Smirnov, such as [70] and [71]. However, no technical studies were found on how to optimize the estimation of the actuarial tables to be adopted, considering increases and reductions in the probabilities of death and disability [72], which is widely accepted by current legislation. The following steps were followed (methodological proposal):

- Step 1 creating a trusted database;
- Step 2 define/choose a heuristic to be applied to the data;
- Step 3 database heuristic adherence test;
- Step 4 selection of the best model for the study;
- Step 5 selection of the computational model; and
- Step 6 analysis of results.

3.1. Creation of SMIB

In the development of the remuneration studies, the MD realized that the lack of detailed information on military payroll expenses was the major hindrance to negotiations with the Ministry of Planning, Budget and Management (MPBM) and, consequently, the major problem for the monitoring and evaluation of the financial impact of the proposed adjustments or of changes in the legislation in force. In order to reduce this deficiency and make it possible to monitor the effects of provisional measure (PM) n° 2.215/2001 [73], SMIB was created.

From the year of its creation, SMIB was perfected and managed by the Secretariat of Co-ordination and Institutional Organization (SCIO), through the advisory office, Department of Coordination, Organization and Legislation (DCOL) and, currently, the Compensation Division, so that it serves the MD as a managerial tool in the development of several studies.

With this, SMIB is the only database that allows consolidated calculations of the three forces, providing the calculation of financial impacts arising from measures that may alter the remuneration policy of the military and its pensioners. It is possible to understand the strategic importance of SMIB to the armed forces.

The analysis of large amounts of data by man is not feasible without the aid of appropriate computational tools. Therefore, it is essential to provide tools that help the man in the task of analyzing, interpreting, and relating these data, so that strategies can be developed and selected for action in each field of application [74].

Initially, the platform used for the SMIB was SQL Server 2000 from the Microsoft Corporation, which contain data as of January 2001, taking up space of approximately 20 gigabytes, 25% of the total dedicated server capacity (80 gigabytes). New data are stored per month, with approximately 200 megabytes, or 0.25% of the total server space, which is equivalent to the annual data addition of 3% of the storage capacity of that server. The information available in the SMIB also allows the MD to attend the various administrative queries requested and the institutional demands required of other government or private bodies, as shown in Figure 2.

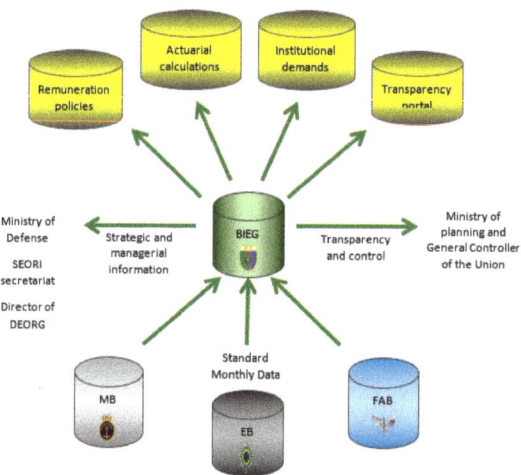

Figure 2. Strategic and Management Information Bank (SMIB).

In order to improve the SMIB, some minimum requirements were established, mainly to improve the quality of management information contained in the bank, not forgetting the reliability and standardization of the data. The requirements are:

- Greater consistency of information based on the maintenance of a unique historical basis;
- Higher reliability of the database, these being correct and applicable in any situation;
- Ability to consolidate information, with the possibility of aggregating remunerative installments of various forms;
- Ability to detail the remuneration structure of the military, with the possibility of explaining the composition of the military remuneration; and
- Ability to detail payroll by nature of expenses (NE), which provides greater precision in comparisons with the federal government's integrated financial administration system (FGIFAS).

In this sense, in order to keep the database reliable, meetings are held annually to discuss possible improprieties in some data sent by the forces and to discuss suggestions for improvements and improvements to correct these inconsistencies. With each modification introduced, new instructions are given to provide data, aiming at maintaining the standardization of information. Before sending the data to the MD, the forces are able to verify the results obtained by these routines and, when necessary, rectify them.

The criticisms of the database were established based on general rules and that the occurrences resulting from the application of them are in fact inconsistencies, since there may be specific cases in each force that justify some occurrences without representing impropriety.

3.2. Heuristics

3.2.1. The Probabilistic Multidecrements

The pension and social security systems of countries that require the solvency of social security entities require the measurement of contributions and future payments of active, inactive, and pensioners, whose technical nomenclature is the actuarial projection of revenues and expenses.

In order to comply with rigid regulations established by [75], in this area, the manager needs to determine the mortality and disability tables that best represent the expectations of decrements, that is, death and disability of the study population.

The graph shown in Figure 3, shows that an active individual is subject to joint probabilities of dying, or being invalidated. Each vertex of the graph establishes a state in which the military can meet (active, reserved, married, retired, with children, etc.). It is often said that this individual is subjected to probabilistic multidecrements.

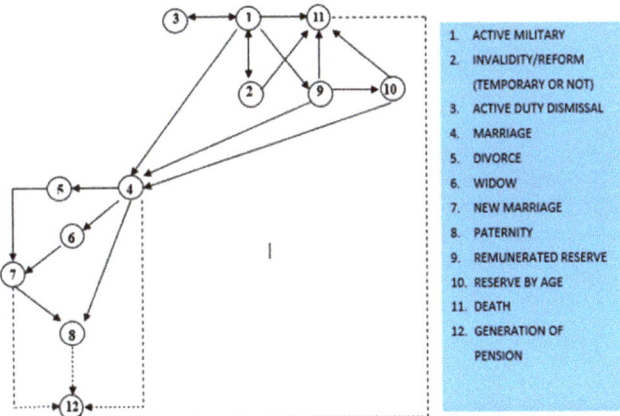

Figure 3. Biometric and social states.

Thus, Figure 3 shows that:

- An active military (state 1) can be declared invalid (state 2), marry (state 4), go to reserve (state 9), resign (state 3), or die (state 11);
- An invalid military (state 2) can return to active (state 1), marry (state 2), or pass away (state 11);
- If the military member resigns (state 3), he leaves the system and does not generate a pension;
- A married soldier (state 4) can divorce (state 5), become a widower (state 6), or become a parent (state 8). Once married, the dotted line shows that the military can generate a pension (state 12);
- A divorced military (state 5) may enter into a new marriage (state 7);
- A widowed soldier (state 6) may contract a new marriage (state 7);
- A military who contracted a new marriage (state 7) can become a parent state 8);
- A military man who became a father (state 8) can generate a pension (state 12) as indicated by the dotted line;
- A military in the Remunerated Reserve (state 9) can contract marriage (state 4), go to the reserve by age (state 10), or die (state 11);
- A military in the reserve by age (state 10) may marry (state 4) or die (state 11); and

- Generation of pension (state 12) can be generated by marriage (state 4), by a new marriage (state 7), and by paternity (state 8) once the military passed away (state 12).

3.2.2. The Actuarial Tables

De Witt in the Netherlands, and Grauns and Halley in England, advanced in the studies of probability and demographics related to human longevity. According to [76], only in 1815, Milne created the first table of life that contemplated probabilities of death (q_x) and survival (p_x).

Such a table was drawn up on the basis of the observed mortality of the inhabitants of Carlisle, England. According to [77], numerous tables were drawn up for different regions and countries around the world because of their crucial importance for the analysis of sociological, population, economic, and biometric factors.

For [78], every product, whether in the social security area or the living area, is supported by the mortality tables. Starting from a closed number of participants, called the "root", in which the gender can be taken into account, the mortality table reveals the number of people living annually at each age, that is, it is a board determined by annual mortality or survival rates. The construction of these tables can be derived from the insurers' experience or using the census data.

Currently, professionals in the area have access to dozens of mortality and disability tables for different populations and different breeding dates. In this way, the professional must choose among the numerous existing tables that present the greatest accuracy and precision in relation to the decreases observed in the population of the private pension entity under study [79].

The actuarial tables help in the performance of various sociological and economic calculations [80], such as calculating the life expectancy of assets, inactive and invalid, the average number of people that will be invalidated, population density, measurement of economically active population, and others. The most important actuarial tables for social security entities are: the mortality table of invalid, table of disability, and table of mortality of invalids, which are detailed below [81].

3.2.3. The Mortality Tables

According to [82], the actuarial calculus works by providing means to calculate insurance premiums related to life and social security costs [83]. The most traditional element of this technique is the mortality table, whose function is to give life expectancy for a given (whole) age in the interval [0.1]. This probability distribution is called the survival function, represented in (2):

$$S(x) = P[X > x] \qquad (2)$$

For [84], in the last decades, actuaries and demographers used increasingly sophisticated methods for predicting mortality.

Mortality tables, also known as survival tables, are intended to represent the actual probability of death (q_x) of a given population, and such death probabilities are determined by the age of the individuals in the population.

The mortality table or life table is the most complete tool for analyzing the mortality of a population. Another important aspect of the study of mortality is the analysis of the various socioeconomic characteristics, such as the composition of the workforce, age population, and the regulation of social security systems [85].

3.2.4. Invalidity Entry Tables

Invalidity entry tables are intended to represent the actual probability that a valid (i_x) is due to a fortuitous event. These probabilities are defined according to the age of the individuals in the population. In addition to the probabilities of invalidity, these tables provide the average number of people who theoretically will be invalidated by age in a particular closed population, in addition to other statistical information that can be extracted by algebraic calculations [86].

3.2.5. Tables of Invalidity Mortality

The mortality tables for invalids are applied exclusively to the participants who are no longer active because they contracted some incapacity that does not allow them to exercise their work activity. Such boards are intended to represent the actual probability of death of this specific group of participants by age [87]. In addition to the probabilities of death of invalids, these tables provide the average number of deceased and survivors by age in a given closed population, the expected life expectancy of an incapable participant, as well as additional information that can be obtained through math operations [88,89].

3.2.6. Selection of the Model

The methodology consists of the application of 199 adhesion tests for each actuarial board analyzed, that is, the adhesion of the board, and 198 variations of the board are verified, which represents 99 aggravations and 99 different reliefs. The worsening rates vary from 1% to 99%, which increase the chances of death/disability of all ages from 1% ($[q_x \text{ or } i_x] \times 0.99$), respectively.

Thus, the reductions tested consist of reducing the odds of all ages from 1% ($[q_x \text{ or } i_x] \times 0.99$) to 99% ($[q_x \text{ or } i_x] \times 1.01$). The actuarial tables of mortality and invalidity that were analyzed in this study are presented in Tables 1 and 2. The specifics of the actuarial tables used in this research can be found on the Society of Actuaries (SOA).

Table 1. Valid mortality tables used.

CS0-41	CSO-58	CSO-80	AT-49	AT-50	AT-55
AT-71	American Experience	GAM-1971	SGB-51	SGB-71	SGB-75
IAPC	Hunter Semitropical	Rentiers Français	Grupal Americana	USTP-61	GKM-70
GKM-80	ALLG-72	X-17	CSG-60	Prudential 1950	GAM 1994 Male
RP-2000-1992 Base-Male Aggregate	AT-2000	AT-2000 F	AT-83	AT-83 male	UP-84
UP94Men	UP94Woman	UP-94 MT-M-ANB	GRM-80	GRF-80	GRM-95
GRF-95	BR-EMSsb-v.2010-m	BR-EMSsb-v.2010-f	BR-EMSmt-v.2010-m	BR-EMSmt-v.2010-f	BR-EMSsb-v.2015-m
BR-EMSsb-2015-f	BR-EMSmt-2015-m	BR-EMSmt-2015-f	CSO2001MALE	CSO2001FEMALE	IBGE-2011-M
IGBE-2011-F	IBGE-2011	IBGE-2012-M	IBGE-2012-F	IBGE-2012	-

Table 2. Invalidity and death tables for invalids used.

Invalidity and Mortality Tables for Invalids Used					
IAPB-57 Weak	IAPB-57 Strong	Zimmermann	Zimmermann (Ferr. Germans)	Zimmermann (Empre. Write.)	Grupal Americana
Álvaro Comings	TASA-1927	Prudential (Ferr. Retired.)	IBA (Railways)	Muller	Hunter's
IAPB-57 (AJUST/ITAU)	Winklevoss	Bentzien	IAPC	IAPB-57	ALLG72
USTP61	Rentiers Français	X17	-	-	-

In this way, tests are performed for three different groups, valid mortality, invalidity mortality, and invalidity, in order to determine the actuarial tables that have the best adherence to data coming from a specific database of the Ministry of Defense (MD).

Initially, the probabilities referring to the original mortality/disability tables, as shown in Tables 1 and 2, are structured in matrices, through a computational application developed in C, for each group studied. In Brazil, the category of military professionals does not resemble any other professional category because it has its own characteristics, especially regarding biometric data. Such specificities require the development of said application.

Table 1 presents the main existing actuarial tables [53], which were analyzed in order to obtain the one most adherent to the data of the Brazilian military.

These matrices have two dimensions, the first one referring to the tables being analyzed (47 for mortality of valid and 21 for invalidity and mortality of invalids) and the second corresponding to the possible ages of the participants (0–125 years).

The matrix shown in Figure 4 is considered the base matrix to achieve the 99 aggravated boards and the 99 additional mitigated boards, which, when generated by multiplicative terms, result in a three-dimensional matrix.

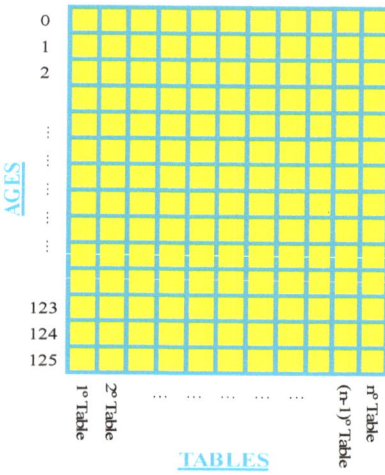

Figure 4. Matrix of original actuarial boards.

Thus, the cube shown in Figure 5 is a conceptual model called the "Adherence Cube", represented by a three-dimensional matrix that contains the original, aggravated, and undeserved death/invalidity probabilities.

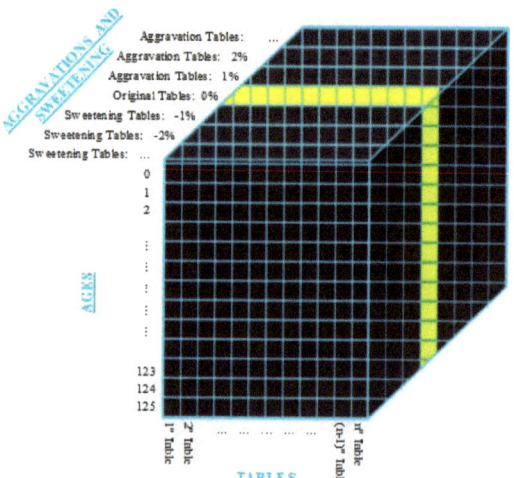

Figure 5. Adherence Cube.

Therefore, the first dimension represents the actuarial tables presented in Tables 1 and 2, the second dimension means the ages of the participants, and the third dimension corresponds to the original table with its respective aggravations and redemptions.

After determining all odds of death/disability, the application starts performing the adhesion tests according to (1). A grip test is applied for each actuarial table generated, considering that it varies from age zero to age 125 years. In this sense, 9353 tests ([47 different actuarial tables] × [1 original board + 99 aggravated boards + 99 allowable boards]) are necessary to perform the validity test for adherence of valid mortality tables. Accordingly, for conducting the invalidity and invalidity mortality tests, there are 4179 tests ([21 boards] × [1 original board + 99 aggravated boards + 99 boards granted]).

In this way, the board that has the best adherence to the data is the x^2, calculated as less than the x^2 (true null hypothesis), and it has the lowest statistical value among all the results obtained. Therefore, it is concluded that the distribution of deaths or disability entry of the Brazilian Armed Forces is more adherent to the distribution of a certain actuarial table.

The developed actuarial application provides as a result of the actuarial calculations a two-dimensional matrix, signaling in green all the tables in which the null hypothesis was considered true; however, the board with the best adherence to the AF mortality/disability events is indicated in red and exemplified in Figure 6.

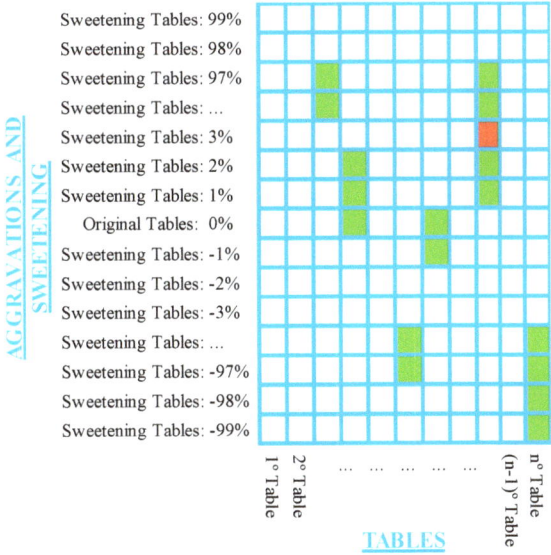

Figure 6. Results obtained with the developed application.

3.3. Computational Model

The actuarial calculus is a mathematical method that uses financial, economic, and probability concepts to measure the number of resources and contributions necessary to pay future benefits of the insureds of the social security funds and institutes, also called social security own regimes, which seeks the balance between the financial results and the actuarial projection. The maintenance of this balance is of paramount importance, especially in times of economic crisis.

The actuarial projections of income and expenses for a pension and pension entity are intended to quantify the estimated future costs of payment of benefits and the estimated future income from participant contributions. These projections are important for entities and governments to provision such monetary amounts for subsequent years, ensuring actuarial balance and reducing the risk of illiquidity. As exposed in [90], when contributions are properly defined, planning tends to have a financial–actuarial equilibrium [45].

Pension and social security institutions project future costs and revenues over a 75-year time horizon; however, nothing prevents the projection from being calculated at 80 or 100 years. The main assumptions that impact this actuarial calculation are: mortality table of invalids, table of mortality of invalids, table of disability, turnover rate, wage growth, rate of inflation, and replacement of assets.

3.4. Parallel Computing

Faced with the limitations of sequential computing, we opted for parallel computing, so that the results of the actuarial projections of the armed forces could be generated in an acceptable time, in order to support the senior administration of the armed forces in matters related to pension reform with the government federal.

In order to support the development and use of a computational application for the actuarial calculation, we sought knowledge in areas related to parallel computing, focusing on the creation of a computational environment capable of propitiating the actuarial projections in a timely manner. According to [91], parallel computing is a kind of computing in which multiple calculations are performed in several parallel, rather than sequential, processing units [92,93]. The idea here is to replace a large mass of processing in a single CPU by smaller processing in several CPUs [94].

The adoption of a methodology that uses parallel computing resources in the development of an application to calculate actuarial projections can, by extrapolating the results achieved within the scope of the armed forces, considerably shorten the time needed to obtain results and reduce the costs of organizations with the contracting of third-party services.

The exact percentage of time reduction achieved by parallel computing in actuarial problems will depend on a variety of factors, including the size of the problem, the number of processors used, and the efficiency of the algorithms used. However, substantial reductions in processing time can often be achieved, sometimes on the order of several orders of magnitude.

Although we have not found specific studies on reducing processing times in actuarial science, the academic literature presents some studies that use parallel computing to reduce processing time in complex problems, such as:

Cader et al. [95] focused on software-based acceleration for plagiarism detection using CPU/GPU. The authors gained $45\times$ speed-up compared to the CPU. Hossain and Assiri [96] proposed a facial expression recognition framework with the incorporation of parallelism, and the processing time speeds up three times faster. López et al. [97] proposed the use of RGB point clouds estimated from structure from motion (SfM) as the input for building thermal point clouds. The authors reported up to 96.73% less processing time. Morishima [98] proposed a subgraph-based anomaly detection method to perform the detection using a part of the blockchain data. According to the author, the proposed method was $11.1\times$ faster than an existing GPU-based method without lowering the detection accuracy. Zhang [99] presented a method that parallelizes Bayesian computation using distributed computing on Apache Spark across a cluster of computers. According to the author, the distributed algorithm achieved as much as 65 times performance gain over the non-parallel method.

These papers demonstrate the potential benefits of parallel computing in reducing processing time in actuarial problems, although the exact percentage of time reduction will vary depending on the specific problem and implementation. Analyzing these findings, we obtained a good starting point for understanding the use of parallel computing in reducing processing time in actuarial problems and the potential for speed-up. The exact percentage of reduction in processing time may vary depending on the specific problem and the parallel computing method used.

3.4.1. Parallel Programming with C

Current architectures may contain two, four, six, or more complex processing cores, and are very much employed in exploring parallelism at the instruction and thread level. In theory, such architectures could be extended to tens or even hundreds of cores in the future, but they run into two main obstacles: the difference between processor and memory speeds, known as memory walls, and excessive heat generation due to high frequencies necessary for the operation of such architectures [100].

Multi-core processors (color) were on the market for many years and are currently available on most devices. However, many developers continue to do what the same thing: create programs that use a single stream of isolated sequential control inside a program called a thread. This means that not all processing power available on the machine is used. Most currently commercialized computers have a four-core and four-core processor, or six-core and eight-core processors. By purchasing a computer with such features, users pay for extra processing power. However, by providing a program that uses a single thread, the developer does not allow the use of this extra processing capacity.

Kirk and Hwu [101] point out that it is a simple task to achieve a ten-fold speed up when an application makes use of data parallelism. A computation is said to be parallel when a program runs on a multiprocessor machine in which all processors share access to available memory, i.e., the same address on different processors corresponds to the same memory location. Golov and Rönnbäck [102] make similar comments.

Multi-threaded processing is not new to experienced C # developers, but it is not always easy to develop programs that use all the available processing power. In addition, the evolution of programming languages facilitated the work of developers by simplifying the implementation of parallel programming.

In order to advance the use of parallel programming, it is important to establish two important concepts: synchronous execution and asynchronous execution. A good insight into these two modes of execution is basic knowledge to improve the performance of your applications. When executing a synchronous operation, the program executes all the tasks in sequence, as shown in Figure 7. When firing the execution, each task will only be executed after the previous task ends.

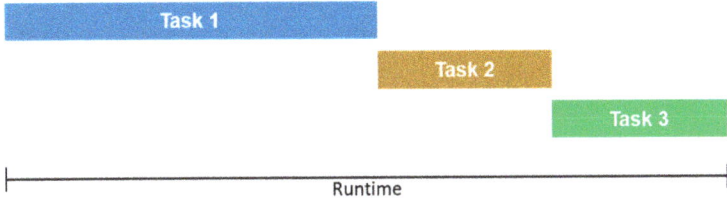

Figure 7. Synchronous execution.

When executing an operation in asynchronous mode, the program triggers the tasks when necessary, and they are started and closed concomitantly to the execution of other tasks, as shown in Figure 8.

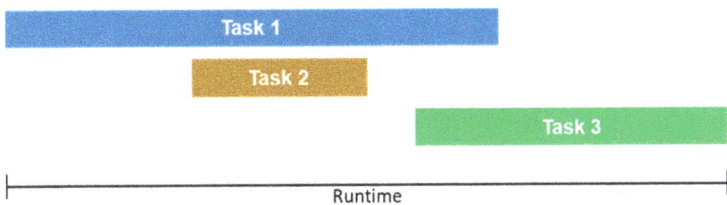

Figure 8. Synchronous execution.

As it induces image analysis, the same tasks running asynchronously will require a shorter execution time than when executed in a synchronous manner, for the simple fact that there is no need for one task to "wait" for another task to start. Waiting, in this case, would only be acceptable if there were a dependency relationship between the tasks; that is, if a task depended, for example, on a calculation that another task, still in execution, is producing.

From the previous paragraph it is possible to deduce that the use or not of the parallel programming should be evaluated by the developer. In some situations, its use can be quite beneficial by decreasing the execution times and producing the results. However, in other situations, its unbalanced use may even degrade application performance. Since the implementation of parallel programming with C # requires the explicit insertion in the code of specific instructions of parallels, it is up to the developer to decide when and where to use such instructions.

The question may arise as to why many developers still choose to run synchronously if asynchronous execution takes less time. The answer to such a question is not simple. What can be said straight away is that with asynchronous programming, the developer has some new challenges:

Synchronize tasks. Assuming that in Figure 7 it is necessary to start a task only after the other two are finished, it would be necessary, in this case, to create a wait mechanism to wait for all tasks to finish before performing the new task.

Solve competition problems. If a shared resource exists, such as a list that is written to a task and read into another task, you would need to create a mechanism to ensure that the list is kept in a known state.

Adapt to a new programming logic. Since there is no logical sequence, tasks can end at any time and you no longer have control of which ends first.

Asynchronous programming requires a paradigm shift on the part of the developer. Its adoption, however, has some advantages. One of the most significant is the non-crash of the user interface (UI), as the tasks can be executed in the background. Another advantage is the ability to use all the cores of the machine, making better use of its resources.

3.4.2. Asynchro Programming with Async and Await

It is possible to avoid performance bottlenecks and improve the overall response of software using asynchronous programming. However, traditional techniques for writing asynchronous applications can be tricky, making it difficult to develop, debug, and maintain.

Asynchrony is essential for activities exposed to a potential block, such as when the application accesses the web. Access to a web resource is sometimes slow or subject to delays. If such activity is blocked within a synchronous process, the entire application will be on hold. In an asynchronous process, the application can continue to perform another task, which does not rely on the web resource, until the task exposed to a potential block ends.

Async and await, keywords in C #, are the core of asynchronous programming. Using these two words, one can use the features of the .NET framework or the Windows runtime to create an asynchronous method almost as easily as creating a synchronous method.

Figure 9 shows part of an asynchronous routine. When using the async keyword, you can write your code the same way you write the synchronous code because the compiler takes care of all the complexity and frees the programmer to write program logic.

```
async Task<int> AccessTheWebAsync()
{
    HttpClient client = new HttpClient();
    Task<string> getStringTask = client.GetStringAsync("http://msdn.microsoft.com");
    DoIndependentWork();
    string urlContents = await getStringTask;
    return urlContents.Length;
}
```

Figure 9. Asynchronous routine.

To use this routine, you should expect your return using the await keyword, as in the example: "string urlContents = await client.GetStringAsync ()". Following these guidelines, when the compiler encounters a method with the expression await, which marks the point at which the method cannot continue until the expected asynchronous operation completes, it starts running in the background and continues to run other tasks. When the routine is complete, execution returns on the instruction following the routine call.

C # language enhancements with the async and await keywords restore the sequential order of code while using system resources efficiently. There are still some relevant aspects to be observed, such as concurrency or task synchronization, but these are minor compared to the work required to create a good program that uses parallel processing. Parallelism is to divide for multiple processors that work concurrently; parallelism is used for computing tasks and accelerates the efficiency [103].

The use of the techniques described here helps a lot in the creation of programs that make use of parallel computing and that better use the resources of the system.

3.5. The Software Developed

In the context of pension benefits, the actuarial and financial assumptions represent a formal set of estimates for events: biometric, financial, economic, demographic, social, etc. The choice and use of actuarial assumptions that are not committed to the reality to which the participants, sponsors, and entities are subject may lead to incorrect costs, leading to technical deficits or surpluses, as well as overexposure to risks or underexposure to them. The use of more conservative assumptions may lead to higher initial costs, albeit with lower risks of rising costs. On the other hand, the adoption of less conservative assumptions should be made with the knowledge of the risk that they may not be confirmed, allowing for critical solvency problems at a future date.

The actuarial assumptions will always be criteria that are preferably permeated by common sense, remembering that excess safety margins are as burdensome as the excesses of risks that one intends to assume. Both lead to the incapacity to pay, sometimes participants and/or sponsors, or the own provident entity or benefit plan.

Figure 10 summarizes the classification of the actuarial assumptions of the armed forces. The economic and biometric assumptions make up the active choices, given that the manager has an effective capacity to interfere with them, modifying them to each actuarial evaluation, and choosing them according to their perception. Generic premises, on the other hand, do not submit to the manager's perception, varying according to an external reality.

The concepts of parallel computing presented were used in the armed forces actuarial software V 1.1. (AFAS), giving it the ability to demand a low computational effort to produce the results of the actuarial projections. Figure 11 shows the AFAS execution flow for the calculation of the actuarial projections, showing how the data are computed in parallel until the results are obtained.

The data stored in the application DB are put into memory by a parallel data loading process, filling all the data structures required for the calculations. Once these structures are complete, three parallel large tasks (TASK) demand the necessary data from the RAM memory much faster than the HD. The tasks are carried out simultaneously, the ACTIVE MILITARY task being responsible for the calculations referring to the active military, the INACTIVE MILITARY task responsible for the calculations referring to the inactive military, and the PENSIONER task responsible for calculations referring to military pensioners.

Each TASK above performs for each operation on the lists (arrays) in which iterations are executed in parallel and the state of the loop is monitored and manipulated. In addition, the parallel task library (PTL) dynamically scales the degree of concurrency to use all available processors in the most efficient way.

The work developed focused on optimizing the computational application of the actuarial calculation to produce the actuarial projections of the pensioners of the armed forces. In this sense, any and all access to the hard disk (HD) was eliminated during the execution of the calculations.

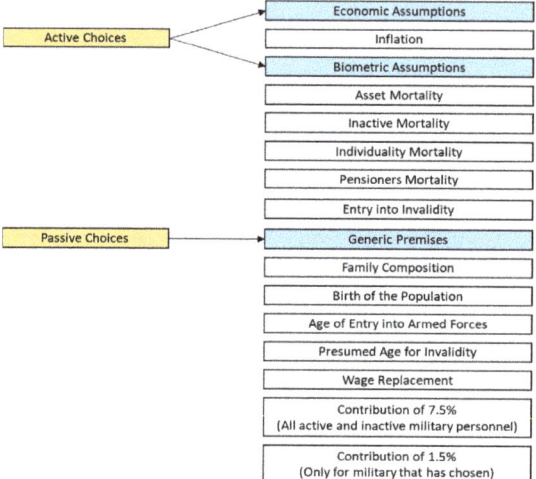

Figure 10. Actuarial assumptions of the AF.

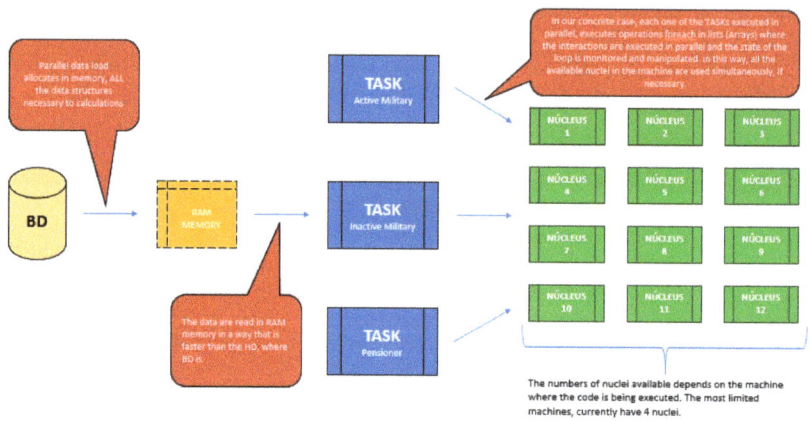

Figure 11. Armed forces actuarial software (AFAS).

To achieve this, a technique was developed which loads all the data necessary for the calculations into the computer memory as soon as the application is started. During the application load the data are read from the respective database tables and are generated from SQL queries, and then persisted in structures (arrays) in memory. Once loaded, the data are only read in these structures until the application is closed, which makes the data reading and writing processes very fast.

This technique proved to be efficient, due to the fact that the HD is much slower than RAM. While a DDR4-2400MHZ (1606R) module communicates with the processor at a theoretical speed of 4200 MB/s, the sequential read speed of the current HDs hardly exceeds the 233 MB/s mark. In addition to this, the HD access time, ie., the time required to locate the information and initiate the transfer, is considerably higher than that of the RAM.

While memory is spoken at access times of less than ten nanoseconds, most HDs work with access times greater than ten milliseconds. This causes the HD performance to be much lower when reading small files scattered around the disk (as is the case with virtual memory). In many situations, the HD gets to the point of not being able to handle more than two or three hundred requests per second. From the foregoing, it can be understood that the loaded memory arrays already allow their data to be accessed at high speeds, compared to the speeds of access to the hard disk. When the data access methods of such structures are developed using parallel programming techniques, the time required to produce the results is considerably reduced.

Figure 12 shows the AFAS parameter window. In it are inserted the parameters that will compose the actuarial projections.

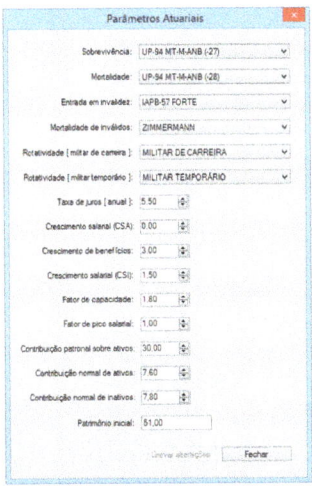

Figure 12. AFAS parameters window.

The actuarial projections are important to understand the future behavior of the population and their respective financial flow of payment, using specific actuarial tables for each group and the financial flow.

4. Results

For this study, data from the year 2015 for BN, BA, and BAF were used. Thus, more than one and a half million historical records were analyzed regarding the dates of entry into the armed forces, death, disability, birth, and others, whose numbers are subdivided by active and inactive military personnel, pensioners, and beneficiaries. Said amounts are set forth in Table 3.

Table 3. Quantitative of military active/inactive and pensioners by 2015.

		Invalidity and Mortality Tables for Invalids Used				
IAPB-57 Weak	IAPB-57 Strong	Zimmermann	Zimmermann (Ferr. Germans)	Zimmermann (Empre. Write.)	Grupal Americana	
Álvaro Comings	TASA-1927	Prudential (Ferr. Retired.)	IBA (Railways)	Muller	Hunter's	
IAPB-57 (AJUST/ITAU)	Winklevoss	Bentzien	IAPC	IAPB-57	ALLG72	
USTP61	Rentiers Français	X17	-	-	-	

Through the use of the records presented in Table 1 and the actuarial tables matrix, it was possible to develop a C computational application, with the objective of operationalizing the calculations referring to actuarial projections in a fast and accurate manner.

4.1. Result of Mortality of Assets, Inactive and Pensioners of the Armed Forces

For the active population, inactive, and pensioners of the three armed forces as a whole, there was no actuarial table that had adherence to the observed mortality data in the database, considering all ages. Therefore, it was necessary to apply the adhesion test to representative samples of this population, with the age range between 20 and 90 years, representing 97% of the population data. Thus, the only table that adhered to the observed mortality, for the ages between 20 and 90 years, was the GKM-70 reduced by 61%, as shown in Figure 13.

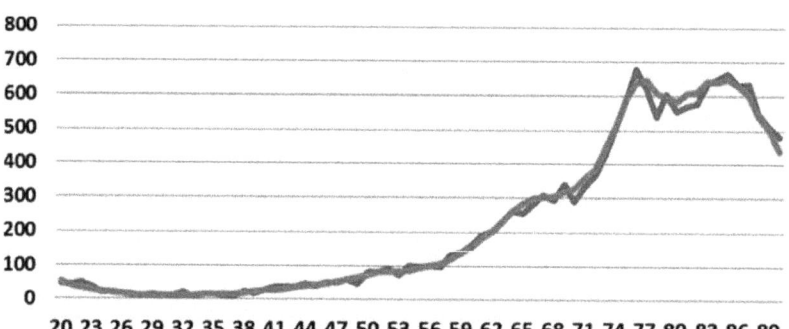

Figure 13. Actuarial table for mortality of active, inactive, and pensioners.

4.2. Results of Invalidity of Mortality of Armed Forces

For the population of invalids of the armed forces, together, there was no actuarial table that had adherence to observed data of mortality in the database, considering all ages. Therefore, it was necessary to apply the adhesion test to representative samples of this population, with the age range between 21 and 93 years, defined empirically, representing 94% of the population data. Consequently, the tables that adhered to the occurrences of death of invalids were: HUNTER'S for all aggravations between 60% and 76%. The board adopted was HUNTER'S aggravated in 68% because it has the best adherence to the mortality of the disabled of the armed forces, as shown in Figure 14.

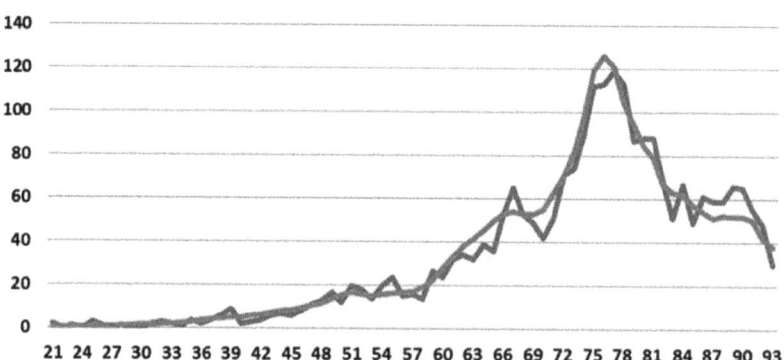

Figure 14. Actuarial table for mortality of invalid military personnel.

4.3. Result of Entry into Disability of the Armed Forces

The table selected to be used as the input for asset impairment was USTP-61 reduced by 49% because it had the lowest chi-square static. To achieve adherence to this table, it was necessary to analyze exclusively the age range between 25 and 41 years, determined empirically, otherwise there would be no adherence to any available actuarial table. Such adherence is shown in Figure 15.

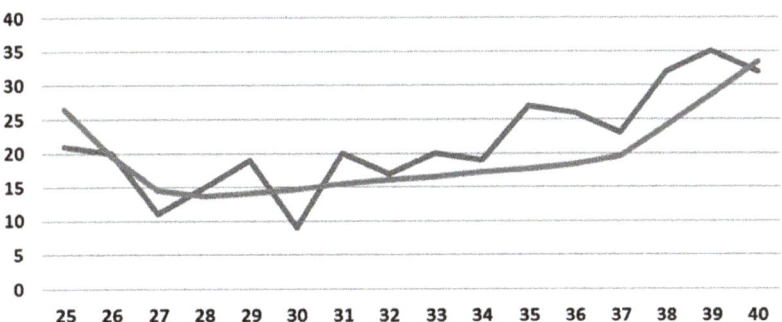

Figure 15. Actuarial table for invalid entry of active military personnel.

In addition to the 49% USTP-61 board, which had the best adhesion, the following actuarial tables also accepted the null hypothesis, but with lower accuracy:

- ALLG-72 for all redemptions between 28% and 39%;
- USTP-61 for all redemptions between 38% and 48%; and
- X17 for all redemptions between 50% and 55%.

Figure 16 shows the decrease in the annual financial cost, mainly due to the fact that it is a population that does not consider the entry of new active military personnel; that is, a closed population. Only those related to the payment of pensions, which have an annual financial balance maintained negative, tending to zero, until the population's extinction were considered as costs. This contributes to the validation of the method proposed in this paper.

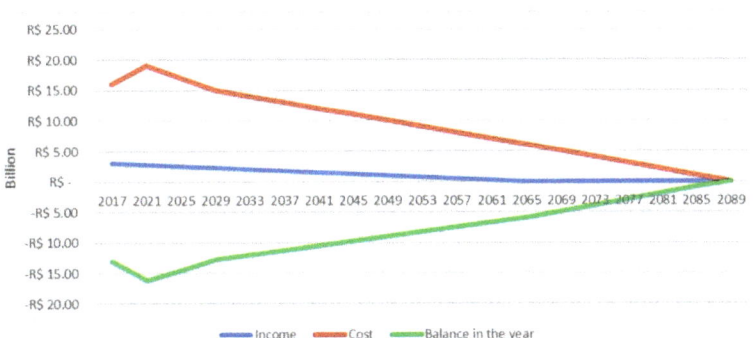

Figure 16. Actuarial projection of revenues and costs, without replacement—for pensioners—AF.

4.4. Processing Time Reduction Results

Table 4 shows the time required for the production of results by the application of the actuarial calculation in two versions. The first version, "Previous Version", does not contemplate any of the techniques, patterns, or features presented in this chapter. The second version, called "Refactored Version", is the final product of the work presented here. In addition, it shows that in all groups analyzed, there was a significant reduction in the time needed to produce the results of the actuarial calculation, notably in the actuarial calculation of present value. The data are presented in three distinct groups, these groups being notably those that require longer processing time, and whose results are of interest to the study under study.

Table 4. Comparison of processing times.

Process	Previous Version [Approximate] HH:MM:SS	Refactored Version [Approximate] HH:MM:SS	Time Reduction (%)
Importing databases.	04:00:00	00:08:00	96.7%
Actuarial calculation of present value.	23:00:00	00:07:00	99.5%
Actuarial projection with a term of 75 years.	16:00:00	00:05:00	99.5%
Total Time	43:00:00	00:20:00	99.2%

In this context, the use of parallel computing techniques and resources proved to be a solution to reduce the computational effort, allowing the use of all the available processing capacity in the computers. An actuarial projection that used to take 43 h can now be completed in 20 min, which represents a reduction of more than 99%. In the specific case of the Brazilian Army, from a mass of data of 500,000 records, it was possible to execute a complex mathematical model with high recursion in about 5 min.

By way of comparison, the results of reducing processing times obtained in this study are better than those presented in the literature, such as those presented in Section 3.4, which shows the relevance and importance of the created software. The percentages of reduction in processing times of the previous studies are consolidated in Table 5.

Table 5. Comparison of processing times with previous studies.

Papers	Time Reduction (%)
Cader et al. [95]	97.7%
Hossain and Assiri [96]	66.7%
López et al. [97]	96.7
Morishima [98]	90.9%
Zhang [99]	98.4%
Our software (AFAS)	99.2%

Analyzing the data in the table above, it is observed that the AFAS presents a superior performance to the systems developed in previous studies, considering the reduction of more than 99% in the processing time. In addition, the created tool allows for finding the actuarial tables that best represent the occurrences of mortality and disability in the military, which makes it unique in the context of the armed forces.

In short, AFAS provides a better dimensioning of military pension costs to be paid by the military pension system in a feasible time due to the application of parallel computing. We emphasize that the implementation of this software allowed the Brazilian Armed Forces to measure the costs of military pensions in a feasible time, which was unfeasible before the creation of the AFAS.

5. Conclusions

Through the development and implementation of actuarial software that optimizes the selection of actuarial mortality and disability tables using the concept of multidimensional arrays and programming structures, we were able to determine the actuarial table that provides the greatest precision and accuracy of the decremental events of a population under study. It should be noted that the greater the adherence, the greater the financial efficiency.

Considering the reduction in processing time through the use of parallel computing, the software proposed in this article performed better than those already presented in the literature, presenting a reduction of more than 99%, allowing a feasible time to carry out actuarial forecasts.

We highlight that no technical studies were found on how to optimize the estimation of the actuarial tables to be adopted, considering aggravations and reductions in the probabilities of death and disability, which is widely accepted by current legislation. Therefore, it is considered the unpublished and unique study in the academic community.

We emphasize that the methodology proposed by this research can be applied in the order actuarial problems. As a limitation of this study, we emphasize that the database was restricted only to the Brazilian Armed Forces. Future studies could apply the proposed methodology in other databases of pensioners, in view of the multidisciplinarity of the presented software.

Author Contributions: Conceptualization, M.d.S. and C.F.S.G.; methodology, M.d.S and E.L.P.J.; software, M.Â.L.M. and I.P.d.A.C.; validation, M.Â.L.M. and I.P.d.A.C.; formal analysis, M.Â.L.M. and E.L.P.J. investigation, M.d.S. and L.P.F.; resources, E.L.P.J. and L.P.F.; data curation, L.P.F.; project administration, C.F.S.G. and M.d.S.; funding acquisition, M.d.S., C.F.S.G. and E.L.P.J. All authors have read and agreed to the published version of the manuscript.

Funding: This research received no external funding.

Institutional Review Board Statement: Not applicable.

Informed Consent Statement: Not applicable.

Data Availability Statement: Not applicable.

Conflicts of Interest: The authors declare no conflict of interest.

References

1. Logullo, Y.; Bigogno-Costa, V.; Silva, A.C.S.d.; Belderrain, M.C. A Prioritization Approach Based on VFT and AHP for Group Decision Making: A Case Study in the Military Operations. *Production* **2022**, *32*. [CrossRef]
2. Do Nascimento Maêda, S.M.; Basílio, M.P.; Pinheiro, I.; d de Araújo costaa, M.Â.; Moreira, L.; dos Santos, M.; Gomes, C.F.S.; de Almeidaa, I.D.P.; de Araújo Costad, A.P. Investments in Times of Pandemics: An Approach by the SAPEVO-M-NC Method. In Proceedings of the 2nd Conference on Modern Management Based on Big Data, MMBD, Quanzhou, China, 8–11 November 2021; and 3rd Conference on Machine Learning and Intelligent Systems, MLIS, Xiamen, China, 8–11 November 2021. pp. 162–168.
3. Morais, D.C.; de Almeida, A.T. Group Decision Making on Water Resources Based on Analysis of Individual Rankings. *Omega* **2012**, *40*, 42–52. [CrossRef]
4. Costa, I.P.D.A.; Costa, A.P.D.A.; Sanseverino, A.M.; Gomes, C.F.S.; Santos, M.D. Bibliometric studies on multi-criteria decision analysis (mcda) methods applied in military problems. *Pesqui. Oper.* **2022**, *42*. [CrossRef]
5. Tenorio, F.M.; Santos, M.D.; Gomes, C.F.S.; Araujo, J.D.C.; De Almeida, G.P. THOR 2 Method: An Efficient Instrument in Situations Where There Is Uncertainty or Lack of Data. *IEEE Access* **2021**, *9*, 161794–161805. [CrossRef]
6. Floriano, C.M.; Pereira, V.; Rodrigues, B.E.S. 3MO-AHP: An Inconsistency Reduction Approach through Mono-, Multi- or Many-Objective Quality Measures. *Data Technol. Appl.* **2022**, *56*, 645–670. [CrossRef]
7. Basilio, M.P.; Pereira, V.; Oliveira, M.W.C.D.; Costa Neto, A.F.D. Ranking Policing Strategies as a Function of Criminal Complaints: Application of the PROMETHEE II Method in the Brazilian Context. *J. Model. Manag.* **2021**, *16*, 1185–1207. [CrossRef]
8. Sharma, H.; Sohani, N.; Yadav, A. Comparative Analysis of Ranking the Lean Supply Chain Enablers: An AHP, BWM and Fuzzy SWARA Based Approach. *Int. J. Qual. Reliab. Manag.* **2022**, *39*, 2252–2271. [CrossRef]
9. Rodrigues, L.V.S.; Casado, R.S.G.R.; Carvalho, E.N.d.; Silva, M.M.; Silva, L.C. Using FITradeoff in a Ranking Problem for Supplier Selection under TBL Performance Evaluation: An Application in the Textile Sector. *Production* **2020**, *30*. [CrossRef]
10. dos Santos, F.B.; dos Santos, M. Choice of Armored Vehicles on Wheels for the Brazilian Marine Corps Using PrOPPAGA. *Procedia Comput. Sci.* **2022**, *199*, 301–308. [CrossRef]
11. Costa, I.P.d.A.; Basílio, M.P.; Maêda, S.M.d.N.; Rodrigues, M.V.G.; Moreira, M.Â.L.; Gomes, C.F.S.; dos Santos, M. Algorithm Selection for Machine Learning Classification: An Application of the MELCHIOR Multicriteria Method. *Front. Artif. Intell. Appl.* **2021**, *341*, 154–161. [CrossRef]
12. Moreira, M.Â.L.; Gomes, C.F.S.; Pereira, M.T.; dos Santos, M. SAPEVO-H2 a Multi-Criteria Approach Based on Hierarchical Network: Analysis of Aircraft Systems for Brazilian Navy. In *Innovations in Industrial Engineering II*; Springer International Publishing: Cham, Switzerland, 2023; pp. 61–74.
13. Santos, N.; Junior, C.d.S.R.; Moreira, M.Â.L.; Santos, M.; Gomes, C.F.S.; Costa, I.P.d.A. Strategy Analysis for Project Portfolio Evaluation in a Technology Consulting Company by the Hybrid Method THOR. *Procedia Comput. Sci.* **2022**, *199*, 134–141. [CrossRef]
14. Song, Z.; Yan, T.; Ge, Y. Spatial Equilibrium Allocation of Urban Large Public General Hospitals Based on the Welfare Maximization Principle: A Case Study of Nanjing, China. *Sustainability* **2018**, *10*, 3024. [CrossRef]

15. Mellem, P.M.N.; Costa, I.P.A.; Costa, A.P.A.; Moreira, M.Â.L.; Gomes, C.F.S.; dos Santos, M.; Corriça, J.V.P. Prospective Scenarios Applied in Course Portfolio Management: An Approach in Light of the Momentum and ELECTRE-MOr Methods. *Procedia Comput. Sci.* **2022**, *199*, 48–55. [CrossRef]
16. Costa, I.P.d.A.; Basílio, M.P.; Maêda, S.M.d.N.; Rodrigues, M.V.G.; Moreira, M.Â.L.; Gomes, C.F.S.; Santos, M. Bibliometric Studies on Multi-Criteria Decision Analysis (MCDA) Applied in Personnel Selection. *Front. Artif. Intell. Appl.* **2021**, *341*, 119–125. [CrossRef]
17. Siegenfeld, A.F.; Bar-Yam, Y. An Introduction to Complex Systems Science and Its Applications. *Complexity* **2020**, *2020*, 6105872. [CrossRef]
18. Ahmed, W.; Najmi, A.; Mustafa, Y.; Khan, A. Developing Model to Analyze Factors Affecting Firms' Agility and Competitive Capability: A Case of a Volatile Market. *J. Model. Manag.* **2019**, *14*, 476–491. [CrossRef]
19. Wu, W. A Revised Grey Relational Analysis Method for Multicriteria Group Decision-Making with Expected Utility Theory for Oil Spill Emergency Management. *Math. Probl. Eng.* **2021**, *2021*, 6682332. [CrossRef]
20. Costa, I.P.d.A.; Moreira, M.Â.L.; Costa, A.P.d.A.; Teixeira, L.F.H.d.S.d.B.; Gomes, C.F.S.; Santos, M.D. Strategic Study for Managing the Portfolio of IT Courses Offered by a Corporate Training Company: An Approach in the Light of the ELECTRE-MOr Multicriteria Hybrid Method. *Int. J. Inf. Technol. Decis. Mak.* **2021**, *21*, 351–379. [CrossRef]
21. Marttunen, M.; Lienert, J.; Belton, V. Structuring Problems for Multi-Criteria Decision Analysis in Practice: A Literature Review of Method Combinations. *Eur. J. Oper. Res.* **2017**, *263*, 1–17. [CrossRef]
22. Moreira, M.Â.L.; Junior, M.A.P.d.C.; Costa, I.P.d.A.; Gomes, C.F.S.; dos Santos, M.; Basilio, M.P.; Pereira, D.A.d.M. Consistency Analysis Algorithm for the Multi-Criteria Methods of SAPEVO Family. *Procedia Comput. Sci.* **2022**, *214*, 133–140. [CrossRef]
23. Doumpos, M.; Zopounidis, C.; Gounopoulos, D.; Platanakis, E.; Zhang, W. Operational Research and Artificial Intelligence Methods in Banking. *Eur. J. Oper. Res.* **2022**, *306*, 1–16. [CrossRef]
24. Silal, S.P. Operational Research: A Multidisciplinary Approach for the Management of Infectious Disease in a Global Context. *Eur. J. Oper. Res.* **2021**, *291*, 929–934. [CrossRef] [PubMed]
25. De Almeida, I.D.P.; de Araújo Costa, I.P.; de Araújo Costa, A.P.; de Pina Corriça, J.V.; Lellis Moreira, M.Â.; Simões Gomes, C.F.; dos Santos, M. A Multicriteria Decision-Making Approach to Classify Military Bases for the Brazilian Navy. *Procedia Comput. Sci.* **2022**, *199*, 79–86. [CrossRef]
26. De Figueiredo, B.H.; dos Santos, M.; Fávero, L.P.L.; Moreira, M.Â.L.; Costa, I.P.d.A. Analysis of Maintenance Activities in Urban Pavement Management Systems Based on Decision Tree Algorithm. *Procedia Comput. Sci.* **2022**, *214*, 712–719. [CrossRef]
27. Pak, T.-Y. Social Protection for Happiness? The Impact of Social Pension Reform on Subjective Well-Being of the Korean Elderly. *J. Policy Model.* **2020**, *42*, 349–366. [CrossRef]
28. Lima, R.C.; Silva, P.F.; Rudzit, G. No Power Vacuum: National Security Neglect and the Defence Sector in Brazil. *Def. Stud.* **2021**, *21*, 84–106. [CrossRef]
29. Maêda, S.M.d.N.; Basílio, M.P.; Costa, I.P.d.A.; Moreira, M.Â.L.; dos Santos, M.; Gomes, C.F.S. The SAPEVO-M-NC Method. *Front. Artif. Intell. Appl.* **2021**, *341*, 89–95. [CrossRef]
30. Jardim, R.; dos Santos, M.; Neto, E.; Muradas, F.M.; Santiago, B.; Moreira, M. Design of a Framework of Military Defense System for Governance of Geoinformation. *Procedia Comput. Sci.* **2022**, *199*, 174–181. [CrossRef]
31. Oxford Analytica. Brazil's pension reform will await electoral outcome. *Expert Brief.* **2018**. [CrossRef]
32. Hoffmann, R. Changes in Income Distribution in Brazil. In *The Oxford Handbook of the Brazilian Economy*; Oxford University Press: New York, NY, USA, 2018; pp. 467–488.
33. Lobato, L.d.V.C.; Costa, A.M.; Rizzotto, M.L.F. Pension Reform: The Fatal Blow to Brazilian Social Security. *Saúde Debate* **2019**, *43*, 5–14. [CrossRef]
34. Costanzi, R.N.; Ansiliero, G.; Da Silva Bichara, J. Survivors' Pensions and Their Impact on the Brazilian Labour Market. *Int. Soc. Secur. Rev.* **2017**, *70*, 19–48. [CrossRef]
35. Wang, L. Fertility and Unemployment in a Social Security System. *Econ. Lett.* **2015**, *133*, 19–23. [CrossRef]
36. Lægreid, P.; Rykkja, L.H. *Societal Security and Crisis Management; Governance Capacity and Legitimacy*; Springer: Berlin/Heidelberg, Germany, 2019.
37. Rejda, G.E. *Social Insurance and Economic Security*; Routledge: London, UK, 2015; ISBN 1315700735.
38. Brockett, P.L.; Zhang, Y. Actuarial (Mathematical) Modeling of Mortality and Survival Curves. In *Handbook of the Mathematics of the Arts and Sciences*; Springer: Cham, Switzerland, 2021. [CrossRef]
39. Santos, M.D.; Gomes, C.F.S.; Martins, E.R.; Costa, I.P.D.A.; Santos, R.C.E.D. Processing Time Reduction of Actuarial Calculus of the Armed Forces: An Application of Parallel Computing. In Proceedings of the IJCIEOM 2020—International Joint Conference on Industrial Engineering and Operations Management, Rio de Janeiro, Brazil, 8–11 July 2020.
40. Zuanazzi, P.T.; Fochezatto, A.; Júnior, M.V.W. Social Security Reform and Personal Saving: Evidence from Brazil. *Int. J. Econ. Financ.* **2018**, *10*. [CrossRef]
41. Nascimento, I.F.d.; Albuquerque, P.H.M. Fair and Balance Rate for Benefits Not Scheduled in Defined Contribution Plans. *Rev. Contab. Finanças* **2021**, *32*, 560–576. [CrossRef]
42. Cuevas, M.A.; Karpowicz, M.I.; Mulas-Granados, M.C.; Soto, M. *Fiscal Challenges of Population Aging in Brazil*; International Monetary Fund: Washington, DC USA, 2017; ISBN 1475595557.

43. Aragão, R.; Linsi, L. Many Shades of Wrong: What Governments Do When They Manipulate Statistics. *Rev. Int. Political Econ.* **2020**, *29*, 88–113. [CrossRef]
44. Roncada, A.L.C. Reforming Old-Age Pension Systems in Developing Countries: Lessons from Latin America. *Braz. J. Political Econ.* **2022**, *20*, 124–145. [CrossRef]
45. De La Peña, J.I.; Fernández-Ramos, M.C.; Garayeta, A.; Martín, I.D. Transforming Private Pensions: An Actuarial Model to Face Long-Term Costs. *Mathematics* **2022**, *10*, 1082. [CrossRef]
46. Godínez-Olivares, H.; Boado-Penas, M.d.C.; Pantelous, A.A. How to Finance Pensions: Optimal Strategies for Pay-as-you-go Pension Systems. *J. Forecast.* **2016**, *35*, 13–33. [CrossRef]
47. Hassani, H.; Unger, S.; Beneki, C. Big Data and Actuarial Science. *Big Data Cogn. Comput.* **2020**, *4*, 40. [CrossRef]
48. Teixeira, L.F.H.d.S.d.B. *Análise Dos Testes de Aderência Em Tábuas Atuariais: Uma Contribuição Para o Sistema de Proteção Social Dos Militares Das Forças Armadas, Dissertação (Mestrado em Engenharia de Produção)—Escola de Engenharia*; Universidade Federal Fluminense: Niterói, RJ, Brazil, 2020.
49. Castro, M.C.d. *Entradas e Saídas No Sistema Previdenciário Brasileiro: Uma Aplicação de Tábuas de Mortalidade*; Universidade Federal de Minas Gerais: Minas Gerais, Brazil, 1997.
50. Vaupel, J.W.; Villavicencio, F.; Bergeron-Boucher, M.-P. Demographic Perspectives on the Rise of Longevity. *Proc. Natl. Acad. Sci. USA* **2021**, *118*, e2019536118. [CrossRef]
51. Queiroz, B.L.; Gonzaga, M.R.; Vasconcelos, A.; Lopes, B.T.; Abreu, D.M.X. Comparative Analysis of Completeness of Death Registration, Adult Mortality and Life Expectancy at Birth in Brazil at the Subnational Level. *Popul. Health Metr.* **2020**, *18*, 11. [CrossRef] [PubMed]
52. Queiroz, B.L.; Ferreira, M.L.A. The Evolution of Labor Force Participation and the Expected Length of Retirement in Brazil. *J. Econ. Ageing* **2021**, *18*, 100304. [CrossRef]
53. Santos, M.D. *Proposta de Modelagem Atuarial Aplicada Ao Setor Militar Considerando Influências Econômicas e Biométricas, Tese de Doutorado Apresentada no Programa de Pós-Graduação em Engenharia de Produção da Universidade Federal Fluminense*; RIUFF: Niterói, Brazil, 2018.
54. Krit, M.; Gaudoin, O.; Remy, E. Goodness-of-Fit Tests for the Weibull and Extreme Value Distributions: A Review and Comparative Study. *Commun. Stat. Simul. Comput.* **2021**, *50*, 1888–1911. [CrossRef]
55. Chu, J.; Dickin, O.; Nadarajah, S. A Review of Goodness of Fit Tests for Pareto Distributions. *J. Comput. Appl. Math.* **2019**, *361*, 13–41. [CrossRef]
56. D'Agostino, R.B.; Stephens, M.A. *Goodness-of-Fit-Techniques*; CRC Press: Boca Raton, FL, USA, 1986; Volume 68, ISBN 0824774876.
57. Lospinoso, J.; Snijders, T.A.B. Goodness of Fit for Stochastic Actor-Oriented Models. *Methodol. Innov.* **2019**, *12*, 2059799119884282. [CrossRef]
58. Assis, J.P.d.; Souza, R.P.d.; Dias Santos, C.T.d. Glossary of Statistics. In *Proceedings of the EdUFERSA*; Vanderbilt University School of Medicine: Nashville, TN, USA, 2019; p. 901.
59. Pho, K.-H. Goodness of Fit Test for a Zero-Inflated Bernoulli Regression Model. *Commun. Stat. -Simul. Comput.* **2022**, 1–16. [CrossRef]
60. Lohse, B.; Mitchell, D.C. Valid and Reliable Measure of Adherence to Satter Division of Responsibility in Feeding. *J. Nutr. Educ. Behav.* **2021**, *53*, 211–222. [CrossRef]
61. Meseguer, J. How Does Mortality Among Disability-Program Beneficiaries Compare with That of the General Population? A Summary of Actuarial Estimates. *Soc. Sec. Bull.* **2021**, *81*, 19.
62. Haberman, S.; Pitacco, E. *Actuarial Models for Disability Insurance*; Routledge: London, UK, 2018; ISBN 1351469045.
63. García-Díaz, V.; Espada, J.P.; Crespo, R.G.; G-Bustelo, B.C.P.; Lovelle, J.M.C. An Approach to Improve the Accuracy of Probabilistic Classifiers for Decision Support Systems in Sentiment Analysis. *Appl. Soft Comput.* **2018**, *67*, 822–833. [CrossRef]
64. Turhan, N.S. Karl Pearson's Chi-Square Tests. *Educ. Res. Rev.* **2020**, *16*, 575–580.
65. Müller, M. Item Fit Statistics for Rasch Analysis: Can We Trust Them? *J. Stat. Distrib. Appl.* **2020**, *7*, 5. [CrossRef]
66. Rokicki, B.; Ostaszewski, K. Actuarial Credibility Approach in Adjusting Initial Cost Estimates of Transport Infrastructure Projects. *Sustainability* **2022**, *14*, 13371. [CrossRef]
67. Kenkel, K.M. Contributor Profile: Brazil. In *Providing for Peacekeeping*; PUC-Rio: Rio de Janeiro, Brazil, 2017.
68. Herodotou, H.; Chen, Y.; Lu, J. A Survey on Automatic Parameter Tuning for Big Data Processing Systems. *ACM Comput. Surv.* **2021**, *53*, 1–37. [CrossRef]
69. Bertsekas, D.; Tsitsiklis, J. *Parallel and Distributed Computation: Numerical Methods*; Athena Scientific: Athena, Greece, 2015; ISBN 1886529159.
70. Arató, M.; Bozsó, D.; Elek, P.; Zempléni, A. Forecasting and Simulating Mortality Tables. *Math. Comput. Model.* **2009**, *49*, 805–813. [CrossRef]
71. Dowd, K.; Cairns, A.J.G.; Blake, D.; Coughlan, G.D.; Epstein, D.; Khalaf-Allah, M. Evaluating the Goodness of Fit of Stochastic Mortality Models. *Insur. Math. Econ.* **2010**, *47*, 255–265. [CrossRef]
72. Ochalek, J.; Wang, H.; Gu, Y.; Lomas, J.; Cutler, H.; Jin, C. Informing a Cost-Effectiveness Threshold for Health Technology Assessment in China: A Marginal Productivity Approach. *Pharmacoeconomics* **2020**, *38*, 1319–1331. [CrossRef] [PubMed]
73. Brasil Medida Provisória No 2.215-10, de 31 de Agosto de 2001. 2001. Available online: https://www.planalto.gov.br/ccivil_03/mpv/2215-10.htm (accessed on 23 February 2023).

74. Goldschmidt, R.; Passos, E.; Bezerra, E. *Data Mining*; Elsevier Brasil: Rio de Janeiro, Brazil, 2015; ISBN 8535278230.
75. Dolatabad, F.R.; Hashemi, F.; Yektatalab, S.; Ayaz, M.; Zare, N.; Mansouri, P. Fatemeh Rahimi et al. Effect of Orem Self-Care Program on Self-Efficacy of Burn Patients Referred to Ghotb-Al-Din-E-Shirazi Burn Center, Shiraz, Iran. *Int. J. Med. Investig.* **2021**, *10*, 135–146.
76. Sutton, W. On the Method Used by Milne in the Construction of the Carlisle Table of Mortality. *J. Inst. Actuar.* **1883**, *24*, 110–129. [CrossRef]
77. Hughes, J. International Public Sector Accounting Standards. In *Handbook of Governmental Accounting*; Routledge: New York, NY, USA, 2008; pp. 513–540.
78. Friedler, L.M.; Newton, L.; Bowers, H.U., Jr.; Gerber, J.C.; Hickman, D.A.; Jones, C.J. NesbittActuarial Mathematics. *Am. Math. Mon.* **1986**, *93*, 489–491. [CrossRef]
79. Storto, C.L.; Gončiaruk, A.G. Efficiency vs. Effectiveness: A Benchmarking Study on European Healthcare Systems. *Econ. Sociol.* **2017**, *10*, 102–115. [CrossRef]
80. Wahlberg, A.; Rose, N. The Governmentalization of Living: Calculating Global Health. *Econ. Soc.* **2015**, *44*, 60–90. [CrossRef]
81. Mennicken, A.; Espeland, W.N. What's New with Numbers? Sociological Approaches to the Study of Quantification. *Annu. Rev. Sociol.* **2019**, *45*, 223–245. [CrossRef]
82. Beechey, S.N. Social Security Tomorrow. In *Social Security and the Politics of Deservingness*; Springer: Berlin/Heidelberg, Germany, 2016; pp. 99–112.
83. Nigri, A.; Levantesi, S.; Marino, M.; Scognamiglio, S.; Perla, F. A Deep Learning Integrated Lee–Carter Model. *Risks* **2019**, *7*, 33. [CrossRef]
84. Russolillo, M. Assessing Actuarial Projections Accuracy: Traditional vs. Experimental Strategy. *Open J. Stat.* **2017**, *7*, 608–620. [CrossRef]
85. Ortega, A. Tablas de Mortalidad; 1987. Available online: https://repositorio.cepal.org/handle/11362/8977 (accessed on 23 February 2023).
86. Spreeuw, J.; Owadally, I.; Kashif, M. Projecting Mortality Rates Using a Markov Chain. *Mathematics* **2022**, *10*, 1162. [CrossRef]
87. Li, Z.; Shao, A.W.; Sherris, M. The Impact of Systematic Trend and Uncertainty on Mortality and Disability in a Multistate Latent Factor Model for Transition Rates. *North Am. Actuar. J.* **2017**, *21*, 594–610. [CrossRef]
88. Lozano, I.A.; Alonso-González, P.J.; Núñez-Velázquez, J.J. Estimation of Life Expectancy for Dependent Population in a Multi-State Context. *Int. J. Environ. Res. Public Health* **2021**, *18*, 11162. [CrossRef]
89. Planchet, F.; Debonneuil, É.; Péju, M. Proposal to Extend Access to Loans for Serious Illnesses Using Open Data. *Risks* **2022**, *10*, 51. [CrossRef]
90. Domínguez-Fabián, I.; del Olmo-García, F.; Miguel, H.-S.; Antonio, J. Reinventing Social Security: Towards a Two-Step Mixed Pension System. In *Economic Challenges of Pension Systems*; Springer: Berlin/Heidelberg, Germany, 2020; pp. 441–472.
91. Almasi, G.S.; Gottlieb, A. *Highly Parallel Computing*; Benjamin-Cummings Publishing Co.: New York, NY, USA, 1994; ISBN 0805304436.
92. Fávero, L.P.; Belfiore, P.; Santos, H.P.; dos Santos, M.; de Araújo Costa, I.P.; Junior, W.T. Classification Performance Evaluation from Multilevel Logistic and Support Vector Machine Algorithms through Simulated Data in Python. *Procedia Comput. Sci.* **2022**, *214*, 511–519. [CrossRef]
93. Junior, C.d.S.R.; Moreira, M.Â.L.; Costa, I.P.d.A.; Gomes, C.F.S.; dos Santos, M.; Silva, F.C.A.; Pereira, R.C.A.; Basilio, M.P.; Pereira, D.A.d.M. Parallel Processing Proposal by Clustering Integration of Low-Cost Microcomputers. *Procedia Comput. Sci.* **2022**, *214*, 100–107. [CrossRef]
94. Junior, C.d.S.R.; Moreira, M.Â.L.; Costa, I.P.d.A.; Gomes, C.F.S.; dos Santos, M.; Silva, F.C.A.; Pereira, R.C.A.; Basilio, M.P.; Pereira, D.A.d.M. IoT Technology Proposal for Multi-Adaptative Sensing Integrated into Data Science and Analytics Scenarios. *Procedia Comput. Sci.* **2022**, *214*, 108–116. [CrossRef]
95. Cader, J.M.A.; Cader, A.J.M.A.; Gamaarachchi, H.; Ragel, R.G. Optimisation of Plagiarism Detection Using Vector Space Model on CUDA Architecture. *Int. J. Innov. Comput. Appl.* **2022**, *13*, 232–244. [CrossRef]
96. Hossain, M.A.; Assiri, B. Facial Expression Recognition Based on Active Region of Interest Using Deep Learning and Parallelism. *PeerJ Comput. Sci.* **2022**, *8*, e894. [CrossRef] [PubMed]
97. López, A.; Jurado, J.M.; Ogayar, C.J.; Feito, F.R. An Optimized Approach for Generating Dense Thermal Point Clouds from UAV-Imagery. *ISPRS J. Photogramm. Remote Sens.* **2021**, *182*, 78–95. [CrossRef]
98. Morishima, S. Scalable Anomaly Detection in Blockchain Using Graphics Processing Unit. *Comput. Electr. Eng.* **2021**, *92*, 107087. [CrossRef]
99. Zhang, Y. Bayesian Analysis of Big Data in Insurance Predictive Modeling Using Distributed Computing. *ASTIN Bull. J. IAA* **2017**, *47*, 943–961. [CrossRef]
100. Hwang, K.; Dongarra, J.; Fox, G.C. *Distributed and Cloud Computing: From Parallel Processing to the Internet of Things*; Morgan Kaufmann: Burlington, MA, USA, 2013; ISBN 0128002042.

101. Kirk, D.B.W.; Mei, W.; Wu, H. *Programming Massively Parallel Processors*; Morgan Kauffman: Burlington, MA, USA, 2010.
102. Golov, N.; Rönnbäck, L. Big Data Normalization for Massively Parallel Processing Databases. *Comput. Stand. Interfaces* **2017**, *54*, 86–93. [CrossRef]
103. Laili, Y.; Zhang, L.; Li, Y. Parallel Transfer Evolution Algorithm. *Appl. Soft Comput.* **2019**, *75*, 686–701. [CrossRef]

Disclaimer/Publisher's Note: The statements, opinions and data contained in all publications are solely those of the individual author(s) and contributor(s) and not of MDPI and/or the editor(s). MDPI and/or the editor(s) disclaim responsibility for any injury to people or property resulting from any ideas, methods, instructions or products referred to in the content.

Article

Probabilistic Coarsening for Knowledge Graph Embeddings

Marcin Pietrasik [1,*] and Marek Z. Reformat [1,2]

1 Department of Electrical and Computer Engineering, University of Alberta, Edmonton, AB T6G 2R3, Canada
2 Information Technology Institute, University of Social Sciences, 90-113 Łódź, Poland
* Correspondence: pietrasi@ualberta.ca

Abstract: Knowledge graphs have risen in popularity in recent years, demonstrating their utility in applications across the spectrum of computer science. Finding their embedded representations is thus highly desirable as it makes them easily operated on and reasoned with by machines. With this in mind, we propose a simple meta-strategy for embedding knowledge graphs using probabilistic coarsening. In this approach, a knowledge graph is first coarsened before being embedded by an arbitrary embedding method. The resulting coarse embeddings are then extended down as those of the initial knowledge graph. Although straightforward, this allows for faster training by reducing knowledge graph complexity while revealing its higher-order structures. We demonstrate this empirically on four real-world datasets, which show that coarse embeddings are learned faster and are often of higher quality. We conclude that coarsening is a recommended prepossessing step regardless of the underlying embedding method used.

Keywords: knowledge graph; embedding; coarsening

MSC: 68T30

Citation: Pietrasik, M.; Reformat, M.Z. Probabilistic Coarsening for Knowledge Graph Embeddings. Axioms **2023**, 12, 275. https://doi.org/10.3390/axioms12030275

Academic Editors: Cheng-Shian Lin, Chien-Chang Chen and Yi-Hsien Wang

Received: 21 January 2023
Revised: 26 February 2023
Accepted: 1 March 2023
Published: 6 March 2023

Copyright: © 2023 by the authors. Licensee MDPI, Basel, Switzerland. This article is an open access article distributed under the terms and conditions of the Creative Commons Attribution (CC BY) license (https://creativecommons.org/licenses/by/4.0/).

1. Introduction

Knowledge bases have received considerable research attention in recent years, demonstrating their utility in areas ranging from question answering [1,2] to knowledge generation [3–5] to recommender systems [6]. These knowledge bases are underpinned by graph structures called knowledge graphs, which describe facts as a collection of triples that relate two entities via a predicate. Advances in artificial intelligence have spurred the need to find representations of knowledge graphs that can be easily and accurately reasoned with by machines. Perhaps the most common approach to this is knowledge graph embedding, which transforms a knowledge graph into a low-dimensional embedding space, thereby providing a representation that is both intuitive and highly operable. Many [2–5,7,8] knowledge graph embedding methods have been proposed in recent years, each excelling at capturing different aspects of the knowledge graph's structure and semantics. Relatively less work has been performed on methods for preprocessing a knowledge graph prior to embedding. It has been shown on simple graphs, however, that hierarchically coarsening prior to embedding yields higher-quality embeddings [9,10]. This provides the motivation for our work, namely to investigate whether or not such an approach can improve embeddings for knowledge graphs. Specifically, we propose a simple embedding meta-strategy that can be applied to any arbitrary embedding method. Our strategy first reduces an input knowledge graph—henceforth referred to as a base graph—to a coarsened graph, along with a mapping between the entities in each knowledge graph. Coarse embeddings are then learned on the coarse graph and mapped back down as base embeddings. They may then be fine-tuned on the base graph to reintroduce information that was lost in the coarsening procedure. Figure 1 outlines the flow of this approach. The hypothesized rationale for coarsening is multifactorial, as pointed out in [9,10]. Although largely untested empirically in these works, it may be summarized as follows:

- Coarsening reduces knowledge graph size whilst preserving the global structure, potentially revealing higher-order features.
- Training schemes that rely on stochastic gradient descent may learn embeddings that fall in local minima. Initializations learned on the coarse graph may be more resistant to this problem.
- Structurally equivalent entities are embedded jointly in coarse graphs, reducing training complexity.

We evaluate our proposed strategy on the entity classification task using four real-world datasets and perform a pairwise comparison against common embedding methods. The results indicate that embedding on a coarse graph produces faster and, in many cases, higher-quality embeddings.

In summary, the contributions of our paper are as follows. To the best of our knowledge, we are the first to use coarsening as an explicit preprocessing strategy for generating knowledge graph embeddings. To this end, we propose a novel probabilistic coarsening procedure that reduces knowledge graph size while preserving its global structure. The results of our empirical evaluation allow us to conclude that coarsening is a recommended strategy regardless of the underlying embedding method being used.

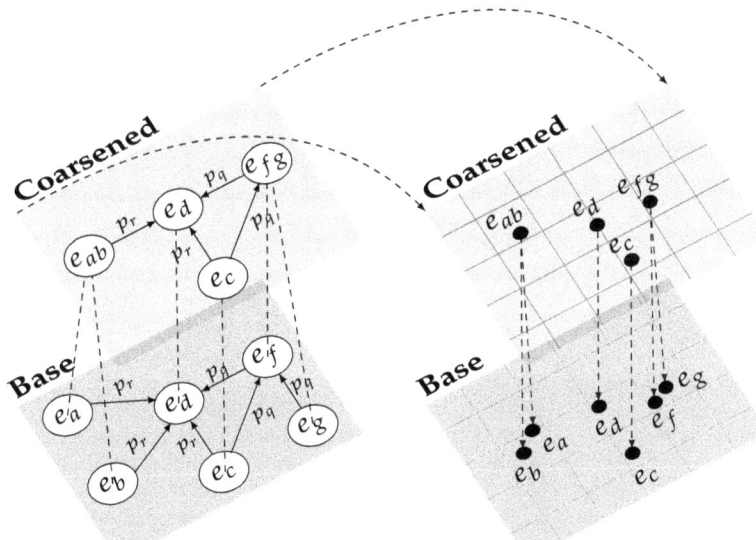

Figure 1. Toy example demonstrating our proposed embedding strategy. The logical flow is guided by dashed line arrows, starting in the bottom left corner and proceeding clockwise.

2. Related Work

Research in graph representation, including graph embeddings, has a long history rooted in mathematics with early methods discussed in [11]. More recently, deep learning has been leveraged for graph embeddings to achieve state-of-the-art results. For instance, DeepWalk [12], Large-scale Information Network Embedding [13], and node2vec [14] sample random walks on a graph and treat them as input words to the skip-gram language model [15]. The intuition behind this approach is that nodes that are sampled in the same random walks are more similar semantically and should have similar embeddings. Another class of deep approaches, Graph Convolution Networks (GCN) [16,17], utilize the convolution operator to learn neighbourhood information for graph entities. Extensions and derivatives of GCNs are ample; for a comprehensive discussion of these methods, we refer readers to [18]. Autoencoders use neural networks to reduce input to a latent embedding before reconstructing the embedding back to the original input. This approach has shown success in generating graph embeddings in [6,19].

Meta-strategies that preprocess graphs into hierarchies before applying embedding methods have been shown to produce higher-quality embeddings at reduced training complexity. The first of these proposed, HARP [9], sequentially reduces the input graph into a hierarchy of progressively coarser graphs. These coarse graphs are then embedded, starting with the coarsest graph such that their embeddings serve as the initialization of the graph directly below it in the hierarchy. This idea was extended in Multi-Level Embedding [10] and GOSH [20], both of which modify the coarsening procedure. In the case of MILE, a hybrid of Structural Equivalence Matching and Normalized Heavy Edge Matching [21] is utilized for coarsening. Furthermore, GCNs are used to refine learned embeddings when moving down the coarse hierarchy to initialize embeddings.

Knowledge graphs present structural traits that render the aforementioned methods ill-suited for their embedding. Specifically, knowledge graphs are directed and labelled in their relations between entities. In light of this, much research has been devoted to developing methods that account for these complexities. For instance, RDF2Vec [7] uses breadth-first graph walks on the skip-gram model to generate embeddings. This model generates embeddings in which entities that are in lower-order neighbourhoods of one another are more proximal in the embedding space. Being one of the first and most popular embedding approaches, it has received significant research attention and extensions, such as KG2Vec [22], Triple2Vec [23], and RDF2Vec_oa [24]. GCNs have been extended to knowledge graphs with the Relational Graph Convolution Network (R-GCN) [3], which aggregates predicate-specific convolutions of the original model. As with RDF2Vec, its success attracted much attention and many extensions, including the Relational Graph Attention Network [25], which leverages graph attention mechanisms and QA-GNN [26], which incorporates contextual information for question and answering tasks. ConvE [5] also leverages the convolution operator in a neural framework by stacking embeddings as a matrix and convolving them in two dimensions. This approach is capable of learning highly expressive embeddings while achieving computational efficiency [27]. Translation-based methods apply the intuition that subject embeddings should be near object embeddings when translated by valid corresponding predicates. These models were pioneered by TransE [4], which was subsequently improved upon to address its challenges in modelling certain types of relations, such as one-to-many and many-to-one [28–34]. Two of these extensions, TransR [29] and TransH [28], are described later on in the paper. Factorization models, such as RESCAL [8] and DistMult [35], learn embeddings by factorizing the knowledge graph adjacency tensor into the product of entity embeddings and relation-specific translation matrices. In bilinear models, such as the two mentioned, the embedded representation of the relations forms a two-dimensional matrix. Non-bilinear factorization models, such as HolE [36] and TuckER [37], do not share this property. Deep reinforcement learning has also shown promise in this domain with MINERVA [2], which learns knowledge graph paths to find the correct entity in incomplete triples. A recent and comprehensive discussion of knowledge graph embedding methods can be found in [38].

3. Proposed Strategy

We define a knowledge graph, $\mathcal{K}$, as a collection of triples such that each triple relates a subject entity, e_s, to an object entity, e_o, via a predicate, p_r. In this view, $\mathcal{K} := \{(e_s, p_r, e_o)\} \in \mathcal{E} \times \mathcal{P} \times \mathcal{E}$ where $e \in \mathcal{E}$ is the set of entities and $p \in \mathcal{P}$ is the set of predicates. The task of knowledge graph embedding is to find a function, f, which maps each entity to the embedding space $f : \mathcal{E} \mapsto \mathbb{R}^{|\mathcal{E}| \times d}$ where d is the dimensionality of the embedding space such that $d << |\mathcal{E}||\mathcal{P}|$. Most embedding methods also embed predicates, although their formulation is highly variable.

We employ the notation used in [39] wherein a knowledge graph is interpreted by a set of entities and the tags that annotate them. In this view, a tag t, is defined as a predicate-entity pair that describes another entity, $t := (p_r, e_o) \mid (e_s, p_r)$. The order between a tag's predicate and entity correspond to whether the tag is incoming or outgoing. Thus, each triple in $\mathcal{K}$ corresponds to two entity-tag mappings. These mappings are expressed as sets such that each entity e_a has a corresponding set of tags that annotate it, denoted as $\mathcal{A}_a$.

Our proposed strategy embeds a base graph via an intermediary coarse graph. In this process, the coarse graph is first generated from the base graph before being embedded. Coarse embeddings are then mapped back down to the base graph and fine-tuned. Our strategy may be divided into the following three steps:

1. **Probabilistic graph coarsening** reduces the base graph to a smaller, coarsened graph and returns an entity mapping between the two graphs.
2. **Coarse graph embedding** applies a predetermined embedding method on the coarse graph to obtain coarse embeddings.
3. **Reverse mapping and fine-tuning** maps coarse embeddings back down to the base graph to obtain base embeddings. Base embeddings may be fine-tuned on the base graph.

The remainder of this section describes each of these steps in detail. The intuition for this process is described visually in Figure 1, while its sequence is outlined in Algorithm 1.

3.1. Probabilistic Graph Coarsening

In this step, the base graph is reduced to create a coarse graph, denoted as $\mathcal{K}'$, such that $|\mathcal{K}'| < |\mathcal{K}|$. This procedure involves collapsing structurally similar entities in $\mathcal{K}$ to one entity cluster in $\mathcal{K}'$. Relations in $\mathcal{K}$ are extended to $\mathcal{K}'$ such that a cluster's relations are the union of its constituent entities' relations. Collapsing entities are divided into two stages, designed to preserve the first-order and second-order proximities of the base graph [13]. This allows the base graph to be reduced of structural redundancies, making it more computationally manageable and potentially revealing its global and most salient features. The mapping between base entities and coarse entities is represented by $\Psi : \mathcal{E} \mapsto \mathcal{E}'$. Coarsening is demonstrated visually on the left half of Figure 1.

3.1.1. Collapsing First-Order Neighbours

Preserving first-order proximity refers to the notion that entities should be embedded proximally to their first-order (i.e., one-hop) neighbours. By collapsing entities with their first-order neighbours, proximity is ensured as collapsed entities share identical embeddings. In undirected, single predicate graphs, edge collapsing [9,40,41] finds the largest subset of edges such that no two edges are incident to the same vertex. Vertices incident to each edge in this set is then collapsed, yielding a graph coarsened to preserve first-order proximity. Edge collapsing may be applied to knowledge graphs by assuming undirected graph relations. This approach proves too liberal in its coarsening, however, since the cost of coarsening is increased in knowledge graphs due to the loss of predicate information. In response, we restrict edge collapsing to entities whose collapsing incurs no loss of predicate information other than predicates that are incident to both entities. Formally, entity e_a is collapsed with e_b if:

$$\{t \in \mathcal{A}_a : e_b \notin t\} \subseteq \{t \in \mathcal{A}_b : e_a \notin t\} \tag{1}$$

First-order entity collapsing is demonstrated in the lower left quadrant of Figure 1, where entity e_g is collapsed with its neighbour e_f to form entity cluster e_{fg} in the coarse graph. We note that entities e_a and e_b are also valid candidates for first-order collapsing with e_d. This demonstrates the necessity of initially performing second-order neighbour collapsing since e_a and e_b are structurally equivalent and thus more similar to one another than to e_d. As such, first-order collapsing is performed after second-order collapsing, as seen in Algorithm 1, where it is captured in lines 11 to 18.

3.1.2. Collapsing Second-Order Neighbours

Second-order (i.e., two-hop) neighbours are two entities that share a first-order neighbour. The rationale for preserving second-order proximity is discussed in [13] and predicated on the intuition that entities that have many common first-order neighbours tend to exhibit similar structural and semantic properties. As such, they should be proximal to one another in the embedding space. In Figure 1, we see that second-order neighbours e_a and e_b have identical tag sets (i.e., $\mathcal{A}_a = \mathcal{A}_b$) and are thus structurally equivalent. Collapsing these entities and embedding them jointly ensures the preservation of second-order proximity in the embedding space while incurring no loss of information. We apply this reasoning to our coarsening procedure. Namely, if two second-order neighbours exhibit a high degree of structural similarity, we collapse them in the coarse graph. We measure the similarity between a pair of second-order neighbours as the Jaccard coefficient between their tag sets:

$$\text{Sim}(e_a, e_c) = \frac{\mathcal{A}_a \cap \mathcal{A}_c}{\mathcal{A}_a \cup \mathcal{A}_c} \qquad (2)$$

where $\text{Sim}(e_a, e_c)$ is the similarity between e_a and e_c such that $0 \leq \text{Sim}(e_a, e_v) \leq 1$. Second-order neighbours are collapsed if their similarity is greater than or equal to a threshold, α, which is chosen such that $0 < \alpha \leq 1$. The value of α dictates the coarseness of the graph, with lower α values resulting in smaller, coarser graphs. This process may be seen as a relaxation of Structural Equivalence Matching (SEM) proposed in [10], which collapses second-order neighbours only if they are structurally equivalent. In other words, SEM is analogous to our method of $\alpha = 1$; collapsing entities e_a and e_c when $\mathcal{A}_a = \mathcal{A}_c$. Second-order collapsing is summarized in lines 2 to 10 of Algorithm 1.

Algorithm 1 Coarse knowledge graph embeddings.

Input: base graph $\mathcal{K}$; collapsing threshold α; random walk count η
Output: base embeddings **E**

1: Initialize $\mathcal{K}'$ and Ψ
2: **for all** $e_a \in \mathcal{E}$ **do**
3:     **for** *iteration* in 1, 2, ..., η **do**
4:        Obtain second order neighbour e_c using (5) and (6)
5:        Calculate $\text{Sim}(e_a, e_c)$ using (2)
6:        **if** $\text{Sim}(e_a, e_c) \geq \alpha$ and $e_c \notin \Psi$ **then**
7:           Collapse e_a with e_c; Update $\mathcal{K}'$ and Ψ
8:        **end if**
9:     **end for**
10: **end for**
11: **for all** $e_a \in \mathcal{E}$ **do**
12:     **for** *iteration* in 1, 2, ..., η **do**
13:        Obtain first order neighbour e_b using (3) and (4)
14:        **if** (1) holds for e_a and $e_a \notin \Psi$ **then**
15:           Collapse e_a into e_b; Update $\mathcal{K}'$ and Ψ
16:        **end if**
17:     **end for**
18: **end for**
19: Obtain coarse embeddings **E'** using (7)
20: **for all** $e_a \in \mathcal{E}$ **do**
21:     Reverse map base embedding **E**$[e_a]$ using (8)
22: **end for**
23: Fine tune base embeddings **E** using (9)

3.1.3. Neighbour Sampling

The pairwise comparison between entities and their first- and second-order neighbourhoods has a worst-case time complexity of $O(|\mathcal{E}|^2)$ and is thus computationally infeasible for large-scale knowledge graphs. To overcome this, we propose a scheme for sampling neighbours using constrained random walks. To obtain a first-order neighbour for entity e_a, we first sample a tag from its tag set:

$$t_1 \sim \text{Uniform}(\mathcal{A}_a) \qquad (3)$$

where t_1 represents one hop in a random walk on the base graph. The first-order neighbour e_b is then extracted from t_1:

$$e_b = t_1 \cap \mathcal{E} \qquad (4)$$

Note that since $t_1 \cap \mathcal{E}$ is a singleton set, we can abuse the $=$ symbol such that $e_b = \{e_b\}$. The predicate $p_r = t_1 \cap \mathcal{P}$ is used as a constraint in sampling a second-order neighbour for e_a. Specifically, given e_a and its first-order neighbour e_b on predicate p_r, we only sample second-order neighbours that are incident to e_b on p_r:

$$t_2 \sim \text{Uniform}(\{t \in \mathcal{A}_b : p_r \in t \wedge e_a \notin t\}) \qquad (5)$$

The second-order neighbour e_c is extracted from t_2 analogously to e_b:

$$e_c = t_2 \cap \mathcal{E} \qquad (6)$$

Sampled neighbours are collapsed if they meet the aforementioned requirements, resulting in a stochastically derived coarse graph.

We sample $\eta \geq 1$ neighbours for each entity, resulting in a $O(|\mathcal{E}|\eta)$ time complexity for our sampling scheme. As a hyperparameter of coarsening, η is chosen a priori allowing for flexibility to account for knowledge graph size. In practice, we see that even small values of η yield encouraging results. The intuition behind this may be summarized as follows:

- Entities that meet the criteria for collapsing are likely to have smaller neighbourhoods.
- Entities that belong to smaller neighbourhoods have a higher chance of getting sampled as candidates for collapsing.

This allows our strategy to be performed with little added computational overhead. We note that reading a dataset has a time complexity of $O(|\mathcal{K}|)$, which may itself be more computationally taxing than coarsening on dense knowledge graphs.

3.2. Coarse Graph Embedding

Having coarsened the base graph, coarse embeddings are obtained by applying an arbitrary embedding method on the coarse graph. Since the coarse graph has all the properties of its base counterpart, no additional changes to the embedding method are necessary, merely a different input. Due to there being fewer entities in the coarse graph than its base counterpart, coarse embeddings may require fewer training steps, resulting in faster training times. We use the notation $f(\mathcal{K}')$ to denote the embedding of coarse graph $\mathcal{K}'$ to yield coarse embeddings $\mathbf{E}'$:

$$\mathbf{E}' = f(\mathcal{K}') \qquad (7)$$

Line 19 in Algorithm 1 places this step in the context of our whole strategy.

3.3. Reverse Mapping and Fine Tuning

Coarse embeddings are extended down as base embeddings $\mathbf{E}$ by reversing the mapping obtained in the coarsening step:

$$\mathbf{E}[e_a] = \mathbf{E}'[\Psi(e_a)] \qquad (8)$$

where $\mathbf{E}[e_a]$ indexes the base embedding for e_a. A consequence of reverse mapping is that entities that were coarsened together share identical embeddings. In applications that rely on the distinction between these entities, this property is not desired. As such, base embedding may be fine-tuned by embedding **E** with respect to the base graph using **E'** as initialisation. This ensures that structural information that was lost in the coarsening process is reintroduced to base embeddings, and collapsed entities become delineated. Furthermore, the training process may be less likely to get stuck in local minima due to its global initialisations. We use the following notation to capture fine-tuning **E** using **E'** as initialisation:

$$\mathbf{E} = f(\mathcal{K}|\mathbf{E}') \qquad (9)$$

Reverse mapping and fine-tuning are described in lines 20 to 23 of Algorithm 1 as the final steps in our strategy.

4. Evaluation

We evaluate our strategy on the entity classification task performed in [3,7], which involves embedding a knowledge graph and using the embeddings to infer entity labels. Our strategy is compared pairwise against the baseline methods used in the embedding step. This allows us to measure whether our coarsening strategy is justified in comparison to using the baseline methods conventionally. We use three baseline methods to evaluate our strategy: RDF2Vec, R-GCN, and TransE. In performing our evaluation, we extend the code provided in [3,42] and publish it online for replication (https://sites.ualberta.ca/~pietrasi/coarse_embeddings.zip (accessed on 3 March 2023).

4.1. Datasets

We use four canonical datasets from [3,7] in our evaluation: MUTAG, AIFB, BGS, and AM. Each dataset consists of a knowledge graph in Resource Description Framework format and labels for a subset of its entities. We mirror [3] in removing knowledge graph relations, which are on predicates that correlate strongly with their labels. Statistics for each dataset are provided in Table 1. What follows is a brief description of each dataset.

- **MUTAG** depicts the properties and interactions of molecules that may or may not be carcinogenic. We remove the labelling predicate isMutagenic from the dataset.
- **AIFB** reports the work performed at the AIFB research group and labels its members by affiliation. We remove predicates, employs, and affiliation.
- **BGS** captures geological data from the island of Great Britain and is used to predict the lithogenicity of rocks. As such, we remove the hasLithogenesis predicate.
- **AM** describes and categorises artefacts in the Amsterdam Museum. We remove the materials predicate as it correlates with artefact labels.

Table 1. Summary of datasets used in this paper.

Dataset	MUTAG	AIFB	BGS	AM
Triples	74,227	29,043	916,199	5,988,321
Entities	23,644	8285	333,845	1,666,764
Predicates	23	45	103	133
Labelled	340	176	146	1000
Classes	2	4	2	11

4.2. Procedure

Embeddings were learned using each of the baseline embedding methods on the base graph and on the coarse graph as per our strategy. To assess the quality of these embeddings, entity classification was performed by training a support vector machine on 80% labelled entities and testing on the remaining 20% using splits provided in [7]. We use the accuracy of classification on the testing entities as the metric of our strategy's performance. To account for stochasticity in this process, embeddings were learned and evaluated ten times for each dataset.

To obtain optimal results, we set aside 20% of the training entities as validation for hyperparameter selection and to prevent overfitting. In magnanimity, we used embedding hyperparameters, which were selected on validation results obtained on the base graphs. For coarsening hyperparameters, we performed exploration on $\alpha \in \{0.25, 0.5, 0.75, 1\}$ and used $\eta = 10$ in all of our experiments. The optimal hyperparameters for each dataset and baseline method may be found with our published code.

4.3. Results

The results of our evaluation are summarised in Table 2. We use the notation $C(x)$ to refer to our strategy applied to baseline embedding method x. Our strategy improved on the baseline in 10 of the 12 experiments, 7 of which were statistically significant. Furthermore, we were able to achieve state-of-the-art performance on three of the four datasets, albeit using different baseline methods.

Table 2. Results of pairwise comparison between our strategy and baseline embedding methods as measured by accuracy (mean ± standard deviation) obtained on testing entities for each dataset. Asterisk (*) indicates superior performance as per Student's t-test at a 0.05 level of significance. Underline indicates top performance on the dataset, regardless of the baseline method.

Method	MUTAG	AIFB	BGS	AM
RDF2Vec	0.7500 ± 0.0392	0.9111 ± 0.0117	0.7828 ± 0.0327	0.8758 ± 0.0143
C(RDF2Vec)	0.7956 ± 0.0340	0.9167 ± 0.0000	0.8828 ± 0.0178	0.8778 ± 0.0211
Change	6.1% *	0.6%	12.8% *	0.2%
R-GCN	0.7397 ± 0.0286	0.9528 ± 0.0264	0.8345 ± 0.0424	0.8833 ± 0.0197
C(R-GCN)	0.7294 ± 0.0242	0.9694 ± 0.0088	0.8690 ± 0.0317	0.8828 ± 0.0138
Change	−1.4%	1.7% *	4.1% *	−0.1%
TransE	0.7397 ± 0.0422	0.8722 ± 0.0397	0.6793 ± 0.0371	0.4207 ± 0.0143
C(TransE)	0.7412 ± 0.0368	0.9056 ± 0.0299	0.7759 ± 0.0335	0.4955 ± 0.0179
Change	0.3%	3.8% *	14.2% *	17.7% *

Although extensive comparisons between the baseline methods with and without the application of our strategy are outside the scope of this paper, we suggest possible reasons for the improved results and how employing coarsening may overcome certain limitations present in the baselines. The main difference in using our strategy in conjunction with RDF2VEC is in how it changes the sequences obtained from the random walks on the knowledge graph. Because densely connected entities are less likely to be collapsed in the coarsening process, they are more likely to be sampled in walks on the coarsened graph. This bears some similarity to RDF2VEC Light [43], which only performs walks on entities of interest if we assume that densely connected entities are more likely to be of interest. Furthermore, on all four datasets, we see a larger reduction in the percentage of entities as opposed to triples. This too changes the nature of sampled walks, namely in that predicates are more likely to be sampled. The difference between sampling entities versus predicates was discussed in [44] and termed e-walks and p-walks, respectively. In short, it was shown that e-walks are better at capturing the relatedness of entities, and p-walks are better at capturing their semantic similarity. Because coarsening changes the sampled walks in the direction of p-walks, our strategy is theorised to be better at capturing semantic similarity between entities. In general, the idea of biasing random walks in order to improve the performance of RDF2VEC is well studied and extensively evaluated in [45]. The advantage of using our strategy in conjunction with a R-GCN baseline is that of parameter reduction. Recall that R-GCN relies on computations made on the adjacency matrix of the knowledge graph. Such a formulation results in an increasing number of parameters as the size of the knowledge graph increases, making its scalability poor for very large datasets. By coarsening the knowledge graph, we reduce the number of trainable parameters in the model, improving its efficiency. We note, however, that our strategy appears to perform worse on R-GCN relative to the other baselines. The reason for this may be that coarsening produces graphs with a larger proportion of highly connected hub entities, which is a structural weakness of R-GCN as pointed out by its authors. The limitations of the translational assumption inherent to the TransE model is not addressed by our strategy directly, as the underlying embedding procedure is never changed. These include the inability to properly handle relational patterns such as one-to-many, many-to-one, inverse, and symmetric relations and were largely addressed by subsequent models in the translational family, such as the aforementioned TransR and TransH models. Specifically, TransR finesses the issue of entities and predicates being embedded in the same space by introducing a separate predicate embedding space. Entities are then projected to the predicate space by a predicate-specific projection matrix, and the original translation assumptions of the TransE model are applied. This solves the problem of embedding entities, which may or may not be similar to one another depending on their predicate context. TransH was proposed to handle the problem of embedding one-to-many and many-to-one relationships. To this end, it too introduced the notion of predicate-specific projections, although unlike TransR, entities and predicates were mapped in the same space. In contrast to these approaches, our strategy may be seen as improving on TransE indirectly, namely by augmenting the input data. One-to-many and many-to-one relationships are likely candidates for second-order collapsing, ensuring tight embeddings of these entities by TransE. Such a feature does not rectify TransE's challenges in handling these types of relationships but merely accepts its inadequacy and ensures that less computation is spent on embedding these entities. This is also the case for symmetrical relationships whose entities are candidates for first-order collapsing. Thus, in order to overcome the obstacles of TransE, it would be advised to apply our strategy in conjunction with one of its successors, which explicitly deals with the limitations mentioned. We note that despite our strategy's positive impact in regard to the aforementioned limitations, it is formulated to be embedding-method agnostic. As such it does not inherently seek to overcome the limitations of any particular embedding method. Finally, we see that datasets with knowledge graphs that have a higher degree of reduction at $\alpha = 0.5$ and $\eta = 10$ perform better. This is because not all knowledge graphs are equally suitable candidates for coarsening. Namely, knowledge graphs that exhibit a high degree of structural equivalency between entities lose less information in the coarsening process. We see this in the AIFB and BGS datasets, where more than half of their entities get collapsed in the coarsening step, as shown in Table 3.

Table 3. Percent reduction in coarse graphs relative to base graphs at $\alpha = 0.5$ and $\eta = 10$.

Dataset	MUTAG	AIFB	BGS	AM
Triples	52,179	20,134	501,722	4,080,981
Change	−29.7%	−30.7%	−45.2%	−31.8%
Entities	16,115	2801	78,335	944,759
Change	−31.8%	−66.2%	−76.5%	−43.3%
Predicates	23	43	97	129
Change	0%	−4.4%	−5.8%	−3.0%

Figure 2 plots the performance of our strategy compared to baselines when increasing the number of training steps performed. Due to computational constraints, we trained the embeddings up to fifty epochs. It is possible that given enough training, baseline methods could catch up in performance to our coarsening strategy, as can be seen on the AM dataset using TransE. This, however, still demonstrates that coarse graphs produce quality embeddings faster than embedding on base graphs. This is further confirmed by RDF2Vec on AIFB and AM and R-GCN on MUTAG, which show similar trendlines to the coarsened counterpart requiring fewer training steps. This suggests that our strategy is faster to train than its baseline counterparts.

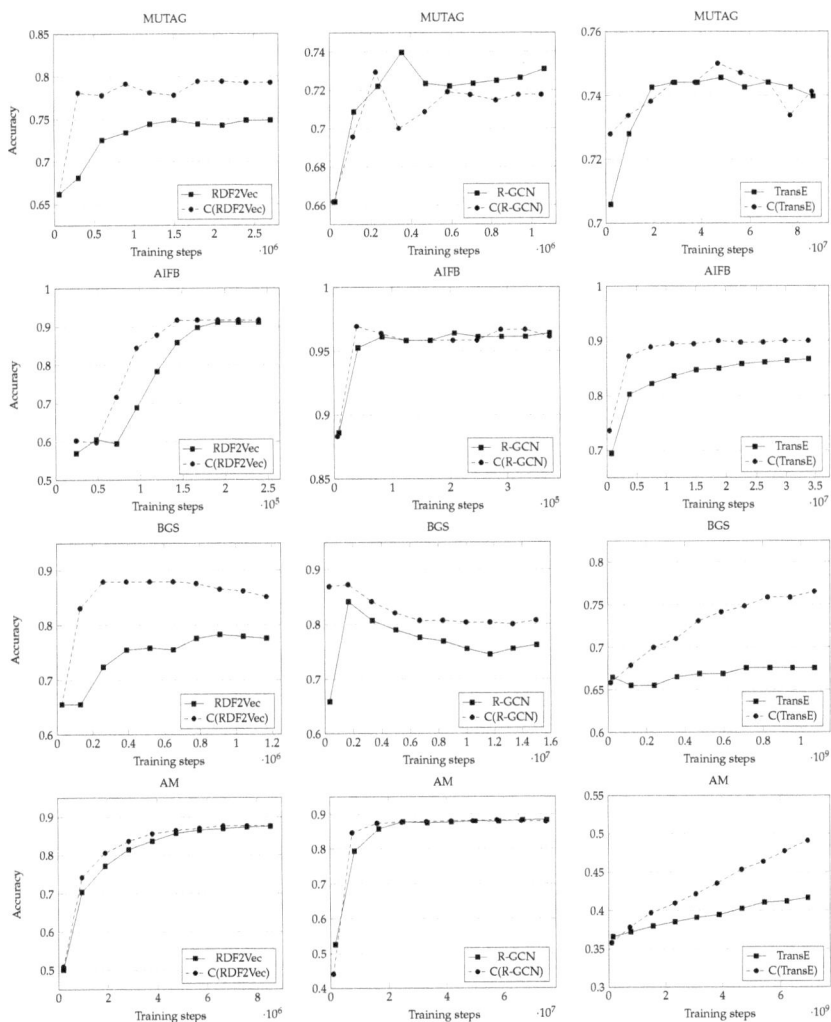

Figure 2. Pairwise comparison between the baseline method and our strategy demonstrating performance (accuracy) as a function of the number of training steps performed for each dataset.

5. Conclusions

We introduced a simple meta-strategy for embedding knowledge graphs that relies on coarsening as a preprocessing step to obtain a reduced knowledge graph prior to embedding. To this end, we adapted existing graph coarsening concepts to knowledge graphs and introduced a novel entity collapsing and neighbour sampling scheme. Our evaluation demonstrates that such an approach results in faster and, oftentimes, more accurate knowledge graph embeddings. Coupled with the fact that our strategy incurs little overhead costs, we conclude that graph coarsening is a recommended preprocessing step before applying any existing knowledge graph embedding method.

Despite the encouraging results, there are still limitations to our work and avenues for future work. The evaluation of the reverse mapping procedure could be performed by a simple pairwise comparison. Specifically, comparing the embedding quality with and without reverse mapping and fine-tuning. We anticipate, however, that on the entity classification task, such a comparison would not be indicative of the extent to which information is regained in this step. This is because entity classification is performed on a subset of graph entities that are highly connected and thus unlikely to be collapsed in the coarsening process. This is due to the requirements for collapsing and their satisfaction being more likely by peripheral entities. As such, the embeddings of classified entities will not change during the reverse mapping and fine-tuning process. This brings attention to another limitation, namely that of evaluating the strategy on different downstream tasks, such as the commonly used link prediction task. In this task, triples not present in the knowledge graph are inferred by assigning a score to reflect the likelihood of observing such a triple. This task was not originally handled by RDF2Vec, whose principal function was data mining. It has been shown more recently [46] that RDF2Vec can be adapted to the link prediction task. As such, testing our strategy on this task is a worthwhile endeavour. Finally, future improvements to our work may be made by proposing alternate coarsening schemes, such as those which leverage graph clustering or community detection. These models present the opportunity for more intelligent collapsing of nodes, which may improve the efficiency of our overall strategy. To this end, models such as KDComm [47], Bayesian Symmetric NMF [48], the Multilayer Stochastic Blockmodel [49], and the Multilayer Mixed Membership Stochastic Blockmodel [50] can be utilized. One of the challenges to overcome if these models were to be integrated with our strategy would be that of computational efficiency. In general, the process by which these models induce communities from the knowledge graph is more expensive than our approach. This would be further exacerbated if multi-step coarsening were to be employed.

Author Contributions: Conceptualisation, M.P. and M.R.; methodology, M.P.; software, M.P.; validation, M.P.; formal analysis, M.P.; investigation, M.P.; resources, M.P and M.R.; data curation, M.P.; writing—original draft preparation, M.P.; writing—review and editing, M.R.; visualisation, M.P.; supervision, M.R.; project administration, M.R.; funding acquisition, M.R. All authors have read and agreed to the published version of the manuscript.

Funding: This research received no external funding.

Institutional Review Board Statement: Not applicable.

Data Availability Statement: Data may be obtained from: https://sites.ualberta.ca/~pietrasi/coarse_embeddings.zip (accessed on 3 March 2023).

Conflicts of Interest: The authors declare no conflict of interest.

References

1. Bordes, A.; Usunier, N.; Chopra, S.; Weston, J. Large-scale simple question answering with memory networks. *arXiv* **2015**, arXiv:1506.02075.
2. Das, R.; Dhuliawala, S.; Zaheer, M.; Vilnis, L.; Durugkar, I.; Krishnamurthy, A.; Smola, A.; McCallum, A. Go for a walk and arrive at the answer: Reasoning over paths in knowledge bases using reinforcement learning. *arXiv* **2017**, arXiv:1711.05851.
3. Schlichtkrull, M.; Kipf, T.N.; Bloem, P.; Van Den Berg, R.; Titov, I.; Welling, M. Modeling relational data with graph convolutional networks. In *European Semantic Web Conference*; Springer: Cham, Switzerland, 2018; pp. 593–607.
4. Bordes, A.; Usunier, N.; Garcia-Duran, A.; Weston, J.; Yakhnenko, O. Translating embeddings for modeling multi-relational data. *Adv. Neural Inf. Process. Syst.* **2013**, *26*, 2787–2795.
5. Dettmers, T.; Minervini, P.; Stenetorp, P.; Riedel, S. Convolutional 2d knowledge graph embeddings. *arXiv* **2017**, arXiv:1707.01476.
6. Bellini, V.; Schiavone, A.; Di Noia, T.; Ragone, A.; Di Sciascio, E. Knowledge-aware autoencoders for explainable recommender systems. In Proceedings of the 3rd Workshop on Deep Learning for Recommender Systems, Vancouver, BC, Canada, 6 October 2018.
7. Ristoski, P.; Paulheim, H. Rdf2vec: Rdf graph embeddings for data mining. In *International Semantic Web Conference*; Springer: Cham, Switzerland, 2016; pp. 498–514.
8. Nickel, M.; Tresp, V.; Kriegel, H.P. A three-way model for collective learning on multi-relational data. In Proceedings of the 28th International Conference on Machine Learning, Bellevue,WA, USA, 28 June–2 July 2011.
9. Chen, H.; Perozzi, B.; Hu, Y.; Skiena, S. Harp: Hierarchical representation learning for networks. In Proceedings of the 32nd AAAI Conference on Artificial Intelligence, New Orleans, LA, USA 2–7 February 2018; pp. 2127–2134.
10. Liang, J.; Gurukar, S.; Parthasarathy, S. Mile: A multi-level framework for scalable graph embedding. *arXiv* **2018**, arXiv:1802.09612.
11. Archdeacon, D. Topological graph theory. *Surv. Congr. Numer.* **1996**, *115*, 18.
12. Perozzi, B.; Al-Rfou, R.; Skiena, S. Deepwalk: Online learning of social representations. In Proceedings of the 20th ACM SIGKDD International Conference on Knowledge Discovery and Data Mining, New York, NY, USA, 24–27 August 2014; pp. 701–710.

13. Tang, J.; Qu, M.; Wang, M.; Zhang, M.; Yan, J.; Mei, Q. Line: Large-scale information network embedding. In Proceedings of the 24th International Conference on World Wide Web, Florence, Italy, 18–22 May 2015.
14. Grover, A.; Leskovec, J. node2vec: Scalable feature learning for networks. In Proceedings of the 22nd ACM SIGKDD International Conference on Knowledge Discovery and Data Mining, San Francisco, CA, USA, 13–17 August 2016; pp. 855–864.
15. Mikolov, T.; Sutskever, I.; Chen, K.; Corrado, G.S.; Dean, J. Distributed representations of words and phrases and their compositionality. *Adv. Neural Inf. Process. Syst.* **2013**, *26*, 3111–3119.
16. Duvenaud, D.K.; Maclaurin, D.; Iparraguirre, J.; Bombarell, R.; Hirzel, T.; Aspuru-Guzik, A.; Adams, R.P. Convolutional networks on graphs for learning molecular fingerprints. *Adv. Neural Inf. Process. Syst.* **2015**, *28*, 2224–2232.
17. Kipf, T.N.; Welling, M. Semi-supervised classification with graph convolutional networks. *arXiv* **2016**, arXiv:1609.02907.
18. Wu, Z.; Pan, S.; Chen, F.; Long, G.; Zhang, C.; Philip, S.Y. A comprehensive survey on graph neural networks. *IEEE Trans. Neural Netw. Learn. Syst.* **2020**, *32*, 4–24. [CrossRef]
19. Simonovsky, M.; Komodakis, N. Graphvae: Towards generation of small graphs using variational autoencoders. In *International Conference on Artificial Neural Networks*; Springer: Cham, Switzerland, 2018; pp. 412–422.
20. Akyildiz, T.A.; Aljundi, A.A.; Kaya, K. Gosh: Embedding big graphs on small hardware. In Proceedings of the 49th International Conference on Parallel Processing (ICPP), Edmonton, AB, Canada, 17–20 August 2020; pp. 1–11.
21. Karypis, G.; Kumar, V. Multilevel k-way partitioning scheme for irregular graphs. *J. Parallel Distrib. Comput.* **1998**, *48*, 96–129. [CrossRef]
22. Wang, Y.; Dong, L.; Jiang, X.; Ma, X.; Li, Y.; Zhang, H. KG2Vec: A node2vec-based vectorization model for knowledge graph. *PLoS ONE* **2021**, *16*, e0248552. [CrossRef]
23. Fionda, V.; Pirró, G. Triple2Vec: Learning Triple Embeddings from Knowledge Graphs. In Proceedings of the AAAI Conference on Artificial Intelligence, New York, NY, USA, 7–12 February 2020.
24. Portisch, J.; Paulheim, H. Putting rdf2vec in order. In Proceedings of the International Semantic Web Conference (ISWC 2021): Posters and Demo, Virtual Conference, 24–28 October 2021.
25. Busbridge, D.; Sherburn, D.; Cavallo, P.; Hammerla, N.Y. Relational graph attention networks. *arXiv* **2019**, arXiv:1904.05811.
26. Yasunaga, M.; Ren, H.; Bosselut, A.; Liang, P.; Leskovec, J. QA-GNN: Reasoning with Language Models and Knowledge Graphs for Question Answering. In *2021 Conference of the North American Chapter of the Association for Computational Linguistics: Human Language Technologies*; Association for Computational Linguistics: Stroudsburg, PA, USA, 2021; pp. 535–546.
27. Alshahrani, M.; Thafar, M.A.; Essack, M. Application and evaluation of knowledge graph embeddings in biomedical data. *PeerJ Comput. Sci.* **2021**, *7*, e341. [CrossRef]
28. Wang, Z.; Zhang, J.; Feng, J.; Chen, Z. Knowledge graph embedding by translating on hyperplanes. In Proceedings of the AAAI Conference on Artificial Intelligence, Portsmouth, NH, USA, 21–26 June 2014, Volume 28.
29. Lin, Y.; Liu, Z.; Sun, M.; Liu, Y.; Zhu, X. Learning entity and relation embeddings for knowledge graph completion. In Proceedings of the AAAI Conference on Artificial Intelligence, Austin, TX, USA, 25–30 January 2015; Volume 29.
30. Ji, G.; He, S.; Xu, L.; Liu, K.; Zhao, J. Knowledge graph embedding via dynamic mapping matrix. In *53rd Annual Meeting of the Association for Computational Linguistics and the 7th International Joint Conference on Natural Language Processing (Volume 1: Long Papers)*; Association for Computational Linguistics: Stroudsburg, PA, USA, 2015; pp. 687–696.
31. Xiao, H.; Huang, M.; Hao, Y.; Zhu, X. TransA: An adaptive approach for knowledge graph embedding. *arXiv* **2015**, arXiv:1509.05490.
32. Nguyen, D.Q.; Sirts, K.; Qu, L.; Johnson, M. STransE: a novel embedding model of entities and relationships in knowledge bases. In *2016 Conference of the North American Chapter of the Association for Computational Linguistics: Human Language Technologies*; Association for Computational Linguistics: Stroudsburg, PA, USA, 2016; pp. 460–466.
33. Ebisu, T.; Ichise, R. Toruse: Knowledge graph embedding on a lie group. In Proceedings of the AAAI Conference on Artificial Intelligence, New Orleans, LA, USA, 2–7 February 2018; Volume 32.
34. Sun, Z.; Deng, Z.H.; Nie, J.Y.; Tang, J. RotatE: Knowledge Graph Embedding by Relational Rotation in Complex Space. In Proceedings of the International Conference on Learning Representations, New Orleans, LA, USA, 6–9 May 2019.
35. Yang, B.; Yih, W.t.; He, X.; Gao, J.; Deng, L. Embedding entities and relations for learning and inference in knowledge bases. *arXiv* **2014**, arXiv:1412.6575.
36. Nickel, M.; Rosasco, L.; Poggio, T. Holographic embeddings of knowledge graphs. In Proceedings of the AAAI Conference on Artificial Intelligence, Phoenix, AZ, USA, 12–17 February 2016; Volume 30.
37. Balazevic, I.; Allen, C.; Hospedales, T. TuckER: Tensor Factorization for Knowledge Graph Completion. In *2019 Conference on Empirical Methods in Natural Language Processing and the 9th International Joint Conference on Natural Language Processing (EMNLP-IJCNLP)*; Association for Computational Linguistics: Stroudsburg, PA, USA, 2019; pp. 5185–5194.
38. Ji, S.; Pan, S.; Cambria, E.; Marttinen, P.; Yu, P.S. A survey on knowledge graphs: Representation, acquisition and applications. *arXiv* **2020**, arXiv:2002.00388.
39. Pietrasik, M.; Reformat, M. A Simple Method for Inducing Class Taxonomies in Knowledge Graphs. In *European Semantic Web Conference*; Springer: Cham, Switzerland, 2020; pp. 53–68.
40. Hendrickson, B.; Leland, R.W. A Multi-Level Algorithm For Partitioning Graphs. *SC* **1995**, *95*, 1–14.
41. Karypis, G.; Kumar, V. A fast and high quality multilevel scheme for partitioning irregular graphs. *SIAM J. Sci. Comput.* **1998**, *20*, 359–392. [CrossRef]

42. Han, X.; Cao, S.; Xin, L.; Lin, Y.; Liu, Z.; Sun, M.; Li, J. OpenKE: An Open Toolkit for Knowledge Embedding. In Proceedings of the 2018 Conference on Empirical Methods in Natural Language Processing: System Demonstrations, Brussels, Belgium, 31 October–4 November 2018.
43. Portisch, J.; Hladik, M.; Paulheim, H. RDF2Vec Light—A Lightweight Approach for Knowledge Graph Embeddings. In Proceedings of the International Semantic Web Conference, Posters and Demos, Virtual Conference, 1–6 November 2020.
44. Portisch, J.; Paulheim, H. Walk this way! entity walks and property walks for rdf2vec. In *The Semantic Web: ESWC 2022 Satellite Events: Hersonissos, Crete, Greece, 29 May–2 June 2022, Proceedings*; Springer: Cham, Switerland, 2022; pp. 133–137.
45. Cochez, M.; Ristoski, P.; Ponzetto, S.P.; Paulheim, H. Biased graph walks for RDF graph embeddings. In Proceedings of the 7th International Conference on Web Intelligence, Mining and Semantics, Amantea, Italy, 19–22 June 2017; pp. 1–12.
46. Portisch, J.; Heist, N.; Paulheim, H. Knowledge graph embedding for data mining vs. knowledge graph embedding for link prediction–two sides of the same coin? *Semant. Web* **2022**, *13*, 399–422. [CrossRef]
47. Bhatt, S.; Padhee, S.; Sheth, A.; Chen, K.; Shalin, V.; Doran, D.; Minnery, B. Knowledge graph enhanced community detection and characterization. In Proceedings of the twelfth ACM International Conference on Web Search and Data Mining, Melbourne, VIC, Australia, 11–15 February 2019; pp. 51–59.
48. Shi, X.; Qian, Y.; Lu, H. Community Detection in Knowledge Graph Network with Matrix Factorization Learning. In *Web and Big Data: APWeb-WAIM 2019 International Workshops, KGMA and DSEA, Chengdu, China, August 1–3. 2019, Revised Selected Papers 3*; Springer: Cham, Switzerland, 2019; pp. 37–51.
49. Paul, S.; Chen, Y. Consistent community detection in multi-relational data through restricted multi-layer stochastic blockmodel. *Electron. J. Stat.* **2016**, *10*, 3807–3870. [CrossRef]
50. De Bacco, C.; Power, E.A.; Larremore, D.B.; Moore, C. Community detection, link prediction, and layer interdependence in multilayer networks. *Phys. Rev. E* **2017**, *95*, 042317. [CrossRef] [PubMed]

Disclaimer/Publisher's Note: The statements, opinions and data contained in all publications are solely those of the individual author(s) and contributor(s) and not of MDPI and/or the editor(s). MDPI and/or the editor(s) disclaim responsibility for any injury to people or property resulting from any ideas, methods, instructions or products referred to in the content.

Article

A Multiple Linear Regression Analysis to Measure the Journal Contribution to the Social Attention of Research

Pablo Dorta-González

Institute of Tourism and Sustainable Economic Development (TIDES), Campus de Tafira, University of Las Palmas de Gran Canaria, 35017 Las Palmas de Gran Canaria, Spain; pablo.dorta@ulpgc.es

Abstract: This paper proposes a three-year average of social attention as a more reliable measure of the social impact of journals since the social attention of research can vary widely among scientific articles, even within the same journal. The proposed measure is used to evaluate a journal's contribution to social attention in comparison to other bibliometric indicators. This study uses Dimensions as a data source and examines research articles from 76 disciplinary libraries and information science journals through multiple linear regression analysis. This study identifies socially influential journals whose contribution to social attention is twice that of scholarly impact, as measured by citations. In addition, this study finds that the number of authors and open access have a moderate effect on social attention, while the journal impact factor has a negative effect and funding has a small effect.

Keywords: altmetrics; social mentions; multiple linear regression; public attention to research; socially influential journal

MSC: 62P25

1. Introduction

Several factors influence the relationship between the public attention a paper receives and its scholarly impact. The academic impact is primarily influenced by the perceived quality of the research, the reputation of the authors, their institutions, and the journals in which they publish. Social attention, on the other hand, is influenced by a broader range of factors, including the topic of the publication, the demographics of the authors who are active on social media, and the current trends and interests of the general public. For example, topics that are controversial or trending tend to generate a lot of social attention, regardless of the scholarly impact of the publication.

Since the term "altmetrics" was first coined in 2010 [1], both theoretical and practical research has been conducted in this area [2]. In addition, governments are now encouraging researchers to engage in activities that have a social impact, such as those that bring economic, cultural, and health benefits [3].

While altmetric data can increase citation rates by accelerating the accumulation of citations after publication [4], they show only a moderate correlation with Mendeley readership [5] and a weak or negligible correlation with other altmetric indicators and citations [6,7]. Consequently, altmetrics may capture different types of impact beyond citation impact [8].

There are many and varied factors that influence the public exposure of research [2]. These include collaboration, research funding, mode of access to the publication, citation, and journal impact factor, which will be discussed below.

Collaboration is becoming increasingly important in scientific research as it allows the combination of knowledge and skills to generate new ideas and research avenues [9]. Co-authorship analysis of research papers is a valid method for studying collaboration [10]. While researchers have increased their production of research articles in recent decades, the number of co-authors has also increased, resulting in a steady publication rate [11,12].

Collaborative research has been associated with higher citation rates and more impactful science [13]. Scientists who collaborate more often tend to have higher h-indices [14]. In addition, both citation and social attention increase with co-authorship, although the influence becomes less significant as the number of collaborators increases [15].

Funding is another important input into the research process. The authors found that 43% of the publications acknowledge funding, with considerable variation between countries [16]. They also found that publications that acknowledge funding are more highly cited. However, citations are only one side of a multidimensional concept, such as research impact, and alternatives have been considered to complement the impact of research. Other authors conclude that there is a positive correlation between funding and usage metrics, but with differences between disciplines [17].

Another factor to consider when analyzing research performance is the type of publication access. The impact advantage of open access is probably because greater access allows more people to read articles that they would not otherwise read. However, the true causality is difficult to establish because there are many possible confounding factors [18,19].

In this context, in this present paper, I quantify the contribution of the journal to societal attention to research. I compare this contribution with other bibliometric and impact indicators discussed earlier, such as collaboration, research funding, type of access, citation, and journal impact factor. To this end, I propose a measure of social influence for journals. This indicator is a three-year average of the social attention given to articles published in the journal. The data source is Dimensions, and the units of study are research articles in library and information science. The methodology used is multiple linear regression analysis.

2. Social Attention to Research and Traditional Metrics

In the field of research evaluation, scholars have studied the impact of research papers. However, traditional metrics such as citation analysis, impact factors, and h-index tend to focus only on the academic use of research papers and ignore their social impact on the Internet [20]. Web 2.0 has transformed social interaction into a web-based platform that allows two-way communication and real-time interaction, creating an environment in which altmetrics has emerged as a new metric to measure the impact of a research paper. The term "altmetrics" was first introduced in 2010 by Priem, who also published a manifesto on the subject [1]. However, the correlation between citation counts and alternative metrics is complicated because neither are direct indicators of research quality, making it nearly impossible to achieve a perfect correlation unless they are unbiased [21].

Some research studies have focused on exploring the correlation between traditional citation metrics and alternative metrics [21,22]. Such studies are important for understanding how research performance is evaluated, particularly with respect to measuring impact through citation counts and altmetric attention scores (AAS). While citation counts have been the primary means of assessing research performance, the importance of AAS is increasing in today's social media-driven world. This is because citation counts have limitations, such as delays in adding a publication to citation databases and potential biases due to self-citation.

A study compared citation data from 3 databases (WoS, Scopus, and Google Scholar) for 85 LIS journals and found that Google Scholar citation data had a strong correlation with altmetric attention, while the other 2 databases showed only a moderate correlation [23]. However, for the nine journals that were consistently present in all three databases, there was a positive but not significant correlation between citation score and altmetric attention. Although there was no correlation between citation count and altmetric score, a study found a moderate correlation between journal impact factor and citation count, a weak correlation between journal tweets and impact factor, and a strong correlation between journal tweets and altmetric score [24].

3. Materials and Methods

This study employed a rigorous and systematic process for collecting and analyzing bibliometric data using the Dimensions database to ensure that the results were reliable, valid, and informative for the field of library and information science.

- Unit of Analysis: The unit of analysis for this study is the "research article" in the field of library and information science.
- Data Source: The data source for this study is the Dimensions database, which provides social attention data at the article level. This database was selected because of its comprehensive coverage of scholarly publications in a variety of disciplines.
- Journal Selection: The JCR Journal Impact Factor in the Web of Science database was used to select journals in the library and information science category. Of the 86 journals identified in the 2020 edition, 10 journals were excluded because they were not indexed in the Dimensions database. This step ensured that only high-quality, peer-reviewed journals were included in the analysis. The final dataset included 76 library and information science journals. These journals were selected based on their relevance and impact on the field.
- Timeframe: Research articles indexed in the Dimensions database between 2012 and 2021 were included in the analysis. This timeframe ensured that the analysis covered recent publications, while also allowing for the collection of sufficient data.
- Search Criteria: In the Dimensions database, the following search criteria were used for each journal X. Source Title was set to X, Publication Type was set to Article, and Publication Year was set to the range 2012 to 2021.
- Final Dataset: All retrieved records were then exported to a file in CSV (comma-separated values) format. The export file contained data on each research article's bibliographic information, social attention metrics, and other relevant variables.
- Data Collection: Data was collected on 6 June 2022. A total of 49,202 research articles were analyzed in this study.

Note that Altmetric is the source of altmetric data in Dimensions, and it is one of the earliest and most popular altmetric aggregator platforms. Digital Science launched this platform in 2011, and it tracks and aggregates mention and views of scholarly articles from various social media channels, news outlets, blogs, and other platforms. It also calculates a weighted score, called the 'altmetric attention score', in which each mentioned category contributes differently to the final score [25].

The altmetric attention score measures the amount of social attention an article receives from sources such as mainstream and social media, public policy documents, and Wikipedia. It assesses the online presence of the article and evaluates the discussions surrounding the research. To avoid confusion, this paper uses the term "social attention score" or simply "social attention" is used to refer to this metric.

This paper proposes a journal-level measure of social attention to research. This measure is defined as the average social attention of articles over a three-year window. Note that the Dimensions database does not provide journal-level impact indicators. Therefore, I included another measure of journal impact in the dataset. I used the Journal Impact Factor provided by the JCR Web of Science database for 2020, the year available at the time of data collection.

The methodology consists of a multiple linear regression analysis. Thus, the dependent variable is the social attention of the article, and the independent variables are the proposed measure of the social attention of the journal, the number of authors, the type of access to the publication {open access = 1, closed = 0}, the funding of the research {funded = 1, unfunded = 0}, the citations of the article, and the impact factor of the journal.

4. Results

The article-level dataset is described in Table 1. The information in this table is presented according to the time elapsed since publication (in average years from publication to the time of data collection in the first half of 2022). It can be observed that the maximum social attention of scientific research in library and information science is reached on average 4 years after its publication, with an average score of 5.57. However, there are no significant differences after the second year. The highest values, more than five points, are observed between the second and sixth year after publication. Nevertheless, the marginal variation between years is only relevant in the second year, with an increase of 0.97 points compared to the first year.

Table 1. Descriptive statistics of the dataset at the article level. Category: Library and Information Science. Data source: Dimensions.

Years Since Pub.*	Year of Pub.	Num. Art.	Num. Authors (Mean)	OA Art. (%)	Funded Art. (%)	Citations (Mean)	Art. Social Attention	
							Mean Score	Marg. Var.
1	2021	6156	3.15	39.57%	23.93%	2.79	4.41	
2	2020	5687	3.10	44.43%	26.01%	9.14	5.39	0.97
3	2019	4880	2.88	43.03%	23.55%	11.87	5.31	−0.08
4	2018	4811	2.73	43.17%	22.49%	14.94	5.57	0.26
5	2017	4897	2.63	45.01%	21.14%	16.91	5.17	−0.40
6	2016	4592	2.72	42.29%	18.47%	20.61	5.51	0.34
7	2015	4521	2.64	39.02%	20.97%	23.14	4.92	−0.58
8	2014	4551	2.67	37.84%	19.12%	22.73	3.89	−1.03
9	2013	4613	2.45	34.92%	17.86%	24.36	3.33	−0.57
10	2012	4494	2.37	34.40%	15.20%	25.77	2.57	−0.75
All		49,202	2.76	40.50%	21.12%	16.52	4.63	

* Average years from publication to the time of data collection in the first half of 2022.

Table 1 also shows how the average number of authors per article in library and information science has gradually increased over the past decade, from an average of 2.37 authors per article in 2012 to an average of 3.15 authors per article in 2021. This 33% increase in co-authorship in a decade is remarkable. The increase in co-authorship may partially explain the 37% increase in research article production over the decade in the Library and Information Science category, from just under 4500 articles in 2012 to more than 6100 articles in 2021.

In the dataset, 40% of the articles are open access, and 21% of publications indicate in the acknowledgments section that the authors have received some form of funding, with a sustained increase in most of the years analyzed. In terms of citations, the increase observed in Table 1 was to be expected, from 2.8 cites per article in the first year after the publication to an average of 25.8 cites at the end of the decade. Significant marginal increases are observed up to the seventh year after publication, highlighting the increase of 6.35 citations that occurs in the second year.

4.1. Journal Social Attention: Definition and Consistency of the Indicator

When aggregating the data at the journal level, I observed a large interannual variability in the average social attention per article when the time window was reduced to a single year. That is, for each journal, the average social attention of the articles in a single year differs significantly from that of the articles in the previous and subsequent years of the series. This large variability in the average social attention of each journal over time means that the one-year average is not a consistent measure of social attention for journals. This weakness observed for social media mentions also occurs for other citation-based indicators, such as the impact factor, with short time windows.

One reason for this high interannual variability is the low correlation between the individual scores of articles and the average scores of journals when the time window in which citations or mentions are collected is short. Thus, a small proportion of articles from each journal receive a large proportion of scientific citations and social mentions. In order to increase the consistency of a measure by partially reducing the interannual variability, it is often chosen in bibliometrics to increase the size of the window for counting observations (citations or mentions). In the case of the impact factor, the various databases thus provide indicators for two, three, four, and even five years.

In this study, I chose a three-year window as a compromise between the advantages and disadvantages of considering large time windows. That is, four-year and five-year windows require a long waiting period before social attention can be measured for a journal, while a two-year window still produces a high interannual variability in the dataset.

Therefore, I propose the following definition for the social attention measure at the journal level. The journal social attention in year y counts the social attention received in years $y-2$, $y-1$, and y for research articles published in those years ($y-2$, $y-1$, and y) and divides it by the number of research articles published in those years ($y-2$, $y-1$, and y). For example, the journal social attention in 2021 counts the social attention received in 2019–2021 for research articles published in 2019–2021 and divides it by the number of research articles published in 2019–2021.

The journal-level dataset is described in Table 2. This table also includes the measure of the journal social attention. Due to space limitations, I only show the information corresponding to the year 2020 for the production and impact indicators (the last year available at the time of data collection) and the year 2021 for the journal social attention (time window 2019–2021). The graphical description of the data is shown in Figures 1 and 2.

Table 2. Description of the dataset at the journal level in the subject category Library and Information Science (JCR). Data sources: Web of Science and Dimensions.

	Journal	Num. Art. 2020	JIF 2020	JIF Percentile 2020	JIF Quartile 2020	5-Year JIF 2020	Journal Social Attention 2021
1	ASLIB J INFORM MANAG	54	1.903	44.12	Q3	2.343	1.83
2	CAN J INFORM LIB SCI	5	0.000	0.59	Q4	0.420	0.78
3	COLL RES LIBR	52	2.381	52.35	Q2	2.204	5.55
4	DATA TECHNOL APPL	51	1.667	39.41	Q3	1.667	0.37
5	ELECTRON LIBR	56	1.453	34.71	Q3	1.540	0.36
6	ETHICS INF TECHNOL	64	4.449	74.71	Q2	3.925	10.70
7	EUR J INFORM SYST	64	4.344	71.18	Q2	7.130	6.43
8	GOV INFORM Q	71	6.695	91.18	Q1	8.293	7.66
9	HEALTH INFO LIBR J	45	2.154	47.65	Q3	2.187	6.25
10	INFORM SOC-ESTUD	32	0.311	8.82	Q4	0.313	0.39
11	INFORM MANAGE-AMSTER	91	7.555	94.71	Q1	9.183	2.48
12	INFORM ORGAN-UK	15	6.300	90	Q1	5.866	6.24
13	INFORM DEV	74	2.049	46.47	Q3	2.205	0.99
14	INFORM PROCESS MANAG	237	6.222	88.82	Q1	5.789	2.06
15	INFORM RES	75	0.780	20.59	Q4	1.197	1.42
16	INFORM SOC	25	4.571	77.06	Q1	3.936	6.94
17	INFORM SYST J	49	7.453	93.53	Q1	8.814	7.05
18	INFORM SYST RES	69	5.207	82.94	Q1	6.888	7.54
19	INFORM TECHNOL MANAG	15	1.533	38.24	Q3	2.627	0.19
20	INFORM TECHNOL PEOPL	121	3.879	67.65	Q2	4.238	1.65
21	INFORM TECHNOL LIBR	27	1.160	27.65	Q3	1.351	8.90
22	INFORM TECHNOL DEV	66	4.250	70	Q2	4.221	6.06
23	INT J COMP-SUPP COLL	18	5.108	80.59	Q1	4.966	4.09
24	INT J GEOGR INF SCI	162	4.186	68.82	Q2	4.645	3.66
25	INT J INFORM MANAGE	203	14.098	99.41	Q1	13.074	4.99

Table 2. Cont.

	Journal	Num. Art. 2020	JIF 2020	JIF Percentile 2020	JIF Quartile 2020	5-Year JIF 2020	Journal Social Attention 2021
26	INVESTIG BIBLIOTECOL	39	0.475	13.53	Q4	0.535	0.27
27	J ACAD LIBR	104	1.533	38.24	Q3	2.023	5.03
28	J COMPUT-MEDIAT COMM	25	5.410	85.29	Q1	9.953	25.01
29	J DOC	98	1.819	40.59	Q3	1.988	3.43
30	J ENTERP INF MANAG	128	5.396	84.12	Q1	5.839	0.26
31	J GLOB INF MANAG	38	1.373	33.53	Q3	1.550	0.75
32	J GLOB INF TECH MAN	14	3.519	66.47	Q2	2.631	0.94
33	J HEALTH COMMUN	94	2.781	59.41	Q2	3.468	8.44
34	J INF SCI	120	3.282	65.29	Q2	2.904	2.38
35	J INF TECHNOL-UK	21	5.824	86.47	Q1	9.439	2.28
36	J INFORMETR	77	5.107	79.41	Q1	5.421	7.12
37	J KNOWL MANAG	162	8.182	97.06	Q1	8.720	0.60
38	J LIBR INF SCI	123	1.992	45.29	Q3	2.009	2.47
39	J MANAGE INFORM SYST	40	7.838	95.88	Q1	8.335	3.53
40	J ORGAN END USER COM	23	4.349	72.35	Q2	2.808	0.08
41	J SCHOLARLY PUBL	19	1.512	35.88	Q3	1.245	3.77
42	J STRATEGIC INF SYST	16	11.022	98.24	Q1	11.832	1.37
43	J AM MED INFORM ASSN	209	4.497	75.88	Q1	5.178	14.38
44	J ASSOC INF SCI TECH	150	2.687	54.71	Q2	3.854	8.09
45	J ASSOC INF SYST	47	5.149	81.76	Q1	6.780	2.06
46	J AUST LIB INF ASSOC	28	0.725	19.41	Q4	0.851	1.64
47	J MED LIBR ASSOC	60	3.180	61.76	Q2	3.874	4.57
48	KNOWL MAN RES PRACT	106	2.744	58.24	Q2	3.027	1.24
49	KNOWL ORGAN	34	1.000	25.29	Q4	0.979	0.18
50	LEARN PUBL	53	2.506	53.53	Q2	2.659	20.19
51	LIBR INFORM SCI RES	32	2.730	57.06	Q2	2.778	5.15
52	LIBR HI TECH	83	2.357	51.18	Q2	2.065	1.32
53	LIBR QUART	26	1.895	42.94	Q3	2.277	1.27
54	LIBR RESOUR TECH SER	3	0.424	12.35	Q4	0.541	0.45
55	LIBR TRENDS	38	1.311	31.18	Q3	1.354	5.70
56	LIBRI	25	0.521	14.71	Q4	0.706	0.75
57	MALAYS J LIBR INF SC	20	1.250	28.82	Q3	1.320	0.00
58	MIS QUART	58	7.198	92.35	Q1	12.803	0.84
59	MIS Q EXEC	17	4.371	73.53	Q2	7.563	6.12
60	ONLINE INFORM REV	82	2.325	50	Q3	2.883	3.92
61	PORTAL-LIBR ACAD	36	1.067	26.47	Q3	1.285	1.93
62	PROF INFORM	169	2.253	48.82	Q3	2.285	6.99
63	QUAL HEALTH RES	192	3.277	64.12	Q2	5.038	7.03
64	REF USER SERV Q	27	0.650	17.06	Q4	0.581	0.22
65	REF SERV REV	38	0.831	22.94	Q4	1.221	1.74
66	RES EVALUAT	20	2.706	55.88	Q2	3.434	12.70
67	RESTAURATOR	13	0.296	7.65	Q4	0.427	0.11
68	REV ESP DOC CIENT	29	1.276	30	Q3	1.259	2.71
69	SCIENTOMETRICS	454	3.238	62.94	Q2	3.702	7.97
70	SERIALS REV	36	0.324	10	Q4	0.425	1.53
71	SOC SCI COMPUT REV	93	4.578	78.24	Q1	5.194	11.99
72	SOC SCI INFORM	28	0.714	18.24	Q4	0.966	4.48
73	TELECOMMUN POLICY	84	3.036	60.59	Q2	3.500	9.72
74	TELEMAT INFORM	91	6.182	87.65	Q1	6.769	3.61
75	TRANSINFORMACAO	23	0.648	15.88	Q4	0.561	5.20
76	Z BIBL BIBL	19	0.125	1.76	Q4	0.071	0.31

Note. The shade of green corresponds to the magnitude of each number relative to the other values in its column. As such, the larger the number, the deeper the green hue used to represent it.

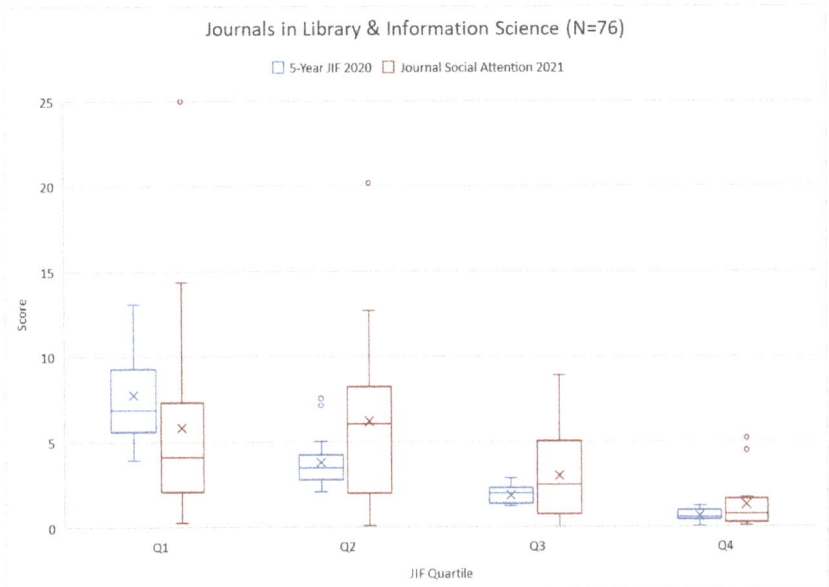

Figure 1. The 5-year Journal Impact Factor (2020 edition) and the Journal Social Attention (2021 edition) by JIF quartiles. The mean is represented by a cross. The differences between the groups are all significant ($p < 0.01$), except between Q1 and Q2 for Social Attention.

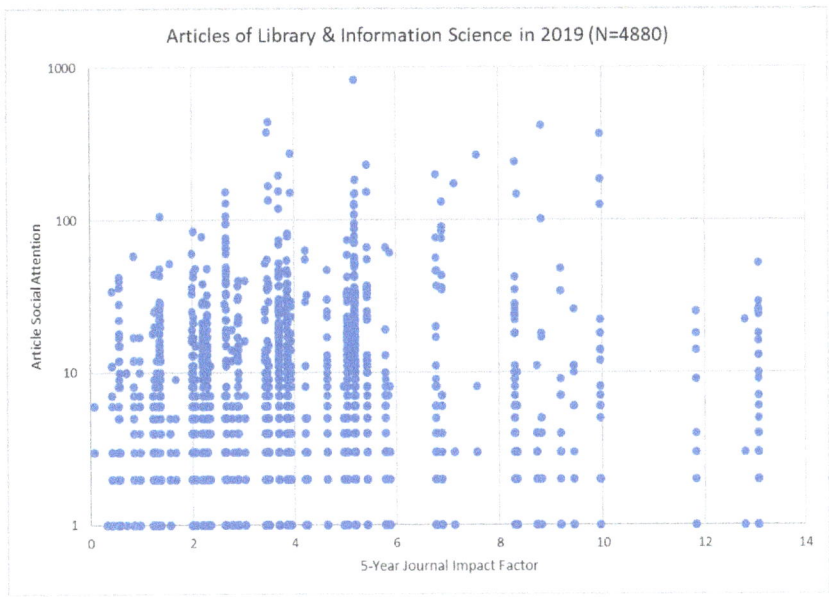

Figure 2. Social attention (logarithmic scale) of articles published in 2019, as a function of the journal's 5-year impact factor (2020 edition), in the Library and Information Science category.

A box-and-whisker plot by quartile for the 5-year journal impact factor (2020 edition) and the journal social attention (2021 edition) is shown in Figure 1. The differences between the groups are all significant for the journal social attention ($p < 0.01$), except between Q1 and Q2. Note that the journal social attention decreases in groups Q2 to Q4 as the journals reduce their impact factors. This trend is observed in both the mean and the median, and even in the remaining quartiles of the distribution represented by the boxes and whiskers in the figure. However, this is not the case when moving from Q1 to Q2.

As can also be seen in Figure 1, the distributions in the group of journals with a higher impact factor (Q1) are highly skewed, especially with respect to social attention. Note that the mean, represented by the cross, is much higher than the median, represented by the central line in the box.

Figure 2 shows the enormous variability in social attention, regardless of the journal's impact factor. Note that in the group of medium-impact journals (Q2 and Q3), there are articles that receive a lot of social attention.

4.2. Multiple Linear Regression Analysis

I would like to know if and how the social attention of articles can be predicted from the social attention of journals and several bibliometric characteristics. The description of the variables can be found in Table 3.

Table 3. Variables and description in the Multiple Linear Regression model.

Name	Measure	Variable Description
Article Social Attention	Altmetric attention score for research articles published in 2019	Natural number $N = \{0, 1, 2, ...\}$
Journal Social Attention	Journal social attention 2021: average altmetric attention score for research articles published in 2019–2021	Positive real number $R^+_0 = [0, +\infty)$
Num. Authors	Number of authors for research articles published in 2019	Positive natural number $N^+ = \{1, 2, 3, ...\}$
OA Article	Type of access to the research articles published in 2019	Dichotomous {open access = 1, closed = 0}
Funded Article	Research funding declared in the acknowledgments section for the research articles published in 2019	Dichotomous {funded = 1, unfunded = 0}
Article Citations	Times cited in Dimensions for research articles published in 2019	Natural number $N = \{0, 1, 2, ...\}$
Journal Impact Factor	5-year journal impact factor in the 2020 issue of JCR	Positive real number $R^+_0 = [0, +\infty)$

The dependent variable is the article social attention for publications in the year 2019, in short, "article social attention". The independent variables are the journal social attention (2021), the number of authors for publications in the year 2019, the type of access to these publications {open access = 1, closed = 0}, the funding of the research {funded = 1, unfunded = 0}, the article citations, and the journal impact factor (2020 edition).

I checked for missing values in the descriptive statistics of all variables (see Table 4 for the mean and standard deviation). Note that I have N = 4880 independent observations in the dataset. The distributions in the histograms are likely for all variables and there are no missing values. I have also checked for curvilinear relationships or anything unusual in the plot of the dependent variable against each independent variable.

Table 4. Means, SDs, and Pearson correlations between the dependent and all independent variables.

Variable	Mean	SD	1	2	3	4	5	6	7
1. Article Social Attention	5.31	22.42		0.22 **	0.09 **	0.10 **	0.04 **	0.10 **	0.03 *
2. Journal Social Attention	5.08	4.29			0.20 **	0.19 **	0.20 **	0.03 *	0.15 **
3. Num. Authors	2.88	2.10				0.07 **	0.33 **	0.11 **	0.19 **
4. OA Article (1, Closed = 0)	0.43	0.50					0.04 **	0.00	−0.11 **
5. Funded Article (1, Unfunded = 0)	0.24	0.42						0.11 **	0.17 **
6. Article Citations	11.87	26.62							0.39 **
7. Journal Impact Factor	4.24	3.03							

* $p < 0.05$. ** $p < 0.01$.

Note that each independent variable has a significant linear relationship with the article's social attention (see Table 4). Therefore, the multiple linear regression model could estimate the article's social attention from all independent variables simultaneously. I checked the correlations between the variables (Table 4). The absolute correlations are low (none of the correlations exceeds 0.39), and multicollinearity problems are discarded for the actual regression analysis.

In general, the observed correlations are low. The highest correlations are between article citations and journal impact factor (0.39) and between the number of authors and funding (0.33). All other correlations are below 0.22. The only negative correlation is observed between the type of access and the impact factor.

The regression model according to the b-coefficients in Table 5 is as follows:

$$\text{Article\_Social\_Attention}\_i = 0.74 \cdot \text{Journal\_Social\_Attention}\_i + 0.41 \cdot \text{Num\_Authors}\_i \\ + 1.75 \cdot \text{OA\_Article}\_i + 1.55 \cdot \text{Funded\_Article}\_i \\ + 0.09 \cdot \text{Article\_Citations}\_i - 0.78 \cdot \text{JIF}\_i \quad (1)$$

where Article_Social_Attention_i denotes the predicted social attention for article i, $i = 1, 2, \ldots, 4880$.

Table 5. Regression coefficients predicting Article Social Attention. Standard multiple linear regression analysis.

Variable	B (Coeff.)	95% CI	β (Standardized Coeff.)	t	p (Sig.)
Constant	0	-	0	-	-
Journal Social Attention	0.741	[0.595, 0.887]	0.207	9.956	0.000
Num. Authors	0.412	[0.215, 0.609]	0.051	4.093	0.000
OA Article (1, Closed = 0)	1.755	[1.040, 2.471]	0.048	4.811	0.000
Funded Article (1, Not = 0)	1.552	[0.358, 2.746]	0.022	2.548	0.011
Article Citation	0.090	[0.079, 0.101]	0.104	16.373	0.000
Journal Impact Factor	−0.784	[−0.969, −0.600]	−0.044	−8.336	0.000

Note. Adjusted R-square $R^2_{adj} = 0.197$ (N = 4880, $p = 10^{-4}$). CI = confidence interval for B.

R-squared is the proportion of the variance in the dependent variable accounted for by the model. I have reported the adjusted R-squared in Table 5. In this model, $R^2_{adj} = 0.197$. This is considered acceptable by social science standards. Furthermore, since the p-value found in the ANOVA is $p = 10^{-3}$, I conclude that the entire regression model has a non-zero correlation.

Note that each b-coefficient in Equation (1) indicates the average increase in social attention associated with a one-unit increase in a predictor, all else equal. Thus, a 1-point increase in social attention to the journal is associated with a 0.74 increase in social attention to the article.

Similarly, an additional co-author increases the social attention of a study by an average of 0.41 points. Furthermore, 1 additional citation increases the social attention of an article by an average of 0.09 points, or, alternatively, every 10 citations increase the social attention of a study by 0.9 points, all else being equal. Similarly, a 1-point increase in the journal's impact factor is associated with a 0.78 decrease in the social attention to the article.

For the dichotomous variables, a 1 unit increase in open access is associated with an average 1.75 point increase in the social attention to the article. Note that open access is coded in the dataset as 0 (closed access) and 1 (open access). Therefore, the only possible 1 unit increase for this variable is from closed (0) to open (1). Therefore, I can conclude that the average social attention for open articles is 1.75 points higher than for closed articles (all other things being equal). Similarly, the average social attention for funded articles is 1.55 points higher than for unfunded articles, all else being equal.

The statistical significance column (Sig. in Table 5) shows the 2-tailed p-value for each b-coefficient. Note that all of the b-coefficients in the model are statistically significant ($p < 0.05$), and most of them are highly statistically significant with a p-value of 10^{-3}. However, the b-coefficients do not indicate the relative strength of the predictors. This is because the independent variables have different scales. The standardized regression coefficients or beta coefficients, denoted as β in Table 5, are obtained by standardizing all the regression variables before calculating the coefficients and are, therefore, comparable within and across regression models.

Thus, the 2 strongest predictors in the coefficients are the social attention of the journal ($\beta = 0.207$) and the citations received by the article ($\beta = 0.104$). This means that the journal is the factor that contributes the most to the social attention of the research, about twice as much as the citations received. In addition, the number of authors in the research ($\beta = 0.051$) contributes about half as much as citations and slightly more than open access to the publication ($\beta = 0.048$). Journal impact factor ($\beta = -0.044$) contributes as much as open access but in the opposite direction. Finally, research funding ($\beta = 0.022$) contributes half as much as the impact factor.

Regarding the multiple regression assumptions, each observation corresponds to a different article. Therefore, I can consider them independent observations. The regression residuals are approximately normally distributed in the histogram. I also checked the assumptions of homoscedasticity and linearity by plotting the residuals against the predicted values. This scatterplot shows no systematic pattern, so I can conclude that both assumptions hold.

5. Discussion

Social attention to research is crucial for understanding the impact and dissemination of scientific research beyond traditional citation-based metrics and has practical implications for academic publishing, funding decisions, and science communication.

First, it provides a measure of the impact of scientific articles beyond traditional citation-based metrics, such as the number of times an article is shared, downloaded, or discussed on social media platforms. This can help researchers, publishers, and funding agencies better understand the impact and reach of their research. Second, social attention to research can provide insights into how scientific information is disseminated and consumed by different audiences, which can inform public engagement and science communication strategies. Third, social attention research can highlight emerging trends and issues in science and technology that can guide future research agendas and funding decisions.

The results suggest that public attention to research occurs mainly in the first year after publication and to a lesser extent in the second year. However, a more detailed analysis of the dataset shows that the largest increase in social attention is observed in the first months after its publication.

Some considerations can be made about the negative signs observed in the interannual marginal variation (decrease in the average social attention compared to the previous year). This decrease could be due to several factors. First, the increasing use of social networks and the growing number of platforms from which social attention is collected. Second, the social attention of research is measured with regularly updated data on the social presence on the Internet (from June 2022 in the dataset). Since some mentions in social media may be ephemeral and disappear after a while (unlike citations in the databases that index the documents), the negative signs in the marginal variation could also be due to this circumstance. Finally, the observations (research articles) differ between years, so this result is, therefore, plausible.

The average number of authors per article in library and information science has gradually increased over the last decade, from an average of 2.37 authors per article in 2012 to an average of 3.15 authors in 2021. This 33% increase in co-authorship in a decade is relevant in terms of social attention, as discussion on the web is often driven by the authors of the research. More authors, therefore, mean more presence on social networks.

In the dataset, 40% of library and information science publications are open access. In addition, 21% of the publications indicate in the acknowledgments section that the authors have received some form of funding, with a sustained increase over the years. Note that this percentage of funded articles in LIS is half the average for all research fields [12].

The social attention of journals decreases in quartiles Q2 to Q4 as journals reduce their impact factors. However, there are no significant differences between the two highest quartiles (Q1 and Q2). This means that the journals that are most cited by researchers are not necessarily the ones that receive the most social attention. Note that this may be due to the subject category analyzed. For example, in the Library and Information Science category, there are also prestigious journals in the second quartile. This is the case, for example, for the journal *Scientometrics*. Journals with low obsolescence are penalized by the impact factor compared to other journals with higher obsolescence, which accumulate most of their citations in the first years after publication [26].

I found low correlations between the variables. The highest correlations are between citation count and journal impact factor (0.39) and between the number of authors and funding (0.33). All other correlations are lower than 0.22. The only negative correlation is observed between the type of access and journal impact factor. This is because, in the library and information science category, open access publishing is not yet widespread among the journals with the highest impact factors. Surprisingly, however, there is no correlation between access type and citations. In other words, open-access articles do not receive more citations than closed articles. The reason for this is the same as that mentioned above. Open access in library and information science is not generalized in high-impact journals, which are those with the greatest visibility of research [27].

I observed that a 1-point increase in the social attention of the journal is associated with an average 0.74 increase in the social attention of the article, all else equal. Similarly, an additional co-author contributes an average 0.41 increase in the social attention of the research. Furthermore, every 10 citations increase the social attention of a paper by 0.9 points, all else being equal. I also concluded that the average social attention for open articles is 1.75 points higher than for closed articles, all else being equal. Similarly, the average social attention for funded articles is 1.55 points higher than for unfunded research.

The finding that a 1-point increase in the journal impact factor is associated with a 0.78 decrease in the social attention to the article suggests that there is a negative relationship between the 2 metrics. One possible explanation for this finding is that the number of citations, which is the basis of the journal impact factor, is an indicator of the influence of research in the academic world. The academic impact of a publication is determined by several factors, such as the reputation of the authors, the standing of the institutions with which they are affiliated, and the perceived importance and quality of the research. Therefore, journals with high impact factors tend to publish research that is more specialized and may be of interest primarily to researchers in a particular field, resulting in fewer social mentions.

However, social attention is influenced by a wider range of factors, including the topic of the publication and the current trends and interests of the general public. For example, controversial or fashionable topics tend to generate a lot of social attention, regardless of the journal impact factor of the publication. Therefore, papers in high-impact factor journals that do not address current social trends or controversial topics may not receive as much social attention as papers in low-impact factor journals that do address such topics.

Another factor that may contribute to the negative correlation between the journal impact factor and the social attention of a paper is the demographics of the authors who are active on social media. Younger researchers tend to be more active on social media than their more established counterparts, and they may be more likely to publish in low-impact journals due to their less extensive research experience. This could also contribute to the negative correlation between the two measures.

In summary, the negative association between the journal impact factor and the social attention of a paper can be explained by the different factors that influence the two metrics. While the journal impact factor is primarily influenced by academic factors such as the reputation of the authors and their institutions, the social attention of a paper is influenced by a wider range of factors, including the subject of the publication and the demographics of the authors.

The standardized regression coefficients indicate that the social attention of the journal and the citations received by the article are the two strongest predictors of the social attention of the article. The analysis shows that the journal is the most influential factor, contributing about twice as much as the citations received. The number of authors in the research contributes about half as much as the citations and slightly more if the publication is open access. The impact factor of the journal has a similar influence as open access but in the opposite direction. Finally, research funding contributes about half as much as the impact factor.

There are some points to note regarding hybrid indicators and the "altmetric attention score" used in this research. A hybrid indicator can combine different sources to create a single score [25]. However, hybrid indicators are not robust and, therefore, should not be used to evaluate researchers, especially for hiring or internal promotions. In this study, the indicator was used to evaluate the research process rather than the researchers themselves.

6. Conclusions

Understanding societal attention to research is important because it can help researchers identify emerging or pressing societal issues, prioritize research questions, and engage with stakeholders and the public. It can also inform efforts to communicate research findings to a broader audience, promote evidence-based policy, and increase public trust in science.

Although most of the social attention to research occurs in the first year, even in the first few months, a robust measure with low variability over time is preferable for identifying socially influential journals. This paper proposes a three-year average of social attention as a measure of social influence for journals. I used a multiple linear regression analysis to quantify the contribution of journals to the social attention of research in comparison to other bibliometric indicators. Thus, the data source was Dimensions, and the unit of study was the research article in disciplinary journals of Library and Information Science.

As a main result, the factors that best explain the social attention of the research are the social attention of the journal and the number of citations. There are socially influential journals, and their contribution to the social attention of the article multiplies by two the effect attributed to the academic impact measured by the number of citations. Furthermore, the number of authors and open access has a moderate effect on the social attention of research. Funding has a small effect, while the impact factor of the journal has a negative effect.

It should be emphasized that low R-squared values may indicate that the predictions of an article's social attention are not very accurate. In addition, altmetric indicators have the advantage of measuring different types of impact beyond scholarly citations, and they have the potential to identify earlier evidence of impact, making them valuable for self-assessment. Furthermore, they are useful for investigating scholarships, as in this study. Nevertheless, it is important to use social attention with caution, as it can provide a limited and biased perspective on all forms of social impact.

This study analyzed a specific area of research over a specific period of time. However, in order to apply the findings to other areas, it is recommended that further studies be conducted with more diverse data. In terms of future research directions, incorporating author characteristics, such as research experience, h-index, affiliations, and social media presence, into the model could provide insights into the social impact of their research and its correlation with citations received. In addition, the inclusion of these and other variables may improve the model's R-squared.

Funding: This research received no external funding.

Data Availability Statement: Data sourced from Dimensions, an interlinked research information system provided by Digital Science (accessed on 6 June 2022).

Acknowledgments: Access to advanced features of the database allowed by Digital Science.

Conflicts of Interest: The author declares no conflict of interest.

References

1. Priem, J.; Taraborelli, D.; Growth, P.; Neylon, C. Altmetrics: A Manifesto. 2010. Available online: http://altmetrics.org/manifesto/ (accessed on 2 February 2023).
2. Sugimoto, C.R.; Work, S.; Larivière, V.; Haustein, S. Scholarly use of social media and altmetrics: A review of the literature. *J. Assoc. Inf. Sci. Technol.* **2017**, *68*, 2037–2062. [CrossRef]
3. Thelwall, M. Measuring societal impacts of research with altmetrics? Common problems and mistakes. *J. Econ. Surv.* **2021**, *35*, 1302–1314. [CrossRef]
4. Fang, Z.; Costas, R. Studying the accumulation velocity of altmetric data tracked by Altmetric.com. *Scientometrics* **2020**, *123*, 1077–1101. [CrossRef]
5. Zahedi, Z.; Haustein, S. On the relationships between bibliographic characteristics of scientific documents and citation and Mendeley readership counts: A large-scale analysis of Web of Science publications. *J. Informetr.* **2018**, *12*, 191–202. [CrossRef]
6. Bornmann, L. Alternative metrics in scientometrics: A meta-analysis of research into three altmetrics. *Scientometrics* **2015**, *103*, 1123–1144. [CrossRef]
7. Costas, R.; Zahedi, Z.; Wouters, P. Do "altmetrics" correlate with citations? Extensive comparison of altmetric indicators with citations from a multidisciplinary perspective. *J. Assoc. Inf. Sci. Technol.* **2015**, *66*, 2003–2019. [CrossRef]
8. Wouters, P.; Zahedi, Z.; Costas, R. Social media metrics for new research evaluation. In *Springer Handbook of Science and Technology Indicators*; Glänzel, W., Moed, H.F., Schmoch, U., Thelwall, M., Eds.; Springer: Berlin/Heidelberg, Germany, 2019; pp. 687–713. [CrossRef]
9. Heinze, T.; Kuhlmann, S. Across institutional boundaries? Research collaboration in German public sector nanoscience. *Res. Policy* **2008**, *37*, 888–899. [CrossRef]
10. Glänzel, W.; Schubert, A. Analysing scientific networks through co-authorship. In *Handbook of Quantitative Science and Technology Research*; Moed, H.F., Glänzel, W., Schmoch, U., Eds.; Springer: Dordrecht, The Netherlands, 2004; pp. 257–276. [CrossRef]
11. Fanelli, D.; Larivière, V. Researchers' individual publication rate has not increased in a century. *PLoS ONE* **2016**, *11*, e0149504. [CrossRef]
12. Lee, S.; Bozeman, B. The impact of research collaboration on scientific productivity. *Soc. Stud. Sci.* **2005**, *35*, 673–702. [CrossRef]
13. Bote, V.P.G.; Olmeda-Gómez, C.; De Moya-Anegón, F. Quantifying the benefits of international scientific collaboration. *J. Am. Soc. Inf. Sci. Technol.* **2013**, *64*, 392–404. [CrossRef]
14. Parish, A.J.; Boyack, K.W.; Ioannidis, J.P.A. Dynamics of co-authorship and productivity across different fields of scientific research. *PLoS ONE* **2018**, *13*, e0189742. [CrossRef] [PubMed]
15. Dorta-González, P.; Dorta-González, M.I. Collaboration effect by co-authorship on academic citation and social attention of research. *Mathematics* **2022**, *10*, 2082. [CrossRef]
16. Costas, R.; van Leeuwen, T.N. Approaching the "reward triangle": General analysis of the presence of funding acknowledgments and "peer interactive communication" in scientific publications. *J. Am. Soc. Inf. Sci. Technol.* **2012**, *63*, 1647–1661. [CrossRef]
17. Zhao, S.X.; Lou, W.; Tan, A.M.; Yu, S. Do funded papers attract more usage? *Scientometrics* **2018**, *115*, 153–168. [CrossRef]
18. Dorta-González, P.; Santana-Jiménez, Y. Prevalence and citation advantage of gold open access in the subject areas of the Scopus database. *Res. Eval.* **2018**, *27*, 1–15. [CrossRef]
19. Dorta-González, P.; Dorta-González, M.I. Contribution of the open access modality to the impact of hybrid journals controlling by field and time effects. *J. Data Inf. Sci.* **2022**, *7*, 57–83. [CrossRef]
20. Smith, R. Measuring the social impact of research: Difficult but necessary. *Br. Med. J.* **2001**, *323*, 528. [CrossRef]
21. Thelwall, M. Interpreting correlations between citation counts and other indicators. *Scientometrics* **2016**, *108*, 337–347. [CrossRef]
22. Sud, P.; Thelwall, M. Evaluating altmetrics. *Scientometrics* **2014**, *98*, 1131–1143. [CrossRef]
23. Ezema, I.J.; Ugwu, C.I. Correlating research impact of library and information science journals using citation counts and altmetrics attention. *Inf. Discov. Deliv.* **2019**, *47*, 143–153. [CrossRef]
24. Rong, L.Q.; Lopes, A.J.; Hameed, I.; Gaudino, M.; Charlson, M.E. Examining the correlation between Altmetric score and citation count in the anaesthesiology literature. *Br. J. Anaesth.* **2020**, *125*, e223–e226. [CrossRef] [PubMed]
25. How Is the Altmetric Attention Score Calculated? Available online: https://help.altmetric.com/support/solutions/articles/6000233311-how-is-the-altmetric-attention-score-calculated- (accessed on 2 February 2023).
26. Dorta-González, P.; Gómez-Déniz, E. Modeling the obsolescence of research literature in disciplinary journals through the age of their cited references. *Scientometrics* **2022**, *127*, 2901–2931. [CrossRef]
27. Dorta-González, P.; González-Betancor, S.M.; Dorta-González, M.I. Reconsidering the gold open access citation advantage postulate in a multidisciplinary context: An analysis of the subject categories in the Web of Science database 2009–2014. *Scientometrics* **2017**, *112*, 877–901. [CrossRef]

Disclaimer/Publisher's Note: The statements, opinions and data contained in all publications are solely those of the individual author(s) and contributor(s) and not of MDPI and/or the editor(s). MDPI and/or the editor(s) disclaim responsibility for any injury to people or property resulting from any ideas, methods, instructions or products referred to in the content.

Article

Automatic Classification of Coronary Stenosis Using Feature Selection and a Hybrid Evolutionary Algorithm

Miguel-Angel Gil-Rios [1], Claire Chalopin [2], Ivan Cruz-Aceves [3,*], Juan-Manuel Lopez-Hernandez [4], Martha-Alicia Hernandez-Gonzalez [5] and Sergio-Eduardo Solorio-Meza [6]

1. Departamento de Tecnologías de la Información, Universidad Tecnológica de León, Blvd. Universidad Tecnológica 225, Col. San Carlos, León 37670, Mexico; mgil@utleon.edu.mx
2. Faculty of Engineering and Health, University of Applied Sciences and Arts, 37085 Göttingen, Germany; claire.chalopin@hawk.de
3. CONACYT, Center for Research in Mathematics (CIMAT), A.C., Jalisco S/N, Col. Valenciana, Guanajuato 36000, Mexico
4. División de Ingenierías (DICIS), Campus Irapuato-Salamanca, Universidad de Guanajuato, Carretera Salamanca-Valle de Santiago km 3.5 + 1.8 km, Comunidad de Palo Blanco, Salamanca 36885, Mexico; jmlopez@ugto.mx
5. Unidad Médica de Alta Especialidad (UMAE), Hospital de Especialidades No. 1, Centro Médico Nacional del Bajío, IMSS, León 37320, Mexico; martha.hernandez@imss.gob.mx
6. División Ciencias de la Salud, Campus León, Universidad Tecnológica de México, Blvd. Juan Alonso de Torres 1041, León 37200, Mexico; sergio_solorio@my.unitec.edu.mx
* Correspondence: ivan.cruz@cimat.mx

Abstract: In this paper, a novel method for the automatic classification of coronary stenosis based on a feature selection strategy driven by a hybrid evolutionary algorithm is proposed. The main contribution is the characterization of the coronary stenosis anomaly based on the automatic selection of an efficient feature subset. The initial feature set consists of 49 features involving intensity, texture and morphology. Since the feature selection search space was $O(2^n)$, being $n = 49$, it was treated as a high-dimensional combinatorial problem. For this reason, different single and hybrid evolutionary algorithms were compared, where the hybrid method based on the Boltzmann univariate marginal distribution algorithm (BUMDA) and simulated annealing (SA) achieved the best performance using a training set of X-ray coronary angiograms. Moreover, two different databases with 500 and 2700 stenosis images, respectively, were used for training and testing of the proposed method. In the experimental results, the proposed method for feature selection obtained a subset of 11 features, achieving a feature reduction rate of 77.5% and a classification accuracy of 0.96 using the training set. In the testing step, the proposed method was compared with different state-of-the-art classification methods in both databases, obtaining a classification accuracy and Jaccard coefficient of 0.90 and 0.81 in the first one, and 0.92 and 0.85 in the second one, respectively. In addition, based on the proposed method's execution time for testing images (0.02 s per image), it can be highly suitable for use as part of a clinical decision support system.

Keywords: Boltzmann distribution; coronary angiograms; feature selection; simulated annealing; stenosis classification; support vector machine

1. Introduction

Coronary heart disease is the main cause of morbidity all over the world [1]. Consequently, it is highly important for coronary stenosis to be detected and diagnosed by cardiologists and addressed in computational science. Nowadays, X-ray coronary angiography is the main source of decision making in stenosis diagnosis. In order to detect coronary stenosis, a specialist performs an exhaustive visual examination of the entire angiogram, and based on their knowledge, the stenosis regions are labeled. In order to illustrate the challenging and laborious task carried out by the specialist in terms of the visual examination of coronary angiograms, in Figure 1, a set of X-ray angiograms along with manually detected stenosis regions is presented.

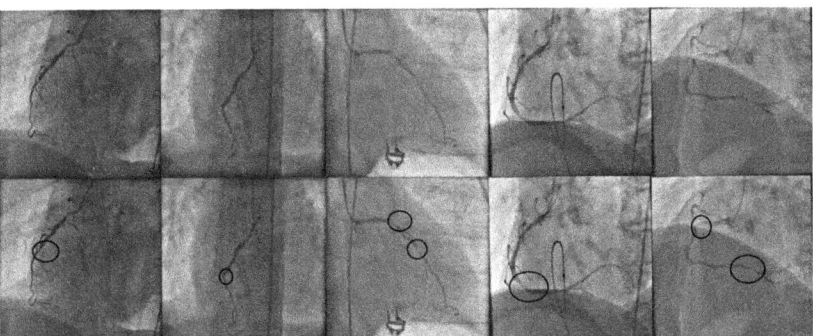

Figure 1. (**First row**): set of X-ray coronary angiograms and the corresponding stenosis regions manually detected by cardiologist (**second row**).

The main disadvantages of working with X-ray coronary angiograms are the high noise levels and low-contrast regions, which make automatic vessel identification, measurement and classification tasks difficult. Moreover, for the automatic stenosis classification problem, some approaches have been reported. The method proposed by Saad [2] detects the presence of atherosclerosis in a coronary artery image using a vessel-width variation measure. The measurements are computed from a previously segmented image containing only vessel pixels and its corresponding skeleton in order to determine the vessel center line, from which the orthogonal line length of a fixed-size window is computed, moving through the image. Kishore and Jayanthi [3] applied a manually fixed-size window from an enhanced image. The vessel pixels were measured, adding them to intensity values in order to obtain a coronary stenosis grading measure. Other approaches make use of the Hessian matrix properties to enhance or extract vessel trees at the first stage. For instance, the works of Wan et al. [4], Sameh et al. [5], and Cervantes-Sanchez et al. [6] applied the Hessian matrix properties in order to enhance vessel pixels in coronary angiograms. The response image allows for the measurement and extraction of features related with vessel shapes that are used for the automatic classification and grading of coronary stenosis.

The use of classification techniques and search metaheuristics are additional approaches that have been used to address vessel disease problems. Cervantes-Sanchez et al. [7] proposed a Bayesian-based method using a $3D$ feature vector that was extracted from the image histogram in order to classify stenosis cases. Taki et al. [8] achieved a competitive result in the categorization of calcified and noncalcified coronary artery plaques using a Bayesian-based classifier. The proposal of Welikala et al. [9] works with retinal vessels, applying a genetic algorithm to reduce the number of needed features that perform a correct classification of proliferative diabetic retinopathy cases. Sreng et al. [10], proposed a hybrid simulated annealing method to select relevant features that are then used with an ensemble bagging classifier in order to produce a suitable screening of the eye. The method of Chen et al. [11] works with a $6D$ feature vector related with the morphology of bifurcated vessels in order to detect coronary artery disease. A fuzzy criterion was used by Giannoglou et al. [12] in order to select features in characterization of atherosclerotic plaques, and Wosiak and Zakrzewska [13], proposed an automatic feature selection method by integrating correlation and clustering strategies in cardiovascular disease diagnosis.

On the other hand, emergent evolution of deep learning techniques such as the convolutional neural network (CNN) have made it possible for them to be applied to the coronary artery disease problem [14]. CNN contains a set of layers (convolutional layers) focused on the automatic segmentation of the image in order to keep only the data that allow the CNN to achieve correct classification rates [15–17]. Antczak and Liberadzki [18], proposed a method that is able to generate synthetic coronary stenosis and nonstenosis patches in order to improve the CNN training rates. The strategy proposed by Ovalle et al. [19] makes use of a transfer learning [20–22] strategy in order to achieve correct training and classification rates with complex CNN architectures. One of the main drawbacks of CNN is the need for large-instance databases in order to achieve correct training rates. Data augmentation techniques [23–27] are commonly used as a way to generate large amounts of instances that are used in the training and testing of the CNN. In addition, it is difficult for a CNN to identify which features are really useful for a correct classification and what they represent [28,29].

In the present paper, a novel method for the automatic classification of coronary stenosis based on feature selection and a hybrid evolutionary algorithm in X-ray angiograms is presented. The proposed method uses the evolutionary computation technique for addressing the high-dimensional problem of selecting an efficient subset of features from a bank of 49 features, where the problem is a computational complexity of $O(2^n)$. To select the best evolutionary technique, different population-based strategies were compared in terms of feature reduction and classification accuracy using a training set of coronary stenosis images. From the comparative analysis, the Boltzmann univariate marginal distribution algorithm (BUMDA) and simulated annealing (SA) were selected for further analysis. In the experiments, two different databases were used. The first database was provided by the Mexican Institute of Social Security (IMSS), and it contains 500 images. The second database corresponds to Antczak [18], which is publicly available and contains 2700 patches. Finally, the proposed method was compared with different state-of-the-art classification methods in terms of classification accuracy and Jaccard coefficient, working with both databases in order to show the classification robustness achieved by the subset of 11 features, which were obtained from the feature selection step using the hybrid BUMDA-SA evolutionary technique.

The remaining of this paper is as follows. In Section 2, the background methodology is described. Section 3 presents the proposed method and the hybrid approach that performs the automatic feature selection task. In Section 4, the experiment details and results are described, and finally, conclusions are given in Section 5.

2. Methods

In this section, the strategies and techniques related to the proposed method are described in detail. Section 2.1 starts describing feature selection techniques from the literature in order to extract distinct types of them, such as texture, intensity and morphology. Consequently, in Section 2.2, the Boltzmann univariate marginal distribution algorithm and the simulated annealing strategies are described, since they comprise the hybrid evolutionary approach used in the automatic feature selection stage. Finally, in Section 2.3, the support vector machine technique is described, because it is used as the classifier in order to determine if a given instance, which is composed of a feature vector, is classified as positive (stenosis case) or negative (nonstenosis case).

2.1. Feature Extraction

In digital image processing, feature extraction is an important task, because it allows properties or interest objects of an image (global features) to be described, and it is also possible to extract features from specific regions (local features) [30,31]. Different feature types can be extracted from an image, as reported in [32–34]. Based on their type, features can be classified as being related to texture, intensity or morphology.

2.1.1. Texture Features

Texture features have had high relevance in different cardiovascular problems [9,35–39]. The most widely used approach in texture feature extraction for grayscale images is the gray-level co-occurrence matrix (GLCM) [40–43]. The GLCM measures the frequency of variation between gray levels from a given point in the image. It is represented as a matrix, whose rows and columns correspond to the intensity pixels of the entire image or a region from it. The variation frequencies are computed based on a specific spatial relationship (offset) denoted by $(\Delta x, \Delta y)$ between a pixel with intensity i and another pixel with intensity j, as follows:

$$C_{\Delta x, \Delta y}(i,j) = \sum_{x=1}^{n}\sum_{y=1}^{m} \begin{cases} 1, \text{if } I(x,y) = i \text{ and } I(x + \Delta x, y + \Delta y) = j \\ 0, \text{otherwise} \end{cases}, \quad (1)$$

where $C_{\Delta x, \Delta y}(i,j)$ is the frequency at which two pixels with intensities i and j at an specific offset $(\Delta x, \Delta y)$ occur; n and m represent the height and width of the image, respectively. $I(x,y)$ and $I(x + \Delta x, y + \Delta y)$ are the pixel values in image I.

In addition, the Radon transform is also used for texture analysis in medical image processing and feature extraction [44–46]. The Radon transform is an alternative way to represent an image. Instead of the original spatial domain of the image, the Radon transform is the projection of the image intensity along with a radial line oriented at some specific angle. It can be computed as follows:

$$R(\rho, \theta) = \int_{-\infty}^{\infty} \int_{-\infty}^{\infty} f(x,y)\delta(\rho - x\cos\theta - y\sin\theta)dxdy, \quad (2)$$

where $R(\rho, \theta)$ is the Radon transform of a function $f(x,y)$ at an angle θ; $\delta(r)$ is the Dirac delta function, which is zero, except when $r = 0$ and $\delta(\rho - x\cos\theta - y\sin\theta)$ in the definition of the Radon transform forces the integration of $f(x,y)$ along the line $\rho - x\cos\theta - y\sin\theta = 0$.

2.1.2. Shape Features

Shape-based features allow measurable information to be extracted about different aspects related to the shape of the arteries, such as the length of a segment, its tortuosity, the number of bifurcations of a segment, the vessel width, etc. However, in order to obtain correct data from shape-based features, a previous segmentation of the original image is required to discriminate noninterest information such as noise and background. In the present work, the Frangi method [47] was used in order to extract vessel information. The Frangi method works with the Hessian matrix, which is the result of the second-order derivative of a Gaussian kernel that is convolved with the original image. The Gaussian kernel is represented as follows:

$$G(x,y) = -exp\left(-\frac{x^2 + y^2}{2\sigma^2}\right), \quad \|y\| < L/2, \quad (3)$$

where σ is the spread of the Gaussian profile and L is the length of the vessel segment.
The resultant Hessian matrix is expressed as follows:

$$H = \begin{pmatrix} H_{xx} & H_{xy} \\ H_{yx} & H_{yy} \end{pmatrix}, \quad (4)$$

where H_{xx}, H_{xy}, H_{yx} and H_{yy} are the different convolution responses of the original image with each second-order partial derivative of the Gaussian kernel.
The segmentation function defined by Frangi for 2D vessel detection is as follows:

$$f(x) = \begin{cases} 0 & \text{if } \lambda_2 > 0, \\ exp\left(-\frac{R_b^2}{2\alpha^2}\right)\left(1 - exp\left(\frac{S^2}{2\beta^2}\right)\right) & \text{elsewhere.} \end{cases} \quad (5)$$

The α parameter is used with R_b to control the shape discrimination. The β parameter is used by S^2 for noise elimination. R_b and S^2 are calculated as follows:

$$R_b = \frac{|\lambda_1|}{|\lambda_2|}, \quad (6)$$

$$S^2 = \sqrt{\lambda_1^2 + \lambda_2^2},\tag{7}$$

where λ_1 and λ_2 are the eigenvalues of Hessian matrix.

Since the filter response of the Frangi method can be represented as a grayscale image, an automatic thresholding strategy has to be applied in order to classify vessel and nonvessel pixels. In the Otsu method [48], the threshold value is computed automatically based on the pixel intensities, from which a weighted sum of variance of the two classes is performed. The threshold is computed as follows:

$$\sigma_w^2(t) = w_0(t)\sigma_0^2(t) + w_1(t)\sigma_1^2(t),\tag{8}$$

where w_0 and w_1 weights are the probabilities of the two classes separated by a threshold t, and σ_0^2 and σ_1^2 are the statistical variances of w_0 and w_1, respectively.

On the other hand, several vessel shape-based features are computed from the skeleton of the arteries. In order to extract the vessel skeleton from a previously enhanced image, the medial axis transform is widely used. It is commonly implemented using the Voronoi method, expressed as follows:

$$R_k = \{x \in X | d(x, P_k) \leq d(x, P_j) \text{ for all } j \neq k\},\tag{9}$$

where R_k is the Voronoi region associated with the site P_k (a tuple of nonempty subsets in space X), which contains the set with all points in X whose distance to P_k is not greater than their distance to the other sites P_j. j is any index different from k. $d(x, P_k)$ is a closeness measure from point x to point P_k. In this part, as a measure of closeness, the Euclidean distance is the most commonly used norm, which is defined as follows:

$$D(p, q) = \sqrt{\sum_{i=1}^{n}(p_i - q_i)^2}\tag{10}$$

where $D(p, q)$ is the Euclidean distance between points p and q, i is the value of the points in each corresponding dimension and n is the number of dimensions in which p and q are represented.

2.2. Metaheuristics

Selecting features that are relevant for classification in a specific problem is a challenging task. The total number of different feature combinations that can occur is denoted by 2^n, where n is the number of features involved in the studied problem. In this context, the use of search metaheuristics and evolutionary strategies are convenient for addressing the problem.

2.2.1. Simulated Annealing

The simulated annealing (SA) algorithm is a stochastic optimization technique that was inspired from the annealing procedure in metallurgy and ceramics. The goal is a reduction in defects in solid materials by performing controlled heating and cooling steps. In the annealing process, the material is exposed to high temperatures. When a determined temperature is reached, the material is exposed to a controlled cooling process, keeping an optimal equilibrium of their molecules at all times through its correct alignment. The heating and cooling procedures are decisive in order to obtain the final structure; if the initial temperature was not high enough or the cooling process was too slow or too fast, the resultant material will present defects called metastable states. Kirkpatrick et al. [49] adapted the procedure to the computational field. It is useful for combinatorial and continuous problems where the search space is high-dimensional and difficult to explore exhaustively. The algorithm starts with an initial random solution. In each iteration, the parameters T_{min}, T_{max} and T_{step} are used to generate a new solution by varying the old one according to a probability that depends on the current temperature and the decreasing ΔE

parameter, based on the objective function. The probability is computed by applying the Boltzmann distribution as follows:

$$P(\Delta E, T) = \frac{f(s') - f(s)}{T},\qquad(11)$$

where $P(\Delta E, T)$ is the probability based on the Boltzmann distribution; $f(s')$ is the response of the objective function evaluating the current solution denoted by s'; $f(s)$ is the value of the objective function evaluated with the previous solution (denoted by s).

The simulated annealing pseudocode is described in Algorithm 1.

Algorithm 1: Simulated annealing pseudocode.

Input:
T_{max} /* Max temperature value */
T_{min} /* Min temperature value */
T_{step} /* Temperature variation from T_{max} to T_{min} */
begin
    $s = s_0$ /* Generate a random solution */
    $T_{current} = T_{max}$
    while $T_{current} > T_{min}$ **do**
        /* Select a random element */
        $s_{new} = selectRandom(s)$
        if $P(E(s), E(s_{new}), T_{current}) \geq generateRandom(0,1)$ **then**
            $s = s_{new}$
        end
        $T_{current} = T_{current} - T_{step}$
    end
end
Output: The final state s

2.2.2. Boltzmann Univariate Marginal Distribution Algorithm

The Boltzmann univariate marginal distribution algorithm (BUMDA) [50] is an evolutionary computation technique from the family of estimation of distribution algorithms (EDAs) [51]. In EDAs, new populations are generated based on the probability distribution over the search space of the current generation [52]. BUMDA uses the Boltzmann probability distribution, which makes use of the mean and variance as follows:

$$\mu = \sum_j W(X_j) x_j, \text{ where } W(X_j) = \frac{g(X_j)}{\sum_{X_j} g(X_j)},\qquad(12)$$

$$v = \sum_j W'(X_j)(X_j - \mu)^2, \text{ where } W'(X_j) = \frac{g(X_j)}{\sum_{X_j} g(X_j) + 1},\qquad(13)$$

where μ y v are the objective function mean and variance obtained from the population, respectively. $g(X_j)$ is the value of the objective function obtained by the individual j^{th}, which belongs to population X. Consequently, similar to UMDA [53], a fraction of the best individuals are considered to generate the new population. However, in BUMDA, the selection rate for the new population is computed according to a selection threshold θ, as follows:

$$\theta^{t+1} = \begin{cases} f(x_{npop}) & \text{if } t = 1, \\ f(x_{\frac{npop}{2}}) & \text{if } f(x_{\frac{npop}{2}}) >= \theta^t, \\ f(x_i) & \text{when } f(x_i) >= \theta^t \Big|_{i=\frac{npop}{2}+1}^{npop}, \end{cases} \qquad(14)$$

where npop is the population size.

Only those individuals whose objective function value is higher or equal than θ^{t+1} will be considered for the Boltzmann distribution and the generation of the new population. The BUMDA pseudocode is described in Algorithm 2.

Algorithm 2: BUMDA pseudocode

Input:
D /* Problem dimension */
n_{pop} /* Population size */
N_{gen} /* Number of generations */
begin
    Initialize $t = 0$, $X^t \sim U(0,1)$
    Evaluate $F^t = f(X^t)$
    Select $[X_{best}, X^t]$ = sort X^t, according to an objective function.
    while $t < N_{gen}$ **do**
        for $i = 1 \ldots D$ **do**
            $p_i = \sum_{j=1}^{n_{set}} x_{i,j}$
        end
        Set $P = [p_1, p_2, \ldots, p_D]$
        Select individuals for new generation by applying Equation (14)
        Generate new population using μ and ν, which were calculated previously:
        $X^{t+1} = [X^{t+1}_{1:(n_{pop}-1)} = \text{random\_normalized}\,(\mu, \nu), x_{best}]$
        Set $t = t+1$
        Evaluate $F^t = f(X^t)$
        Select $[X_{best}, X^t]$ = sort X^t, according to an objective function.
    end
end
Output: x_{best} /* The best solution achieved */

BUMDA presents several advantages with respect to another population-based metaheuristics. For instance, in BUMDA, only the population size and the max number of generations are required, because the selection rate is computed automatically. In addition, the use of the Boltzmann distribution helps to generate populations with widely dispersed individuals, which decreases the risk of falling into a local-optima solution.

2.3. Support Vector Machines

Support vector machines (SVMs) are supervised learning strategies designed at first as lineal separators for binary classification [54,55]. When the instances are not linearly separable (classifiable) in their original representation space, the SVM projects the instances from their original representation space to higher-dimensional orders, where the linear classification can be made [56]. In order to perform the projections, the SVM makes use of those instances lying in both sides of the separation line (2D), plane (3D) or hyperplane (4D or higher). The hyperplane depends only on the support vectors and not on any other observations. The projection of the training instances in a space χ to a higher-dimensional feature space $\mathcal{F}$ is performed via a Mercer kernel operator. For given training data $x_1, \ldots, x_n$, that are vectors in some spaces $\chi \subseteq \mathbb{R}^d$; the support vectors can be considered as a set of classifiers expressed as follows [57]:

$$f(x) = \left(\sum_{i=1}^{n} \alpha_i K(x_i, x) \right). \tag{15}$$

When K satisfies the Mercer condition [58], it can be expressed as follows:

$$K(u, v) = \Phi(u) \cdot \Phi(v), \tag{16}$$

where $\Phi : \chi \to \mathcal{F}$ and "·" denotes an inner product. With this assumption, f can be rewritten as follows:

$$f(x) = w \cdot \Phi(x),$$
$$w = \sum_{i=1}^{n} \alpha_i \Phi(x_i). \tag{17}$$

3. Proposed Method

The proposed method consists of the steps of feature extraction, automatic feature selection, feature subset testing and performance evaluation. The first stage is focused in the extraction of 49 features from the image database by considering texture, intensity and morphology feature types. The extracted texture features were those proposed by Haralik [59], and the morphological features were based on Welikala [9]. The bank of 49 features is described below.

1. The minimum pixel intensity present in the patch.
2. The maximum pixel intensity present in the patch.
3. The mean pixel intensity in the patch.
4. The standard deviation of the pixel intensities in the patch.
5–18. Features 5 to 18 are composed of the Haralik features: angular second moment (energy), contrast, correlation, variance, inverse difference moment (homogeneity), sum average, sum variance, sum entropy, entropy, difference variance, difference entropy, information measure of correlation 1, information measure of correlation 2, maximum correlation coefficient.
19–32. The Haralik features applied to the Radon transform response of the patch: angular second moment (energy), contrast, correlation, variance, inverse difference moment (homogeneity), sum average, sum variance, sum entropy, entropy, difference variance, difference entropy, information measure of correlation 1, information measure of correlation 2, maximum correlation coefficient.
33. The Radon ratio-X measure.
34. The Radon ratio-Y measure.
35. The mean of pixel intensities from the Radon transform response of the patch.
36. The standard deviation of the pixel intensities from the Radon transform response of the patch.
37. The vessel pixel count in the patch.
38. The vessel segment count in the patch.
39. Vessel density. The rate of vessel pixels in the patch.
40. Tortuosity 1. The tortuosity of each segment is calculated using the true length (measured with the chain code) divided by the Euclidean length. The mean tortuosity is calculated from all the segments within the patch.
41. Sum of vessel lengths.
42. Number of bifurcation points. The number of bifurcation points within the patch when vessel segments were extracted.
43. Gray-level coefficient of variation. The ratio of the standard deviation to the mean of the gray level of all segment pixels within the patch.
44. Gradient mean. The mean gradient magnitude along all segment pixels within the subwindow, calculated using the Sobel gradient operator applied on the preprocessed image.
45. Gradient coefficient of variation. The ratio of the standard deviation to the mean of the gradient of all segment pixels within the subwindow.
46. Mean vessel width. Skeletonization correlates to vessel center lines. The distance from the segment pixel to the closest boundary point of the vessel using the vessel map prior to skeletonization. This gives the half-width at that point, which is then multiplied by 2 to achieve the full vessel width. The mean is calculated for all segment pixels within the subwindow.

47. The minimum standard deviation of the vessel length, based on the vessel segments present in the patch. The segments are obtained by the tortuosity points along the vessel.
48. The maximum standard deviation of the vessel length, based on the vessel segments present in the patch. The segments are obtained by the tortuosity points along the vessel.
49. The mean of the standard deviations of the vessel length, based on the vessel segments present in the patch. The segments are obtained by the tortuosity points along the vessel.

In Figure 2, the overall hybrid evolutionary proposed method steps are illustrated.

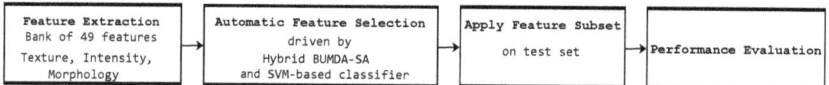

Figure 2. Overall steps of the proposed method based on feature selection to classify coronary stenosis.

In the second step, the automatic feature selection task is performed. It is driven by the proposed hybrid evolutionary strategy involving the BUMDA and SA techniques. In this stage, BUMDA is initialized and iterated until the maximum number of generations is reached. In the third step, the selected feature subset is tested using testing cases, and finally, the obtained classification results are measured based on the accuracy and Jaccard coefficient metrics in order to evaluate their performance.

In Figure 3, the hybrid evolutionary strategy is described in detail. This stage of the proposed method is focused on the automatic feature selection task. It starts with the BUMDA initialization, requiring only the max number of generations and the population size. With BUMDA being a population-based technique, it produces a set of solutions on each iteration. Each solution indicates which features will be used and which will be discarded. Consequently, for each solution, a particular SVM is trained using only the feature subset expressed in the solution. On each BUMDA generation, different SVMs are trained according to each feature vector, which is represented by each individual in the BUMDA population. Based on the SVM training accuracy and the number of selected features, the best individual in each generation is selected. In the next step, the previously selected individual is improved by the SA strategy. Since SA is a single-solution technique, it is useful to improve the best solution produced by the BUMDA. If the SA-obtained result is higher than the best result obtained by BUMDA, its best individual is replaced by the individual improved by the SA. When the max number of BUMDA generations is reached, the individual with the highest fitness value over all generations is selected as the best solution achieved. This solution contains the selected feature subset, which will be directly applied on the test set of coronary stenosis images. In this stage, the use of a hybrid evolutionary strategy based on the BUMDA and SA techniques is relevant, because SA helps to further reduce the number of features represented in the best solution achieved in each BUMDA generation, at the same time keeping the training accuracy rate, or even improving it.

For the experiment, two different image databases were used. The first database was provided by the Mexican Social Security Institute (IMSS) and approved by a local committee under reference R-2019-1001-078. It contains 500 coronary image patches, with a proportion of 50% − 50% for positive and negative stenosis cases. From this database, 400 instances were used for the automatic feature selection stage and the remaining 100 instances were used for testing after this stage ends. All patch sizes were 64 × 64 pixels and were validated by a cardiologist. Figure 4 illustrates sample patches of the IMSS database with their respective vessel segmentation response and skeleton, according to the Frangi method, from which the morphological-based feature extraction task was performed.

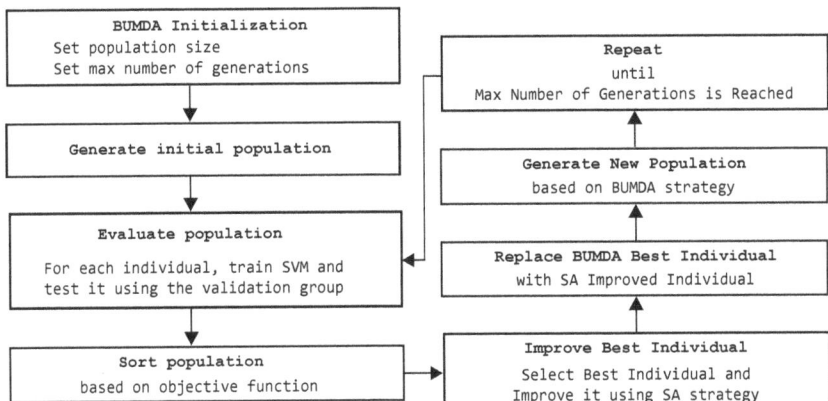

Figure 3. Steps of the proposed hybrid evolutionary method focused in the automatic feature selection task in order to determine the best tradeoff between number of features and classification rate.

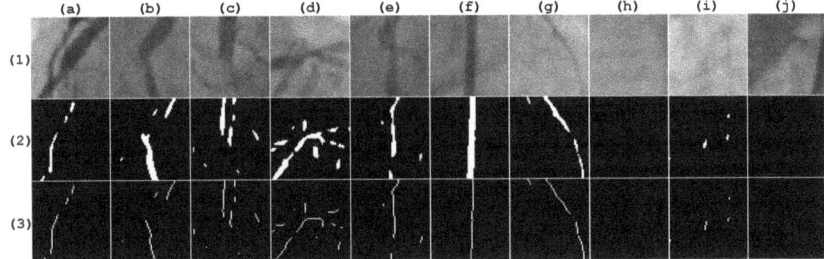

Figure 4. Patches taken from the IMSS database. Row (**1**) contains the original image. Row (**2**) contains the corresponding Frangi response, which is binarized, applying the Otsu method. Row (**3**) contains the corresponding vessel skeleton. Columns (**a**–**e**) are positive stenosis samples. Columns (**f**–**j**) are negative stenosis samples.

The second database was provided by Antczak [18], which is publicly available. It contains 2700 instances, which are also balanced for positive and negative stenosis cases. From this database, 2160 instances (80%) were used for training and the remaining 540 instances were used for testing. Figure 5 illustrates sample patches of the Antczak database with their respective vessel segmentation response and skeleton, according with the Frangi method.

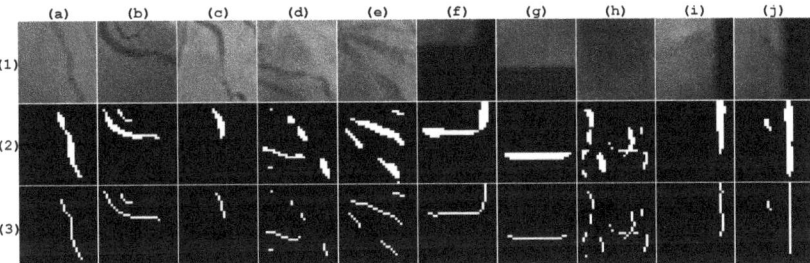

Figure 5. Patches taken from the Antczak database. Row (**1**) contains the original image. Row (**2**) contains the corresponding Frangi response, which is binarized with the Otsu method. Row (**3**) contains the corresponding vessel skeleton. Columns (**a**–**e**) are positive stenosis samples. Columns (**f**–**j**) are negative stenosis samples.

In order to evaluate the performance of the proposed method, the accuracy metric (Acc) and the Jaccard similarity coefficient (JC) were adopted. The accuracy metric considers the fraction of correct classified cases as positive or negative by defining four necessary measures: true-positive cases (TP), true-negative cases (TN), false-positive cases (TP) and false-negative cases. The TP value is the fraction of positive cases classified correctly. The TN value is the fraction of negative cases classified correctly. The FP cases is the fraction of negative cases classified as positive. The FN value is the fraction of positive cases classified as negative. Based on this, the accuracy is computed as follows:

$$Acc = \frac{TP+TN}{TP+TN+FP+FN}, \quad (18)$$

The JC measures the similarity of two element sets. Applying this principle, it is possible to measure the accuracy of a classifier using only positive instances, as follows:

$$JC = \frac{TP}{TP+FP+FN}. \quad (19)$$

It is important to mention that only the IMSS database was used for the automatic feature selection stage. Furthermore, with the Antczak database, only the feature subset obtained by the proposed method was used in order to probe the method's effectiveness. Additionally, classic search techniques from the literature, such as the Tabú search (TS) [60] and the iterated local search (ILS) [61], were also included in the experimentation. For the hybrid approaches, the simulated annealing strategy was used in all experiments in order to improve the best solution achieved for each particular technique.

4. Results and Discussion

In this section, the proposed method for feature selection and automatic classification is evaluated with different state-of-the-art methods using two databases of X-ray angiograms. All the experiments were performed using the Matlab software version 2018 on a computer with an Intel core i7 processor with 8 GB of RAM.

Table 1 describes the parameter settings of the compared methods used in the automatic feature selection stage, considering the same conditions for all of them in order to avoid biased measurements.

The SA strategy was configured with $T_{max} = 1$, $T_{min} = 0$ and $T_{step} = 0.01$. In order to ensure the obtained results, the proposed method was performed with 30 independent trials. For the SVM, 1000 max iterations were established using a cross-validation with $k = 10$. The parameter values for all techniques described previously were set taking into account the tradeoff between the classification accuracy and the execution time required to achieve a solution.

Table 1. Main parameter settings of compared methods in the automatic feature selection stage.

Method	Population Size	Max. Generations	Selection Rate	Trials
UMDA	30	500	0.70	30
GA	30	500	0.70	30
TS	30	500	–	30
ILS	30	500	–	30
BUMDA	30	500	Auto [1]	30
Hybrid GA	30	500	0.70	30
Hybrid TS	30	500	–	30
Hybrid ILS	30	500	–	30
Proposed (BUMDA-SA)	30	500	Auto [1]	30

[1] The selection rate of BUMDA is computed automatically.

In Table 2, a comparative analysis related to the best results obtained by different strategies during the automatic feature selection stage is presented.

Table 2. Comparative analysis of 30 runs between different evolutionary and path-based metaheuristics in terms of accuracy using the training set of the IMSS database. The SVM method was set as the classifier in the experiments.

Feature Selection Method	Number of Features	Accuracy Training		
		Max	Mean	Std. Dev.
None	49	0.90	0.90	0.00
UMDA	20	0.94	0.87	0.02
GA	19	0.96	0.88	0.03
TS	35	0.87	0.82	0.03
ILS	26	0.92	0.83	0.06
SA	27	0.91	0.87	0.02
BUMDA	19	0.95	0.89	0.04
Hybrid GA	13	0.96	0.88	0.06
Hybrid TS	29	0.93	0.84	0.06
Hybrid ILS	22	0.90	0.85	0.02
Proposed (BUMDA-SA)	11	0.96	0.89	0.03

Based on the results described in Table 2, the SVM training efficiency was improved in almost all cases when only a feature subset was used instead of the full set with 49 features. This behavior is because of the difficulty in projecting a high amount of overlapped data to dimensional orders higher than 49-D. Consequently, the proposed method achieved the best result since only 11 of 49 features were selected. This means that 78% of the initial feature set was discriminated, achieving a training rate efficiency of 0.96 at the same time in terms of the accuracy metric. In addition, some of the compared methods presented important variations on the best solution achieved according to the standard deviation accuracy, which gives some evidence of possible local-optima falls in some of the trials. In contrast, the standard deviation for the accuracy of the proposed method was lower, and considering the tradeoff between all measured factors, such as number of selected features, max training accuracy, mean training accuracy and standard deviation accuracy, the proposed method achieved the highest score.

After the automatic feature selection process was performed, in the next stage, the best feature subset, which was achieved by the hybrid BUMDA-SA method, was tested using the test cases from the IMSS and the Antczak databases, separately. Table 3 contains the corresponding confusion matrix, from which the accuracy and Jaccard coefficient metrics are computed.

Table 3. Confusion matrix using 100 test cases from the IMSS database using the proposed method.

		Real Class		
		Positive	Negative	Total
Predicted Class	Positive	44	4	48
	Negative	6	46	52
	Total	50	50	100

In Table 4, a comparative analysis between the proposed method and different state-of-the-art methods is presented, using the test set of 100 images of the IMSS database. The results of the proposed method are described based on the confusion matrix presented in Table 3.

Table 4. Comparison of stenosis classification performance between the proposed method and different methods of the state of the art, using the test set of the IMSS database in terms of the accuracy and Jaccard coefficient.

Method	Number of Features	Reduction Rate	Accuracy	Jaccard Coefficient
GLNet [62]	–	–	0.85	0.78
UNet [63]	–	–	0.87	0.79
CNN-16C [18]	–	–	0.86	0.79
SVM	49	0.00	0.87	0.77
UMDA [61]	20	0.59	0.89	0.80
GA	20	0.61	0.87	0.72
TS	35	0.32	0.80	0.74
ILS	26	0.46	0.82	0.69
SA	27	0.44	0.84	0.72
BUMDA	19	0.61	0.87	0.80
Hybrid GA	13	0.73	0.85	0.72
Hybrid TS	29	0.41	0.78	0.62
Hybrid ILS	22	0.55	0.81	0.68
Proposed (BUMDA-SA)	11	0.78	0.90	0.81

According to the data presented in Table 4, the proposed method achieved the highest classification rate in terms of the accuracy and Jaccard coefficient metrics, whose values were 0.90 and 0.81, respectively. By contrasting the accuracy in the training and testing stages, there is evidence of variation rates corresponding to the compared strategies. In Figure 6, the variation differences in accuracy in the training and testing stages for the contrasted strategies are illustrated.

The values of the accuracy rates show how competitive the feature subset was at classifying stenosis cases. It is remarkable how some feature subsets give evidence of possible overfitting training, such as the Hybrid-TS, since the training accuracy was 0.93 against 0.78 when using testing cases. In contrast, the proposed method achieved a low difference in performance in the training and testing phases compared with the Hybrid-TS and the Hybrid-GA techniques, which was 0.06, indicating that the achieved subset with 11 features is highly suitable for the classification task.

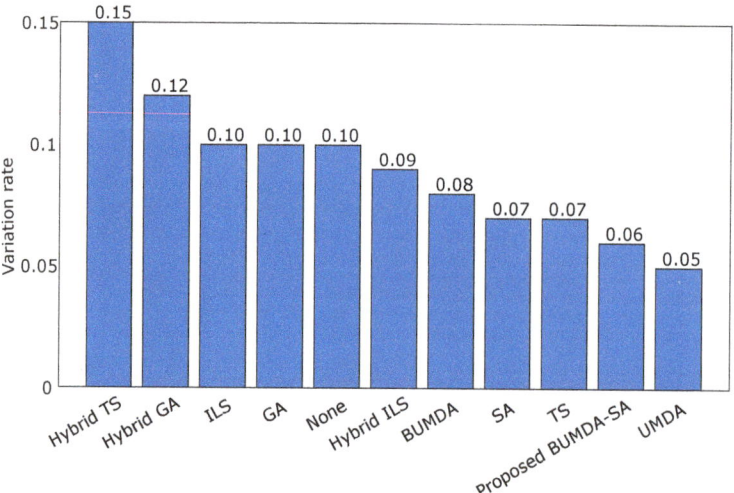

Figure 6. Variation rate computed as the difference in accuracy between training and testing phases for the applied strategies.

In order to evaluate the subset of 11 features achieved by the proposed hybrid BUMDA-SA method in the automatic feature selection stage, the Antczak database was used. In Table 5, the confusion matrix obtained from the proposed method using the Antczak database is presented.

Table 5. Confusion matrix of 700 testing cases, which corresponds to the Antczak database, using the subset of 11 features obtained by the proposed method.

		Real Class		
		Positive	Negative	Total
Predicted Class	Positive	246	18	264
	Negative	25	251	276
	Total	271	269	540

On the other hand, in Table 6, the results obtained by the proposed method and different strategies in the testing stage using the Antczak database are presented.

Based on the results presented in Table 6, the highest accuracy and Jaccard coefficient rates were achieved with the proposed method, whose values were 0.92 and 0.85 respectively. This result is relevant to show that the feature subset found by the proposed hybrid BUMDA-SA method is suitable. Consequently, it is important to mention that according to the results presented in Tables 4 and 6, the GA and UMDA techniques achieved very closed accuracy rates in contrast with the proposed method. However, the reduction rate, which is related to the number of selected features, was overcome by the proposed method when it was contrasted with the other methods. In addition, the proposed method also achieved the highest Jaccard coefficient rate compared with the others. It is important to mention these findings in order to show the importance of the use of a hybrid strategy in this multiobjective problem, where is required to keep or improve a high accuracy rate in the classification task, and at the same time, the use of a minimum number of features.

Table 6. Automatic classification testing rates achieved by the proposed method and different strategies using the Antczak database in terms of accuracy and Jaccard coefficient.

Method	Number of Features	Reduction Rate	Accuracy	Jaccard Coefficient
GLNet [62]	–	–	0.72	0.63
UNet [63]	–	–	0.76	0.72
CNN-16C [18]	–	–	0.86	0.74
SVM	49	0.00	0.69	0.46
UMDA	20	0.59	0.86	0.75
GA	19	0.61	0.85	0.73
TS	35	0.32	0.76	0.57
ILS	26	0.46	0.81	0.66
SA	27	0.44	0.82	0.68
BUMDA	19	0.61	0.88	0.79
Hybrid GA	13	0.73	0.85	0.74
Hybrid TS	29	0.41	0.78	0.64
Hybrid ILS	22	0.55	0.81	0.68
Proposed (BUMDA-SA)	11	0.78	0.92	0.85

Finally, in Table 7, the set of 11 features obtained by the proposed method is described, along with the frequency selection rate obtained from the statistical analysis of the 30 independent runs.

Table 7. Frequency rate and description of the set of 11 features obtained from the proposed hybrid BUMDA-SA method.

Feature Number	Feature Name	Feature Type	Frequency Rate
1	Min	Intensity	0.63
10	Sum Average	Texture	0.47
11	Sum Variance	Texture	0.43
42	Number of Bifurcation Points	Morphological	0.20
24	Radon Sum Average	Texture-Radon	0.13
16	Information Measure of Correlation 1	Texture	0.10
43	Gray Level Coefficient of Variation	Morphological	0.10
48	Max Stdev. of Vessel Length	Morphological	0.10
15	Difference Entropy	Texture	0.07
29	Radon Difference Entropy	Texture-Radon	0.07
48	Radon Information Measure of Correlation 2	Texture-Radon	0.03

According to the results presented in Table 7, the Min, Sum Average and Sum Variance features, which correspond to intensity and texture, have the highest frequency selection rates, followed by the Bifurcation Points and Radon-Sum features, which corresponds to morphology and Radon-based texture, respectively. This analysis is relevant since it allows us to remark on the importance of performing the automatic feature selection process with a high number of features involving different feature types such as texture, intensity and morphology.

5. Conclusions

In this paper, a novel method for the automatic classification of coronary stenosis in X-ray angiograms was introduced. The method is based on feature selection using a hybrid evolutionary algorithm and a support vector machine for classification. The hybrid method was used to explore the high-dimensional search space $O(2^n)$ of a bank of 49 features involving properties of intensity, texture, and morphology. To determine the best evolutionary method, a comparative analysis in terms of feature reduction rate and classification accuracy was performed using a training set of X-ray images. From the analysis, the method using BUMDA and SA achieved the best performance, selecting a subset of 11 features and achieving a feature reduction rate of 77.5%, and a classification accuracy of 0.96. Moreover, two different databases of coronary stenosis were used; the first one was provided by the Mexican Social Security Institute (IMSS), containing 500 images; and the second database is publicly available, with 2700 patches. In the experimental results, the proposed method, using the set of 11 selected features, was compared with different state-of-the-art classification methods, achieving an accuracy and Jaccard coefficient of 0.90 and 0.81 in the first database and 0.92 and 0.85 in the second one, respectively. Finally, it is important to point out that considering the execution time obtained by the proposed method when testing images (0.02 s per image), the proposed method can be useful in assisting cardiologists in clinical practice or as part of a computer-aided diagnostic system.

Author Contributions: Conceptualization, M.-A.G.-R., C.C. and I.C.-A.; methodology, M.-A.G.-R., C.C., I.C.-A. and J.-M.L.-H.; project administration, I.C.-A., C.C. and J.-M.L.-H.; software, M.-A.G.-R., I.C.-A., J.-M.L.-H. and C.C.; supervision, I.C.-A., S.-E.S.-M. and M.-A.H.-G.; validation, S.-E.S.-M., M.-A.H.-G. and I.C.-A.; visualization: J.-M.L.-H., M.-A.H.-G. and S.-E.S.-M.; writing—original draft, M.-A.G.-R., C.C., I.C.-A., J.-M.L.-H., M.-A.H.-G. and S.-E.S.-M. All authors have read and agreed to the published version of the manuscript.

Funding: This research received no external funding.

Institutional Review Board Statement: Not applicable.

Informed Consent Statement: Not applicable.

Data Availability Statement: Not applicable.

Acknowledgments: This work was supported by CONACyT under Project IxM-CONACyT No. 3150-3097.

Conflicts of Interest: The authors declare no conflict of interest.

Abbreviations

The following abbreviations are used in this manuscript:

BUMDA	Boltzmann Univariate Marginal Distribution Algorithm
CNN	Convolutional Neural Network
EDA	Estimation Distribution Algorithm
GA	Genetic Algorithm
ILS	Iterated Local Search
SA	Simulated Annealing
SVM	Support Vector Machine
TS	Tabú Search
UMDA	Univariate Marginal Distribution Algorithm

References

1. Tsao, C. Heart Disease and Stroke Statistics—2022 Update: A Report From the American Heart Association. *Circulation* **2022**, *145*, 153–639. [CrossRef] [PubMed]
2. Saad, I.A. Segmentation of Coronary Artery Images and Detection of Atherosclerosis. *J. Eng. Appl. Sci.* **2018**, *13*, 7381–7387. [CrossRef]
3. Kishore, A.N.; Jayanthi, V. Automatic stenosis grading system for diagnosing coronary artery disease using coronary angiogram. *Int. J. Biomed. Eng. Technol.* **2019**, *31*, 260–277. [CrossRef]
4. Wan, T.; Feng, H.; Tong, C.; Li, D.; Qin, Z. Automated identification and grading of coronary artery stenoses with X-ray angiography. *Comput. Methods Programs Biomed.* **2018**, *167*, 13–22. [CrossRef]
5. Sameh, S.; Azim, M.A.; AbdelRaouf, A. Narrowed Coronary Artery Detection and Classification using Angiographic Scans. In Proceedings of the 2017 12th International Conference on Computer Engineering and Systems (ICCES), Cairo, Egypt, 9–20 December 2017; pp. 73–79. [CrossRef]
6. Cervantes-Sanchez, F.; Cruz-Aceves, I.; Hernandez-Aguirre, A. Automatic detection of coronary artery stenosis in X-ray angiograms using Gaussian filters and genetic algorithms. *AIP Conf. Proc.* **2016**, *1747*, 020005. [CrossRef]
7. Cervantes-Sanchez, F.; Cruz-Aceves, I.; Hernandez-Aguirre, A.; Hernandez-Gonzalez, M.A.; Solorio-Meza, S.E. Automatic Segmentation of Coronary Arteries in X-ray Angiograms using Multiscale Analysis and Artificial Neural Networks. *MDPI Appl. Sci.* **2019**, *9*, 5507. [CrossRef]
8. Taki, A.; Roodaki, A.; Setahredan, S.K.; Zoroofi, R.A.; Konig, A.; Navab, N. Automatic segmentation of calcified plaques and vessel borders in IVUS images. *Int. J. Comput. Assist. Radiol. Surg.* **2008**, *2008*, 347–354. [CrossRef]
9. Welikala, R.; Fraz, M.; Dehmeshki, J.; Hoppe, A.; Tah, V.; Mann, S.; Williamson, T.; Barman, S. Genetic algorithm based feature selection combined with dual classification for the automated detection of proliferative diabetic retinopathy. *Comput. Med. Imaging Graph.* **2015**, *43*, 64–77. [CrossRef]
10. Sreng, S.; Maneerat, N.; Hamamoto, K.; Panjaphongse, R. Automated Diabetic Retinopathy Screening System Using Hybrid Simulated Annealing and Ensemble Bagging Classifier. *Appl. Sci.* **2018**, *8*, 1198. [CrossRef]
11. Chen, X.; Fu, Y.; Lin, J.; Ji, Y.; Fang, Y.; Wu, J. Coronary Artery Disease Detection by Machine Learning with Coronary Bifurcation Features. *Appl. Sci.* **2020**, *10*, 7656. [CrossRef]
12. Giannoglou, V.G.; Stavrakoudis, D.G.; Theocharis, J.B. IVUS-based characterization of atherosclerotic plaques using feature selection and SVM classification. In Proceedings of the 2012 IEEE 12th International Conference on Bioinformatics & Bioengineering (BIBE), Larnaca, Cyprus, 11–13 November 2012; pp. 715–720. [CrossRef]
13. Wosiak, A.; Zakrzewska, D. Integrating Correlation-Based Feature Selection and Clustering for Improved Cardiovascular Disease Diagnosis. *Complexity* **2021**, *2018*, 2520706. [CrossRef]
14. Gudigar, A.; Nayak, S.; Samanth, J.; Raghavendra, U.; A J, A.; Barua, P.D.; Hasan, M.N.; Ciaccio, E.J.; Tan, R.S.; Rajendra Acharya, U. Recent Trends in Artificial Intelligence-Assisted Coronary Atherosclerotic Plaque Characterization. *Int. J. Environ. Res. Public Health* **2021**, *18*, 10003. [CrossRef] [PubMed]
15. Raghavendra, U.; Bhat, N.S.; Gudijar, A. Automated system for the detection of thoracolumbar fractures using a CNN architecture. *Future Gener. Comput. Syst.* **2018**, *85*, 184–189. [CrossRef]

16. Raghavendra, U.; Fujita, H.; Bhandary, S.V.; Gudigar, A.; Hong, T.J.; Acharya, U.R. Deep convolution neural network for accurate diagnosis of glaucoma using digital fundus images. *Inf. Sci.* **2018**, *441*, 41–49. [CrossRef]
17. Ibarra-Vazquez, G.; Olague, G.; Chan-Ley, M.; Puente, C.; Soubervielle-Montalvo, C. Brain programming is immune to adversarial attacks: Towards accurate and robust image classification using symbolic learning. *Swarm Evol. Comput.* **2022**, *71*, 101059. [CrossRef]
18. Antczak, K.; Liberadzki, Ł. Stenosis Detection with Deep Convolutional Neural Networks. *Proc. MATEC Web Conf.* **2018**, *210*, 04001. [CrossRef]
19. Ovalle-Magallanes, E.; Avina-Cervantes, J.G.; Cruz-Aceves, I.; Ruiz-Pinales, J. Transfer Learning for Stenosis Detection in X-ray Coronary Angiography. *Mathematics* **2020**, *8*, 1510. [CrossRef]
20. Azizpour, H.; Sharif Razavian, A.; Sullivan, J.; Maki, A.; Carlsson, S. From Generic to Specific Deep Representations for Visual Recognition. In Proceedings of the IEEE Conference on Computer Vision and Pattern Recognition Workshops, Boston, MA, USA, 7–12 June 2015; pp. 36–45. [CrossRef]
21. Xu, S.; Wu, H.; Bie, R. CXNet-m1: Anomaly Detection on Chest X-rays with Image-Based Deep Learning. *IEEE Access* **2018**, *7*, 4466–4477. [CrossRef]
22. Yadav, S.S.; Jadhav, S.M. Deep convolutional neural network based medical image classification for disease diagnosis. *J. Big Data* **2019**, *6*, 113. [CrossRef]
23. Ding, J.; Chen, B.; Liu, H.; Huang, M. Convolutional Neural Network With Data Augmentation for SAR Target Recognition. *IEEE Geosci. Remote Sens. Lett.* **2016**, *13*, 364–368. [CrossRef]
24. Chlap, P.; Min, H.; Vandenberg, N.; Dowling, J.; Holloway, L.; Haworth, A. A review of medical image data augmentation techniques for deep learning applications. *Med. Imaging Radiat. Oncol.* **2021**, *65*, 545–563. [CrossRef] [PubMed]
25. Garcea, F.; Serra, A.; Lamberti, F.; Morra, L. Data augmentation for medical imaging: A systematic literature review. *Comput. Biol. Med.* **2023**, *152*, 106391. . [CrossRef] [PubMed]
26. Goceri, E. Medical image data augmentation: Techniques, comparisons and interpretations. *Artif. Intell. Rev.* **2023**, [CrossRef]
27. Kebaili, A.; Lapuyade-Lahorgue, J.; Ruan, S. Deep Learning Approaches for Data Augmentation in Medical Imaging: A Review. *J. Imaging* **2023**, *9*, 81. [CrossRef] [PubMed]
28. Knapič, S.; Malhi, A.; Saluja, R.; Främling, K. Explainable Artificial Intelligence for Human Decision Support System in the Medical Domain. *Mach. Learn. Knowl. Extr.* **2021**, *3*, 37. [CrossRef]
29. van der Velden, B.H.; Kuijf, H.J.; Gilhuijs, K.G.; Viergever, M.A. Explainable artificial intelligence (XAI) in deep learning-based medical image analysis. *Med. Image Anal.* **2022**, *79*, 102470. [CrossRef]
30. Trujillo, L.; Olague, G. Automated Design of Image Operators that Detect Interest Points. *Evol. Comput.* **2008**, *16*, 483–507. [CrossRef]
31. Li, Y.; Wang, S.; Tian, Q.; Ding, X. A survey of recent advances in visual feature detection. *Neurocomputing* **2015**, *149*, 736–751. [CrossRef]
32. Tessmann, M.; Vega-Higuera, F.; Fritz, D.; Scheuering, M.; Greiner, G. Multi-scale feature extraction for learning-based classification of coronary artery stenosis. In *Proceedings of the Medical Imaging 2009: Computer-Aided Diagnosis*; Karssemeijer, N.; Giger, M.L., Eds.; International Society for Optics and Photonics, SPIE: Orlando, FL, USA, 2009; Volume 7260, p. 726002. [CrossRef]
33. Olague, G.; Trujillo, L. Interest point detection through multiobjective genetic programming. *Appl. Soft Comput.* **2012**, *12*, 2566–2582. [CrossRef]
34. Fazlali, H.R.; Karimi, N.; Soroushmehr, S.M.R.; Sinha, S.; Samavi, S.; Nallamothu, B.; Najarian, K. Vessel region detection in coronary X-ray angiograms. In Proceedings of the 2015 IEEE International Conference on Image Processing (ICIP), Quebec, Canada, 27–30 September 2015; pp. 1493–1497. [CrossRef]
35. Acharya, U.R.; Sree, S.V.; Krishnan, M.M.R.; Molinari, F.; Saba, L.; Ho, S.Y.S.; Ahuja, A.T.; Ho, S.C.; Nicolaides, A.; Suri, J.S. Atherosclerotic Risk Stratification Strategy for Carotid Arteries Using Texture-Based Features. *Ultrasound Med. Biol.* **2022**, *38*, 899–915. [CrossRef]
36. Pathak, B.; Barooah, D. Texture Analysis based on the Gray-Level Co-Ocurrence Matrix considering possible orientations. *Int. J. Adv. Res. Electr. Electron. Instrum. Eng.* **2013**, *2*, 4206–4212.
37. Faust, O.; Acharya, R.; Sudarshan, V.K.; Tan, R.S.; Yeong, C.H.; Molinari, F.; Ng, K.H. Computer aided diagnosis of Coronary Artery Disease, Myocardial Infarction and carotid atherosclerosis using ultrasound images: A review. *Phys. Medica* **2017**, *33*, 1–15. [CrossRef]
38. Mitchell, C.C.; Korcarz, C.E.; Gepner, A.D.; Nie, R.; Young, R.L.; Matsuzaki, M.; Post, W.S.; Kaufman, J.D.; McClelland, R.L.; Stein, J.H. Retinal vascular tree morphology: A semi-automatic quantification. *J. Am. Heart Assoc.* **2019**, *8*, 912–917. [CrossRef]
39. Ricciardi, C.; Valente, A.S.; Edmunds, K.; Cantoni, V.; Green, R.; Fiorillo, A.; Picone, I.; Santini, S.; Cesarelli, M. Linear discriminant analysis and principal component analysis to predict coronary artery disease. *Health Inform. J.* **2020**, *26*, 2181–2192. [CrossRef]
40. Hernández, B.; Olague, G.; Hammoud, R.; Trujillo, L.; Romero, E. Visual learning of texture descriptors for facial expression recognition in thermal imagery. *Comput. Vis. Image Underst.* **2007**, *106*, 258–269. [CrossRef]
41. Barburiceanu, S.; Terebes, R.; Meza, S. 3D Texture Feature Extraction and Classification Using GLCM and LBP-Based Descriptors. *Appl. Sci.* **2021**, *11*, 2332. [CrossRef]

42. Cheng, K.; Lin, A.; Yuvaraj, J.; Nicholls, S.J.; Wong, D.T. Cardiac Computed Tomography Radiomics for the Non-Invasive Assessment of Coronary Inflammation. *Cells* **2021**, *10*, 879. [CrossRef]
43. Ayx, I.; Tharmaseelan, H.; Hertel, A.; Nörenberg, D.; Overhoff, D.; Rotkopf, L.T.; Riffel, P.; Schoenberg, S.O.; Froelich, M.F. Myocardial Radiomics Texture Features Associated with Increased Coronary Calcium Score-First Results of a Photon-Counting CT. *Diagnostics* **2022**, *12*, 1663. [CrossRef]
44. Murphy, L.M. Linear feature detection and enhancement in noisy images via the Radon transform. *Pattern Recognit. Lett.* **1986**, *4*, 279–284. [CrossRef]
45. Mallat, S. *A Wavelet Tour of Signal Processing*; 3rd ed.; Elsevier: Amsterdam, The Netherlands, 2009; Chapter 13, pp. 699–752.
46. Timothy-G, F. The Radon Transform. In *The Mathematics of Medical Imaging*; Technical University of Denmark: Lyngby, Denmark, 2015; pp. 13–37. [CrossRef]
47. Frangi, A.; Nielsen, W.; Vincken, K.; Viergever, M. Multiscale vessel enhancement filtering. In *Medical Image Computing and Computer-Assisted Intervention (MICCAI'98)*; Springer: Berlin/Heidelberg, Germany, 1998; pp. 130–137. [CrossRef]
48. Otsu, N. A Threshold Selection Method from Gray-Level Histograms. *IEEE Trans. Syst. Man Cybern.* **1979**, *9*, 62–66. [CrossRef]
49. Kirkpatrick, S.; Gelatt, C.D.; Vecchi, M.P. Optimization by simulated annealing. *Science* **1983**, *220*, 671–680. [CrossRef]
50. Valdez-Peña, S.I.; Hernández, A.; Botello, S. A Boltzmann based estimation of distribution algorithm. *Inf. Sci.* **2013**, *236*, 126–137. [CrossRef]
51. Gu, W.; Wu, Y.; Zhang, G. A hybrid Univariate Marginal Distribution Algorithm for dynamic economic dispatch of units considering valve-point effects and ramp rates. *Int. Trans. Electr. Energy Syst.* **2015**, *25*, 374–392. [CrossRef]
52. Dang, D.C.; Lehre, P.K.; Nguyen, P.T.H. Level-Based Analysis of the Univariate Marginal Distribution Algorithm. *Algorithmica* **2017**, *81*, 668–702. [CrossRef]
53. Hashemi, M.; Reza-Meybodi, M. Univariate Marginal Distribution Algorithm in Combination with Extremal Optimization (EO, GEO). In *International Conference on Neural Information Processing*; Springer: Berlin/Heidelberg, Germany, 2011; pp. 220–227. [CrossRef]
54. Cortes, C.; Vapnik, V. Support-Vector Networks. *Mach. Learn.* **1995**, *20*, 273–297. [CrossRef]
55. Cristianini, N.; Shawe-Taylor, J. *An Introduction to Support Vector Machines and Other Kernel-Based Learning Methods*; Cambridge University Press: Cambridge, UK, 2000.
56. Noble, W.S. What is a support vector machine? *Nat. Biotechnol.* **2006**, *24*, 1565–1567. [CrossRef]
57. Tong, S.; Chang, E. Support Vector Machine Active Learning for Image Retrieval. In *Proceedings of the Ninth ACM International Conference on Multimedia*; Association for Computing Machinery: New York, NY, USA, 2001; pp. 107–118. [CrossRef]
58. Burges, C.J. A Tutorial on Support Vector Machines for Pattern Recognition. *Data Min. Knowl. Discov.* **1998**, *2*, 121–167. [CrossRef]
59. Haralick, R.; Shanmugam, K.; Dinstein, I. Textural Features for Image Classification. *IEEE Trans. Syst. Man Cybern.* **1973**, *SMC-3*, 610–621. [CrossRef]
60. Johnson, D.S.; Papadimitriou, C.H.; Yannakakis, M. How easy is Local Search? *J. Comput. Syst. Sci.* **1988**, *37*, 79–100. [CrossRef]
61. Gil-Rios, M.A.; Cruz-Aceves, I.; Cervantes-Sánchez, F.; Guryev, I.; López-Hernández, J.M. Automatic enhancement of coronary arteries using convolutional gray-level templates and path-based metaheuristics. *Recent Trends Comput. Intell. Enabled Res.* **2021**, *1*, 129–152.
62. Szegedy, C.; Liu, W.; Jia, Y.; Sermanet, P.; Reed, S.; Anguelov, D.; Erhan, D.; Vanhoucke, V.; Rabinovich, A. Going Deeper with Convolutions. *arXiv* **2014**, arXiv:1409.4842.
63. Harouni, A.; Karargyris, A.; Negahdar, M.; Beymer, D.; Syeda-Mahmood, T. Universal multi-modal deep network for classification and segmentation of medical images. In Proceedings of the 2018 IEEE 15th International Symposium on Biomedical Imaging (ISBI 2018), Washington, DC, USA, 4–7 April 2018; pp. 872–876. [CrossRef]

Disclaimer/Publisher's Note: The statements, opinions and data contained in all publications are solely those of the individual author(s) and contributor(s) and not of MDPI and/or the editor(s). MDPI and/or the editor(s) disclaim responsibility for any injury to people or property resulting from any ideas, methods, instructions or products referred to in the content.

Article

Proposed Shaft Coupling Based on RPRRR Mechanism: Positional Analysis and Consequences

Stelian Alaci [1,*], Ioan Doroftei [2], Florina-Carmen Ciornei [1], Ionut-Cristian Romanu [1], Toma-Marian Ciocirlan [1] and Mariana-Catalina Ciornei [3,4,*]

[1] Mechanics and Technologies Department, "Stefan cel Mare" University of Suceava, 720229 Suceava, Romania; florina.ciornei@usm.ro (F.-C.C.); ionutromanucristian@usm.ro (I.-C.R.); marian.ciocirlan1@student.usv.ro (T.-M.C.)
[2] Mechanical Engineering, Mechatronics and Robotics Department, "Gheorghe Asachi" Technical University, 700050 Iasi, Romania; idorofte@mail.tuiasi.ro
[3] Physiology Department, "Carol Davila" University of Medicine and Pharmacy, 020021 Bucharest, Romania
[4] Faculty of Medical Engineering, University "Politehnica" of Bucharest, 060042 București, Romania
* Correspondence: stelian.alaci@usm.ro (S.A.); catalina.ciornei@umfcd.ro (M.-C.C.)

Abstract: This study proposes a solution for the transmission of rotation motion between two shafts with crossed directions. For constructive simplicity, the solutions including the planar pair were preferred and, from the two variants, namely structurally symmetric, revolute–planar–revolute (RPR), or asymmetric RRP, the last was selected. The resulting solution, RPRRR, is a non-Denavit-Hartenberg (non-D-H) mechanism. The D-H methodology is laborious since the structure of the equivalent mechanism is more complex than the actual one. For this reason, in the present paper, the kinematic analysis of the mechanism uses geometrical conditions of existence of the planar pair. The system is solved analytically and two main conclusions result: for a set of constructive data and a stipulated position of the driving element, two different assembling positions exist and a rotation motion occurs in the final revolute joint, but in the internal revolute pairs, the motion is oscillatory. The correctness of the theoretical results was corroborated by a CATIA model. The mechanism was also constructed and smooth running was noticed. Two main concerns were considered for the design of the mechanism: avoiding mechanical interference between the elements and estimating the stresses and deformations.

Keywords: shaft coupling; planar pair; revolute pair; D–H algorithm; CAD design; numerical simulation

MSC: 70B15; 70B10; 00A06; 65D17

Citation: Alaci, S.; Doroftei, I.; Ciornei, F.-C.; Romanu, I.-C.; Ciocirlan, T.-M.; Ciornei, M.-C. Proposed Shaft Coupling Based on RPRRR Mechanism: Positional Analysis and Consequences. *Axioms* **2023**, *12*, 707. https://doi.org/10.3390/axioms12070707

Academic Editors: Cheng-Shian Lin, Chien-Chang Chen and Yi-Hsien Wang

Received: 9 June 2023
Revised: 14 July 2023
Accepted: 18 July 2023
Published: 20 July 2023

Copyright: © 2023 by the authors. Licensee MDPI, Basel, Switzerland. This article is an open access article distributed under the terms and conditions of the Creative Commons Attribution (CC BY) license (https:// creativecommons.org/licenses/by/ 4.0/).

1. Introduction

One of the key objectives of the Theory of Machines and Mechanisms is to propose solutions for the transmission of motion between two elements—driving and driven—belonging to a mechanical structure [1]. Regarding the motion of the driving element, it should be as simple as possible [2,3], such as rotation or sliding for most of cases, depending on the type of the actuating motor; but the motion of the final element can be from simple to complex [4]. We must emphasize that the evolution of mathematics was at least spectacular in the last century and notions which seemed to be pointless proved to be applicable for everyday life. Can be reminded here the theory of distributions [5], fractional derivative [6], matrix analysis [7], chaos theory [8], etc. To the above considerations, we can add Gaudi's observation [9] that in nature there are no straight lines, a remark that highlights the nonlinear character of our world, evidenced by rather different topics: non-linear vibrations [10], green energy [11], semiconductor materials [12], dynamics of non-Newtonian fluids [13], music [14], sports [15], and so on. The same spectacular development of analysis methods was achieved in the domain of the spatial mechanisms theory. We can mention the screw theory [16–18], the dual numbers theory [19], the quaternions algebra [20], the dual quaternions method [21], and the tensor matrix method [22,23].

Two main directions are met in engineering applications: either the final element belongs to a mechanism and therefore the kinematics will depend on the motion of the driving element and on the constructive parameters of the mechanism, or the final element appertains to a robotic structure wherein the binary elements present a simple shape [24–26] (open kinematic chain) and the motion of the final element is ensured by the action of multiple driving pairs from the structure of the robot [27]—with the well-known examples of multiple-axes CNC machines [28,29] and medical devices and robots [30–36]. Contrasting with the robotic kinematic chain, in the case of mechanisms, the task of obtaining an imposed motion law of the final element is more difficult due to the fact that the driving element performs a simple motion. Here, the project design engineer must choose a certain structure for the intermediate coupling chain [37]; moreover, they must perform the dimensional optimization for the elements from the chosen structure [38–40], with the aim of ensuring for the driven element the imposed law of motion at a specified precision. When the transmission of rotation motion between two shafts with crossed axes is desired [41,42], the direct coupling of the shafts represents the simplest structural solution. A simple structural calculus reveals that a class 1 pair must be created between the two shafts, materialized by a Hertzian point contact [43–45]. To this class of mechanisms belong the cam mechanisms [46] and the gear mechanisms [47–51] (which are particular cases of cam mechanisms). The coupling pair ensures five simple, possible motions: sliding in the common tangent plane after two directions and rotations, two about two axes from the tangent plane and one about an axis normal to this plane. The solution is extremely simple from a structural point of view but, regarding functional aspects, it has as main disadvantages: high contact stresses—which produce wear and energy losses due to friction [52–54] and contact hysteresis [55]—and the complicated geometries of the elements. A frequently utilized compromise in the kinematical analysis of spatial mechanisms consists in replacing the class 1 pair with an equivalent kinematic chain, constructed by elements joined with pairs of lower mobility, usually lower pairs (cylindrical, spherical, or planar) [56–58]. The case in which the sphere–plane contact from a tripodic mechanism [59–62] was replaced by a binary element that makes the initial elements a planar pair and a spherical pair is presented in [63]. Another example is presented in [64], where the swash plate mechanism was studied by two kinematic analysis methods. The first manner considers the actual mechanism and applies the geometrical conditions of definition for the sphere–plane pair. The second manner studies an equivalent mechanism of Denavit–Hartenberg (D–H) type [65], obtained as a result of replacing the class 1 pair with a fictive kinematical chain containing only binary elements joined by cylindrical pairs (rotation or prismatic) in D–H condition. Next, the D–H algorithm is applied for the kinematic analysis of the equivalent mechanism. The direct approach, based on the definition condition of the class 1 pair, is simpler than the method of "homogenous operators" proposed by Denavit and Hartenberg [66], or other methods, equivalent to this, such as the dual matrix method [67,68], the method of dual quaternions [69,70], the screw theory [71], or other algorithms [72–75], which have the drawback of leading to cumbersome systems of trigonometric equations, difficult or impossible to solve analytically. This aspect can be overcome by using numerical methods; for example, Uicker et al. [76] present a matrix iterative procedure, fast convergent, based on the D–H algorithm.

Section 2 presents the theoretical basis upon which the structure of the proposed mechanism was chosen. For constructive simplicity, the solutions including the planar pair were preferred and, from the two variants, namely structurally symmetric, revolute–planar–revolute (RPR), or asymmetric RRP, the last was selected. The result is the mechanism for the coupling of the two crossed shafts is the RPRRR solution which, due to the presence of a planar pair that does not have a rotation axis with a well-stipulated direction, is a non-Denavit–Hartenberg (non-D–H) mechanism. The kinematical analysis is performed and the angular displacements from the revolute pairs and motions from the planar pair are found by analytical calculus. The next section, Section 3, presents both the models of the studied mechanism in Mathcad and CATIA but also the prototype constructed in the laboratory. The final section draws the main conclusions, from which the RPRRR mechanism is evidenced by its constructive simplicity, low fabrication costs, and high reliability due to the presence of lower pairs.

2. Materials and Methods

2.1. Structural Considerations

The transmission of rotation motion from a driving axis 1 to a driven axis n is a problem often encountered in engineering applications. Generally, the motion of the driving element is obtained from a motor with constant rotation velocity (combustion engine, electric motor, etc.). From a geometric point of view, the transmission of motion from the axis 1 to the axis n is characterized by the relative position between the input and output axes, expressed, for the most general case of crossed axes, by the twisted angle α_{1n} and the length of the common normal a_{1n}, as represented in Figure 1. The particular cases can be obtained from this general schematic: for $\alpha_{1n} = 0$, the shafts are parallel and for $a_{1n} = 0$, the shafts are intersecting. Between the input shaft (1) and the output shaft (n), a kinematic chain can be interposed in order to ensure the coupling. The characteristics of the intermediate coupling chain will influence the transmission ratio.

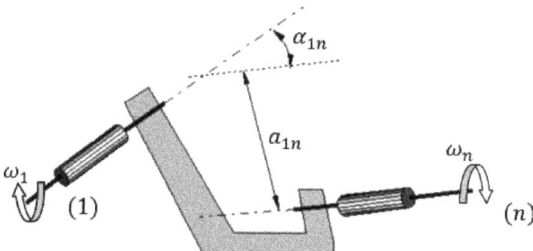

Figure 1. Coupling scheme of two crossed shafts, (1) and (n); the driving shaft (1) has a rotational speed ω_1 and the driven shaft (n) has the output rotational speed ω_n; a_{1n} is the common normal and α_{1n} is the twisted angle bteweeen the input and output shafts.

The quality of the motion transmission is considered by the transmission ratio i_{1n} defined as

$$i_{1n} = \frac{\omega_1}{\omega_n}. \tag{1}$$

Dependent on the requirements imposed to the transmission ratio, the coupling between the driven and driving axis can be achieved directly or by means of an intermediate kinematic chain. Considering economic and functional criteria, the structure of the intermediate chain must contain a reduced number of elements—as less as possible—and the kinematic pairs between the elements should have a high reliability. For a transmission wherein a unique driving element exists, the mobility must be 1. In the general coupling case, the mobility is found using the following relation:

$$M_f = (6-f)(n-1) - \sum_{k=f+1}^{n}(k-f)c_k \tag{2}$$

where n is the number of elements, including the immobile element, f is the family of the mechanism—defined as the number of common constraints—and c_k is the number of kinematic pairs of the k class. Here, for the general case of a transmission of 0 family, for a direct coupling, in the relation (2) the number of elements is $n = 3$ and it also requires the presence of two revolute pair of class 5, for joining each of the two shafts to the ground. The relation (2) is applied for this case:

$$\sum_{k=1}^{5} kc_k = 1 \tag{3}$$

The unique solution of Equation (3) is $k = 1$ and, from here, the conclusion is that, for a general case, the coupling between two shafts must be accomplished by means of a class 1 pair. When a middle element is interposed between the two shafts, is results in $n = 4$ and the conclusion is as follows:

$$\sum_{k=1}^{5} kc_k = 7. \tag{4}$$

The 7 degrees of freedom can be placed in pairs of any class; therefore, the number of structural solutions increases. Akbil [61] presents the solution of tripod coupling with curve–curve-type contacts. The same structural solution is applied in [59] where point–surface-type contact is used for a tripod coupling. Evidently, by increasing to 2 the number of elements of the intermediate chain, the number of structural solutions will increase significantly, according to the following relation:

$$\sum_{k=1}^{5} kc_k = 13 \tag{5}$$

But knowing that the coupling kinematic chain contains 2 elements, it results that only three pairs will exist in the structure of the coupling kinematic chain. More than this, the relation (5) shows that the pairs of class c_1 or c_2 cannot be present in the structure of the coupling kinematic chain. This can be proved by examples; for instance, when accepting a class 2 pair, $c_2 = 1$, the sum of classes of the other two pairs would be 11; therefore, the relation (5) cannot be satisfied because the maximum value of the class of a pair is 5. Therefore, the remaining possible structural solutions are

$$c_3 = 1, c_4 = 0, c_5 = 2; \tag{6}$$

$$c_3 = 0, c_4 = 2, c_5 = 1 \tag{7}$$

The present work considers the first structural solution, relation (6), for which the kinematic chain contains a planar pair and two revolute pairs. This selected structural solution RPRRR is shown in Figure 2, using standard convention [77]. A particular feature to be mentioned about this mechanism is the parallelism of the axes of the revolute pairs, formed between the element 2 and the neighboring elements.

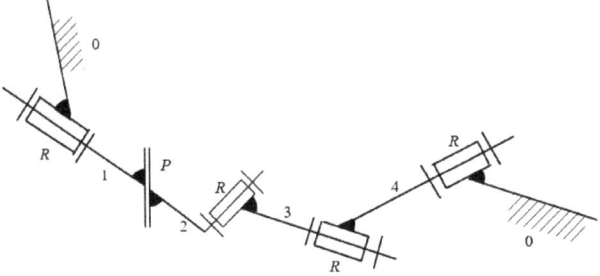

Figure 2. The coupling solution, RPRRR: kinematical diagram with graphical symbols.

2.2. Kinematic Analysis of the Proposed Structural Solution

2.2.1. Principle of the Denavit–Hartenberg Methodology

Denavit and Hartenberg [65,66] proposed a solution for the kinematic analysis of spatial kinematic chains, based on the transformation of the coordinates of a point when a reference system is changed into another. In a general case, the coordinate transformation of a point from a Cartesian reference system into another coordinate system is described by a 3×3 type matrix, R_{12}, that specifies the rotation of the axes of the new system with respect to the old ones and by a 3×1 type displacement vector, d_{12}, that stipulates the position of the new origin O_2 with respect to the initial origin O_1. The drawback of the method resides in the non-homogenous relations resulting from combining the transformations, when a third coordinate system is interposed between the initial and final frame:

$$\begin{bmatrix} x_1 \\ y_1 \\ z_1 \end{bmatrix} = d_{12} + R_{12} \begin{bmatrix} x_2 \\ y_2 \\ z_2 \end{bmatrix}. \tag{8}$$

Or, concentrated

$$x_2 = d_{12} + R_{12} x_2 \tag{9}$$

The direct transformation from the frame 3 to system 1 and then, by means of the system 2, is written as

$$x_1 = d_{13} + R_{13} x_3 = d_{12} + R_{12} x_2 = d_{12} + R_{12}(d_{23} + R_{23} x_3) = d_{13} + R_{12} d_{23} + R_{12} R_{23} x_3. \tag{10}$$

By identification, it results that

$$d_{13} = d_{12} + R_{12} d_{23};\ R_{13} = R_{12} R_{23}. \tag{11}$$

The relation (11) confirms the non-homogeneous character of the relation of composition of displacements. As emphasized above, the concepts introduced in abstract mathematics proved to be applicable in modern engineering problems; in the case of spatial kinematics, Denavit and Hartenberg regarded the displacement from a coordinate system to another as a gliding in the plane $x_4 = 1$ from the quadri-dimensional space (x_1, x_2, x_3, x_4), with gliding performed along a tri-dimensional sub-space in which the motion of the mechanism is completed. The transformation (relation 8) is now re-written as

$$\begin{bmatrix} x_1 \\ y_1 \\ z_1 \\ 1 \end{bmatrix} = \begin{bmatrix} R_{12} & d_{12} \\ 0 & 1 \end{bmatrix} \begin{bmatrix} x_2 \\ y_2 \\ z_2 \\ 1 \end{bmatrix}. \tag{12}$$

Or, in concentrated manner:

$$X_1 = T_{12} X_2. \tag{13}$$

The relations (4) can now be written as

$$X_1 = T_{13} X_3 = T_{12}(T_{23} X_3) = (T_{12} T_{23}) X_3. \tag{14}$$

From here,

$$T_{13} = T_{12} T_{23} \tag{15}$$

Relation (15) attests to the fact that the artifice proposed by Denavit and Hartenberg, that is, the matrices describing the transformation of coordinates from a frame to another, is described using a matrix product respecting the succession in the order of transition from a frame to another and so the methodology was named the method of "homogenous operators". The restriction imposed by the Denavit–Hartenberg (D–H) method consists in accepting the hypothesis that, in the structure of the kinematic chain, only cylindrical pairs C exist, with their particular forms of revolution R and translation T. The hypothesis permits that, by conforming the selection of coordinate frames attached to the elements of the mechanism, the relative position of two coordinate systems should be described by four parameters instead of six parameters required in the general case. In fact, each of the coordinate systems has the Oz axis directed along the axis of the pair and the Ox axis along the common normal of two consecutive axes. The transition from a frame to the next one is made by a roto-translation of parameters θ and s with respect to the current Oz

axis followed by a roto-translation of parameters α and a with respect to the Ox axis of the succeeding frame. The two displacements are described by the operators:

$$Z(\theta, s) = \begin{bmatrix} \cos\theta & -\sin\theta & 0 & 0 \\ \sin\theta & \cos\theta & 0 & 0 \\ 0 & 0 & 1 & s \\ 0 & 0 & 0 & 1 \end{bmatrix} \qquad (16)$$

and

$$X(\alpha, a) = \begin{bmatrix} 1 & 0 & 0 & a \\ 0 & \cos\alpha & -\sin\alpha & 0 \\ 0 & \sin\alpha & \cos\alpha & 0 \\ 0 & 0 & 0 & 1 \end{bmatrix}. \qquad (17)$$

The coordinates are transformed from frame 2 into frame 1 with the following relation:

$$\begin{bmatrix} x_1 \\ y_1 \\ z_1 \\ 1 \end{bmatrix} = Z(\theta_1, s_1) X(\alpha_{12}, a_{12}) \begin{bmatrix} x_2 \\ y_2 \\ z_2 \\ 1 \end{bmatrix}. \qquad (18)$$

or concentrated as

$$X_1 = Z(\theta_1, s_1) X(\alpha_{12}, a_{12}) X_2. \qquad (19)$$

Relation (18) was written according to the notation of axes by Yang [70]. Explicitly, the Ox axes and the corresponding parameters α and a are denoted using two indices, corresponding to the two Oz axes intersected by the current axis as common normal. Moreover, Yang proposes that, for cylindrical pairs, the displacements about the Oz axis, (θ, s), also have two indices in order to specify the constant displacement. Thus, the matrix $Z(\theta_1, s_1)$ will represent the roto-translation motion from the cylindrical pair with as axis the line z_1 while $Z(\theta_1, s_{11})$ will represent the rotation from the revolute pair and $Z(\theta_{11}, s_1)$ will represent the sliding from the prismatic pair.

Another advantage of the Denavit–Hartenberg methodology resides in the manner in which the inverse matrices of $Z(\theta, s)$ and $X(\alpha, a)$ are calculated, specifically by the plain change in the signs of the arguments. For instance, relation (18) can be written as

$$X_2 = (Z(\theta_1, s_1) X(\alpha_{12}, a_{12}))^{-1} X_1 = X(-\alpha_{12}, -a_{12}) Z(-\theta_1, s_1) X_1. \qquad (20)$$

Apparently restrictive, due to the hypothesis requiring only cylindrical pairs in the structure of the kinematic chain (the D–H mechanism condition), the methodology can be applied to any kinematic chain after all the pairs, other than the cylindrical ones, which were structurally equivalated by successions of cylindrical pairs.

For the mechanism with the structural scheme presented in Figure 2, which is a non-D–H mechanism due to the incidence of the planar pair P, the method becomes appropriate after the planar pair P is equivalated by two prismatic pairs on different directions and a revolute pair with the normal direction for both of these directions. Thus, a kinematic chain consisting of 7 elements and 7 kinematic pairs of class 5 is obtained. The drawback of this equivalation is the fact that the matrix closure equations have a large number of factors (in the present case, this equation contains 7 factors of 7a type, so a product of 14 matrices) that lead to systems of cumbersome trigonometrical equations. These systems can rarely be solved analytically, only for particular situations, and in most of cases, they require numerical procedures for solving. Furthermore, the system of equations has multiple solutions, corresponding to all possible assembling positions of the kinematic chain, and a methodology for selecting the suitable assembling solutions is necessary. According to the mentioned problems, for the mechanism equivalent to the mechanism seen in Figure 2, a trigonometric system of six equations with six unknowns will be obtained, whose analytical solving is expected to be difficult or rather impossible.

2.2.2. Kinematic Analysis of the Proposed Mechanism

In order to avoid the issues related to these cumbersome systems of equations resulting from equivalations, the approach of the actual mechanism and the direct application of the conditions of definition of the planar pair are proposed. The planar pair can be realized in several modes. In the present case, the planar pair between elements 3 and 4 will exist when three non-colinear points from element 3 will also appertain to a plane attached to element 4. In Figure 3, the planar pair is made between the plane $(x_3 y_3)$ and the plane $(x_4 z_4)$ from element 4. The normal to the plane parallel to the axes y_3 and y_4 is denoted n_4 and the equation of the plane is

$$n_4 \cdot (r - r_O) = 0 \qquad (21)$$

where r is the position vector of a current point from the plane $(x_3 z_3)$ and r_0 is the position vector of a reference point from the same plane. A point from the plane $x_3 y_3$ belongs to the plane of Equation (8) if its coordinates verify Equation (8). For this purpose, the coordinates of a point belonging to element 3 are first brought in system 4, and after that, relation (8) is applied. The preferential selection of the orientation of the axes of the coordinate systems from Figure 3 simplifies the conditions of existence of the planar pair.

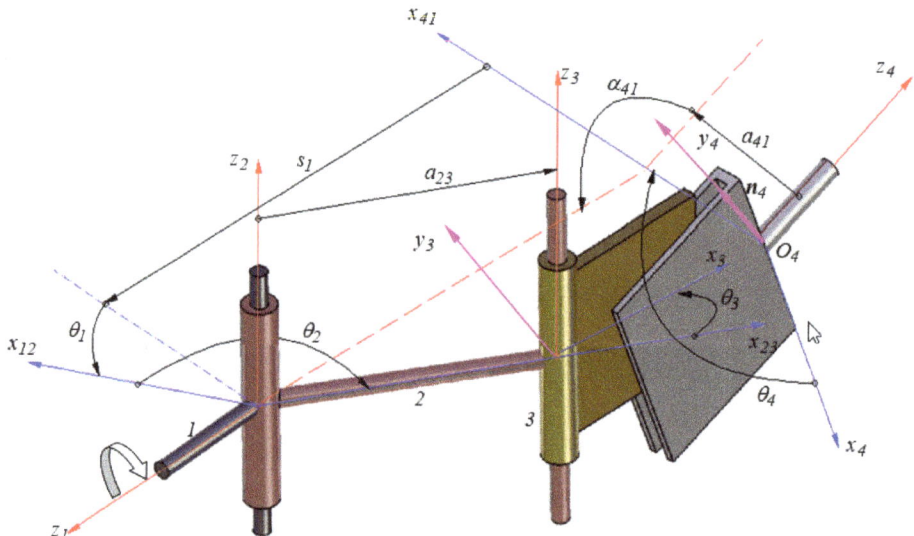

Figure 3. Kinematic and constructive parameters of the coupling mechanism.

From Figure 3, it can be observed that a point from the plane $x_3 z_3$ will belong to the plane $x_4 z_4$ if, after the coordinate transformation, the following condition is satisfied:

$$y_4 = 0. \qquad (22)$$

It is noticed that, instead of a system of six equations, a system of three equations is obtained, from imposing the condition that Equation (21) (or Equation (22)) is satisfied by three distinct points. In order to obtain the transformation relation, the matrix describing the displacement of frame 3 is necessary. This cannot be obtained directly; a succession of D–H transformations must be applied in the following order: $4 \to 1 \to 2 \to 3$. Specifically,

$$T_{43} = Z(\theta_4, s_4) X(\alpha_{41}, a_{41}) Z(\theta_1, s_1) X(\alpha_{12}, a_{12}) Z(\theta_2, s_2) X(\alpha_{23}, a_{23}) Z(\theta_3, s_3). \qquad (23)$$

2.2.3. Finding the Motions from the Revolute Pairs

Concerning the rotation motions from the pairs, the rotation from the driving pair θ_1 is known, while θ_2, θ_3, and θ_4 are unknown. Except for the angles ($\theta_k, k = 1, 4$), all the other parameters from Equation (23) are constant, and some of them are zero:

$$s_2 = s_3 = s_4 = 0;\ a_{12} = 0;\ \alpha_{01} = -\frac{\pi}{2},\ \alpha_{12} = \frac{\pi}{2},\ \alpha_{23} = 0. \tag{24}$$

The form of the equations of the system representing the condition of the planar pair can be simplified by choosing the three points in particular positions: the origin of the system 3: $M_1(0,0,0)$; a point form the axis Ox_3: $M_2(x_3,0,0)$; and a point from the axis Oz_3: $M_3(0,0,z_3)$. The relation of coordinate transformation of a point is applied for transition from system 3 to system 4:

$$\begin{bmatrix} x_4 \\ y_4 \\ z_4 \\ 1 \end{bmatrix} = T_{43} \begin{bmatrix} x_3 \\ y_3 \\ z_3 \\ 1 \end{bmatrix} \tag{25}$$

and for the points $M_1, M_2,$ and M_3, the ordinate y_4 in frame 4 must be zero; thus, the following system of equations is obtained, using Mathcad software [78]:

$$\begin{cases} a_{23}\cos\theta_1\cos\theta_2\sin\theta_4 + a_{23}\cos\alpha_{41}\sin\theta_1\cos\theta_2\cos\theta_4 - a_{23}\sin\alpha_{41}\sin\theta_2\cos\theta_4 - s_1\sin\alpha_{41}\cos\theta_4 + a_{41}\sin\theta_4 = 0 \\ x_3\cos\theta_1\cos\theta_2\cos\theta_3\cos\theta_4 + a_{23}\cos\theta_1\cos\theta_2\sin\theta_4 + x_3\cos\alpha_{41}\sin\theta_1\cos\theta_2\cos\theta_3\cos\theta_4 \ldots \\ +a_{23}\sin\theta_1\cos\alpha_{41}\cos\theta_2\cos\theta_4 - x_3\sin\alpha_{41}\sin\theta_2\cos\theta_3\cos\theta_4 - a_{23}\cos\theta_4\sin\alpha_{41}\sin\theta_2 \ldots \\ -x_3\cos\theta_1\sin\theta_2\sin\theta_3\sin\theta_4 - x_3\cos\alpha_{41}\sin\theta_1\sin\theta_2\sin\theta_3\cos\theta_4 - x_3\sin\alpha_{41}\cos\theta_2\sin\theta_3\cos\theta_4 \ldots \\ -s_1\sin\alpha_{41}\cos\theta_4 + a_{41}\sin\theta_4 = 0 \\ a_{23}\cos\theta_1\cos\theta_2\sin\theta_4 + a_{23}\cos\alpha_{41}\sin\theta_1\cos\theta_2\cos\theta_4 - a_{23}\sin\alpha_{41}\sin\theta_2\cos\theta_4 .. \\ +z_3\sin\theta_1\sin\theta_4 - z_3\cos\alpha_{41}\cos\theta_1\cos\theta_4 - s_1\sin\alpha_{41}\cos\theta_4 + a_{41}\sin\theta_4 = 0. \end{cases} \tag{26}$$

System (26) takes a simpler form if the first equation is subtracted from the last two equations:

$$\begin{cases} a_{23}\cos\theta_1\cos\theta_2\sin\theta_4 + a_{23}\cos\alpha_{41}\sin\theta_1\cos\theta_2\cos\theta_4 - a_{23}\sin\alpha_{41}\sin\theta_2\cos\theta_4 - s_1\sin\alpha_{41}\cos\theta_4 + a_{41}\sin\theta_4 = 0 \\ \cos\theta_1\cos\theta_2\cos\theta_3\sin\theta_4 + \cos\alpha_{41}\sin\theta_1\cos\theta_2\cos\theta_3\cos\theta_4 - \sin\alpha_{41}\sin\theta_2\cos\theta_3\cos\theta_4 \ldots \\ -\cos\theta_1\sin\theta_2\sin\theta_3\sin\theta_4 - \cos\alpha_{41}\sin\theta_1\sin\theta_2\sin\theta_3\cos\theta_4 - \sin\alpha_{41}\cos\theta_2\sin\theta_3\cos\theta_4 = 0 \\ \sin\theta_1\sin\theta_4 - \cos\alpha_{41}\cos\theta_1\cos\theta_4 = 0. \end{cases} \tag{27}$$

The Equation (27) now have the following significance: the first equation imposes that the origin O_3 of the frame $x_3y_3z_3$ is positioned in the plane $y_4 = 0$ while the last two equations impose that the vectors M_1M_2 and M_1M_3 are parallel to the plane x_4z_4. The system (27) can be solved analytically:

$$\theta_4 = \operatorname{atan} \frac{\cos\alpha_{41}\cos\theta_1}{\sin\theta_1} + k\pi, k \in Z. \tag{28}$$

From a physical perspective, relation (28) does not have multiple solutions because the term $k\pi$ does not alter the orientation of the plane of symmetry of the driven element but, at most, reverses the orientation of the normal n_4. Relation (28) can be re-written as follows:

$$\tan\theta_4 = \frac{\cos\alpha_{41}}{\tan\theta_1} \tag{29}$$

and it is identical to the relation between the position parameters of the driven and driving elements of the Cardan transmission [1]. Relation (29) highlights the fact that the transmission ratio of the mechanism depends only on the constructive parameter α_{41}, and the remaining constructive parameters of the mechanism must not satisfy special precision conditions. With a known θ_4 angle, from the first equation of the system (27), the angle θ_2 can be obtained, since the coefficients $A(\theta_1), B(\theta_1), C(\theta_1)$ are now known; thus,

$$\theta_2 = 2atan\frac{B(\theta_1) \pm \sqrt{B(\theta_1)^2 + A(\theta_1)^2 - C(\theta_1)^2}}{A(\theta_1) - C(\theta_1)} + k\pi, k \in \mathbf{Z} \quad (30)$$

where

$$\begin{aligned}A(\theta_1) &= a_{23}[cos\alpha_{41}sin\theta_1 cos\theta_4 + sin\theta_4\, cos\theta_1];\\ B(\theta_1) &= -a_{23}sin\alpha_{41}cos\theta_4;\\ C(\theta_1) &= a_{41}sin\theta_4 - s_1 sin\alpha_{41}cos\theta_4.\end{aligned} \quad (31)$$

Equation (30) shows that, this time, from a physical point of view, for a stipulated position of the θ_1 angle of the driving element, there are two different assembling solutions for element 2.

The second Equation (27) makes it possible to find the rotation angle θ_3 with the following relation:

$$\theta_3(\theta_1) = atan[P(\theta_1)/Q(\theta_1)] + k\pi \quad (32)$$

where

$$\begin{aligned}P(\theta_1) &= cos\theta_1 cos\theta_2 sin\theta_4 + cos\alpha_{41}sin\theta_1 cos\theta_2 cos\theta_4 - sin\alpha_{41}sin\theta_2 cos\theta_4;\\ Q(\theta_1) &= cos\theta_1 sin\theta_2 sin\theta_4 + cos\alpha_{41}sin\theta_1 sin\theta_2 cos\theta_4 + sin\alpha_{41}cos\theta_2 cos\theta_4.\end{aligned} \quad (33)$$

Relation (33) shows that, similar to element 3, a unique assembly solution exists. As a conclusion, for a given position of the driving element, only two different assembling positions of the mechanism exist, presented in Figure 4, with the remark that the plane faces of part 3 from the two variants must be coplanar. The mechanism was modelled in CATIA.

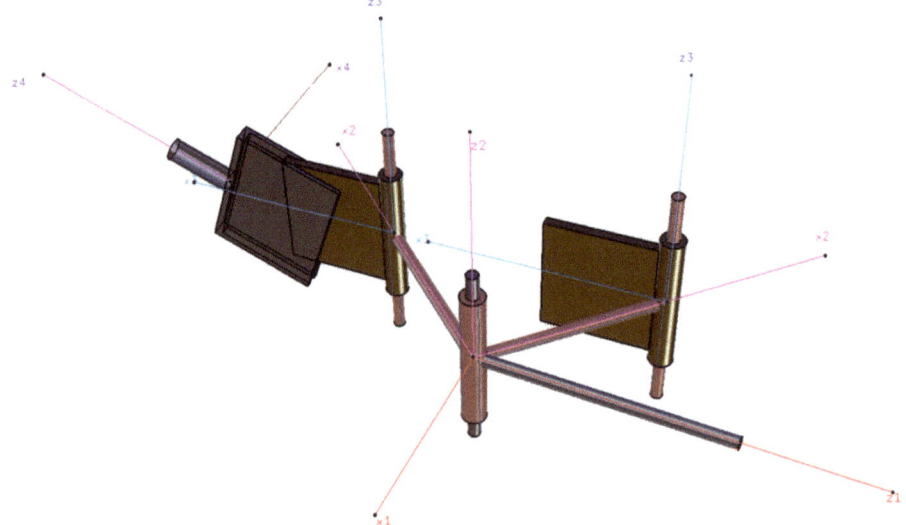

Figure 4. The two alternatives of mechanism assembly.

The variations in the angles θ_4, θ_2, and θ_3 as functions of the position angle of the driving element are presented in Figure 5, and it is noticed that the plot of the θ_4 angle presents jumps which are not actual, caused by the multiform character of the function $atan(x)$ from relation (28). In these jump-points, as seen in Figure 5b,c, the mechanism passes from an assembling position to another, which is in fact impossible. To overcome this aspect, the θ_4 angle is redefined to eliminate the discontinuities. Ensuring a continuous variation of the θ_4 angle is reflected to the variation of the other two angles θ_2 and θ_3, which will also not present discontinuities any more, as seen in Figure 6.

$$\theta_4 = \int_0^{\theta_1} \frac{d\theta_4(\theta_1)}{d\theta_1} d\theta_1 \quad (34)$$

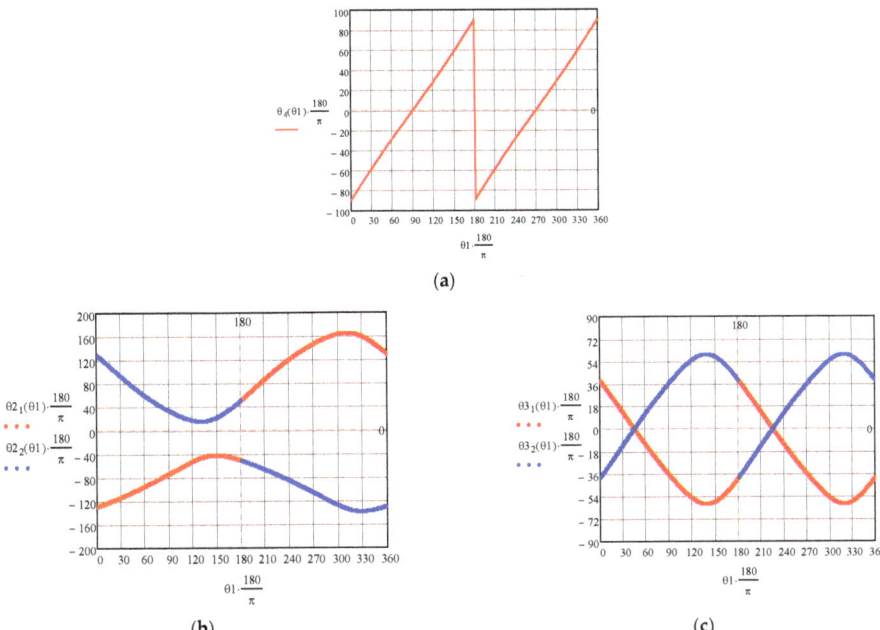

Figure 5. The angles from the revolute pairs of the mechanism: (**a**) variation in angle θ_4, relation (28); (**b**) variation in angle $\theta2_1$ and $\theta2_2$ corresponding to the two asssembly options; (**c**) variation in angle $\theta3_1$ and $\theta3_2$ corresponding to the two asssembly options.

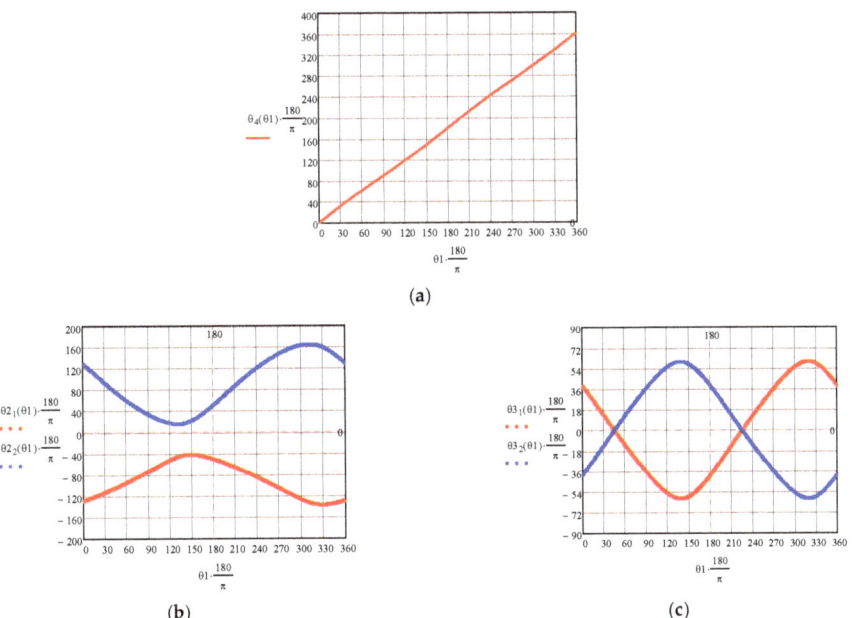

Figure 6. The rotation angles from the joints of the mechanism: (**a**) plot of angle θ_4, relation (34); (**b**) variation in θ_2 angle for the two assembly options, $\theta2_1$ and $\theta2_2$; (**c**) variation in the θ_3 angle for the two assembly options, $\theta3_1$ and $\theta3_2$.

Interesting consequences result from the analysis of the angular velocity variations, represented by the curves in Figures 7 and 8. In Figure 7 is presented the variation in the angular velocity of the driven element $\frac{\dot{\theta}_4}{\dot{\theta}_1}$ obtained by the derivative of relation (29) with respect to time, both analytically and by modelling the mechanism in a specialised software. The two plots are similar and this fact confirms the correctness of relation (32). Additionally, the transmission ratio of the mechanism is the same as the one of a Cardan coupling having the same angle between axes, with the mention that the present coupling can transmit motion between crossed axes.

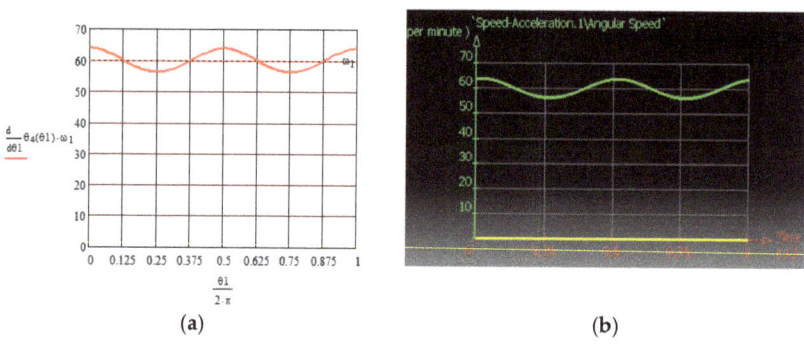

Figure 7. Variation in the transmission ratio: (**a**) analytical result; (**b**) numerical simulation.

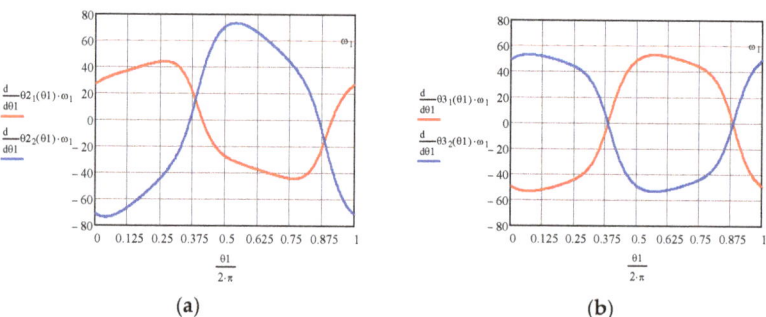

Figure 8. The angular velocities from the intermediate revolute pairs: (**a**) variation in ω_2 ($\theta 2_1$ and $\theta 2_2$ assembling options); (**b**) variation in ω_3 ($\theta 3_1$ and $\theta 3_2$ assembling options).

Regarding the motions from the other two revolute joints, when the two assembling solutions of the transmission are considered, the motions from pair 3 are identical but of opposite sign, but the motions from pair R_2 are completely different. This fact allows for selecting, from the two positions, the assembly variant for which the motion from pair R_2 leads to minimal dynamic effects, this choice not affecting the quality of transmission.

The magnitude of the rotational speed of the driving element is not relevant because the study of the mechanism was performed only through a kinematics point of view. The variations in all positional parameters from the kinematic pairs are proportional to this input driving rotational speed.

2.2.4. Finding the Motion from the Planar Pair

The planar pair is a c_3 joint (Class 3), so between the two elements forming the joint, there are $6 - c_k = 3$ degrees of freedom, which permit for two translations in the plane of the pair and a rotation performed around an axis normal to the plane of the planar pair. The motion from the planar pair is fully characterized if the motion of a point from an element with respect to the other element and the variation in the angle between two straight lines from the contact plane, each line belonging to an element of the pair, are known. All these parameters should be stipulated as functions of the angle θ_1 of the driving element and of the constructive parameters of the mechanism. A point of coordinates $M(x_3, 0, z_3)$ from element 3 is considered, which describes in the coordinate system 4 a trajectory defined by the parametric equations:

$$\begin{bmatrix} x_4 \\ 0 \\ z_4 \\ 1 \end{bmatrix} = T_{43} \begin{bmatrix} x_3 \\ 0 \\ z_3 \\ 1 \end{bmatrix} \quad (35)$$

Relation (35) is developed; therefore, the parametric equations of the trajectory of a point from the plane x_3z_3 in the plane x_4z_4 are obtained:

$$\begin{cases} x_4(\theta_1, x_3, z_3) = x_3[\cos\theta_1\cos\theta_2\cos\theta_3\cos\theta_4 - \cos\alpha_{41}\sin\theta_1\cos\theta_2\cos\theta_3\sin\theta_4 + \sin\alpha_{41}\sin\theta_2\cos\theta_3\sin\theta_4... \\ +\cos\alpha_{41}\sin\theta_1\sin\theta_2\sin\theta_3\sin\theta_4 - \cos\theta_1\sin\theta_2\sin\theta_3\cos\theta_4 + \sin\theta_3\sin\theta_4\sin\alpha_{41}\cos\theta_2]... \\ +z_3[\sin\theta_1\cos\theta_4 + \cos\alpha_{41}\cos\theta_1\sin\theta_4] + s_1\sin\alpha_{41}\sin\theta_4 + a_{41}\cos\theta_4... \\ +a_{23}[\sin\alpha_{41}\sin\theta_2\sin\theta_4 + \cos\theta_1\cos\theta_2\cos\theta_4 - \cos\alpha_{41}\sin\theta_1\cos\theta_2\sin\theta_4] \\ z_4(\theta_1, x_3, z_3) = x_3[\sin\alpha_{41}\sin\theta_1\cos\theta_2\cos\theta_3 + \cos\alpha_{41}\sin\theta_2\cos\theta_3 - \sin\theta_3\sin\alpha_{41}\sin\theta_1\sin\theta_2 + \sin\theta_3\cos\alpha_{41}\cos\theta_2]... \\ -z_3\sin\alpha_{41}\cos\theta_1 + a_{23}[\sin\alpha_{41}\sin\theta_1\cos\theta_2 + \cos\alpha_{41}\sin\theta_2] + s_1\cos\alpha_{41}. \end{cases} \quad (36)$$

In Figure 9, the trajectory of the origin of the system $O_3x_3y_3z_3$ in the plane x_4z_4 attached to element 4 is plotted, as in the particular case $x_3 = 0; z_3 = 0$ in relation (36).

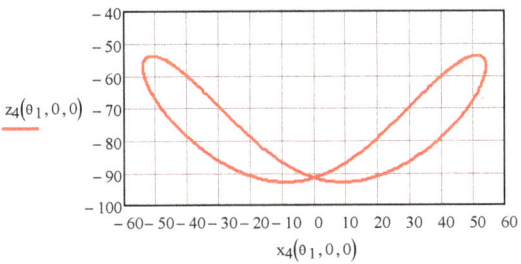

Figure 9. The trajectory of the origin of the system $O_3x_3y_3z_3$.

To find the rotation motion from the pair, it is sufficient to specify the variation in time of the angle between two straight lines belonging to the planes that form the planar pair. Aiming at this, the angle made by the versors i_3 and i_4 is found, considering that versor i_3 is defined by two points from the quadro-dimensional space by $\begin{bmatrix} 1 & 0 & 0 & 1 \end{bmatrix}^T$ and $\begin{bmatrix} 0 & 0 & 0 & 1 \end{bmatrix}^T$ and the projections of versor i_3 on the axes of the coordinate system 4 are given by the following relation:

$$\begin{bmatrix} i_3 \cdot i_4 \\ i_3 \cdot j_4 \\ i_3 \cdot k_4 \\ 0 \end{bmatrix} = T_{43} \left\{ \begin{bmatrix} 1 \\ 0 \\ 0 \\ 1 \end{bmatrix} - \begin{bmatrix} 0 \\ 0 \\ 0 \\ 1 \end{bmatrix} \right\}. \quad (37)$$

After the calculus is made, it results that

$$\begin{cases} i_3 \cdot i_4 = \cos\theta_{34}(\theta_1) = \cos\theta_1\cos\theta_2\cos\theta_3\cos\theta_4 - \cos\alpha_{41}\sin\theta_1\cos\theta_2\cos\theta_3\sin\theta_4... \\ +\sin\alpha_{41}\sin\theta_2\cos\theta_3\sin\theta_4... \\ -\cos\theta_1\sin\theta_2\sin\theta_3\cos\theta_4 + \cos\alpha_{41}\sin\theta_1\sin\theta_2\sin\theta_3\sin\theta_4 + \sin\alpha_{41}\cos\theta_2\sin\theta_3\sin\theta_4 \\ i_3 \cdot j_4 = 0 \\ i_3 \cdot k_4 = \sin\theta_{34}(\theta_1) = \sin\alpha_{41}\sin\theta_1\cos\theta_2\cos\theta_3 + \cos\alpha_{41}\sin\theta_2\cos\theta_3... \\ -\sin\alpha_{41}\sin\theta_1\sin\theta_2\sin\theta_3 + \cos\alpha_{41}\cos\theta_2\sin\theta_3. \end{cases} \quad (38)$$

Relation (38) allow for finding the rotation angle $\theta_{34}(\theta_1)$ from the higher pair. It should be mentioned that, since the motion of the mechanism is periodic, with the angular period 2π, an inverse trigonometrical function of two arguments is recommended to be used. With a known angle of rotation, the angular velocity is obtained with the following relation:

$$\omega_{43} = \omega_1 \frac{d}{d\theta_1}\left[\frac{atan(sin\alpha_{43})}{cos\alpha_{43}}\right]. \tag{39}$$

One must emphasize that, while the angular velocities ω_{34} and ω_{43} are identical but of opposite sign, it results from the definition of the two angles θ_{34} and θ_{43} that the relative motions of the origins O_3 and O_4 in the contact plane of the planar pair differ. To sustain this, based on relation (35), one can write the relation of transformation of the coordinates of a point from the plane x_4z_4 to the plane x_3z_3:

$$\begin{bmatrix} x_3 \\ 0 \\ z_3 \\ 1 \end{bmatrix} = T_{43}^{-1} \begin{bmatrix} x_4 \\ 0 \\ z_4 \\ 1 \end{bmatrix} \tag{40}$$

where the calculus of the homogenous operator T_{43}^{-1} is made simply, applying relation (35); which results in

$$\begin{cases} x_3(\theta_1, x_4, z_4) = x_4[cos\theta_1 cos\theta_2 cos\theta_3 cos\theta_4 - cos\theta_1 sin\theta_2 sin\theta_3 cos\theta_4 - cos\alpha_{41} sin\theta_1 cos\theta_2 cos\theta_3 sin\theta_4... \\ +cos\theta_{41} sin\theta_1 sin\theta_2 sin\theta_3 sin\theta_4 + sin\alpha_{41} sin\theta_2 cos\theta_3 sin\theta_4 + sin\alpha_{41} cos\theta_2 sin\theta_3 sin\theta_4]... \\ +z_4[sin\alpha_{41} sin\theta_1 cos\theta_2 cos\theta_3 + cos\alpha_{41} sin\theta_2 cos\theta_3 - sin\alpha_{41} sin\theta_1 sin\theta_2 sin\theta_3 + cos\alpha_{41} cos\theta_2 sin\theta_3]... \\ -s_1[cos\theta_3 sin\theta_2 + sin\theta_3 cos\theta_2] - a_{23} cos\theta_3 \\ z_3(\theta_1, x_4, z_4) = x_4[cos\theta_4 sin\theta_1 + cos\alpha_{41} cos\theta_1 sin\theta_4] - z_4 sin\alpha_{41} cos\theta_1 - a_{41} sin\theta_1. \end{cases} \tag{41}$$

Two main conclusions can be drawn:

- The angular velocity ω_4 has a constant sign and presents a periodic variation, which attests to the fact that, in the final pair, the motion is rotatory (Figure 7).
- In the other internal pairs of the mechanism, the angular velocities ω_2, ω_3 (Figure 8a,b), and ω_{34} (Figure 10b) present periodic changes in sign in a bounded domain, showing that, in the inner revolute pairs and in the planar pair, oscillatory motions happen.

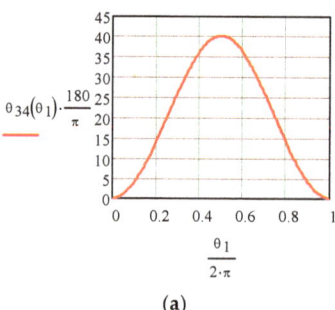
(a)

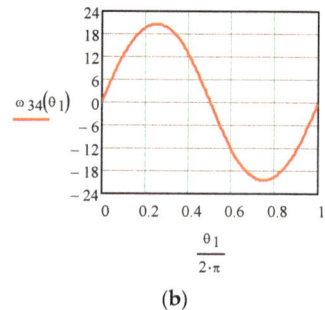
(b)

Figure 10. The variation in the rotation motion from the planar pair: (**a**) rotation angle; (**b**) angular velocity.

In the obtained relations (41), the particular case $x_4 = 0$, $z_4 = 0$ gives the trajectory of the origin O_4 in the plane x_3z_3, which is represented in Figure 11a. The simulation software was applied to obtain the same curve, presented in Figure 11b, and an excellent concordance between the two curves is remarked.

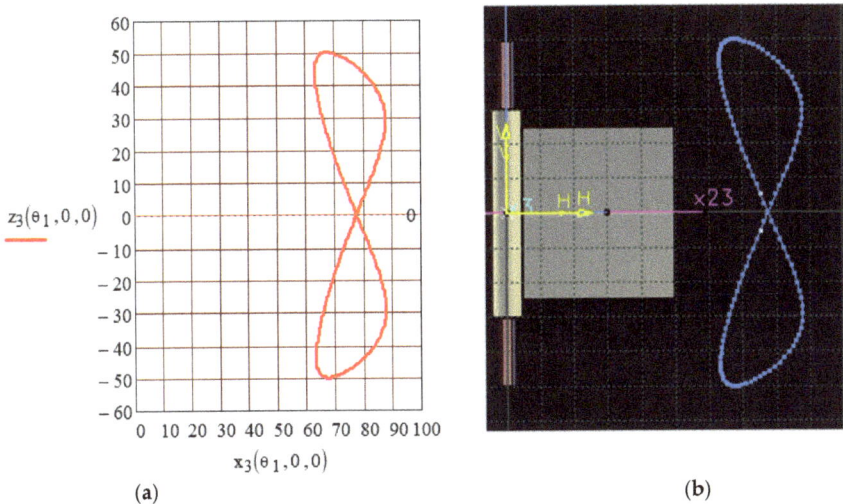

Figure 11. The trajectory of the origin O_4 of the coordinate frame fixed to the final element with respect to the plane x_3z_3: (**a**) analytical curve; (**b**) simulation curve.

The quantitative comparison between the two trajectories can be made when Cartesian coordinate wireframes, spaced at 10 mm, are attached to each plot.

3. Results and Discussions

A laboratory device was designed and constructed for the study of the RPRRR transmission and for future dynamic studies. The design was accomplished using the CATIA Dassault software. The designed constructive solution and the laboratory device are presented in Figure 12.

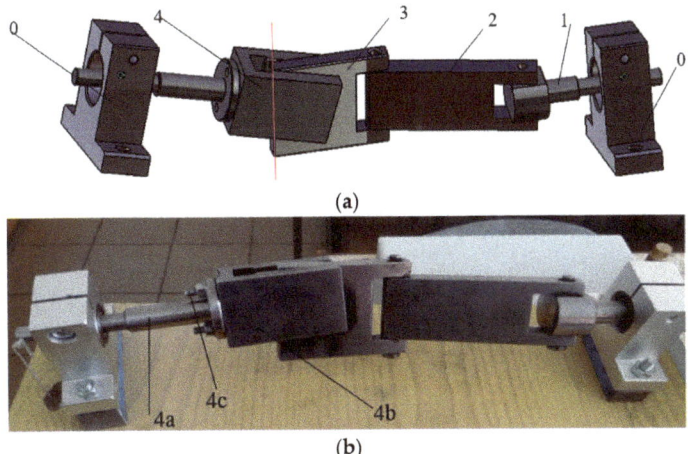

Figure 12. The designed RPRRR transmission: (**a**) CAD model: ground 0, driving element 1, intermediate elements 2 and 3, driven element 4; (**b**) laboratory device: output shaft 4a, part with channel 4b, assembly screw 4c.

From the designing point of view, there are two important aspects:

Avoiding the mechanical interference between the elements of the mechanism. The risk that the edge Δ_3 of element 3 touches the bottom of the rectangular channel from element 4 is shown in Figure 13. It is required for the bottom of the channel to be placed outside the envelope of segment Δ_3. Concerning the interference of element 4 upon element 3, it cannot happen due to the constructive shape of element 3 that has a constant thickness; therefore, segment Δ_4 attached to element 4 never interferes with any of the points of element 3. But there is the possibility that segment Δ_4 interferes with the plane surface Σ_2 of element 2. To avoid this interference, it is necessary that segment Δ_4 and the straight line Δ_{23} (resulting from the intersection of the surfaces Σ_3 and Σ_2) do not intersect. This straight line is mobile in space. To avoid the interference between element 4 and element 2, the envelope of segment Δ_4 must always be placed on the left side of segment Δ_{23}, represented in Figure 13. From the presented considerations, it results that, for an accurate design of the mechanism, the envelopes of the segments Δ_3 and Δ_4 described with respect to element 4 and 3, respectively, must be found. These can be obtained by applying relations (36) and (40), because the parameters x_3, z_3, x_4, and z_4, respectively, must be chosen in a manner that the points of coordinates (x_3, y_3) and (x_4, y_4) are placed on the segments Δ_3 and Δ_4 respectively. The illustration of the procedure is shown in Figures 14 and 15.

In Figure 14a is presented the envelope of segment Δ_3 obtained with relation (36) and the envelope of segment Δ_4 based on relation (39) is shown in Figure 15a. The same envelopes were obtained by CAD simulation using the DMU-Kinematics CATIA module. In Figures 14b and 15b were also represented the elements 4 and 3, respectively, which can take part in the interference phenomenon. From these plots, it results that the mechanism is correctly designed from the point of view of avoiding interference.

Another occurring problem consists in limiting the stresses and strains from the elements of the mechanisms. Next, the elements forming the planar pair are under special attention. From Figure 12, it can be seen that, for technological reasons, element 4 was made from two parts: the shaft 4a and the prismatic part 4b, assembled by two screws. These screws also have a safety character, as torque limiters. The coupling should not transmit a torsion moment greater than M_{tmax}; the diameter d of the screws was chosen as they are the first parts to break, protecting the parts with higher production costs.

$$M_{tmax} = \tau_f n \frac{\pi d_{int}^2}{4} \frac{D}{2} \qquad (42)$$

where τ_f is the admissible shear stress of the material of the screws, n is the number of screws (here $n = 2$), d_{int} is the inner diameter of the thread, and D is the diameter needed for mounting the screws. Relation (25) is used for dimensioning the diameter of the assembling screws.

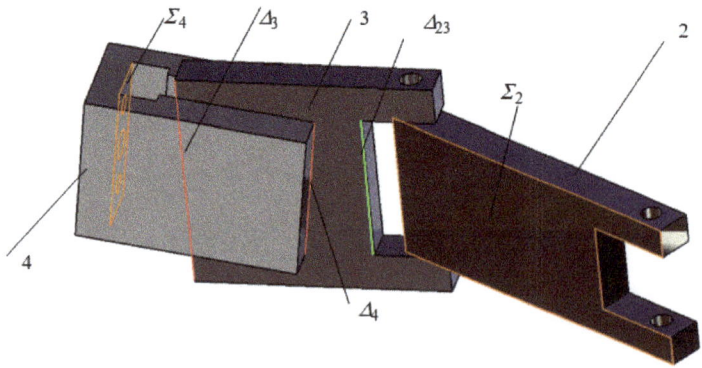

Figure 13. Possible mechanical interferences in the proposed mechanism.

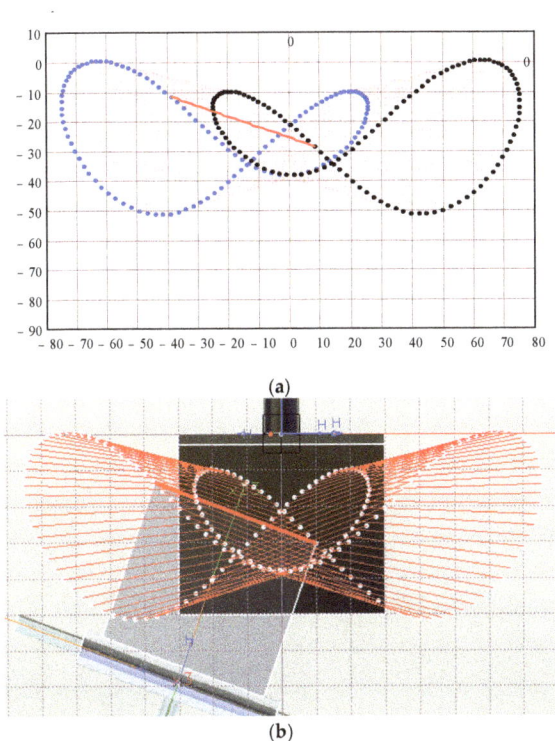

Figure 14. The envelope of the position of a segment of element 3 in the contact plane of the planar pair: (**a**) Mathcad result; (**b**) CAD simulation.

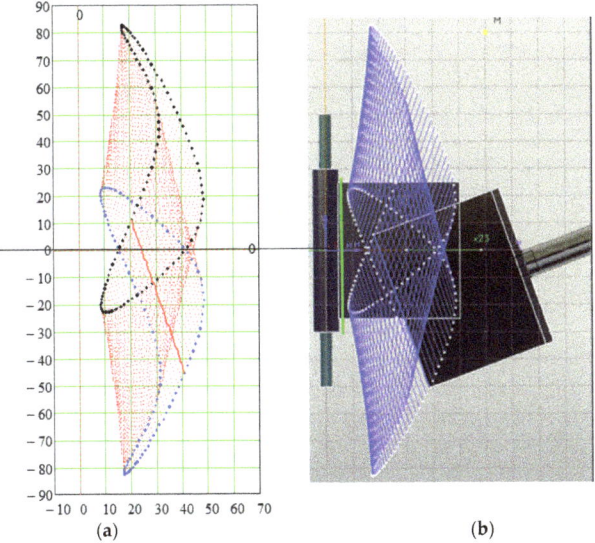

Figure 15. The envelope of the position of a segment of element 4 in the contact plane of the planar pair: (**a**) Mathcad result; (**b**) CAD simulation.

The assembly of the parts creating the planar pair is considered next. The finite element module from CATIA software was used to find the stresses and the displacements from the two parts when a moment of torsion is transmitted. As support schematics, part 3 was considered clamped on cylindrical surfaces Σ_3 that create the revolute pairs and the torque is applied by means of the cylindrical surface Σ_{4b} that assembles the parts 4a and 4b. To exemplify the design, it was considered that element 4b is loaded by a torque $M_t = 100$ Nm. The calculus was made for the linear elastic domain and the value of the torque was arbitrarily chosen. For another stipulated value of the torque, the stresses and deformations will result by simply applying the proportionality principle. In Figure 16a are presented the loading scheme and the main dimensions of the two parts. The optimized mesh of the two parts, made using the CATIA FEA module, is presented in Figure 16b. It must be mentioned that the software performs the analysis considering the materials in the linear elastic domain. This restriction has the advantage of proportionality between the loads and stresses, on one side, and stresses and deformations on the other side. Therefore, if in a real situation a stress or deformation exceeds the admissible value from the elastic domain, by simply diminishing the load, the stress/deformation can be adjusted to a desired value.

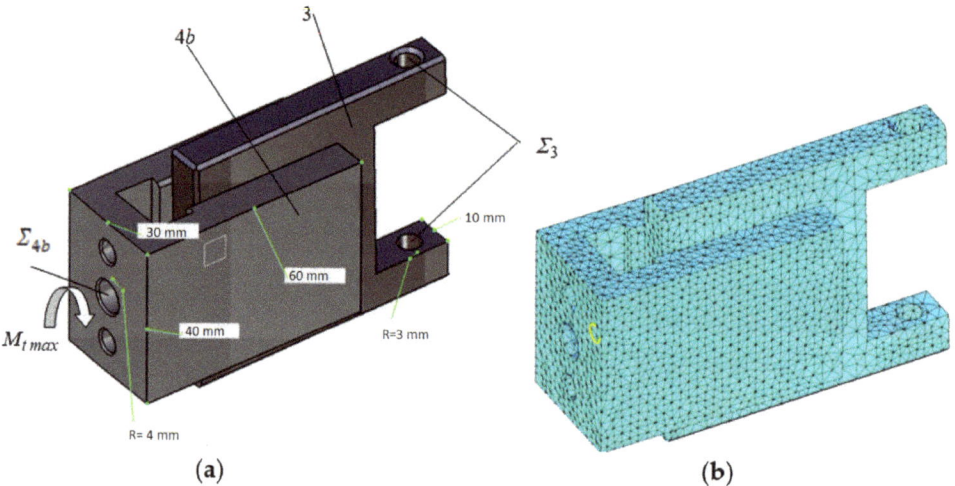

Figure 16. The elements of the planar pair: (**a**) main dimensions and loading scheme; (**b**) FEA mesh obtained in CATIA.

The von Mises equivalent stress distribution from the assembly of the planar pair is presented in Figure 17 and it can be observed that the maximum stress obtained $8.3 \cdot \frac{10^8 N}{mm^2}$ exceeds the yield stress of the steel, $\sigma_{Ysteel} = 2.5 \cdot \frac{10^8 N}{mm^2}$. Therefore, the two parts must be re-designed. For this purpose, the equivalent von Mises stresses from each part are represented separately, as seen in Figure 18. It is remarked that part 3 does not suffer plastic deformations because the yield stress is not reached and the part to be re-designed is element 4b. A similar methodology is applied for deformations. The total deformations of the assembly of the pair are presented in Figure 19, which highlights the total maximum deformation, and in Figure 20 are presented the deformations from each part.

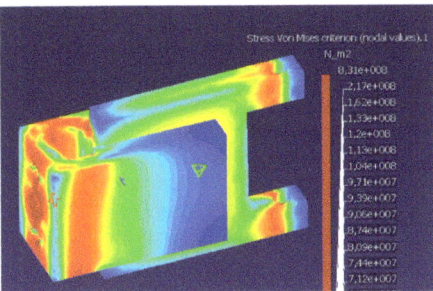

Figure 17. Von Mises stresses in the assembly of the planar pair loaded by M_{tmax}.

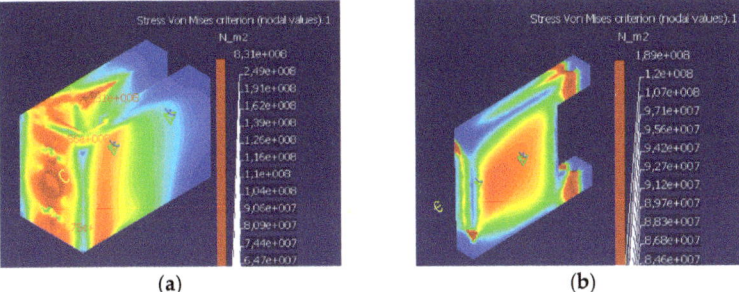

Figure 18. Von Mises stresses in the parts of the planar pair: (**a**) part 4b; (**b**) part 3.

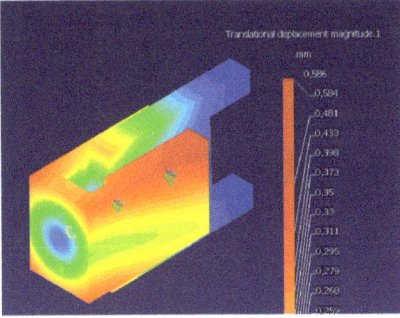

Figure 19. Total deformations in the assembly of planar pair.

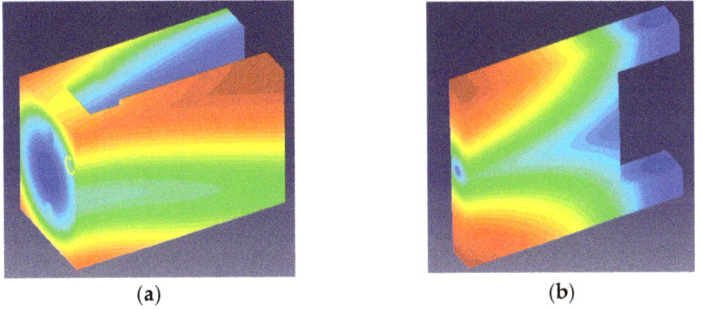

Figure 20. Total deformations in the parts of planar pair (**a**) total deformations of part 4b; (**b**) total deformations of part 3.

4. Conclusions

The present work proposes a solution for the transmission of rotation motion between two shafts with crossed directions. The proposed coupling cannot be replaced by a Cardan coupling since the Cardan transmission is a spherical linkage which can be used only for shafts with intersecting axes. The RPRRR mechanism is suited for the most general case, when the axes of the shafts are crossed (non-intersecting).

Analyzing, by structural considerations, the possibility of transmitting motion between two crossed axes via a kinematic chain consisting of two elements and three kinematic pairs, the conclusion that multiple structural solutions exist is reached.

The condition of high reliability implies dropping the higher pairs, where point or linear contact exists between the elements of the pair. Therefore, the possible remaining structural solutions are either a kinematic chain with two class 4 pairs and a class 5 pair, or a kinematic chain with two class 5 pairs and a class 3 pair (with variants in planar and spherical pairs). For constructive simplicity, the solutions including the planar pair were chosen and, from the two variants, namely structurally symmetric, revolute–planar–revolute (RPR), or asymmetric RRP, the last was chosen. Consequently, the coupling mechanism of the two crossed axes is the RPRRR mechanism which, due to the presence of a planar pair that does not have a rotation axis with a well-stipulated direction, is a non-D–H mechanism.

The Denavit–Hartenberg mechanisms (D–H) have in their structure only cylindrical pairs (with particular variants of revolute, translation or helicoidal) and the kinematic analysis is performed using a well-established methodology which, based on the matrix equation of closure of kinematic chain, makes it possible to find the kinematic parameters characterizing all the kinematic pairs. The methodology is applicable to the non-D–H mechanism, requiring that all non-cylindrical pairs are replaced by kinematic chains containing only cylindrical joints.

The methodology is laborious since the structure of the equivalent mechanism is more complex than the actual one. For this reason, in the present paper, the kinematic analysis of the mechanism uses geometrical conditions to create the planar pair. It results in a system of three scalar equations that makes it possible to find the motions from the revolute pairs of the mechanism based on known driving motion.

Two main conclusions are drawn after solving the system: for a set of constructive data and a stipulated position of the driving element, two different assembling positions exist and a rotation motion exists in the final revolute joint but, in the internal revolute pairs, the motion is oscillatory. The motion from the planar pair is fully described by the position of a point belonging to an element of the pair with respect to the other element and by the angle between two straight lines appertaining to each of the elements. To solve this problem, the relation of coordinate transformation of a point, when the coordinate frames are changed, under the form of homogenous operators, is proposed by Denavit and Hartenberg.

In order to validate the theoretical results, the mechanism was designed and animated using CAD simulation software. The concordance between the analytical and the numerical results provided by the software confirms the correctness of the analytical expressions. The presented coupling mechanism can be used as a general solution for two crossed shafts, with the mention that high torques are envisaged. For instance, equipment working in hard conditions (mining, agriculture, civil engineering, etc.).

The mechanism was also constructed and a noiseless, smooth running was noticed; dynamic aspects and constructive optimization are aimed for further studies.

Two main concerns were considered for the design of the mechanism: avoiding mechanical interference between the elements of the planar pair and estimating the stresses and deformations occurring in the parts of the pair. The first problem was solved using the transformation relations of the coordinates of a point when the system of coordinates is changed. Thus, the envelopes of different edges of an element with respect to another were found. The problem of stresses and deformations estimation was solved using a finite element analysis software. The stresses and deformations from the elements of the planar pair were found for a moment of torsion of stipulated maximum value that should be transmitted by the pair.

The proposed coupling solution, the RPRRR mechanism, presents as main advantages the constructive simplicity, which is reflected in manufacturing low costs and high reliability due to the presence of lower pairs in the structure.

The main objectives of future research are the optimization of constructive parameters of the mechanism in order to obtain a minimum variation in the transmission ratio and finding the theoretical and experimental efficiency of the transmission.

Author Contributions: Conceptualization, S.A. and I.D.; methodology, F.-C.C. and I.-C.R.; software, S.A., I.-C.R. and T.-M.C.; validation, S.A. and T.-M.C.; writing—original draft preparation, S.A. and F.-C.C.; writing—review and editing, M.-C.C. and I.D.; supervision, S.A. and M.-C.C. All authors have read and agreed to the published version of the manuscript.

Funding: This research received no external funding.

Data Availability Statement: Not applicable.

Conflicts of Interest: The authors declare no conflict of interest.

References

1. Uicker, J.J., Jr.; Pennock, G.R.; Shigley, J.E. *Theory of Machines and Mechanisms*, 4th ed.; Oxford University Press: New York, NY, USA, 2010; pp. 368–370.
2. Sclater, N. *Mechanisms and Mechanical Devices Sourcebook*, 5th ed.; McGraw Hill: New York, NY, USA, 2011; pp. 109–110.
3. Tsai, L.-W. *Mechanism Design: Enumeration of Kinematic Structures According to Function*; CRC Press: Boca Raton, FL, USA, 2000; 328p.
4. Phillips, J. *Freedom in Machinery*; Cambridge University Press: Cambridge, UK, 2007; 448p.
5. Schwartz, L. Theorie des distributions et transformation de Fourier. *Ann. Univ. Grenoble-Sect. Sci. Math. Phys.* **1948**, *23*, 7–24.
6. Ata, E.; Kıymaz, O. New generalized Mellin transform and applications to partial and fractional differential equations. *Int. J. Math. Comput. Eng.* **2023**, *1*, 45–66. [CrossRef]
7. Horn, R.A.; Johnson, C.R. *Matrix Analysis*, 2nd ed.; Cambridge University Press: New York, NY, USA, 2012; pp. 43–75.
8. Dilao, R. *Dynamical System and Chaos: An Introduction with Applications*; Springer Nature Switzerland AG: Cham, Switzerland, 2023; pp. 105–132.
9. Lorenzi, M.G.; Francaviglia, M. Art & Mathematics in Antoni Gaudi's architecture: "La Sagrada Família". *J. Appl. Math.* **2010**, *3*, 125–146.
10. Zhu, N.; Tian, J. Numerical simulation of vortex vibration in main girder of cable-stayed bridge based on bidirectional fluid–structure coupling. *Appl. Math. Nonlinear Sci.* **2022**. ahead of print. [CrossRef]
11. Yan, L. Application of renewable energy decorative materials in modern architectural design under low-carbon concept. *Appl. Math. Nonlinear Sci.* **2022**. ahead of print. [CrossRef]
12. Bi, S.; Ye, X.; Shao, Y. Electronic properties of diamond semiconductor materials: Based on response surface model. *Appl. Math. Nonlinear Sci.* **2023**. ahead of print. [CrossRef]
13. Irgens, F. *Rheology and Non-Newtonian Fluids*; Springer: New York, NY, USA, 2013; pp. 143–167.
14. Wang, Y. Numerical Simulation and Characteristic Analysis of Music Based on Nonlinear Equations. *Appl. Math. Nonlinear Sci.* **2023**. ahead of print. [CrossRef]
15. Chi, J.; Alahmadi, D. Badminton players' trajectory under numerical calculation method. *Appl. Math. Nonlinear Sci.* **2022**, *7*, 217–228. [CrossRef]
16. Ball, R.S. *The Theory of Screws; A Study in the Dynamics of Rigid Body*; Hodges, Foster and CO: Dublin, Ireland, 1876; pp. 38–43.
17. Phillips, J. *Freedom in Machinery*; Cambridge University Press: Cambridge, UK, 1984; pp. 45–58.
18. Clifford, W.K. Preliminary Sketch of Bi-quaternions. *Proc. Lond. Math. Soc.* **1873**, *4*, 381–395.
19. Angeles, J. The Application of Dual Algebra to Kinematic Analysis. In *Computational Methods in Mechanical Systems—NATO ASI Series F*; Springer-Verlag Berlin Heidelberg: Berlin, Germany, 1998; Volume 161, pp. 3–32. ISBN 978-3-662-03729-4_1.
20. Hamilton, W.R. On quaternions, or on a new system of imaginaries in algebra. *Phil. Magaz. J. Sci.* **2009**, *25*, 489–495.
21. Yang, A.T. Application of Quaternion Algebra and Dual Numbers to the Analysis of Spatial Mechanisms. Ph.D. Thesis, Columbia University, New York, NY, USA, 1963.
22. Ho, C.Y. Tensor analysis of spatial mechanisms. *IBM J. Res. Dev.* **1966**, *10*, 207–212. [CrossRef]
23. Mangeron, D.; Drăgan, B. Kinematic study with new matrix-tensor methods for four link spatial mechanisms. *Rev. Mech. Appl.* **1962**, *7*, 1539–1551.
24. Baigunchekov, Z.; Laribi, M.A.; Carbone, G.; Mustafa, A.; Amanov, B.; Zholdassov, Y. Structural-Parametric Synthesis of the RoboMech Class Parallel Mechanism with Two Sliders. *Appl. Sci.* **2021**, *11*, 9831. [CrossRef]

25. Barbin, E.; Menghini, M.; Volkert, K. *Descriptive Geometry, The Spread of a Polytechnic Art—The Legacy of Gaspard Monge*; Springer Nature: Cham, Switzerland, 2019; pp. 3–18.
26. Yoshikawa, T. *Foundations of Robotics: Analysis and Control*; MIT Press: Cambridge, MA, USA, 2003; pp. 259–262.
27. Davidson, J.K.; Hunt, K.H. *Robots and Screw Theory: Applications of Kinematics and Statics to Robotics*; Oxford University Press Inc.: New York, NY, USA, 2004; pp. 59–94.
28. Lee, R.S.; Lin, Y.H. Development of universal environment for constructing 5-axis virtual machine tool based on modified D–H notation and OpenGL. *Robot. Comput.-Integr. Manuf.* **2010**, *26*, 253–262. [CrossRef]
29. Tsai, C.Y.; Lin, P.D. The mathematical models of the basic entities of multi-axis serial orthogonal machine tools using a modified Denavit–Hartenberg notation. *Int. J. Adv. Manuf. Technol.* **2009**, *42*, 1016–1024. [CrossRef]
30. Benignus, C.; Buschner, P.; Meier, M.K.; Wilken, F.; Rieger, J.; Beckmann, J. Patient Specific Instruments and Patient Individual Implants—A Narrative Review. *J. Pers. Med.* **2023**, *13*, 426. [CrossRef]
31. Greco, C.; Weerakkody, T.H.; Cichella, V.; Pagnotta, L.; Lamuta, C. Lightweight Bioinspired Exoskeleton for Wrist Rehabilitation Powered by Twisted and Coiled Artificial Muscles. *Robotics* **2023**, *12*, 27. [CrossRef]
32. Lenarčič, J.; Bruno Siciliano, B. *Advances in Robot Kinematics*; Springer: Cham, Switzerland, 2020; pp. 1–6, 98–108. [CrossRef]
33. Doroftei, I.; Cazacu, C.-M.; Alaci, S. Design and Experimental Testing of an Ankle Rehabilitation Robot. *Actuators* **2023**, *12*, 238. [CrossRef]
34. Yang, G.; Zhang, H.; Zhang, L. Study of frictional wear properties of materials for mechanical seals. *Appl. Math. Nonlinear Sci.* **2023**. ahead of print. [CrossRef]
35. Vorro, J.; Bush, T.R.; Rutledge, B.; Li, M. Kinematic measures during a clinical diagnostic technique for human neck disorder: Inter- and intraexaminer comparisons. *BioMed Res. Int.* **2013**, *2013*, 950719. [CrossRef]
36. Yoon, K.; Cho, S.-M.; Kim, K.G. Coupling Effect Suppressed Compact Surgical Robot with 7-Axis Multi-Joint Using Wire-Driven Method. *Mathematics* **2022**, *10*, 1698. [CrossRef]
37. Zhang, J.; Ng, N.; Scott, C.E.H.; Blyth, M.J.G.; Haddad, F.S.; Macpherson, G.J.; Patton, J.T.; Clement, N.D. Robotic arm-assisted versus manual unicompartmental knee arthroplasty. *Bone Jt. J.* **2022**, *104*, 541–548. [CrossRef]
38. Hunt, K.H. *Kinematic Geometry of Mechanisms*; Oxford University Press: Oxford, UK, 1990; pp. 30–51.
39. Angeles, J. *Spatial Kinematic Chains: Analysis–Synthesis–Optimization*; Springer: Berlin/Heidelberg, Germany, 1982; pp. 189–218.
40. McCarthy, J.M.; Soh, G.S. *Geometric Design of Linkages*; Springer: Berlin/Heidelberg, Germany, 2010; pp. 253–279.
41. Yi, L.; Leinonen, T. On the Dimensional Synthesis of Spatial Four-and Five-Bar Linkage, Romansy 14: Theory and Practice of Robots and Manipulators, Proceedings of the Fourteenth CISM-IFToMM Symposium; Bianchi, G., Guinot, J.-C., Rzymkowski, C., Eds.; Springer: Vienna, Austria, 2002; pp. 407–419. [CrossRef]
42. Segreti, A. Mechanism for the Transmission of Rotary Movement between two Shafts having Non-Parallel, Non-Coplanar Axes. U.S. Patent WO 02/103220 A2, 27 December 2002.
43. Seherr-Thoss, H.C.; Schmelz, F.; Aucktor, E. *Universal Joints and Driveshafts. Analysis, Design, Applications*, 2nd ed.; Springer: Berlin/Heidelberg, Germany, 2006; pp. 53–79; discussion 109–245.
44. Gladwel, G.M.L. *Contact Problems in the Classical Theory of Elasticity*; Sijthoff & Noordhoff: Hague, The Netherlands, 1980; p. 716.
45. Hills, D.A.; Nowell, D.; Sackfield, A. *Mechanics of Elastic Contacts*; Elsevier Butterworth-Heinemann: Oxford, UK, 1993; pp. 198–226.
46. Johnson, K.L. *Contact Mechanics*; Cambridge University Press: Cambridge, UK, 1985; pp. 84–106. [CrossRef]
47. Gonzales-Palacios, M.A.; Angeles, J. *Cam Synthesis*; Springer: Dordrecht, The Netherlands, 1993; pp. 37–53.
48. Inurritegui, A.; Larranaga, J.; Arana, A.; Ulacia, U. Load distribution and tooth root stress of highly crowned spherical gear couplings working at high misalignment angles. *J. Mech. Mach. Theory* **2023**, *179*, 105104. [CrossRef]
49. Inurritegui, A.; Larranaga, J.; Arana, A.; Ulacia, U. Numerical-experimental analysis of highly crowned spherical gear couplings working at high misalignment angles. *J. Mech. Mach. Theory* **2023**, *183*, 105260. [CrossRef]
50. Inurritegui, A.; Larranaga, J.; Arana, A.; Ulacia, U. Spherical gear coupling design space analysis for high misalignment applications. *Mech. Mach. Theory* **2022**, *173*, 104837. [CrossRef]
51. Litvin, F.L.; Fuentes, A. *Gear Geometry and Applied Theory*; Cambridge University Press: Cambridge, UK, 2004; pp. 441–474.
52. Vullo, V. *Gears, Volume 1: Geometric and Kinematic Design*; Springer: Cham, Switzerland, 2021; pp. 139–151.
53. Alaci, S.; Muscă, I.; Pentiuc, Ș.-G. Study of the Rolling Friction Coefficient between Dissimilar Materials through the Motion of a Conical Pendulum. *Materials* **2020**, *13*, 5032. [CrossRef] [PubMed]
54. Popov, V.L. *Contact Mechanics and Friction. Physical Principles and Applications*; Springer: Berlin/Heidelberg, Germany, 2010; pp. 55–69.
55. Alaci, S.; Cerlinca, D.A.; Ciornei, F.C.; Filote, C.; Frunza, G. Experimental Highlight of Hysteresis Phenomenon in Rolling Contact. *J. Phys. Conf. Ser.* **2015**, *585*, 012010. [CrossRef]
56. Hayes, M.J.D.; Rotzoll, M.; Bucciol, Q.; Copeland, A.A. Planar and spherical four-bar linkage vi−vj algebraic input–output equations. *J. Mech. Mach. Theory* **2023**, *182*, 105222. [CrossRef]
57. Luzi, L.; Sancisi, N.; Parenti-Castelli, V. The Potential of the 7R-R Closed Loop Mechanism to Transfer Motion Between Two Shafts with Varying Angular Position. In *Interdisciplinary Applications of Kinematics. Mechanisms and Machine Science*; Kecskeméthy, A., Geu Flores, F., Carrera, E., Elias, D., Eds.; Springer: Cham, Switzerland, 2019; Volume 71, pp. 185–195. [CrossRef]
58. Watanabe, K.; Sekine, T.; Nango, J. Kinematic Analysis of RSCR Spatial Four-Link Mechanisms. *Trans. Jpn. Soc. Mech. Eng. Ser. C* **1997**, *63*, 2482–2489. [CrossRef]

59. Urbinati, F.; Pennestrì, E. Kinematic and Dynamic Analyses of the Tripode Joint. *Multibody Syst. Dyn.* **1998**, *2*, 355–367. [CrossRef]
60. Akbil, E.; Lee, T.W. On the motion characteristics of tripode joints. Part 1: General case; Part 2: Applications. *ASME J. Mech. Transm. Autom. Des.* **1984**, *106*, 228–241. [CrossRef]
61. Lobontiu, N.; Hunter, J.; Keefe, J.; Westenskow, J. Tripod mechanisms with novel spatial Cartesian flexible hinges. *J. Mech. Mach. Theory* **2022**, *167*, 104521. [CrossRef]
62. Wang, X.F.; Chang, D.G.; Wang, J.Z. Kinematic investigation of tripod sliding universal joints based on coordinate transformation. *Multibody Syst. Dyn.* **2009**, *22*, 97–113. [CrossRef]
63. Alaci, S.; Ciornei, F.C.; Filote, C. Considerations upon a New Tripod Joint Solution. *Mechanika* **2013**, *19*, 567–574. [CrossRef]
64. Alaci, S.; Pentiuc, R.D.; Ciornei, F.C.; Buium, F.; Rusu, O.T. Kinematics analysis of the swash plate mechanism. *IOP MSE* **2019**, *568*, 012017.
65. Hartenberg, R.; Denavit, J. *Kinematic Synthesis of Linkages*, 1st ed.; McGraw-Hill Inc.: New York, NY, USA, 1964; pp. 343–368.
66. Denavit, J.; Hartenberg, R.S. A kinematic notation for lower-pair mechanisms based on matrices. *J. Appl. Mech.* **1955**, *22*, 215–221. [CrossRef]
67. Alaci, S.; Pentiuc, R.D.; Doroftei, I.; Ciornei, F.C. Use of dual numbers in kinematical analysis of spatial mechanisms. Part II: Applying the method for the generalized Cardan mechanism. *IOP MSE* **2019**, *568*, 12032. [CrossRef]
68. Fischer, I. *Dual-Number Methods in Kinematics, Statics and Dynamics*; CRC Press: New York, NY, USA, 1999; pp. 54–95.
69. McCarthy, J.M. *Introduction in Theoretical Kinematics*, 3rd ed.; MIT Press: Cambridge, MA, USA, 2018; pp. 103–108.
70. Yang, A.T.; Freudenstein, F. Application of Dual-Number Quaternion Algebra to the Analysis of Spatial Mechanisms. *J. Appl. Mech.* **1964**, *31*, 300–308. [CrossRef]
71. Dimentberg, F.M. *The Screw Calculus and Its Applications in Mechanics*; Foreign Technology Division Translation FTD-HT-23-1965; U.S. Department of Commerce: Washington, DC, USA, 1969; pp. 1632–1667.
72. Angeles, J. *Rational Kinematics*; Springer: New York, NY, USA, 1998; pp. 12–34.
73. Cao, A.; Jing, Z.; Ding, H. A general method for kinematics analysis of two-layer and two-loop deployable linkages with coupling chains. *J. Mech. Mach. Theory* **2020**, *152*, 103945. [CrossRef]
74. Molotnikov, V.; Molotnikova, A. Kinematic Analysis of Mechanisms. In *Theoretical and Applied Mechanics*; Springer Nature: Cham, Switzerland, 2023; pp. 299–310. [CrossRef]
75. Roupa, I.; Gonçalves, S.B.; Silva, M.T. Kinematics and dynamics of planar multibody systems with fully Cartesian coordinates and a generic rigid body. *J. Mech. Mach. Theory* **2023**, *180*, 105134. [CrossRef]
76. Uicker, J.J., Jr.; Denavit, J.; Hartenberg, R.S. An Iterative Method for the Displacement Analysis of Spatial Mechanisms. *J. Appl. Mech.* **1964**, *31*, 309–314. [CrossRef]
77. *EN ISO 3952-1*; Kinematic Diagrams—Graphical Symbols. Part 1. The European Standard: Geneva, Switzerland, 2019; pp. 1–25.
78. Maxfield, B. *Engineering with Mathcad*; Butterworth-Heinemann, Elsevier: Oxford, UK, 2006; pp. 287–289.

Disclaimer/Publisher's Note: The statements, opinions and data contained in all publications are solely those of the individual author(s) and contributor(s) and not of MDPI and/or the editor(s). MDPI and/or the editor(s) disclaim responsibility for any injury to people or property resulting from any ideas, methods, instructions or products referred to in the content.

Article

An Exploration and Exploitation-Based Metaheuristic Approach for University Course Timetabling Problems

Rakesh P. Badoni [1], Jayakrushna Sahoo [2], Shwetabh Srivastava [3], Mukesh Mann [4], D. K. Gupta [5], Swati Verma [6], Predrag S. Stanimirović [7,8,*], Lev A. Kazakovtsev [8,9] and Darjan Karabašević [10,*]

1. Department of Mathematics, École Centrale School of Engineering, Mahindra University, Hyderabad 500043, India; rakeshbadoni@gmail.com or rakesh.badoni@mahindrauniversity.edu.in
2. Department of Computer Science & Engineering, Indian Institute of Information Technology Kottayam, Kottayam 686635, India; jsahoo@iiitkottayam.ac.in
3. CMP Degree College, University of Allahabad, Prayagraj 211002, India; shwetabhiit@gmail.com or shwetabh.math@cmpcollege.ac.in
4. Department of Computer Science & Engineering, Indian Institute of Information Technology, Sonepat 131029, India; mukesh.maan@iiitsonepat.ac.in
5. Department of Mathematics, Indian Institute of Technology Kharagpur, Kharagpur 721302, India; dkg@maths.iitkgp.ernet.in
6. CSIR-National Institute of Oceanography, Panaji 403004, India; swati.geo09@gmail.com or vswati@nio.org
7. Faculty of Sciences and Mathematics, University of Niš, 18000 Niš, Serbia
8. Laboratory "Hybrid Methods of Modelling and Optimization in Complex Systems", Siberian Federal University, Prosp. Svobodny 79, 660041 Krasnoyarsk, Russia; levk@bk.ru
9. Institute of Informatics and Telecommunications, Reshetnev Siberian State University of Science and Technology, 31 Krasnoyarskiy Rabochiy Av., 660037 Krasnoyarsk, Russia
10. Faculty of Applied Management, Economics and Finance, University Business Academy in Novi Sad, Jevrejska 24, 11000 Belgrade, Serbia
* Correspondence: pecko@pmf.ni.ac.rs (P.S.S.); darjan.karabasevic@mef.edu.rs (D.K.)

Abstract: The university course timetable problem (UCTP) is known to be NP-hard, with solution complexity growing exponentially with the problem size. This paper introduces an algorithm that effectively tackles UCTPs by employing a combination of exploration and exploitation strategies. The algorithm comprises two main components. Firstly, it utilizes a genetic algorithm (GA) to explore the search space and discover a solution within the global optimum region. Secondly, it enhances the solution by exploiting the region using an iterated local search (ILS) algorithm. The algorithm is tested on two common variants of UCTP: the post-enrollment-based course timetable problem (PE-CTP) and the curriculum-based course timetable problem (CB-CTP). The computational results demonstrate that the proposed algorithm yields competitive outcomes when compared empirically against other existing algorithms. Furthermore, a t-test comparison with state-of-the-art algorithms is conducted. The experimental findings also highlight that the hybrid approach effectively overcomes the limitation of local optima, which is encountered when solely employing GA in conjunction with local search.

Keywords: timetabling; metaheuristics; genetic algorithm; iterated local search; local search; perturbation

MSC: 68W50; 90C59

Citation: Badoni, R.P.; Sahoo, J.; Srivastava, S.; Mann, M.; Gupta, D.K.; Verma, S.; Stanimirović, P.S.; Kazakovtsev, L.A.; Karabašević, D. An Exploration and Exploitation-Based Metaheuristic Approach for University Course Timetabling Problems. *Axioms* **2023**, *12*, 720. https://doi.org/10.3390/axioms12080720

Academic Editor: Hsien-Chung Wu

Received: 6 June 2023
Revised: 16 July 2023
Accepted: 22 July 2023
Published: 25 July 2023

Copyright: © 2023 by the authors. Licensee MDPI, Basel, Switzerland. This article is an open access article distributed under the terms and conditions of the Creative Commons Attribution (CC BY) license (https://creativecommons.org/licenses/by/4.0/).

1. Introduction

Timetabling is an important and challenging area of research with diverse applications in education, enterprises, sports, transportation, human resources planning, and logistics. According to [1], timetabling refers to the allocation of given resources, subject to constraints, to objects placed in space–time, aiming to maximize the number of satisfied desirable objectives. These high-dimensional, multi-objective combinatorial optimization problems have received significant attention from the scientific community because manually generating timetables is laborious and time-consuming, often resulting in ineffective and costly schedules. Therefore, the development of automated timetabling systems is crucial to reducing errors, accelerating the creation process, and maximizing desirable objectives. Among the various forms of timetabling problems, the educational timetabling problem stands out as one of the most extensively studied. Finding a universal and effective solution for this problem is challenging due to its complexity, varying constraints, and evolving requirements.

The *university course timetabling problem* (UCTP) is a multidimensional assignment problem that involves assigning students and teachers to events (or courses), which are then allocated to appropriate timeslots and rooms. The UCTP can be categorized into two categories: post-enrollment-based course timetabling problems (PE-CTPs) and curriculum-based course timetabling problems (CB-CTPs). PE-CTP, sometimes referred to as "event timetabling", focuses on assigning events to timeslots and resources (rooms and students) to avoid conflicts between events, timeslots, and rooms. The timetable is constructed after student enrollment to ensure all students can attend the events they are enrolled in. On the other hand, CB-CTP was first introduced in the Second International Timetabling Competition (ITC2007) [2] and is a weekly assignment problem that involves scheduling a specific number of lectures for various university courses within a given number of time periods and a set of rooms. Each day is divided into a fixed number of timeslots, and a period refers to a combination of a day and a timeslot. The total number of scheduling periods per week is determined by multiplying the number of days per week by the number of timeslots per day. Each course must be scheduled at different periods. Additionally, a set of curricula consists of groups of courses with shared students, and conflicts between courses are resolved based on the curricula rather than student enrollment data.

The main difference between these two variants of the UCTP is that in the PE-CTP, all objectives and constraints are based on the student's enrollment in various course events, whereas in the CB-CTP, all objectives and constraints are associated with the curriculum conception, which is a set of courses that form a complete assignment for a group of students. An illustration of a student's preference in the PE-CTP can be seen in the statement, "A student should have multiple events in a day." Similarly, for the CB-CTP, a teacher's preference can be exemplified by the statement, "A teacher prefers to have no more than two consecutive lectures." These timetabling problems involve two types of constraints: hard and soft. Hard constraints are those that must be satisfied under any circumstances. A timetable is considered feasible if it successfully satisfies all hard constraints. On the other hand, soft constraints are more flexible and can be violated if necessary, but it is desirable to minimize these violations due to associated penalty costs. The lower the total value of the penalty cost, the higher the quality of the timetable. Thus, the main objective is to create a high-quality schedule with minimal penalties for violations of soft constraints.

Educational timetabling has been studied for over 60 years, beginning with Gotlieb [3]. Over the years, many solution approaches have been proposed by researchers. Carter et al. [4] provided an overview of the primary solution approaches for the UCTP and roughly divided them into four categories: constraint-based, sequential, clustered, and metaheuristic methods. In recent years, metaheuristic algorithms have been successfully applied for both variants of the UCTP and are classified into local area-based and population-based approaches. Local area-based algorithms, also called single-point algorithms, focus more on exploitation than exploration [5]. These algorithms work iteratively on a single solution and may not thoroughly explore the entire solution space. Examples of local area-based algorithms include tabu search (TS), iterated local search (ILS), very large neighborhood search (VLNS), and simulated annealing (SA). On the other hand, population-based algorithms, also known as multiple-point algorithms, are good at exploration rather than exploitation [6]. These algorithms maintain multiple solutions within a population and employ a selection process to update the solutions. They extensively search the entire solution space to find a globally optimal solution and are sometimes referred to as global area-based algorithms. Consequently, these algorithms do not focus solely on individuals with good fitness within a population but instead explore the entire solution space to identify potential solutions. However, premature convergence is the main disadvantage of such types of algorithms. Commonly utilized population-based algorithms for timetabling problems include the genetic algorithm (GA), artificial bee colony (ABC), particle swarm optimization (PSO), and ant colony optimization (ACO).

Driven by these discoveries and acknowledging that exploration, carried out through population-based algorithms, and exploitation, executed via local area-based algorithms, are two significant attributes of an optimization algorithm, which complement each other and necessitate fine-tuning between them, we propose a hybrid metaheuristic algorithm named GAILS, for solving PE-CTP and CB-CTP. The algorithm iteratively explores the search space, finds the global optimum region using GA, and then employs ILS to obtain the global optimum solution by exploiting this region. The GA generally fails to reach a global optimum because it repeatedly explores various sub-parts of the search space, leading to a long execution time. Additionally, the GA incorporates a local search (LS) which tends to become trapped in a local optimum quickly. Therefore, when dealing with a large search space, the GA might either fail to converge to a global optimum solution or require a significant amount of time due to the possibility of getting trapped in a local optimum. At this juncture, ILS is used to escape from the local optimum by applying perturbations to the current solution. This allows one to maintain a proper balance between the merits of these algorithms. Consequently, GA emphasizes exploration and diversification, while ILS concentrates on the exploitation and intensification of the search space. Various crossover and mutation operators, as well as neighborhood and perturbation moves, are utilized by the algorithm to generate new solutions.

The superiority of GAILS can be attributed to its hybridization of two complementary approaches. It initiates the search by using GA with an LS approach to explore the search space and identify the global optimum region, which is prone to becoming trapped in a local optimum. To overcome this challenge, ILS is employed, introducing perturbations to the current solution and facilitating escape from local optima. Furthermore, we conducted experimental investigations with varying time limits to demonstrate GAILS' capability to evade local optima. The results affirm the effectiveness of our proposal, as the solution quality improves with increased time. Additionally, we evaluate the algorithm's performance on benchmark problem instances of differing complexity, employing the fitness function value as a metric and comparing it with other algorithms using a t-test.

The structure of this paper is as follows: In Section 1, an introduction is provided. Section 2 contains a brief literature review of the related work on PE-CTP and CB-CTP. The PE-CTP and CB-CTP, along with their mathematical formulation, are explained in Section 3. Section 4 covers the description of the GAILS algorithm. Implementation and testing of GAILS on different benchmark problem instances with varying complexity are performed in Section 5. Finally, conclusions are summarized in Section 6.

2. Related Work

In different subsections of this section, the earlier research on the two UCTP versions, PE-CTP and CB-CTP, is discussed in detail.

2.1. Related Work on PE-CTP

The history of the educational scheduling problem can be traced back over six decades, starting with [3]. Over the years, numerous researchers have proposed different solution approaches and tested them on real-world problem instances. Despite significant progress in this field, researchers have faced difficulties when comparing their algorithms with existing state-of-the-art solutions due to differing problem formulations and instances used by each researcher. To address this issue, the International Metaheuristic Network organized the First International Timetabling Competition (ITC2002) in 2002. The objective was to simulate a realistic scenario where students have priorities when selecting events, and the timetable is constructed based on these preferences. Since then, these artificially generated enrollment-based course timetable problem instances have become the standard in the research community. Various researchers have utilized these instances to demonstrate the effectiveness of their novel techniques.

Socha et al. [7] utilized the same data generator to produce eleven instances of PE-CTP. They proposed the MAX-MIN ant system, which incorporates a local search routine optimized by creating an appropriate construction graph. The pheromone value determined the allocation of events to timeslots within specified bounds. The authors concluded that the MAX-MIN ant system outperformed random restart local search when applied to a set of typical problem instances. Rossi et al. [8] conducted a fair comparison of five different metaheuristic algorithms for solving the PE-CTP by using a common solution representation and standard neighborhood structure. Their empirical investigation revealed that each metaheuristic has distinct capabilities in satisfying hard and soft constraints, and an approach suitable for hard constraints may not be appropriate for optimizing soft constraints. Ref. [9] introduced a TS hyper-heuristic where heuristics compete to be selected by the hyper-heuristic.

Burke et al. [10] introduced an investigation into a simple, generic hyper-heuristic method for solving the PE-UCTP. They employed a set of widely used constructive heuristics, specifically graph coloring heuristics. The main characteristic of their method is to utilize a TS approach to alter the permutations of six graph coloring heuristics before creating a timetable. The outcomes of the approach improved further when a higher number of low-level heuristics were applied. In [11], an adaptive randomized descent algorithm (ARDA), which employs an adaptive criterion to escape from local optimal solutions, is described. Ref. [12] proposed a basic harmony search algorithm (BHSA) that takes advantage of the benefits of population-based algorithms by identifying the promising region in the search space using memory consideration and randomness. The proposed approach also used the benefits of local area-based algorithms by fine-tuning the search space region. They also introduced two modifications to the BHSA and proposed a modified harmony search algorithm (MHSA). The first modification involved considering memory, while the second modification aimed to enhance the functionality of the pitch adjustment operators by replacing the acceptance rule from a 'random walk' to a 'first improvement' and 'side walk' approach.

The approach by Cambazard et al. [13] for PE-CTP utilized constraint programming techniques and LS. They demonstrated the advantages of applying a list-coloring relaxation to the problem. They achieved the best constraint programming approach through various investigations and maintained the original problem decomposition. Additionally, they introduced lower bounds to estimate the costs related to the soft constraints in the problem. Motivated by the perception of a gravitational emulation local search algorithm, ref. [14] proposed a new population-based local search (PB-LS) heuristic for their solution. The authors integrated a multi-neighborhood particle collision algorithm and an adaptive randomized descent algorithm into their proposed approach, aiming to address the constraints of population-based algorithms. Ref. [15] proposed an integer linear programming-based heuristic to solve a real-world PE-CTP arising in an institution in Buenos Aires, Argentina. The algorithm produced high-quality results and provided generalizations to other related problems in the literature. Ref. [16] proposed a two-stage approach for solving the PE-CTP. The first phase focused on obtaining a feasible solution by satisfying all the hard constraints. In the second phase, they aimed to improve the solution quality by minimizing violations of soft constraints. To execute this two-phased approach, they employed an enhanced version of the SA with a reheating algorithm called simulated annealing with improved reheating and learning (SAIRL). Additionally, they introduced a reinforcement learning-based approach to establish an effective neighborhood structure for search operations.

Over the years, many hybrid approaches by hybridizing a local area-based algorithm within a population-based algorithm have gained much interest [17]. Such hybridization aims to achieve an equilibrium between exploration and exploitation of the search space to achieve the benefits of population-based and local area-based approaches. Ref. [18] proposed GA with a repair function and local search for solving PE-CTP. They presented a new repair function capable of transforming an unfeasible timetable into a feasible one. The local search algorithm was employed before the next generation to enhance timetable quality. A hybrid evolutionary algorithm employing hybridization between a memetic algorithm and a randomized iterative improvement local search was given by [19]. They reduced the exploration ability of the search space by excluding the crossover operator from the memetic algorithm. Ref. [20] suggested a guided search genetic algorithm (GSGA) consisting of a guided search strategy and a local search technique for their solution. The guided search strategy introduced offspring into the population based on a data structure that stores information extracted from previous competent individuals. Subsequently, the LS technique is employed to enhance the overall quality of individual outcomes. Ref. [21] further proposed an extended guided search genetic algorithm (EGSGA) by introducing a new local search strategy in addition to the original local search strategy used in GSGA.

Ref. [22] proposed a hybrid metaheuristic algorithm that combines an electromagnetic-like mechanism and the great deluge algorithm for solving both variants of UCTP. The electromagnetic-like mechanism is a population-based stochastic global optimization approach that simulates the attraction, physics, and repulsion of sample points in moving toward optimality. The great deluge algorithm is a local search strategy that allows the worst solutions to be accepted by an upper boundary. The dynamic force estimated from the attraction–repulsion mechanism is used as a declining rate to update the search procedure. Ref. [23] presented a hybrid metaheuristic approach that combines the great deluge and tabu search. They proposed their solution approach for both PE-CTP and CB-CTP. The algorithm is divided into two parts, construction and improvement, and four different neighborhood moves are employed. Ref. [24] proposed a new hybrid algorithm that combines GA with local search and uses events based on groupings of students. Ref. [25] proposed a solution for the PE-CTP that is motivated by particle swarm optimization and implemented in the basic artificial bee colony algorithm. The algorithm was hybridized with the great deluge algorithm to enhance local exploitation capabilities and improve global exploration quality. This approach achieved equilibrium by using a combination of these techniques. Ref. [26] developed a new hybrid method that combines genetic-based discrete particle swarm optimization with local search and tabu search approaches for solving the PE-CTP.

A hybrid approach based on the improved parallel GA and LS (IPGALS) is proposed to solve the PE-CTP by [27]. The GA is enhanced by incorporating LS. IPGALS adopts a timetable representation, guaranteeing the preservation of hard constraints. The proposed approach is run parallel to enhance the GA searching process due to various problem constraints. The algorithm was tested on benchmark PE-CTP problem instances, and the results were compared to other methods previously used to solve PE-CTP, and it was found to be very effective. Ref. [28] proposed a review paper regarding the most recent scientific approaches applied to the UCTP. The study demonstrates different methodologies researchers use to solve the problem based on when they were created and what data they used. The paper also discusses the challenges and opportunities while solving the UCTP. They have found that metaheuristic approaches are widely favored, with hybrid and hyper-heuristic approaches subsequently employed to achieve effective outcomes. They also observed that the most advanced techniques found in the scientific literature are not always used in the real world, probably because they are not adaptable enough.

2.2. Related Work on CB-CTP

After successfully organizing ITC2002, the research community in the field of timetabling organized the Second International Timetabling Competition (ITC2007) in 2007 [2]. During this event, they introduced three tracks for educational timetabling problems, with the third track focusing on curriculum-based course timetabling applied to Italian universities. For this track, several datasets were derived from real-world examples provided by the University of Udine. These datasets primarily emphasized lecturers' preferences rather than students', as is the case in PE-CTP.

By nature, CB-CTP is a highly constrained and complicated combinatorial optimization problem extensively studied by a large number of researchers [22,29–33]. They classified them first, along with their mathematical formulations, and then proposed several solutions approaches. In general, there is no known efficient deterministic polynomial-time algorithm for their solution, and they are solved by a variety of exact and heuristic approaches. Ref. [4] discussed their main solution approaches and roughly divided them into four categories: constraint-based, sequential, clustered, and generalized search (metaheuristics) methods. In constraint-based approaches [29,34], these problems are represented as constraint satisfaction problems (CSPs) and solved using CSP-solving approaches. Ref. [29] proposed to formulate the timetabling instance of CB-CTP as CSP instances and applied a general-purpose CSP solver to find solutions. The solver effectively handled weighted constraints using a hybrid algorithm combining tabu search and ILS. Ref. [35] introduced a constraint-based solver approach for CB-CTP that included multiple local search approaches working in three stages.

Ref. [31] proposed a two-stage integer linear programming (ILP) model for the solution of CB-CTP. The approach involves decomposing the problem into two stages, each represented by a distinct ILP model. In the first stage, the objective is to assign lectures to time periods, whereas the assignment of lectures to rooms is performed in the second stage by considering room stability. In the first stage, the assignment is performed without considering rooms, minimum working days, curriculum compactness, or minimizing penalties for room capacity. The representation of CB-CTPs as graphs is demonstrated in [36], where vertices and connections correspond to the lectures of courses and the constraints between them. Subsequently, graph coloring algorithms are employed to solve these CB-CTPs. Although this kind of approach (sequential heuristics) has demonstrated greater efficiency in small-sized problem instances, it seems ineffective in large-sized problem instances. Ref. [37] have proposed a satisfiability (SAT) model to solve a real-world CB-CTP at a Mexican university. Ref. [38] proposed a harmony search algorithm for the solution of CB-CTP. In the execution of their algorithm, the process of improvisation consists of memory consideration, random consideration, and pitch adjustment. A high-level object-oriented model called QuikFix has been proposed by [39] for the solution of CB-CTP. A repair-based heuristic is used in their approach, and certain structural constraints and significant neighborhood moves are applied in the problem domain's search space.

Other extensively explored areas, such as the adaptive approaches, metaheuristics, multi-criteria, and case-based reasoning discussed by [40], are also used to solve these problems. In recent years, metaheuristic approaches and hybrid approaches have been extensively used to solve CB-CTP. These metaheuristic approaches are motivated by nature and apply nature-like processes to obtain optimal or near-optimal solutions. These approaches are generally categorized as local area-based (ILS, TS, SA, and VLNS) and population-based (GA, ACO, ABC, and PSO) algorithms. According to [41], an ABC algorithm has four phases: initialization, the employed bee phase, the onlooker bee phase, and the scout bee phase. Ref. [42] proposed a new swarm intelligence algorithm based on ABC to solve the CB-CTP. Their algorithm works in two phases. The first phase is used to obtain a feasible solution by satisfying all the hard constraints. In contrast, the second phase is used to satisfy as many soft constraints as possible without violating any hard constraints. Ref. [32] proposed an adaptive tabu search (ATS) algorithm for their solution by the hybridization of TS and ILS. The algorithm uses two neighborhood structures, namely

SimpleSwap and *KampeSwap*, and a standard tabu list to prevent the cycling of previously visited solutions for both moves.

Ref. [30] proposed a two-phase approach for resolving the CB-CTP problem in their publication. The first phase involved utilizing a robust single-stage simulated annealing method for problem-solving, while in the second phase, an extensive and statistically sound methodology was designed and applied for the parameter tuning process. This resulted in a methodology that models the relationship between search method parameters and instance features, allowing for the parameters of unseen instances to be set through a simple inspection. In [43], the CB-CTP was modeled as a bi-criteria optimization problem with two objectives: a penalty function and a robustness metric. The problem was resolved using a hybrid multi-objective genetic algorithm that integrates hill climbing and simulated annealing algorithms with the standard GA approach to produce an accurate approximation of the Pareto-optimal front. Ref. [33] explored the use of generational construction hyper-heuristics for automating the process of low-level construction heuristic generation for CB-CTP. Two hyper-heuristics, an arithmetic hyper-heuristic for evolving arithmetic heuristics and a genetic algorithm hyper-heuristic made up of ten problem attributes for generating hierarchical heuristics, were implemented and applied to solve CB-CTP.

Ref. [44] presented an answer set programming-based approach, termed a teaspoon, for solving the CB-CTP. In this approach, the system first reads a CB-CTP instance of a standard input format and converts it into a set of answer set programming facts. These facts are then combined with the first-order encoding for CB-CTP solving, which any off-the-shelf ASP system can subsequently solve. Ref. [45] proposed a novel competition-guided multi-neighborhood local search (CMLS) algorithm for solving the CB-CTP. The proposed algorithm consists of three main contributions. First, it combines different neighborhoods uniquely by selecting only one at each iteration. This helps find a balance between finding many options and being efficient with time. Second, the algorithm uses two rules to determine the likelihood of selecting a neighborhood. Lastly, CMLS has a restart strategy where two different local search procedures are used and the best result is used as the starting point for the next search. An extensive and systematic review of the utilization of metaheuristic approaches used for UCTPs has been proposed by [46]. They thoroughly review, summarize, and categorize these approaches while introducing a classification for hybrid metaheuristic methods. Additionally, their study critically analyzes these methods' advantages and limitations, highlighting the challenges, gaps, and potential areas for future research.

3. Problem Formulation

This section outlines the two variants of UCTPs, namely, the PE-CTP and the CB-CTP, and presents their mathematical formulations. The UCTP is a multi-dimensional assignment problem where students and teachers are assigned to events (or courses), which are then allocated to appropriate timeslots and rooms. In the subsequent subsections, we delve into the PE-CTP and CB-CTP individually.

3.1. Post-Enrollment Based Course Timetabling Problem

This section provides an explanation of the PE-CTP, along with its mathematical formulation. The PE-CTP is characterized as a multi-dimensional assignment problem wherein students select events, such as lectures, tutorials, and laboratories. These events must be allocated to a certain number of timeslots (9 per day for 5 days) and rooms, with the goal of minimizing constraint violation. Each student selects multiple events, and each room has a specific capacity and various features. The resolution to this problem entails assigning the events to suitable timeslots and rooms that fulfill the specified hard constraints, as described below.

1. Each student can attend only one event at any given timeslot.
2. Each event must be assigned to a room with enough seating capacity and all the necessary features.

3. Each room can host only one event at a time.

When only hard constraints are present, the goal is to find a feasible solution. In addition, the following soft constraints are considered, the violation of which leads to a certain penalty for the PE-CTP solution.

1. Scheduling an event at the last timeslot of the day should be avoided.
2. A student should not have more than two events in consecutive timeslots daily.
3. Having only one event a day is not recommended for a student.

Next, the mathematical formulation of the PE-CTP can be described. The PE-CTP involves a set E consisting of n events assigned to 45 timeslots (with 9 timeslots per day for 5 days). There is also a set R of m rooms with fixed seating capacity where these events occur. In addition, a set S includes p students who can choose any event from E, and a set F contains q room features required for events in selected rooms. The following notations are used in the formulation of the problem.

- The set of events, denoted as $E = \{e_1, e_2, \ldots, e_n\}$, consists of n events.
- The set of rooms, denoted as $R = \{r_1, r_2, \ldots, r_m\}$, contains m rooms.
- The set of timeslots, denoted as $T = \{t_1, t_2, \ldots, t_{45}\}$, includes 45 timeslots.
- The set of students, denoted as $S = \{s_1, s_2, \ldots, s_p\}$, comprises p students.
- The set of rooming features, denoted as $F = \{f_1, f_2, \ldots, f_q\}$, represents q rooming features.
- $r_i.capacity$ represents the capacity of room r_i.
- A matrix $RF = [rf_{ij}]_{m \times q}$, called a room-feature matrix and represents the feature possessed by the room. Here, $rf_{ij} = 1$, if room r_i is having feature f_j; otherwise, the value is zero.
- The decision variable x_{ijkl} represents student s_i attending the event e_j in the timeslot t_k and in the room r_l. It is defined for i ranging from 1 to p, j ranging from 1 to n, k ranging from 1 to 45, and l ranging from 1 to m.

$$x_{ijkl} = \begin{cases} 1 & \text{if the combination mentioned above is valid,} \\ 0 & \text{otherwise.} \end{cases}$$

- The decision variable y_{ijk} represents an event e_i that takes place in the room r_j with feature f_k. It is defined for $1 \leq i \leq n$, $1 \leq j \leq m$, and $1 \leq k \leq q$.

$$y_{ijk} = \begin{cases} 1 & \text{if the combination mentioned above is valid,} \\ 0 & \text{otherwise.} \end{cases}$$

- The decision variable z_{ij} represents an event e_i that takes place in timeslot t_j and defined for $1 \leq i \leq n$, and $1 \leq j \leq 45$.

$$z_{ij} = \begin{cases} 1 & \text{if the combination mentioned above is valid,} \\ 0 & \text{otherwise.} \end{cases}$$

Now, the mathematical formulation of hard constraints can be described as follows:

1. Each student can attend only one event at any given timeslot.

$$\sum_{j=1}^{n} \sum_{l=1}^{m} x_{ijkl} \leq 1, \ 1 \leq i \leq p; \ 1 \leq k \leq 45.$$

2. Each event must be assigned to a room with enough seating capacity and all the necessary features.

$$\sum_{i=1}^{p} x_{ijkl} \leq r_l.capacity, \ 1 \leq j \leq n; \ 1 \leq k \leq 45; \ 1 \leq l \leq m; \ \text{and}$$

$$y_{ijk} \leq rf_{jk}, \ 1 \leq i \leq n; \ 1 \leq j \leq m; \ 1 \leq k \leq q.$$

3. Each room can host only one event at a time.

$$\sum_{j=1}^{n} x_{ijkl} \leq 1, \ 1 \leq i \leq p; \ 1 \leq k \leq 45; \ 1 \leq l \leq m.$$

Similarly, the soft constraints can be formulated mathematically as follows:

1. Scheduling an event at the last timeslot of the day should be avoided.

$$\sum_{i=1}^{n} z_{ij} = 0, \ j = 9, 18, \ldots, 45.$$

2. A student should not have more than two events in consecutive timeslots daily.

$$\sum_{j=1}^{n}\sum_{l=1}^{m}\sum_{k=a}^{a+2} x_{ijkl} \leq 2, \ 1 \leq i \leq p;$$

$$a = 1, 2, \ldots, 7, 10, 11, \ldots, 16, \ldots, 37, 38, \ldots, 43.$$

3. Having only one event a day is not recommended for a student.

$$\sum_{j=1}^{n}\sum_{l=1}^{m}\sum_{k=d}^{d+8} x_{ijkl} > 1, \ 1 \leq i \leq p; \ d = 1, 10, 19, 28, 37.$$

The objective is to achieve an optimal solution for the PE-CTP by satisfying all the hard constraints and reducing the overall penalty cost of the soft constraint violations. Therefore, the objective function $f(I)$ for an individual solution I can be defined as

$$\min f(I) = \gamma \times hcv(I) + scv(I),$$

where $hcv(I)$ and $scv(I)$ represent the counts of hard and soft constraint violations in solution I, and γ is a constant greater than the maximum potential violation of the soft constraints. To simplify the process, a direct solution representation is used, which involves an integer-valued ordered list of size $|E|$, denoted as $a[i]$, where $1 \leq a[i] \leq 45$ and $1 \leq i \leq |E|$. Each element $a[i]$ represents the timeslot for event e_i. The assignment of rooms is generated using a matching algorithm where a set of events appearing in a timeslot and a pre-processed list of rooms based on their sizes and features are used. A bipartite matching algorithm is employed to obtain a maximum cardinality matching between these two sets, which is determined by using a deterministic network flow algorithm as provided by [47]. The remaining unplaced events are assigned to the room with the fewest events, in order, until all events are assigned. Following these procedures, a similar integer-valued ordered list of size $|E|$, say $b[i]$, where $1 \leq b[i] \leq m$ and $1 \leq i \leq |E|$ is obtained for the event-room assignments. Here, m denotes the total number of rooms. In the case of a tie, the first room is selected. This process leads to a complete assignment of all the events to suitable rooms and timeslots.

3.2. Curriculum-Based Course Timetabling Problem

This subsection presents a description of the CB-CTP and its corresponding mathematical formulation. The CB-CTP refers to a weekly assignment problem that involves the allocation of lectures for multiple courses within a given number of periods and a set of rooms. The day is split into a fixed number of timeslots, and each period is identified as a combination of a day and a timeslot. The total number of scheduling periods per week is determined by multiplying the number of days per week by the number of timeslots per day. It is necessary to schedule each course at different periods, and a set of curricula comprises a group of courses with shared students. In case of conflicts between courses, the curricula are used to resolve the issue instead of relying on student enrollment data. A feasible timetable is one in which all lectures are scheduled within a period and a room while satisfying the following hard constraints.

1. All lectures of a course must take place in distinct rooms and periods.
2. Two lectures cannot occur in the same room during the same period.
3. All lectures for courses taught by the same teacher or within the same curriculum must be scheduled during different time periods. This means that there should not be any overlap of students or teachers during any given period.
4. No lectures for the course can be assigned to a period if the teacher of the course is unavailable for that period.

Also, a penalty is imposed on the timetable for each violation of any of the following soft constraints:

1. The lecture room's capacity should not be exceeded by the number of students attending the course.
2. All lectures in a course should be scheduled in the same room. If this is not possible, the number of occupied rooms should be as low as possible.
3. The lectures of a course should be spread over the given minimum number of days.
4. A curriculum incurs a violation when a lecture is not adjacent to any other lecture of the same curriculum within the same day. This requirement ensures that the student's schedule is as compact as possible.

The aim is to minimize the violation of soft constraints. The problem involves assigning TNL lectures from a set C of n courses to $w = u \times v$ periods. Here, v and u represent the number of timeslots per day and the number of days per week, respectively. Additionally, the problem involves a set R of m rooms with different capacities. Each course $c_i \in C$ comprises $n\ell_i$ lectures, each scheduled at a different period and assigned to a different room. The problem also includes a set Π of x curricula, where each curriculum is a group of courses with common students. The following notations are used to establish the mathematical formulation of CB-CTP.

- $\Pi = \{\pi_1, \pi_2, \ldots, \pi_x\}$ is a set of x curricula.
- $C = \{c_1, c_2, \ldots, c_n\}$ is a set of n courses.
- $D = \{d_1, d_2, \ldots, d_u\}$ is a set of u days in a week.
- $T = \{t_1, t_2, \ldots, t_v\}$ is a set of v timeslots in a day.
- $P = \{p_1, p_2, \ldots, p_w\}$ is a set of w periods, where $w = u \times v$.
- $R = \{r_1, r_2, \ldots, r_m\}$ is a set of m rooms.
- $L = \{\ell_1, \ell_2, \ldots, \ell_{TNL}\}$ is a set of TNL lectures.
- $n\ell_i$ is the total number of lectures for course c_i. Taking $n\ell_0 = 0$, a lecture ℓ_k corresponds to a course c_i for k satisfying $\sum_{j=0}^{i-1} n\ell_j < k \leq \sum_{j=1}^{i} n\ell_j$, $1 \leq i \leq n$. Also, $\sum_{i=1}^{n} n\ell_i = TNL$.
- ns_i is the total number of students taking course c_i.
- $mind_i$ is the minimum number of days for course c_i.
- $r_i.capacity$ represents the capacity of room r_i.
- X_{ijkl} is a decision variable representing that lecture ℓ_i of course c_j takes place in room r_k at period p_l and defined for $1 \leq i \leq n\ell_j$, $1 \leq j \leq n$, $1 \leq k \leq m$, and $1 \leq l \leq w$, as

$$X_{ijkl} = \begin{cases} 1 & \text{if the combination mentioned above is valid,} \\ 0 & \text{otherwise.} \end{cases}$$

- Y_{ijk} is a decision variable representing that lecture ℓ_i of course c_j takes place at period p_k and defined for $1 \leq i \leq n\ell_j$, $1 \leq j \leq n$, and $1 \leq k \leq w$, as

$$Y_{ijk} = \begin{cases} 1 & \text{if the combination mentioned above is valid,} \\ 0 & \text{otherwise.} \end{cases}$$

- Z_{ijk} is a decision variable representing that course c_i takes place in room r_j at period p_k and defined for $1 \leq i \leq n$, $1 \leq j \leq m$, and $1 \leq k \leq w$, as

$$Z_{ijk} = \begin{cases} 1 & \text{if the combination mentioned above is valid,} \\ 0 & \text{otherwise.} \end{cases}$$

- η_{ij} is a decision variable representing that course c_i takes place in room r_j and defined for $1 \leq i \leq n$, and $1 \leq j \leq m$, as

$$\eta_{ij} = \begin{cases} 1 & \text{if the combination mentioned above is valid,} \\ 0 & \text{otherwise.} \end{cases}$$

- una_{ij} is a decision variable representing that course c_i is unavailable at period p_j and defined for $1 \leq i \leq n$, and $1 \leq j \leq w$, as

$$una_{ij} = \begin{cases} 1 & \text{if the combination mentioned above is valid,} \\ 0 & \text{otherwise.} \end{cases}$$

- ξ_{ij} is a decision variable representing that course c_i belongs to curriculum π_j and defined for $1 \leq i \leq n$, and $1 \leq j \leq x$, as

$$\xi_{ij} = \begin{cases} 1 & \text{if the combination mentioned above is valid,} \\ 0 & \text{otherwise.} \end{cases}$$

- μ_{ij} is a decision variable representing that course c_i takes place at period p_j and defined for $1 \leq i \leq n$, and $1 \leq j \leq w$, as

$$\mu_{ij} = \begin{cases} 1 & \text{if the combination mentioned above is valid,} \\ 0 & \text{otherwise.} \end{cases}$$

- ρ_{ij} is a decision variable representing that course c_i takes place in day d_j and defined for $1 \leq i \leq n$, and $1 \leq j \leq u$, as

$$\rho_{ij} = \begin{cases} 1 & \text{if the combination mentioned above is valid,} \\ 0 & \text{otherwise.} \end{cases}$$

- τ_{ij} is a decision variable representing that course of curriculum π_i takes place at period p_j and defined for $1 \leq i \leq x$, and $1 \leq j \leq w$, as

$$\tau_{ij} = \begin{cases} 1 & \text{if the combination mentioned above is valid,} \\ 0 & \text{otherwise.} \end{cases}$$

Now, the mathematical formulation of hard constraints can be described as follows:

1. All lectures of a course must take place in distinct rooms and periods.

$$\sum_{i=1}^{n\ell_j} Y_{ijk} \leq 1, \ 1 \leq j \leq n; \ 1 \leq k \leq w;$$

$$\sum_{i=1}^{n\ell_j} \sum_{k=1}^{w} Y_{ijk} = n\ell_j, \ 1 \leq j \leq n.$$

2. Two lectures cannot occur in the same room during the same period.

$$\sum_{j=1}^{n} \sum_{i=1}^{n\ell_j} X_{ijkl} \leq 1, \ 1 \leq k \leq m; \ 1 \leq l \leq w.$$

3. All lectures for courses taught by the same teacher or within the same curriculum must be scheduled during different time periods. This means that there should not be any overlap of students or teachers during any given period.

$$\sum_{j=1}^{n} \sum_{i=1}^{n\ell_j} \sum_{k=1}^{m} (X_{ijkl} \times \xi_{jy}) \leq 1, \ 1 \leq l \leq w; \ 1 \leq y \leq x.$$

4. No lectures for the course can be assigned to a period if the teacher of the course is unavailable for that period.

$$\sum_{i=1}^{n\ell_j} Y_{ijk} \leq 1 - una_{jk}, \ 1 \leq j \leq n; \ 1 \leq k \leq w.$$

Similarly, the soft constraints can be formulated mathematically as follows:

1. The lecture room's capacity should not be exceeded by the number of students attending the course.

$$\eta_{ij} \times ns_j \leq r_j.capacity, \ 1 \leq i \leq n; \ 1 \leq j \leq m.$$

2. All lectures in a course should be scheduled in the same room. If this is not possible, the number of occupied rooms should be as low as possible.

$$\sum_{k=1}^{w} Z_{ijk} - w \times \eta_{ij} \leq 0, \ 1 \leq i \leq n; \ 1 \leq j \leq m.$$

3. The lectures of a course should be spread over the given minimum number of days.

$$\sum_{j=1}^{v} \mu_{ij} - \rho_{ik} \geq 0, \ 1 \leq i \leq n; \ 1 \leq k \leq u; \text{ and}$$

$$\sum_{j=1}^{u} \rho_{ij} \geq mind_i - H_i, \ 1 \leq i \leq n.$$

Here, H_i will take the value 0 if and only if course c_i takes more than $(mind_i - 1)$ number of days.

4. A curriculum incurs a violation when a lecture is not adjacent to any other lecture of the same curriculum within the same day. This requirement ensures that the student's schedule is as compact as possible.

$$\sum_{i=1}^{n} (\mu_{ij} \times \xi_{ik}) - \tau_{kj} = 0, \ 1 \leq j \leq w; \ 1 \leq k \leq x; \text{ and}$$

$$-\tau_{i(j-1)} + \tau_{ij} - \tau_{i(j+1)} - I_{ij} \leq 0, \ 1 \leq i \leq x; \ 1 \leq j \leq w.$$

Here, $\tau_{i(j-1)}$ is removed for $j = 1, \frac{w}{u} + 1, 2 \times \frac{w}{u} + 1, \ldots, (u-1) \times \frac{w}{u} + 1$, and $\tau_{i(j+1)}$ is removed for $j = \frac{w}{u}, 2 \times \frac{w}{u}, \ldots, u \times \frac{w}{u}$. Also, I_{ij} will take the value 1 if π_i has an isolated lecture at period p_j.

Similar to the PE-CTP, the goal is to attain an optimal solution for the CB-CTP by satisfying all the hard constraints and minimizing the penalty cost of the soft constraint violations. Hence, the objective function $f(I)$ for an individual solution I can be defined as follows:

$$\min f(I) = \gamma \times hcv(I) + scv(I),$$

where the symbols retain their usual meanings. Here also, a direct solution representation is selected. A solution involves an integer-valued ordered list of size TNL, say $a[i]$ ($1 \leq a[i] \leq |P|$ and $1 \leq i \leq$ TNL). Here, list $a[i]$ corresponds to the assigned periods. Taking $n\ell_0 = 0$, the k consecutive entries of $a[i]$, satisfying $\sum_{j=0}^{i-1} n\ell_j < k \leq \sum_{j=1}^{i} n\ell_j$ are corresponding to the periods for all the $n\ell_i$ number of lectures of course c_i. Once the assignments of all the lectures for all the courses to periods are completed, the room assignments are made by using a bipartite matching algorithm. A set of courses appears in a period and a set of rooms based on their sizes. Now, a bipartite matching algorithm is used to obtain a maximum cardinality matching between these two sets using a deterministic network flow algorithm as given by [47]. This solves our CB-CTP by assigning all courses to the appropriate rooms and periods.

4. Proposed Hybrid Metaheuristic Approach

This section develops the proposed exploration and exploitation-based metaheuristic algorithm that combines GA and ILS to find an optimal solution for the UCTP.

The study conducted by Golberg [48] observed that although GAs can identify potential regions for global optima in the search space, they face significant challenges when dealing with highly constrained problems. Moreover, it has been noted [49,50] that hybridizing GA with other optimization techniques can yield even better solutions. Incorporating these findings, we propose an approach for finding optimal solutions for PE-CTP and CB-CTP. Our algorithm aims to reduce the exponential time complexity of GA by combining it with the ILS algorithm, thereby increasing the likelihood of convergence to an optimal solution in the search space. The ILS algorithm refines the GA search and improves the chances of convergence to an optimal solution through successive iterations in various sub-parts of the search space. It is important to note that while GA may generate individuals representing both good and bad search spaces, the ILS algorithm ensures fairness by exploring different sub-parts of the search space.

Let us briefly recall the basic concepts of GA to explain the technical details of our algorithm. This stochastic algorithm is based on the principle of survival of the fittest and is used to iteratively map a population of solutions, known as chromosomes with fitness values, into a new population of solutions known as offspring. It requires the problem-specific encoding of a solution, where genes on chromosomes are characterized by variables. Therefore, it works with a randomly generated population of solutions in the search space and consists of three primary processes: selection, reproduction, and replacement.

In the selection process, more duplications of candidate solutions with higher fitness function values are made to enforce the survival-of-the-fittest mechanism. The reproduction stage uses crossover and mutation operators for the selected parents. In the crossover, segments of two solutions in the population are combined to obtain new and possibly improved solutions. In contrast, a solution is modified locally in a random order in the mutation process. Finally, the original parental population is replaced by a population of offspring solutions generated through the selection and reproduction processes. This replacement includes keeping the best solutions and removing the worst ones. The selection phase ensures better utilization of healthier offspring, while the reproduction phase ensures adequate exploration of the search space. Natural selection ensures the propagation of better fitness function values on chromosomes in future generations. The algorithmic layout of GAILS can be found in Algorithm 1. The complete working procedure of GAILS is shown in the flow chart in Figure 1.

Remark 1. *The algorithms and descriptions provided are designed based on PE-CTP. However, in the case of CB-CTP, the event $e_i \in E$ and timeslot $t_k \in T$ are replaced with lecture $\ell_i \in L$ and period $p_k \in P$, respectively, along with their respective parameters.*

Algorithm 1 The proposed hybrid metaheuristic approach—GAILS

Require: A problem instance I
Ensure: an optimal solution y_{best} for I
1: **begin**
2:   **for** ($i \leftarrow 1$ *to max*) **do**   ▷ randomly generated initial population of size *max*
3:     $y_i \leftarrow$ randomly generated starting solution;
4:     $y_i \leftarrow$ solution obtained by applying LS;   ▷ LS given in Algorithms 3 and 4
5:     compute fitness function value of y_i;
6:   **end for**
7: organize the population of solutions in ascending order based on their fitness function values;
8: $y_{best} \leftarrow y_1$;   ▷ y_1 denotes the finest solution within the population
9: **repeat**
10:    use tournament selection to select two parents from population;
11:    $y \leftarrow$ offspring solution obtained by applying crossover with α rate and mutation with β rate;
12:    **if** ($f(y) < f(y_{best})$) **then**   ▷ $f(y)$ is the fitness function value of y
13:      $y \leftarrow$ solution generated after applying ILS to y;   ▷ ILS given in Algorithm 2
14:    **end if**
15:    $y_{max} \leftarrow y$;   ▷ the worst solution y_{max} is replaced by y in the population of sorted solutions
16:    create and sort the population of solutions in ascending order of their fitness function values;
17:    $y_{best} \leftarrow y_1$;
18: **until** (termination criteria not satisfied);
19: **end**

Since all the variables in both PE-CTP and CB-CTP problems are binary, there is no need for special methods for the solution encoding. Chromosomes in the proposed algorithm are vectors of Boolean values of all decision variables. For the PE-CTP problem: $y_i = (x_{1,1,1,1}, \ldots, x_{p,n,45,m}, y_{1,1,1}, \ldots, y_{n,m,q}, z_{1,1}, \ldots, z_{n,45})$. For the CB-CTP problem: $y_i = (X_{1,1,1,1}, \ldots, X_{n\ell_n,n,m,w}, Y_{1,1,1}, \ldots, Y_{n,\ell_n,w}, Z_{1,1,1}, \ldots, Z_{n,m,w}, \eta_{1,1}, \ldots, \eta_{n,m}, una_{i,j}, \ldots, una_{n,w}, \xi_{1,1}, \ldots, \xi_{n,x}, \mu_{1,1}, \ldots, \mu_{n,w}, \rho_{1,1}, \ldots, \rho_{n,u})$.

By utilizing a uniform distribution, our proposed algorithm produces a population of random solutions with a size of *max*, where each event is assigned a timeslot. As the quality of the initial solutions impacts the final solutions, good initial solutions produce better results in less computation time [51,52]. We applied the LS to each initial population to create a population of good-quality initial solutions. The problem-specified heuristic information from the LS is then used by a steady-state evolution process in which only one pair of parent individuals is chosen for reproduction in each generation. The LS assigns events to timeslots and then uses the matching algorithm to allocate rooms to each event–timeslot pair using three neighborhood operators. Following that, the population of solutions is arranged in ascending order according to their fitness function values, where y_1 represents the best solution. Some individuals with the best fitness function values are randomly selected as parents from the current population. The fitness function $f(I)$ for an individual solution I is given by

$$f(I) = \gamma \times hcv(I) + scv(I),$$

where $hcv(I)$, $scv(I)$, and γ are the counts of violations of hard and soft constraints on I, and a constant greater than the maximum possible violation of soft constraints, respectively. A child solution is generated using a uniform crossover operator with α probability and a mutation operator with β probability over the selected parents. Two individual solutions are chosen from the current population as the parents, using tournament selection with a suitable tournament size to create a child solution using a crossover operator. In our case, for each event, we select the parent with the smaller penalty value and assign their corresponding timeslot and room to the event of the child solution. Finally, a mutation operator is applied to the child solution obtained from the crossover operator.

The mutation operator is defined as a random move in the neighborhood of LS, which is extended with four-cycle permutations of the timeslots corresponding to four different events to complete the neighborhood of LS. Thus, the entire neighborhood consists of four categories of neighborhood moves. In a type 1 move, a random event from a timeslot is selected and moved to another timeslot. A type 2 move involves swapping two randomly chosen events between two different timeslots. A type 3 move selects two timeslots randomly and swaps all the events between them. Lastly, in a type 4 move, three randomly selected events from three different timeslots are permuted in one of the two possible ways.

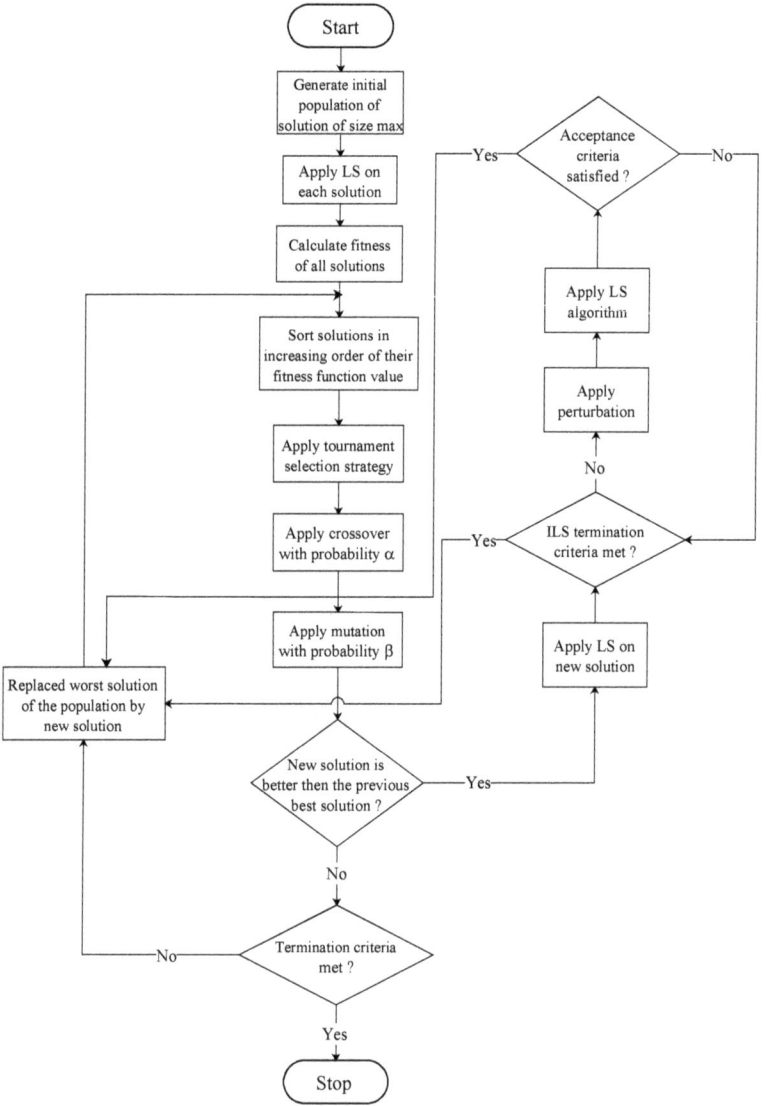

Figure 1. Flow chart of GAILS.

A new solution y is obtained by applying the crossover and mutation operators on the selected parents using tournament selection. If $f(y)$ is less than $f(y_{best})$, the ILS algorithm described in Section 4.1 is applied to y. Here, y_{best} and $f(y_{best})$ correspond to the best solution in the population and the fitness function of the best solution, respectively. Next, the worst solution y_{max} is replaced by the new solution y. The population of solutions is then sorted in increasing order of their fitness function values so that y_1 will be the best solution. This procedure is repeated until a termination criterion is met. Termination criteria may include a time limit, a number of iterations, or achieving an optimal solution with a zero fitness function value. The next subsection discusses the ILS and LS algorithms utilized in the GAILS.

4.1. Iterated Local Search Algorithm

This subsection describes, in brief, the ILS algorithm applied to solve the UCTP. The main disadvantage of LS is that it can become trapped in locally optimal solutions, which are considerably worse than the global optimal solution. It improves the LS algorithm by providing new starting solutions obtained from the current solution using perturbations rather than considering a random restart. Hence, ILS escapes from the local optimal solution by using perturbations. Every single execution of a perturbation in it creates a new solution. The strength of the perturbation is defined as the number of solution components that are modified. It is crucial that the LS algorithm cannot undo the perturbation, or else the solution will fall back into the just-visited local optimal solution. To apply ILS, four components are specified. The first component, "GenerateInitialSolution", modifies y in GAILS to generate the initial solution y_0, which is further improved to a new solution y by applying LS. The second component, "Perturbation", enhances the quality of the current solution y by taking it to some intermediate solution y'. The third component, "LocalSearch", takes solution y' and gives an enhanced solution y''. Finally, the fourth component, "AcceptanceCriteria", selects the solution for the next perturbation, with the acceptance criteria requiring the cost to decrease.

The article ref. [53] proposed that executing a random move within a higher-order neighborhood is more effective for achieving excellent performance in perturbation than moves performed in the LS algorithm. The perturbations should be compatible with the LS algorithm and consider the problem's properties for better results. If the perturbation is too strong, the ILS algorithm may function similarly to a random restart. Conversely, if the perturbation is too small, the LS algorithm will likely return to the previously visited local optimal solution, limiting the diversification of the search space. The solution returned by the AcceptanceCriteria employs this perturbation. The ILS algorithm is described in Algorithm 2.

Algorithm 2 Iterated local search algorithm—ILS

Require: A solution y_0 from the population
Ensure: An enhanced solution y
1: **begin**
2: $y_0 \leftarrow$ GenerateInitialSolution();
3: $y \leftarrow$ apply LS with y_0;
4: **while** (termination criteria not met) **do**
5:     $y' \leftarrow$ Perturbation(y, History);
6:     $y'' \leftarrow$ apply LocalSearch with y';
7:     $y \leftarrow$ AcceptanceCriteria(y, y'', History);
8: **end while**
9: **end**

The ILS method is utilized by starting with the randomly generated initial solution y_0 of PE-CTP. The LS algorithm is applied to y_0 with the help of some designed neighborhoods to obtain an enhanced solution y. The new solution y is then subjected to perturbation to obtain a further improved solution y'. The perturbation employs the search history, referred to as History, to mine the previously discovered local optima, which are used to generate better starting points for LS. After that, LS is applied once more to y' to obtain a further improved solution y''. If the solution y'' satisfies the acceptance criteria based on the specified History, it replaces y'. The ILS method is repeated until the predefined termination criteria used in GAILS are met. In our study, we utilize the following four types of perturbation moves:

Per$_1$: Selecting a different timeslot to a randomly chosen event.

Per$_2$: Swapping timeslots for two randomly chosen events.

Per$_3$: Selecting two timeslots randomly and swapping all their events.

Per$_4$: Selecting three events randomly and permuting them into three distinct timeslots in one of the two possible ways that differ from the existing one.

The random choices mentioned above were selected from a uniform distribution. To determine the strength of the perturbation, each individual random move is performed r times, where $r \in \{1, 5, 10, 20, 40, 50, 100\}$. We have considered three different methods to accept solutions in the AcceptanceCriteria. The initial method, *Random_Walk*, consistently accepts the new solution y'' that LS returns. The second method, *Accept_if_Better*, only accepts a new solution y'' if it is an improvement over the current solution y. The third method is *Simulated_Annealing*, which accepts y'' if it is superior to the current solution; otherwise, it is accepted with a probability determined by $g(y)$. Here, $g(y)$ represents the total count of *hcv* or *scv*, depending on whether solutions y and y'' are feasible. Two methods used for calculating this probability are

M$_1$: $\text{Prob}_1(y, y'') = e^{-\frac{(g(y) - g(y''))}{T}}$

M$_2$: $\text{Prob}_2(y, y'') = e^{-\frac{(g(y) - g(y''))}{T \cdot g(y_{\text{best}})}}$

Here, T and y_{best} represent a temperature parameter and the optimal solution obtained so far. Throughout the execution, the value of T remains constant. Generally, the temperature decreases over time in the SA algorithm to facilitate convergence towards a local minimum. However, when the ILS algorithm incorporates SA, the temperature is maintained at a constant level. The reason is that the ILS algorithm employs a distinct strategy to overcome local minima. Instead of reducing the temperature, the ILS algorithm introduces perturbations to alter the solution randomly. This allows the algorithm to explore new regions of the search space and potentially escape from local minima. Further, the value of T are selected from $\{0.01, 0.1, 1\}$ and $\{0.05, 0.025, 0.01\}$ for M$_1$ and M$_2$, respectively.

4.2. Local Search Algorithm

The classical method of local search is often used to find optimal solutions for many combinatorial optimization problems through two phases. The first phase is called the construction phase, which establishes feasibility. The second phase, the improvement phase, optimizes soft constraints without violating the feasibility of the search space. During the construction phase, the algorithm commences with an empty timetable and systematically builds up a schedule by gradually including one event at a time. Typically, the initial timetable is of poor quality with numerous constraint violations. The improvement phase then gradually enhances the timetable's quality by modifying certain events to achieve a better timetable. The selection of good neighborhoods is a critical aspect of LS.

To solve PE-CTP, the construction and improvement phases of LS are applied to each individual solution. During the construction phase, all possible neighborhood moves are attempted for each event from the list of events associated with *hcv* and ignoring all *scv* until a termination criterion is reached. Termination criteria can be an improvement in the solution or the exhaustion of the pre-specified number of iterations. For simplicity, a portion of the given solution is customized to form a new neighboring solution. In this work, we used a neighborhood consisting of three smaller neighborhoods, N$_1$, N$_2$, and N$_3$, defined as follows:

N$_1$: An operator that randomly chooses a single event and moves this event to a different timeslot that produces the lowest penalty.

N_2: An operator that swaps the timeslots of two randomly selected events.

N_3: An operator that randomly selects two timeslots and swaps all their events.

The neighborhood operator N_2 is applied only when N_1 fails, and N_3 is applied only when both N_1 and N_2 fail. In this context, the term "penalty" refers to the number of violations of hard and soft constraints. The resulting disturbance in room allocation is resolved by applying the bipartite graph matching algorithm to the affected timeslots after each neighborhood move, using its delta-evaluated measure. Delta-evaluation refers to the computation of the *hcv* of events that move within a solution to obtain the fitness function value dispute between the related event's pre- and post-move. If there are no new moves in the neighborhood or the current event has no *hcv*, the construction phase proceeds to the next event. If there is any remaining *hcv* after applying all neighborhood moves to all events, the construction phase ceases to function without discovering a viable solution to the problem. Once a feasible solution is achieved, the improvement phase begins. It operates similarly to the construction phase but focuses on satisfying soft constraints instead of hard constraints. The goal is to minimize the *scv* by applying all neighborhood moves to each event in sequential order without violating hard constraints. In summary, the construction phase provides a feasible solution, while the improvement phase aims to optimize the solution by satisfying as many soft constraints as possible. Algorithms 3 and 4 illustrate the general framework of the LS algorithm in its construction and improvement phases.

Algorithm 3 Construction phase of the local search algorithm

Require: A solution I from the population
Ensure: Either a feasible solution I or the nonexistence of a viable solution
1: **begin**
2: construct a randomly ordered circular list $(e_1, e_2, \ldots, e_n)$ consisting of n events;
3:    $i \leftarrow 0$;   ▷ i is the event counter
4: select event e_i after $i \leftarrow i+1$;   ▷ move to the next event
5: **if** (all neighborhood moves applied to all the events) **then**
6:    **if** ($\exists$ any *hcv* in I) **then**
7:      END LOCAL SEARCH;
8:    **else**
9:      output a feasible solution I and END the construction phase;
10:    **end if**
11: **end if**
12: **if** ((feasible e_i) $\lor$ (no untried move left for e_i)) **then**
13:    goto 4;
14: **end if**
15: *CheckSolution*(e_i, I);   ▷ all neighborhood moves applied and return the solution I
16: **if** (reduced number of *hcv* in I) **then**
17:    make the move;
18:    goto 3;
19: **else**
20:    goto 12;
21: **end if**
22: **end**

Algorithm 4 Improvement phase of the local search algorithm

Require: Solution I from Algorithm 3
Ensure: An optimal solution I
1: **begin**
2: use the circular randomly ordered list $(e_1, e_2, \ldots, e_n)$ of n events generated in Algorithm 3;
3:    $i \leftarrow 0$;   ▷ i is the event counter
4: select event e_i after $i \leftarrow i+1$;   ▷ move to the next event
5: **if** (all neighborhood moves applied to all the events) **then**
6:    END LOCAL SEARCH with an optimal solution I;
7: **end if**
8: **if** ((e_i NOT involved in any *scv*) $\lor$ (no untried move left for e_i)) **then**
9:    goto 4;
10: **end if**
11: *CheckSolution*(e_i, I);   ▷ all neighborhood moves applied and return the solution I
12: **if** (number of *scv* reduced in I without making I infeasible) **then**
13:    make the move;
14:    goto 3;
15: **else**
16:    goto 8;
17: **end if**
18: **end**

Procedure *CheckSolution*(e_i, I)

e_i and I are arguments. Returns I after neighborhood moves

Require: T: the set of 45 timeslots; R: the set of m rooms;
1: **begin**
2: apply N_1 to solution I;
3: **if** (N_1 successful) **then**
4:    generate solution I;
5: **else if** (N_1 to I not successful) $\wedge$ (N_2 to I successful) **then**
6:    apply N_2 to I and generate solution I;
7: **else**
8:    apply N_3 to I and generate solution I;
9: **end if**
10: **for** ($k \leftarrow 1$ *to* 45) **do**
11:    **if** timeslot t_k is effected by either of the move N_1, N_2, or N_3 **then**
12:      use the matching algorithm for events held in t_k to allocate rooms ;
13:    **end if**
14: **end for**
15: delta-evaluate the result of the move;
16: **return** I;
17: **end**

5. Computational Results

In this section, we perform an experimental investigation to assess the performance of our proposed approach, GAILS, compared to several existing algorithms commonly used for solving the UCTP. The fitness function is employed as the measure of performance in all cases. We implemented all algorithms in GNU C++ version 4.5.2 and executed them on a PC with a processing speed of 3.10 GHz and 2 GB of RAM. We conducted experiments using two distinct sets of benchmark problem instances. The first set consists of 11 PE-CTP instances sourced from Socha's benchmark dataset [7]. The second set includes 21 CB-CTP instances from the third track of ITC2007 (UD2). In the following subsections, we address these different problem instances separately.

5.1. Experiments on Socha's Benchmark Dataset

In this subsection, the GAILS algorithm is tested over the 11 problem instances proposed by [7]. The given problem instances comprise a range of 100–400 events. These events must be organized within a timetable that covers 9 timeslots per day for 5 days. Ensuring that the scheduling satisfies both room capacity and room feature constraints is crucial. These instances are divided into five small instances, five medium instances, and one large instance. The parameter values and the detailed description of these problem instances have been presented in Tables 1 and 2.

Table 1. Parameter values for the problem instances of [7].

Class	Small	Medium	Large
Number of events	100	400	400
Number of rooms	5	10	10
Number of students	80	200	400
Number of features	5	5	10
Approximate features per room	3	3	5
Percentage feature use	70	80	90
Maximum events per student	20	20	20
Maximum students per event	20	50	100

Table 2. Description of the problem instances of [7].

Instance	n	m	q	p	Max S/E	Max E/S	Avg. F/R	Avg. F/E
small01	100	5	5	80	15	15	2.8	1.88
small02	100	5	5	80	13	17	3.0	2.02
small03	100	5	5	80	20	13	3.0	2.21
small04	100	5	5	80	12	12	4.4	2.92
small05	100	5	5	80	17	19	3.8	2.80
medium01	400	10	5	200	11	20	2.9	2.355
medium02	400	10	5	200	11	20	3.0	2.33
medium03	400	10	5	200	12	20	3.2	2.525
medium04	400	10	5	200	11	20	3.1	2.493
medium05	400	10	5	200	20	20	3.2	2.535
large	400	10	10	400	30	20	4.8	4.37

S/E: students per event; E/S: events per student; F/R: features per room; F/E: features per event.

The GAILS algorithm is primarily executed on these problem instances, and the best combination of parameters is identified. The population size (δ), tournament size (ω), crossover probability (α), and mutation probability (β) are selected as 10, 5, 0.8, and 0.5, respectively. The different parameters are selected for the ILS depending on the size of the problem instance. For small problem instances, Per_1 with $r = 1$ and M_2 with $T = 0.025$ are used. For medium and large problem instances, Per_1 with $r = 5$ and M_1 with $T = 0.1$ are used. The value of γ in the fitness function is set to 10^6, which indicates that any solution I with $f(I) \geq 10^6$ is infeasible.

To evaluate performance, all small problem instances are run independently for 100 trials, with a specific time-bound in each trial. The lowest fitness function value among them is used as the optimal solution's performance measure. For medium and large problem instances, the trials are fixed at 50 and 20, respectively. The maximum number of iterations in LS is set to 200, 10,000, and 100,000, respectively. Initially, the time limit for all small problem instances is fixed at 2 s.

In Table 3, the results obtained for small problem instances are presented, showcasing the fitness function values of the best solution (f_{min}), the worst solution (f_{max}), and the time taken to achieve the best solution (Time). Notably, in each independent trial, the GAILS algorithm consistently produces the best solution with a fitness value of zero for all small problem instances. The graph in Figure 2 illustrates the relationship between the fitness function values and the time GAILS takes for these small problem instances. It is worth noting that the optimal solution is consistently achieved in a mere 0.2 s.

Table 3. Performance of small problem instances.

Instance	f_{min}	f_{max}	Time
small01	0	0	0.052
small02	0	0	0.016
small03	0	0	0.008
small04	0	0	0.152
small05	0	0	0.020

One of the goals of GAILS is to prevent local optima by incorporating perturbation within ILS. To support our claim, we executed medium problem instances under four different time limits: 900, 1200, 1500, and 12,000 s. This was chosen to examine how time duration affects the solution quality. In Tables 4–7, we present the minimum (f_{min}), maximum (f_{max}), and average (f_{avg}) fitness function values for all trials, along with the standard deviation (ς) and the corresponding time duration. The results demonstrate a significant improvement in fitness function values as the time limit increases. Figure 3 illustrates the best fitness function value attained by GAILS across all medium-sized problem instances for the four time periods. Each instance underwent independent testing for 20 trials, with a time limit of 12,000 s.

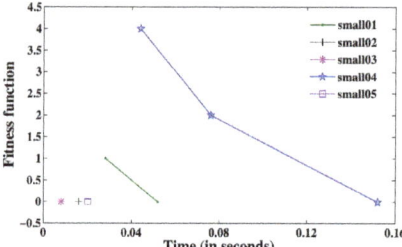

Figure 2. f_{min} versus time for small problem instances.

Table 4. Performance of medium problem instances with a time limit of 900 s.

Instance	f_{min}	f_{max}	f_{avg}	ς	Time
medium01	92	112	102.23	5.538	818.14
medium02	82	120	99.13	9.958	803.51
medium03	122	159	139.77	12.42	857.35
medium04	73	106	90.37	9.397	641.20
medium05	89	128	109.90	12.14	871.69

Table 5. Performance of medium problem instances with a time limit of 1200 s.

Instance	f_{min}	f_{max}	f_{avg}	ς	Time
medium01	85	111	98.43	7.234	1097.41
medium02	78	118	98.73	10.65	1041.31
medium03	112	159	136.87	16.37	1198.55
medium04	69	107	85.97	9.995	1142.16
medium05	77	124	106.23	12.54	1152.59

Table 6. Performance of medium problem instances with a time limit of 1500 s.

Instance	f_{min}	f_{max}	f_{avg}	ς	Time
medium01	78	111	96.50	8.784	1482.74
medium02	75	109	91.27	10.02	1433.71
medium03	102	159	124.17	17.82	1452.59
medium04	60	104	81.97	11.70	1443.61
medium05	70	128	103.70	13.30	1478.37

Table 7. Performance of medium problem instances with a time limit of 12,000 s.

Instance	f_{min}	f_{max}	f_{avg}	ς	Time
medium01	35	52	42.05	5.395	11,755.91
medium02	31	60	40.85	8.362	9893.19
medium03	56	83	68.25	9.453	11,638.80
medium04	35	57	44.05	7.052	11,809.90
medium05	43	66	52.30	8.417	11,498.91

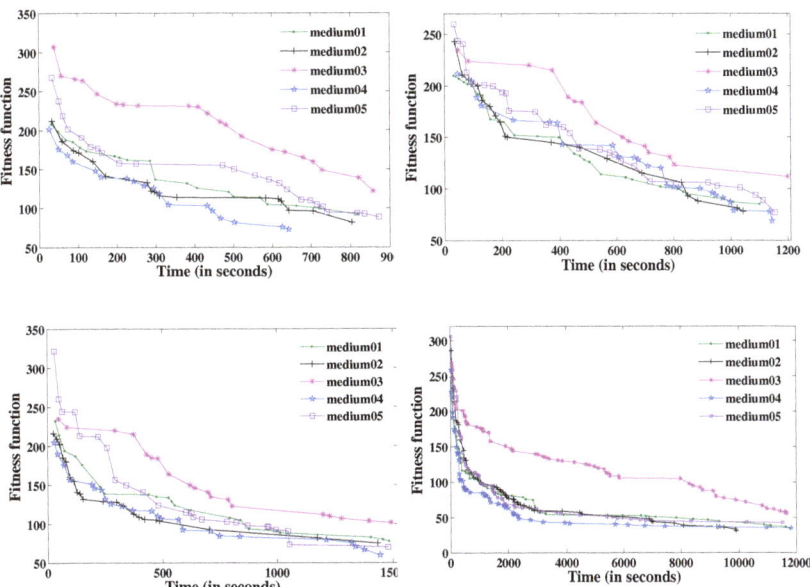

Figure 3. f_{min} versus time for medium problem instances with different time ranges.

Similarly, the large problem instance is executed over three different time limits, taken as 9,000, 12,000, and 15,000 s, and f_{min}, f_{max}, f_{avg}, ς, and time are obtained. These outcomes are presented in Tables 8–10. The best fitness function value versus time obtained by GAILS for the large problem instance over these different time limits is depicted by the graphs in Figure 4.

Table 8. Performance of large problem instance with a time limit of 9000 s.

Instance	f_{min}	f_{max}	f_{avg}	ς	Time (in Seconds)
large	585	708	635.35	40.24	8392.23

Table 9. Performance of large problem instance with a time limit of 12,000 s.

Instance	f_{min}	f_{max}	f_{avg}	ς	Time (in Seconds)
large	580	702	614.95	36.27	11,839.19

Table 10. Performance of large problem instance with a time limit of 15,000 s.

Instance	f_{min}	f_{max}	f_{avg}	ς	Time (in Seconds)
large	572	702	612.6	38.50	14,133.13

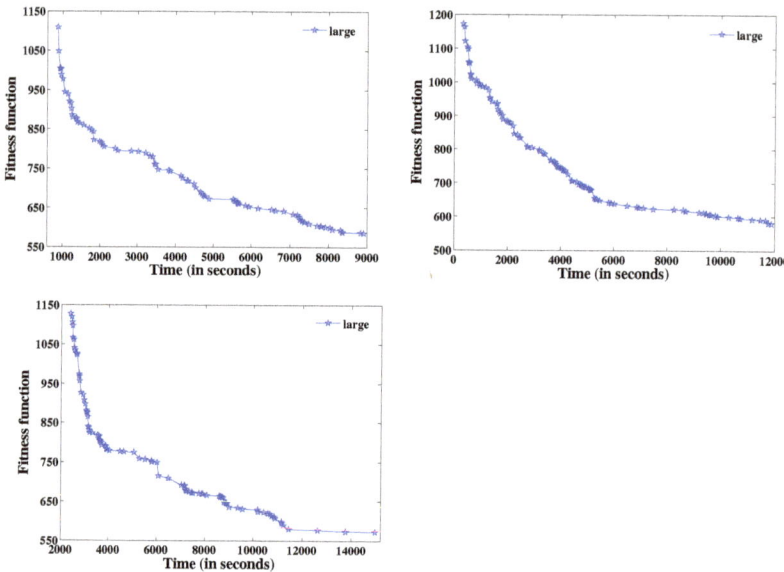

Figure 4. $f_{\min}$ versus time for large problem instance with different time ranges.

Figures 5 and 6 depict boxplots that summarize the outcomes obtained from the medium and large problem instances across various time limits during all the independent trials. The boxplots represent the interquartile range, which is the span between the 25% and 75% quantiles of the data. A bar represents a median, while outliers are indicated using a plus sign.

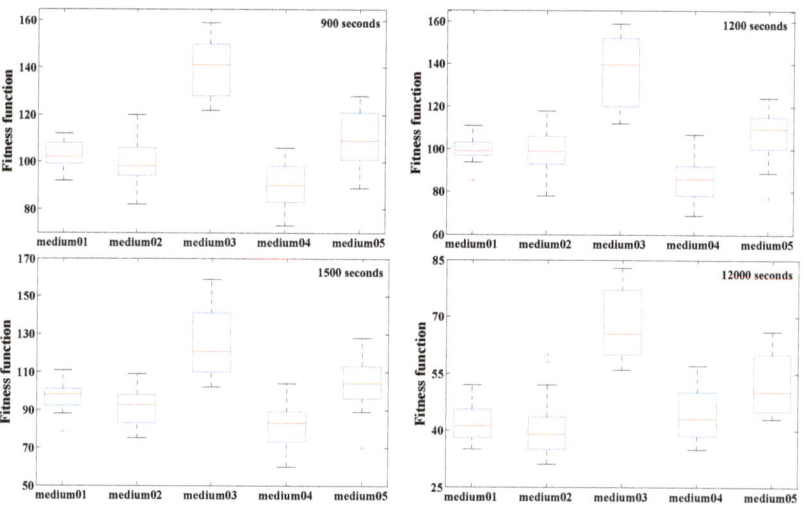

Figure 5. Boxplots of results obtained for medium-sized problems with various time limits.

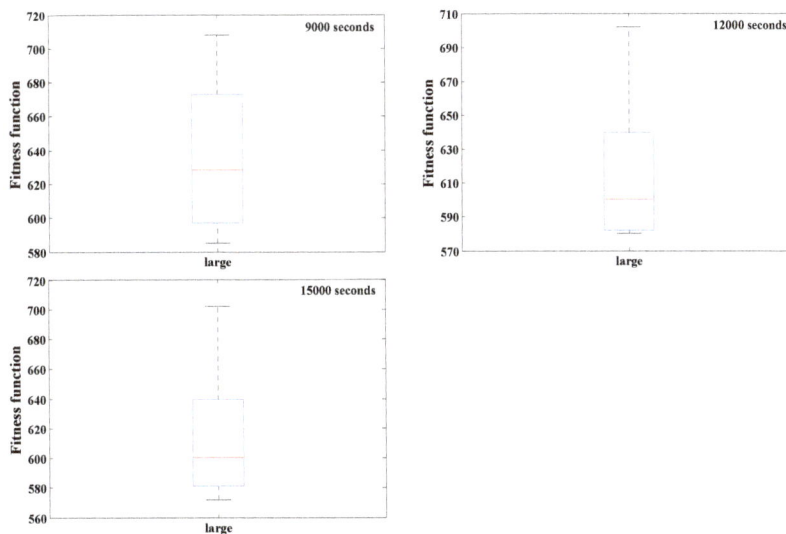

Figure 6. Boxplots of results obtained for large problem instances with various time limits.

5.1.1. Comparative Experiments

In this section, we initially compare the performance of GAILS with ILS, GALS, and NHA [24], as well as the existing algorithms GSGA [20], EGSGA [21], BHSA and MHSA [12]. To ensure a fair comparison, we maintain the same relevant parameters for GALS and ILS as those used in GAILS. For small-sized problem instances, we independently run all algorithms for 100, 50, 50, and 50 trials for GAILS, GALS, ILS, and NHA, respectively. For medium and large-sized problem instances, we independently run GALS and ILS for 50 trials each, while for NHA, this number is limited to 20. Similarly, for GAILS, the figure is 50 for medium-sized problems and 20 for large ones. We restrict the time limit to 2, 900, and 9000 s for small, medium, and large problem instances, respectively, for all algorithms.

We present the comparison of GAILS with GALS, ILS, and NHA through the graphs in Figure 7. The x-axis represents time in seconds, while the y-axis represents the best fitness function value. We give the results obtained by all eight algorithms for all problem instances in terms of f_{min}, f_{max}, f_{avg}, and ς in Table 11. The term $x\%$ Inf. represents the percentage of infeasible solutions over all runs. The comparison results of Figure 7 and Table 11 show that GAILS is more effective than other algorithms, producing lower f_{avg} and ς on most problem instances. In fact, in some cases, the f_{max} obtained by GAILS is better than the f_{min} obtained by other algorithms. These results indicate that GAILS is more reliable than the other algorithms.

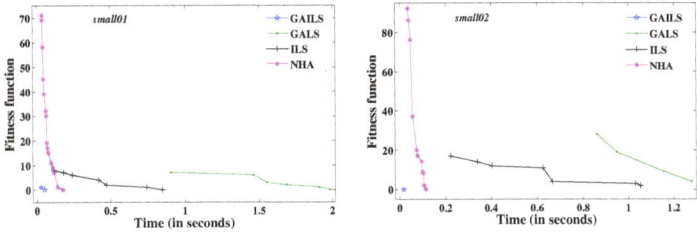

Figure 7. Cont.

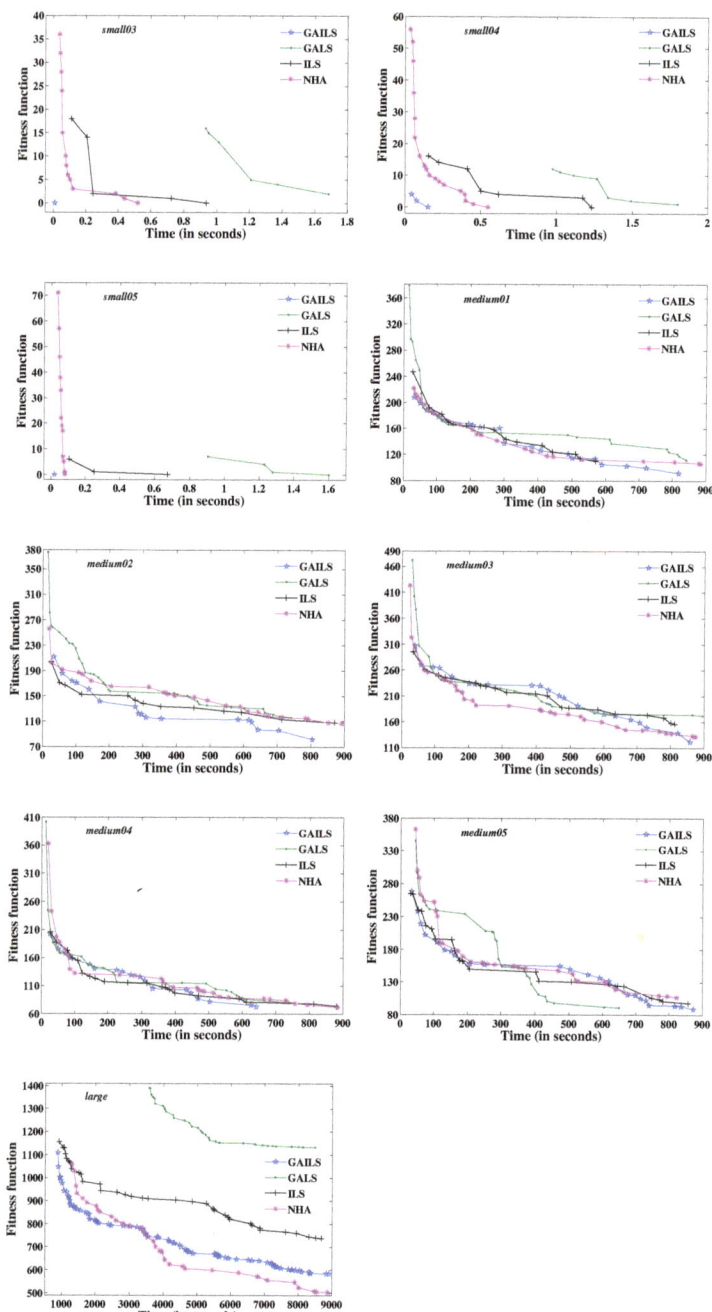

Figure 7. Comparison between GAILS, GALS, ILS, and NHA.

Table 11. Comparison of different algorithms on PE-CTP instances.

Instance		GAILS	GALS	ILS	NHA	GSGA	EGSGA	BHSA	MHSA
small01	f_{min}	0	0	0	0	0	0	3	0
	f_{max}	0	15	17	0	9	4	8	4
	f_{avg}	0	8	7.14	0	2.11	1.71	5	2.5
	ς	0	3.207	3.807	0	3.33	2.42	1.632	1.178
small02	f_{min}	0	4	2	0	0	0	4	0
	f_{max}	0	21	20	0	16	11	9	4
	f_{avg}	0	11.78	10.32	0	2.32	2.01	6.3	2.5
	ς	0	4.117	3.857	0	5.59	3.71	1.494	1.269
small03	f_{min}	0	2	0	0	0	0	2	0
	f_{max}	0	17	21	0	11	2	5	2
	f_{avg}	0	8.98	8.76	0	2.2	1.8	3.7	0.8
	ς	0	3.583	4.547	0	3.21	1.53	1.059	0.788
small04	f_{min}	0	1	0	0	0	0	3	0
	f_{max}	0	14	19	0	11	5	5	3
	f_{avg}	0	7.48	7.58	0	1.84	0.63	3.4	1.2
	ς	0	2.808	4.366	0	2.20	1.89	0.843	0.918
small05	f_{min}	0	0	0	0	0	0	1	0
	f_{max}	0	12	14	0	5	3	4	0
	f_{avg}	0	5.5	4.12	0	0.51	0.55	2.8	0
	ς	0	2.393	2.981	0	1.86	0.82	1.032	0
mediam01	f_{min}	92	112	110	106	240	139	296	168
	f_{max}	112	150	145	147	260	202	318	200
	f_{avg}	102.23	133.7	120.9	131.45	247	142	307.3	179.7
	ς	5.538	11.26	11.51	13.3	9.02	6.384	8.602	10.3
mediam02	f_{min}	82	116	108	107	162	92	236	160
	f_{max}	120	182	140	140	209	134	256	188
	f_{avg}	99.13	138.3	121.3	126.7	172.4	112	245.1	178.67
	ς	9.958	19.43	10.3	9.647	14.49	10.96	6.573	9.772
mediam03	f_{min}	122	172	156	132	242	122	255	176
	f_{max}	159	244	200	185	290	160	286	196
	f_{avg}	139.77	201.5	176.28	151	247	128.4	274.3	182.8
	ς	12.42	20.16	11.5	17.55	6.021	4.832	11.29	7.699
mediam04	f_{min}	73	80	74	72	158	98	231	144
	f_{max}	106	147	120	121	212	112	265	161
	f_{avg}	90.37	116.78	98.4	92.8	162.7	100.2	244.7	153.4
	ς	9.397	18.98	13.79	16.65	17.01	5.451	10.37	7.471
mediam05	f_{min}	89	91	98	107	124	116	207	71
	f_{max}	128	187	166	140	200	151	222	92
	f_{avg}	109.9	153.38	139.6	124.8	128.5	121.3	214.7	80.2
	ς	12.14	24.45	23.04	11.26	23.67	13.29	4.945	8.521
large	f_{min}	585	1133	739	505	801	615	100% Inf.	417
	f_{max}	708	1255	1052	655	921	670	–	530
	f_{avg}	635.35	1189.2	869.15	555	858.2	648.5	–	476.6
	ς	40.24	47.39	99.85	37.54	40.35	19.11	–	37.32

A *t*-test statistical analysis was performed to compare different algorithms, and the results are presented in Table 12. The comparison was conducted with $(n_1 + n_2 - 2)$ degrees of freedom at a significance level of 0.05, where n_1 and n_2 are the sample sizes of the first and second samples, respectively. The *t*-test results are indicated by symbols such as "$s+$", "$s-$", "$+$", "$-$", or "$\sim$" to demonstrate whether the first algorithm is significantly better, significantly worse, insignificantly better, insignificantly worse, or statistically equivalent to the second algorithm, respectively. "Inf." signifies that either or both of the compared algorithms failed to provide a feasible solution for the given problem instance.

The table indicates that GAILS outperforms GALS, ILS, GSGA, and BHSA significantly in all problem instances, and it also performs better than most other algorithms in the majority of cases. This suggests that using only local area- or population-based algorithms is not ideal for solving PE-CTP. Instead, the hybridization of local area-based algorithms with suitable population-based algorithms can significantly improve solution quality.

Table 12. The *t*-test comparison of different algorithms on PE-CTP instances.

Algorithms	s01	s02	s03	s04	s05	m01	m02	m03	m04	m05	l
GAILS vs. GALS	s+	s+	s+	s+	s+	s+	s+	s+	s+	s+	s+
GAILS vs. ILS	s+	s+	s+	s+	s+	s+	s+	s+	s+	s+	s+
GAILS vs. NHA	~	~	~	~	~	s+	s+	s+	+	s+	s−
GAILS vs. GSGA	s+	s+	s+	s+	s+	s+	s+	s+	s+	s+	s+
GAILS vs. EGSGA	s+	s+	s+	s+	s+	s+	s+	s−	s+	s+	+
GAILS vs. BHSA	s+	s+	s+	s+	s+	s+	s+	s+	s+	s+	Inf.
GAILS vs. MHSA	s+	s+	s+	s+	~	s+	s+	s+	s+	s−	s−

Note: Here, *s*, *m* and *l* denotes small, medium, and large respectively.

5.1.2. Comparison with Existing Algorithms

In this segment, we compared the experimental results of the proposed GAILS algorithm with some other existing algorithms and displayed them in Table 13. The running time limits for each independent trial of the small, medium, and large problem instances are taken as 2, 12,000, and 15,000 s, respectively. The description of the compared algorithms under which these outcomes were reported is as follows:

GAILS   The proposed exploration and exploitation-based metaheuristic approach by combining GA with ILS.

B1   The results of a population-based LS heuristic embedded within an LS proposed by [14] were reported from 20 independent trials. Each trial lasted for 120–600 s for small problem instances, while for medium and large problem instances, the duration was 36,000–46,800 s.

B2   The tabu-search hyper-heuristic proposed by [9] involves heuristics competing to be selected by the hyper-heuristic. The results were reported from five independent trials with different iterations: 12,000, 1200, and 5400 for small, medium, and large problem instances, respectively.

B3   Ref. [54] proposed a tabu-based MA, and the results were reported from five independent trials, each with 100,000 iterations per trial. Each trial lasted less than 60 s for small problem instances, while for medium and large problem instances, the duration was 14,400–28,800 s.

B4   Ref. [11] proposed an adaptive randomized descent algorithm called a new heuristic search. The results were reported from 11 independent trials, each with 200,000 iterations. Each trial lasted for 180–600 s for small problem instances, while for medium and large problem instances, the duration was 14,400–32,400 s.

B5   Ref. [55] proposed a randomized iterative improvement algorithm with a composite neighborhood structure. The results were reported from five independent trials with 200,000 iterations per trial. Each trial lasted for a maximum of 50 s for small problem instances, while for medium problem instances, the duration was 28,800 s.

B6   Ref. [22] proposed a hybrid metaheuristic approach that combines an electromagnetic-like mechanism with the great deluge algorithm. The results were reported from five independent trials with 200,000 iterations per trial. For small, medium, and large problem instances, the duration was 90, 7200, and 21,600 s, respectively.

B7   Ref. [56] proposed an extended great deluge algorithm, and the results were reported from ten independent trials, with each trial having 200,000 iterations. For small problems, the best solutions were achieved in 15–60 s.

B8   Ref. [57] proposed a modified great deluge algorithm that uses a non-linear decay of water level. The results were reported from ten independent trials, each with a different duration depending on the problem instance size: 3600, 4700, and 6700 s for small, medium, and large problem instances, respectively.

B9   Ref. [58] proposed a non-linear great deluge hyper-heuristic approach that uses a learning mechanism and a non-linear great deluge acceptance criterion. The

B10   Ref. [12] proposed a modified harmony search algorithm, and the reported results were based on ten independent trials, each with 100,000 iterations.

B11   Ref. [59] proposed a simulation of fish swarm intelligence adapting the biological behavior of fish. The results were reported based on 11 independent trials, with 500,000 iterations per trial.

B12   Ref. [60] proposed a hybridization between the multi-neighborhood particle collision algorithm and adaptive randomized descent algorithm acceptance criteria. The results were reported from 20 independent trials, each consisting of 200,000 iterations.

B13   Ref. [61] proposed the hybridization of the hill-climbing optimizer within the ABC algorithm. The reported results' running time range was measured between 360 and 25,200 s.

B14   Ref. [62] proposed hybridizing the great deluge and ABC algorithms. The findings were derived from 30 independent trials, each taking 900–7200 s for the primary ABC and 3600–14,400 s for the proposed algorithm, depending on the problem instance size.

B15   Ref. [63] proposed a memetic computing technique called the hybrid harmony search algorithm. The reported results did not have a running time limitation; however, the minimum time reported to achieve the solutions was 21,600 s.

B16   Ref. [64] hybridized a non-dominated sorting GA (NSGA-II) with two LS techniques and a TS heuristic. They added an additional LS technique to the existing LS of NSGA-II for further performance enhancement. The outcomes were reported based on 50 independent trials of small and medium problem instances, with a running time of 100 and 1000 s, respectively. Additionally, the large problem instance was reported after 20 runs with a time-bound of 10,000 s.

B17   Ref. [27] proposed a hybrid approach based on the improved parallel genetic algorithm and local search (IPGALS) to solve the PE-CTP. In their approach, the LS is used to strengthen the GA. The result is reported after ten independent executions. They also categorized their parameters into three groups based on the number of events: less than 200, between 200 and 400, and more than 400.

Here, we would like to emphasize that the algorithms referred to earlier, along with the circumstances in which their results were documented, have been widely employed in the literature to evaluate the efficacy of the proposed algorithm. While this method may not be entirely equitable, as the conditions for each algorithm could vary, the reported results may give us a general idea of the proposed algorithm's effectiveness.

Table 13. Comparison results on PE-CTP instances.

Instance	GAILS	B1	B2	B3	B4	B5	B6	B7	B8	B9	B10	B11	B12	B13	B14	B15	B16	B17
small01	0	0	1	0	0	0	0	0	3	0	0	0	0	0	0	0	0	0
small02	0	0	2	0	0	0	0	0	0	4	0	0	0	0	0	0	0	0
small03	0	0	0	0	0	0	0	0	0	6	0	0	0	0	0	0	0	0
small04	0	0	1	0	0	0	0	0	0	6	0	0	0	0	0	0	0	0
small05	0	0	0	0	0	0	0	0	0	0	0	0	0	0	0	0	0	0
medium01	35	41	146	55	82	242	96	80	140	71	168	45	64	73	52	99	127	84
medium02	31	39	173	70	78	161	96	105	130	82	160	40	65	79	45	73	122	99
medium03	56	60	267	102	136	265	135	139	189	137	176	61	91	132	96	130	172	142
medium04	35	39	169	32	73	181	79	88	112	55	144	35	66	69	52	105	110	84
medium05	43	55	303	61	103	151	87	88	141	106	71	49	89	61	56	53	160	112
large	572	463	1166	653	680	100% Inf.	683	730	876	777	417	407	576	462	461	385	904	516

Table 13 shows that GAILS provides the best fitness function values for problem instances medium01, medium02, medium03, and medium05. For the medium04 problem instance, GAILS delivers the second-best fitness function value. Moreover, we have noticed that the solution quality continues to improve as the time restriction extends, a unique characteristic not found in other approaches. This result demonstrates that GAILS can effectively avoid local optima.

5.2. Experiments on ITC2007's Benchmark Dataset of CB-CTP

The proposed approach is tested on the 21 CB-CTP instances as presented and defined in the third track of ITC2007 (UD2). These problem instances are described in Table 14. In order to obtain experimental results for this subsection, each problem instance is run independently for 20 trials by fixing a specific time-bound for each trial. The least fitness function value among them is selected as an optimal solution. The time limit for each independent trial is restricted to 600 s.

Table 14. Description of CB-CTP instances.

Instance	n	TNL	m	v	u	x	MiLDC	MaLDC
comp01	30	160	6	6	5	14	2	5
comp02	82	283	16	5	5	70	2	4
comp03	72	251	16	5	5	68	2	4
comp04	79	286	18	5	5	57	2	4
comp05	54	152	9	6	6	139	2	4
comp06	108	361	18	5	5	70	2	4
comp07	131	434	20	5	5	77	2	4
comp08	86	324	18	5	5	61	2	4
comp09	76	279	18	5	5	75	2	4
comp10	115	370	18	5	5	67	2	4
comp11	30	162	5	9	5	13	2	6
comp12	88	218	11	6	6	150	2	4
comp13	82	308	19	5	5	66	2	3
comp14	85	275	17	5	5	60	2	4
comp15	72	251	16	5	5	68	2	4
comp16	108	366	20	5	5	71	2	4
comp17	99	339	17	5	5	70	2	4
comp18	47	138	9	6	6	52	2	3
comp19	74	277	16	5	5	66	2	4
comp20	121	390	19	5	5	78	2	4
comp21	94	327	18	5	5	78	2	4

MiLDC: Minimum lectures/day/curricula; MaLDC: Maximum lectures/day/curricula.

To find the best combination of parameters for GAILS, we first run trials on all possible combinations of parameters, limiting each trial to 100 s. The values of parameters α and β are selected from $\{0, 0.2, 0.4, 0.5, 0.6, 0.8, 1.0\}$ whereas the value of δ and ω is chosen from $\{5, 10, 20, 50\}$. Similarly, the type of Perturbation and AcceptanceCriterion are selected from the possibilities given in Section 4.1. The best resulting configuration of parameters selected are: $\alpha = 0.8, \beta = 0.5, \delta = 10, \omega = 5$, Perturbation = Per_1 with $r = 5$ and AcceptanceCriterion = M_1 with $T = 0.1$. The maximum number of iterations in the LS is also fixed at 200,000. The results obtained for all the 21 CB-CTP instances out of these 20 independent trials are displayed in Table 15 in terms of $f_{min}, f_{max}, f_{avg}, \varsigma$, and Time. Also, the fitness function values versus time taken by GAILS for eight randomly selected problem instances are depicted by the graphs in Figure 8. The x-axis, in this case, represents time (in seconds), and the y-axis represents the best fitness value.

Table 15. Results obtained for CB-CTP instances.

Instance	f_{min}	f_{max}	f_{avg}	ς	Time (in Seconds)
comp01	5	5	5	0	18.34
comp02	24	55	36.4	11.70	257.62
comp03	72	91	79.8	6.579	436.95
comp04	35	50	43	5.395	373.42
comp05	303	321	314	6.236	440.36
comp06	44	59	50.4	5.254	264.33
comp07	7	26	14.5	6.932	324.46
comp08	39	50	43.4	3.718	450.95
comp09	100	116	107.8	5.073	207.11
comp10	6	24	14.3	6.273	335.82
comp11	0	0	0	0	7.76
comp12	349	367	356.3	6.395	260.39
comp13	65	78	71.5	4.428	392.9
comp14	52	62	56.3	3.529	302.52
comp15	72	94	82.8	7.451	463.62
comp16	31	42	36.7	3.831	293.94
comp17	75	86	79.3	4.001	351.08
comp18	79	94	86.3	5.165	418.52
comp19	62	76	68.3	4.715	302.66
comp20	25	41	30.3	5.187	412.42
comp21	83	107	94.4	8.303	219.11

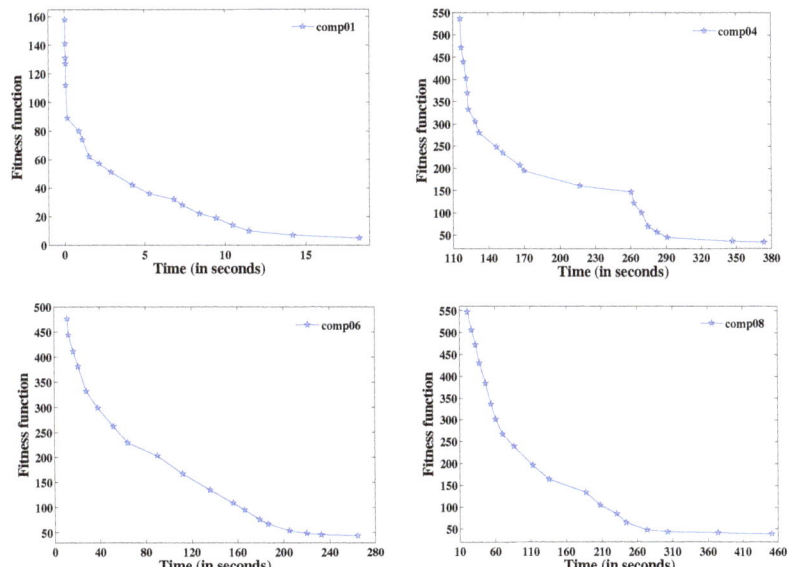

Figure 8. *Cont.*

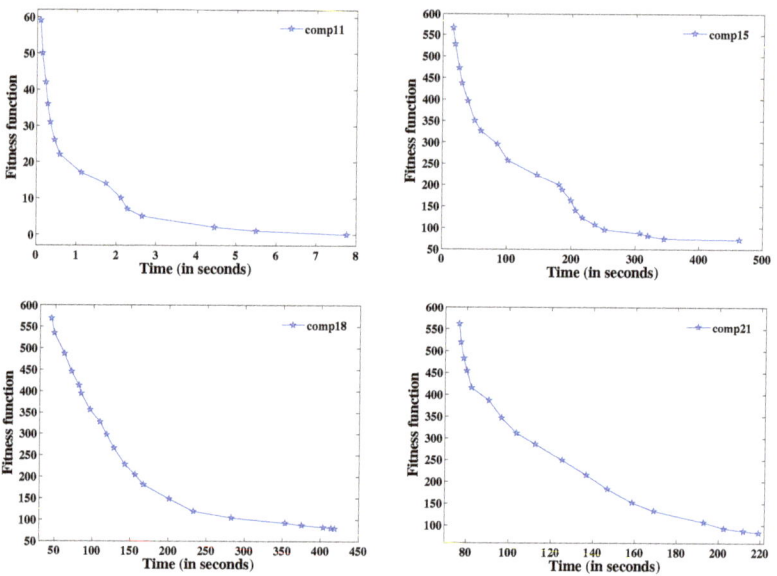

Figure 8. Best fitness function value versus time for CB-CTP instances.

The fitness function values obtained for all 21 instances from all 20 independent trials are summarized by the boxplot in Figure 9.

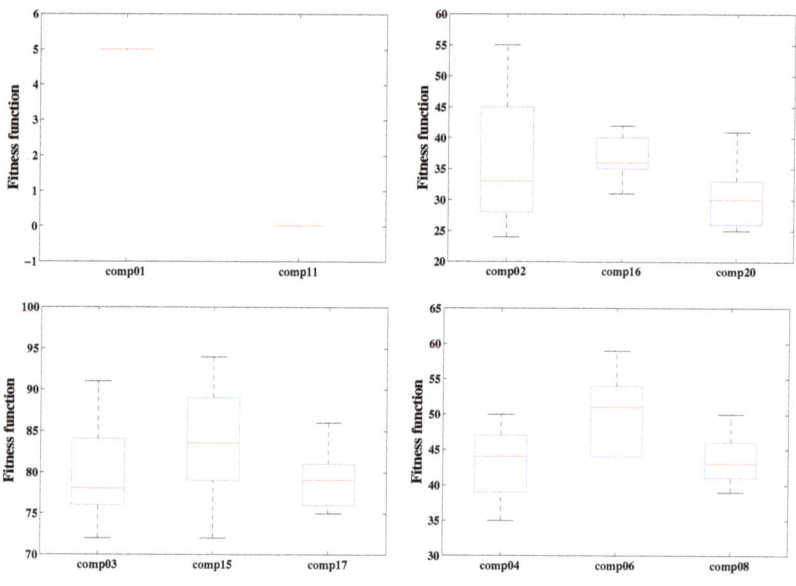

Figure 9. *Cont.*

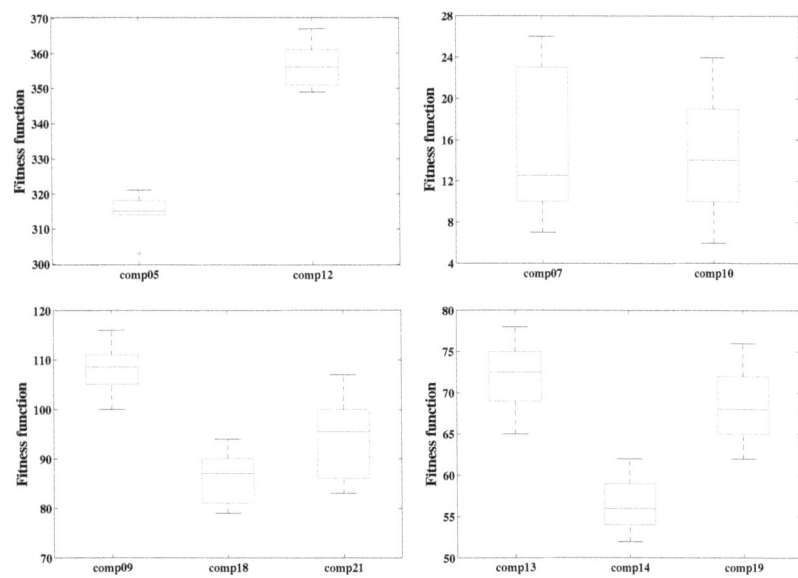

Figure 9. Boxplots of results obtained for CB-CTP instances.

5.2.1. Comparative Experiments

In this segment, we compare the performance of GAILS with the performance of the five finalist algorithms in the third track of ITC2007. These algorithms C1, C2, C3, C4, and C5 were proposed by [29,32,35,39,65], respectively. For all the 21 CB-CTP instances, each of these five algorithms was run independently for ten trials. A ranking was then calculated based on these 50 outcomes for each problem instance. Finally, a ranking was established according to the ranks realized on these 21 CB-CTP instances. Rank-wise, these five finalists were C1, C2, C3, C4, and C5. The detailed results of their outcomes in terms of $f_{min}, f_{max}, f_{avg}$, and ς are given in Table 16.

Table 16. Comparison of different algorithms on CB-CTP instances.

Instance	C1				C2				C3				C4				C5			
	f_{min}	f_{max}	f_{avg}	ς	f_{min}	f_{max}	f_{avg}	ς	f_{min}	f_{max}	f_{avg}	ς	f_{min}	f_{max}	f_{avg}	ς	f_{min}	f_{max}	f_{avg}	ς
comp01	5	5	5	0	5	5	5	0	5	6	5.1	0.316	5	9	6.7	1.059	10	68	27	19.66
comp02	51	70	61.3	6.783	55	74	61.2	5.329	50	76	65.6	7.905	111	168	142.7	21.25	111	146	131.1	11.05
comp03	84	103	94.8	5.922	71	101	84.5	8.086	82	95	89.1	4.932	128	188	160.3	18.18	119	167	138.4	14.64
comp04	37	48	42.8	3.490	43	53	46.9	3.315	35	44	39.2	2.530	72	91	82	6.992	72	110	90.2	10.97
comp05	330	379	343.5	14.62	309	346	326	14.23	312	353	334.5	13.54	410	691	525.4	89.45	426	2000	811.5	628.80
comp06	48	65	56.8	5.350	53	80	69.4	8.656	69	84	74.1	4.408	100	129	110.8	8.377	130	181	149.3	17.20
comp07	20	45	33.9	7.172	28	49	41.5	6.671	42	56	49.8	4.467	57	89	76.6	10.15	110	191	153.4	22.53
comp08	41	55	46.5	4.353	49	58	52.6	2.989	40	50	46	2.828	77	90	81.7	4.448	83	116	96.5	9.733
comp09	109	117	113.1	2.767	105	127	116.5	6.900	110	121	113.3	3.234	150	178	164.1	9.769	139	157	148.9	6.967
comp10	16	27	21.3	4.423	21	48	34.8	9.343	27	49	36.9	6.454	71	96	81.3	7.818	85	122	101.3	12.693
comp11	0	0	0	0	0	0	0	0	0	0	0	0	0	2	0.3	0.675	3	8	5.7	1.337
comp12	333	367	351.6	10.352	343	380	360.1	12.441	351	378	361.6	8.527	442	544	485.1	32.78	408	487	445.3	29.42
comp13	66	81	73.9	4.533	73	87	79.2	4.541	68	82	76.1	4.202	98	125	110.4	9.204	113	145	122.9	10.556
comp14	59	69	61.8	2.936	57	77	65.9	6.226	59	68	62.3	3.433	90	108	99	5.077	84	127	105.9	12.71
comp15	84	103	94.8	5.922	71	101	84.5	8.086	82	95	89.1	4.932	128	188	160.3	18.18	119	138	14.79	
comp16	34	49	41.2	4.826	39	57	49.1	5.567	40	60	50.2	6.477	81	103	92.6	6.620	84	127	107.3	11.98
comp17	83	92	86.6	2.547	91	111	100.7	6.848	102	115	107.3	4.423	124	161	143.4	13.56	152	178	166.6	9.454
comp18	83	102	91.7	5.539	69	93	80.7	6.255	68	80	73.3	3.773	116	145	129.4	9.312	110	142	126.8	11.033
comp19	62	74	68.8	3.676	65	77	69.5	4.353	75	85	79.6	3.373	107	184	132.8	23.612	111	148	125.4	12.633
comp20	27	44	34.3	4.855	47	72	60.9	8.171	61	71	65	3.590	88	109	97.5	6.399	144	201	179.3	17.06
comp21	103	121	108	6.683	106	137	124.7	8.693	123	150	138.1	8.80	174	210	185.3	12.81	169	202	185.8	12.02

In order to compare different algorithms statistically, their t-test comparison was performed, and the obtained results are presented in Table 17. This statistical comparison was implemented by using $n_1 + n_2 - 2$ degree of freedom at 0.05 level of significance, where n_1 and n_2 are the sample sizes of the first and second samples, respectively. The *t*-test comparison of the two algorithms is also demonstrated as "$s+$", "$s-$", "$+$", "$-$", or "$\sim$". The table clearly shows that GAILS outperforms the other algorithms in the majority of the problem instances.

Table 17. The *t*-test comparison of different algorithms on CB-CTP instances.

Instance	GAILS vs. C1	GAILS vs. C2	GAILS vs. C3	GAILS vs. C4	GAILS vs. C5
comp01	$\sim$	$\sim$	$+$	$s+$	$s+$
comp02	$s+$	$s+$	$s+$	$s+$	$s+$
comp03	$s+$	$+$	$s+$	$s+$	$s+$
comp04	$\sim$	$s+$	$s-$	$s+$	$s+$
comp05	$s+$	$s+$	$s+$	$s+$	$s+$
comp06	$s+$	$s+$	$s+$	$s+$	$s+$
comp07	$s+$	$s+$	$s+$	$s+$	$s+$
comp08	$+$	$s+$	$+$	$s+$	$s+$
comp09	$s+$	$s+$	$s+$	$s+$	$s+$
comp10	$s+$	$s+$	$s+$	$s+$	$s+$
comp11	$\sim$	$\sim$	$\sim$	$+$	$s+$
comp12	$\sim$	$+$	$+$	$s+$	$s+$
comp13	$+$	$s+$	$s+$	$s+$	$s+$
comp14	$s+$	$s+$	$s+$	$s+$	$s+$
comp15	$s+$	$+$	$s+$	$s+$	$s+$
comp16	$s+$	$s+$	$s+$	$s+$	$s+$
comp17	$s+$	$s+$	$s+$	$s+$	$s+$
comp18	$s+$	$s-$	$s-$	$s+$	$s+$
comp19	$+$	$+$	$s+$	$s+$	$s+$
comp20	$+$	$s+$	$s+$	$s+$	$s+$
comp21	$s+$	$s+$	$s+$	$s+$	$s+$

It is simple to arrive at the conclusion that an algorithm that relies solely on exploration or exploitation cannot be the best option for solving CB-CTP. Therefore, a suitable choice that can significantly enhance the solution quality of CB-CTP is the hybridization of an exploration-based algorithm (GA) with an appropriate exploitation-based algorithm (ILS).

5.2.2. Comparison with Existing Algorithms

GAILS is now being compared to the 20 existing state-of-the-art algorithms tested on CB-CTP instances. These algorithms are listed in Table 18. The comparison of these algorithms with GAILS is demonstrated in Table 19. Entries in this table signify a feasible solution's measured best fitness function value. Here, the entry "$-$" denotes an untried instance in the experiment.

Table 18. Keys of the algorithms used for comparison.

No.	Key	Algorithm	Reference
1	GAILS	GA with ILS	Proposed method
2	D1	Electromagnetic-like mechanism and great deluge algorithm	[22]
3	D2	Constraint-based solver	[35]
4	D3	Hybrid adaptive TS algorithm	[32]
5	D4	TS algorithm with relaxed stopping condition	[32]
6	D5	Combination of great deluge and TS algorithms	[23]
7	D6	Dynamic TS algorithm	[66]

Table 18. Cont.

No.	Key	Algorithm	Reference
8	D7	Integer programming approach	[67]
9	D8	General purpose constraint satisfaction problem solver	[29]
10	D9	Memetic TS algorithm using random neighborhood	[68]
11	D10	Memetic TS algorithm using general neighborhood	[68]
12	D11	Repair based LS algorithm	[39]
13	D12	Heuristic local search based on the principles of threshold accepting	[65]
14	D13	Hybrid LS algorithm	[69]
15	D14	ABC algorithm	[41]
16	D15	New swarm intelligence algorithm based on the ABC algorithm	[42]
17	D16	Harmony search algorithm	[38]
18	D17	Two mixed-integer programming techniques with flow formulation	[70]
19	D18	Adaptive large neighborhood search	[71]
20	D19	Localized island model GA with dual dynamic migration policy	[72]
21	D20	A competition-guided multi-neighborhood local search algorithm	[45]

Table 19. Comparison results on CB-CTP instances.

Instance	GAILS	D1	D2	D3	D4	D5	D6	D7	D8	D9	D10	D11	D12	D13	D14	D15	D16	D17	D18	D19	D20
comp01	5	5	5	5	5	5	5	13	5	5	5	9	5	5	23	5	322	5	5	5	5
comp02	24	39	43	34	56	39	75	43	50	30	27	103	108	41	190	86	732	8	33	382	39
comp03	72	76	72	70	79	73	93	76	82	70	73	101	115	66	171	101	665	38	71	82	70
comp04	35	35	35	38	38	36	45	38	35	35	39	55	67	35	132	57	577	35	35	38	36
comp05	303	315	298	298	316	309	326	314	312	300	312	370	408	301	1483	377	1297	186	292	5	303
comp06	44	50	41	47	55	43	62	41	69	42	30	112	94	43	237	87	879	16	39	0	42
comp07	7	12	14	19	26	17	38	19	42	8	10	97	56	18	259	61	930	6	12	0	13
comp08	39	37	39	43	42	40	50	43	40	37	37	72	75	39	154	60	645	37	39	0	39
comp09	100	104	103	99	104	104	119	102	110	100	100	132	153	96	190	127	685	74	100	0	100
comp10	6	10	9	16	19	12	27	14	27	7	5	74	66	15	210	51	816	4	11	0	13
comp11	0	0	0	0	0	0	0	0	0	0	0	1	0	0	18	0	179	0	0	0	0
comp12	349	337	331	320	342	334	358	405	351	323	330	393	430	320	583	397	1398	142	310	242	332
comp13	65	61	66	65	72	67	77	68	68	59	62	97	101	64	156	90	694	59	60	0	65
comp14	52	53	53	52	57	54	59	54	59	55	53	87	88	53	165	77	702	44	52	0	53
comp15	72	73	84	69	79	88	87	–	82	70	73	119	128	66	193	92	665	38	67	0	71
comp16	31	32	34	38	46	52	47	–	40	18	18	84	81	28	215	83	827	13	29	32	31
comp17	75	72	83	80	88	88	86	–	102	65	61	152	124	71	206	110	830	44	63	81	69
comp18	79	77	83	67	75	84	71	–	68	72	79	110	116	69	122	97	510	36	65	0	74
comp19	62	60	62	59	64	71	74	–	75	58	57	111	107	60	205	82	608	56	61	75	62
comp20	25	22	27	35	32	34	54	–	61	11	4	144	88	29	263	77	950	0	21	46	28
comp21	83	95	103	105	107	98	117	–	123	86	90	169	174	89	233	74	835	57	92	0	94

Table 19 demonstrates that GAILS can deliver competitive results with current state-of-the-art algorithms. From the obtained results, it can be observed that the appropriate combination of a population-based algorithm emphasizing exploration and a local area-based algorithm emphasizing exploitation can help to reduce the values of the fitness function and produce good results for the CB-CTP in comparison to other existing algorithms.

6. Conclusions

An exploration-and-exploitation-based hybrid approach is proposed by combining GA with ILS to solve the PE-CTP and CB-CTP. This hybrid approach is influential yet straightforward and manages to produce several improved results. The algorithm uses ILS, which utilizes various kinds of moves for neighborhood and perturbation. Furthermore, it enables the refinement of the entire population generated by GA. The algorithm is tested over 11 benchmark PE-CTP instances and 21 benchmark CB-CTP instances in two separate experiments. In the first experiment, all the PE-CTP instances are run, each with different execution times, and the least fitness function value is used as their performance measure. A comparison with existing approaches has been carried out to demonstrate its effectiveness over other approaches. Statistically, t-test comparisons also displayed the dominance of GAILS. In this experiment, it is also observed that the solution quality improves a lot for the extended time limit, establishing that by using the perturbation operator, GAILS is capable of avoiding the local optimal. In the second experiment, the performance of GAILS is measured by running each problem instance for twenty trials, and each trial lasts for 600 s. Its performance is also compared with several other existing algorithms. The computational results show that the proposed algorithm can produce competitive results when compared with existing state-of-the-art algorithms.

Among the timetabling (scheduling) problems, the UCTP is one of the most complex problems, with many decision variables and various soft and hard constraints. Problems with formally simpler problem statements such as the industrial capacity planning [73,74] are sometimes large-scale, and the standard approach of reducing the problem to an integer linear programming problem leads to a huge increase in the number of variables, so in practice, it is necessary to apply various combinations of heuristic algorithms, including evolutionary algorithms, greedy search algorithms, and local search.

Our proposed algorithm gives encouraging results on several instances of rather complex problems of two types. Therefore, further research can be aimed at applying this approach to other scheduling problems; for example, to the problem of capacity utilization planning. The limits of applicability of the proposed approach can be explored and, possibly, extended to other complex optimization problems with Boolean variables for which local search methods are known to be effective.

Author Contributions: Conceptualization, R.P.B., J.S., S.S., M.M., D.K.G., S.V., P.S.S., L.A.K. and D.K.; methodology, R.P.B., J.S., S.S., S.V. and P.S.S.; software, R.P.B., J.S., M.M. and S.V.; validation, R.P.B., J.S., S.S., M.M., D.K.G., S.V., P.S.S., L.A.K. and D.K.; data curation, R.P.B., J.S., S.S., M.M. and S.V.; writing—original draft preparation, R.P.B., J.S., S.S., M.M., D.K.G., S.V., P.S.S., L.A.K. and D.K.; writing—review and editing, P.S.S., L.A.K., D.K.G.; supervision, R.P.B., J.S., D.K.G. and P.S.S.; project administration, R.P.B., J.S., S.S., M.M., D.K.G., S.V., P.S.S., L.A.K. and D.K.; funding acquisition, P.S.S., D.K. All authors have read and agreed to the published version of the manuscript.

Funding: This work is supported by the Ministry of Science and Higher Education of the Russian Federation (Grant No. 075-15-2022-1121).

Data Availability Statement: Data and code will be provided on request to authors.

Acknowledgments: Predrag Stanimirović acknowledges support from the Ministry of Education, Science and Technological Development, Republic of Serbia, grant No. 451-03-47/2023-01/200124 and from the Science Fund of the Republic of Serbia, (No. 7750185, Quantitative Automata Models: Fundamental Problems and Applications-QUAM).

Conflicts of Interest: The authors declare no conflict of interest.

References

1. Wren, A. Scheduling, timetabling and rostering—A special relationship? In *Practice and theory of automated timetabling*; Springer: Cham, Switzerland, 1996; pp. 46–75.
2. Di Gaspero, L.; McCollum, B.; Schaerf, A. *The Second International Timetabling Competition (ITC-2007): Curriculum-Based Course Timetabling (Track 3)*; Technical Report, QUB/IEEE/Tech/ITC2007/CurriculumCTT/v1.0; Queen's University: Belfast, UK, 2007.
3. Gotlieb, C. The construction of class-teacher timetables. In Proceedings of the International Federation of Information Processing Congress, Munich, Germany, 27 August–1 September 1962; Volume 62, pp. 73–77.
4. Carter, M.W.; Laporte, G. Recent developments in practical course timetabling. In *Practice and Theory of Automated Timetabling II*; Springer: Cham, Switzerland, 1998; pp. 3–19.
5. Chiarandini, M.; Birattari, M.; Socha, K.; Rossi-Doria, O. An effective hybrid algorithm for university course timetabling. *J. Sched.* **2006**, *9*, 403–432. [CrossRef]
6. Jat, S.N.; Yang, S. A hybrid genetic algorithm and tabu search approach for post enrolment course timetabling. *J. Sched.* **2011**, *14*, 617–637. [CrossRef]
7. Socha, K.; Knowles, J.; Sampels, M. A max-min ant system for the university course timetabling problem. In *Ant Algorithms*; Springer: Cham, Switzerland, 2002; pp. 1–13.
8. Rossi-Doria, O.; Sampels, M.; Birattari, M.; Chiarandini, M.; Dorigo, M.; Gambardella, L.M.; Knowles, J.; Manfrin, M.; Mastrolilli, M.; Paechter, B.; et al. A comparison of the performance of different metaheuristics on the timetabling problem. In *Practice and Theory of Automated Timetabling IV*; Springer: Cham, Switzerland, 2003; pp. 329–351.
9. Burke, E.K.; Kendall, G.; Soubeiga, E. A tabu-search hyperheuristic for timetabling and rostering. *J. Heuristics* **2003**, *9*, 451–470. [CrossRef]
10. Burke, E.K.; McCollum, B.; Meisels, A.; Petrovic, S.; Qu, R. A graph-based hyper-heuristic for educational timetabling problems. *Eur. J. Oper. Res.* **2007**, *176*, 177–192. [CrossRef]

11. Abuhamdah, A.; Ayob, M. Adaptive randomized descent algorithm for solving course timetabling problems. *Int. J. Phys. Sci.* **2010**, *5*, 2516–2522.
12. Al-Betar, M.A.; Khader, A.T. A harmony search algorithm for university course timetabling. *Ann. Oper. Res.* **2012**, *194*, 3–31. [CrossRef]
13. Cambazard, H.; Hebrard, E.; O'Sullivan, B.; Papadopoulos, A. Local search and constraint programming for the post enrolment-based course timetabling problem. *Ann. Oper. Res.* **2012**, *194*, 111–135. [CrossRef]
14. Abuhamdah, A.; Ayob, M.; Kendall, G.; Sabar, N.R. Population based Local Search for university course timetabling problems. *Appl. Intell.* **2014**, *40*, 44–53. [CrossRef]
15. Méndez-Díaz, I.; Zabala, P.; Miranda-Bront, J.J. An ILP based heuristic for a generalization of the post-enrollment course timetabling problem. *Comput. Oper. Res.* **2016**, *76*, 195–207. [CrossRef]
16. Goh, S.L.; Kendall, G.; Sabar, N.R. Simulated annealing with improved reheating and learning for the post enrolment course timetabling problem. *J. Oper. Res. Soc.* **2019**, *70*, 873–888. [CrossRef]
17. Blum, C.; Roli, A. Metaheuristics in combinatorial optimization: Overview and conceptual comparison. *Acm Comput. Surv. (CSUR)* **2003**, *35*, 268–308. [CrossRef]
18. Abdullah, S.; Turabieh, H. Generating university course timetable using genetic algorithms and local search. In Proceedings of the Third International Conference on Convergence and Hybrid Information Technology (ICCIT'08), Busan, Republic of Korea, 11–13 November 2008; Volume 1, pp. 254–260.
19. Abdullah, S.; Burke, E.K.; McCollum, B. A hybrid evolutionary approach to the university course timetabling problem. In Proceedings of the 2007 IEEE Congress on Evolutionary Computation, Singapore, 25–28 September 2007; pp. 1764–1768.
20. Jat, S.N.; Yang, S. A guided search genetic algorithm for the university course timetabling problem. In Proceedings of the Multidisciplinary International Conference on Scheduling: Theory and Applications IV, Dublin, Ireland, 10–12 August 2009; pp. 180–191.
21. Yang, S.; Jat, S.N. Genetic algorithms with guided and local search strategies for university course timetabling. *IEEE Trans. Syst. Man Cybern. Part Appl. Rev.* **2011**, *41*, 93–106. [CrossRef]
22. Abdullah, S.; Turabieh, H.; McCollum, B.; McMullan, P. A hybrid metaheuristic approach to the university course timetabling problem. *J. Heuristics* **2012**, *18*, 1–23. [CrossRef]
23. Shaker, K.; Abdullah, S.; Alqudsi, A.; Jalab, H. Hybridizing Meta-heuristics Approaches for Solving University Course Timetabling Problems. In *Rough Sets and Knowledge Technology*; Springer: Cham, Switzerland, 2013; pp. 374–384.
24. Badoni, R.P.; Gupta, D.; Mishra, P. A new hybrid algorithm for university course timetabling problem using events based on groupings of students. *Comput. Ind. Eng.* **2014**, *78*, 12–25. [CrossRef]
25. Fong, C.W.; Asmuni, H.; McCollum, B. A hybrid swarm-based approach to university timetabling. *IEEE Trans. Evol. Comput.* **2015**, *19*, 870–884. [CrossRef]
26. Unprasertporn, T.; Lohpetch, D. An Outperforming Hybrid Discrete Particle Swarm Optimization for Solving the Timetabling Problem. In Proceedings of the 12th International Conference on Knowledge and Smart Technology (KST'20), Pattaya, Thailand, 29 January–1 February 2020; pp. 18–23.
27. Rezaeipanah, A.; Matoori, S.S.; Ahmadi, G. A hybrid algorithm for the university course timetabling problem using the improved parallel genetic algorithm and local search. *Appl. Intell.* **2021**, *51*, 467–492. [CrossRef]
28. Chen, M.C.; Goh, S.L.; Sabar, N.R.; Kendall, G. A survey of university course timetabling problem: Perspectives, trends and opportunities. *IEEE Access* **2021**, *9*, 106515–106529. [CrossRef]
29. Atsuta, M.; Nonobe, K.; Ibaraki, T. ITC2007 Track2: An Approach Using General CSP solver. In Proceedings of the Practice and Theory of Automated Timetabling (PATAT 2008), Montreal, QC, Canada, 19–22 August 2008.
30. Bellio, R.; Ceschia, S.; Di Gaspero, L.; Schaerf, A.; Urli, T. Feature-based tuning of simulated annealing applied to the curriculum-based course timetabling problem. *Comput. Oper. Res.* **2016**, *65*, 83–92. [CrossRef]
31. Lach, G.; Lübbecke, M.E. Curriculum based course timetabling: New solutions to Udine benchmark instances. *Ann. Oper. Res.* **2012**, *194*, 255–272. [CrossRef]
32. Lü, Z.; Hao, J.K. Adaptive tabu search for course timetabling. *Eur. J. Oper. Res.* **2010**, *200*, 235–244. [CrossRef]
33. Pillay, N.; Özcan, E. Automated generation of constructive ordering heuristics for educational timetabling. *Ann. Oper. Res.* **2019**, *275*, 181–208. [CrossRef]
34. Badoni, R.P.; Gupta, D.; Lenka, A.K. A new approach for university timetabling problems. *Int. J. Math. Oper. Res.* **2014**, *6*, 236–257. [CrossRef]
35. Müller, T. ITC2007 solver description: A hybrid approach. *Ann. Oper. Res.* **2009**, *172*, 429–446. [CrossRef]
36. Azlan, A.; Hussin, N.M. Implementing graph coloring heuristic in construction phase of curriculum-based course timetabling problem. In Proceedings of the 2013 IEEE Symposium on Computers & Informatics (ISCI), Langkawi, Malaysia, 7–9 April 2013; pp. 25–29.
37. Rangel-Valdez, N.; Torres-Jimenez, J.; Jasso-Luna, J.O.; Rodriguez-Chavez, M.H. SAT Model for the Curriculum-Based Course Timetabling Problem. *Adv. Soft Comput. Tech.* **2013**, *68*, 45–55. [CrossRef]
38. Wahid, J.; Hussin, N.M. Harmony Search Algorithm for Curriculum-Based Course Timetabling Problem. *Int. J. Soft Comput. Softw. Eng.* **2013**, *3*, 365–371.

39. Clark, M.; Henz, M.; Love, B. Quikfix a Repair-Based Timetable Solver. In Proceedings of the 7th International Conference on the Practice and Theory of Automated Timetabling, PATAT, Montréal, QC, Canada, 18–22 August 2008. Available online: http://www.comp.nus.edu.sg/~henz/publications/ps/PATAT2008.pdf (accessed on 1 July 2023).
40. Petrovic, S.; Burke, E.K. University timetabling. In *Handbook of Scheduling: Algorithms, Models, and Performance Analysis*; Leung, J., Ed.; CRC Press: Boca Raton, FL, USA, 2004; Chapter 45; pp. 1–23.
41. Junaedi, D.; Maulidevi, N.U. Solving Curriculum-Based Course Timetabling Problem with Artificial Bee Colony Algorithm. In Proceedings of the First International Conference on Informatics and Computational Intelligence (ICI), Bandung, Indonesia, 12–14 December 2011; pp. 112–117.
42. Agahian, S.; Pehlivan, H.; Dehkharghani, R. Adaptation and Use of Artificial Bee Colony Algorithm to Solve Curriculum-based Course Time-Tabling Problem. In Proceedings of the Fifth International Conference on Intelligent Systems, Modelling and Simulation (ISMS), Langkawi, Malaysia, 27–29 January 2014; pp. 77–82.
43. Akkan, C.; Gülcü, A. A bi-criteria hybrid Genetic Algorithm with robustness objective for the course timetabling problem. *Comput. Oper. Res.* **2018**, *90*, 22–32. [CrossRef]
44. Banbara, M.; Inoue, K.; Kaufmann, B.; Okimoto, T.; Schaub, T.; Soh, T.; Tamura, N.; Wanko, P. *teaspoon*: Solving the curriculum-based course timetabling problems with answer set programming. *Ann. Oper. Res.* **2019**, *275*, 3–37. [CrossRef]
45. Song, T.; Chen, M.; Xu, Y.; Wang, D.; Song, X.; Tang, X. Competition-guided multi-neighborhood local search algorithm for the university course timetabling problem. *Appl. Soft Comput.* **2021**, *110*, 107624. [CrossRef]
46. Abdipoor, S.; Yaakob, R.; Goh, S.L.; Abdullah, S. Meta-heuristic approaches for the University Course Timetabling Problem. *Intell. Syst. Appl.* **2023**, *19*, 200253. [CrossRef]
47. Papadimitriou, C.H.; Steiglitz, K. *Combinatorial Optimization: Algorithms and Complexity*; Courier Dover Publications: Mineola, NY, USA, 1998.
48. Golberg, D.E. *Genetic Algorithms in Search, Optimization, and Machine Learning*; Addion Wesley: Boston, MA, USA, 1989; Volume 1989.
49. Hageman, J.; Wehrens, R.; Van Sprang, H.; Buydens, L. Hybrid genetic algorithm–Tabu search approach for optimising multilayer optical coatings. *Anal. Chim. Acta* **2003**, *490*, 211–222. [CrossRef]
50. Fatourechi, M.; Bashashati, A.; Ward, R.K.; Birch, G.E. A hybrid genetic algorithm approach for improving the performance of the LF-ASD brain computer interface. In Proceedings of the IEEE International Conference on Acoustics, Speech, and Signal Processing, Philadelphia, PA, USA, 23 March 2005; Volume 5, pp. 345–348.
51. Sastry, K.; Goldberg, D.; Kendall, G. Genetic algorithms. In *Search Methodologies*; Springer: Cham, Switzerland, 2005; pp. 97–125.
52. Datta, D.; Deb, K.; Fonseca, C.M. Multi-objective evolutionary algorithm for university class timetabling problem. In *Evolutionary Scheduling*; Springer: Cham, Switzerland, 2007; pp. 197–236.
53. Lourenço, H.R.; Martin, O.C.; Stützle, T. Iterated Local Search. *Sci. Kluwer* **2002**, *57*, 321–353.
54. Turabieh, H.; Abdullah, S. Incorporating tabu search into memetic approach for enrolment-based course timetabling problems. In Proceedings of the Second Conference on Data Mining and Optimization (DMO'09), Kajand, Malaysia, 27–28 October 2009; pp. 115–119.
55. Abdullah, S.; Burke, E.K.; McCollum, B. Using a randomised iterative improvement algorithm with composite neighbourhood structures for the university course timetabling problem. In *Metaheuristics*; Springer: Cham, Switzerland, 2007; pp. 153–169.
56. Mcmullan, P. An extended implementation of the great deluge algorithm for course timetabling. In Proceedings of the International Conference on Computational Science (ICCS'07), Beijing, China, 27–30 May 2007; Springer: Cham, Switzerland, 2007; pp. 538–545.
57. Landa-Silva, D.; Obit, J.H. Great deluge with non-linear decay rate for solving course timetabling problems. In Proceedings of the Fourth International Conference on Intelligent Systems (IS'08), Varna, Bulgaria, 6–8 September 2008; Volume 1, pp. 8–11.
58. Obit, J.; Landa-Silva, D.; Ouelhadj, D.; Sevaux, M. Non-linear great deluge with learning mechanism for solving the course timetabling problem. In Proceedings of the Eighth Metaheuristics International Conference (MIC'09), Hamburg, Germany, 13–16 July 2009.
59. Turabieh, H.; Abdullah, S.; McCollum, B.; McMullan, P. Fish swarm intelligent algorithm for the course timetabling problem. In *Rough Set and Knowledge Technology*; Springer: Cham, Switzerland, 2010; pp. 588–595.
60. Abuhamdah, A.; Ayob, M. MPCA-ARDA for solving course timetabling problems. In Proceedings of the Third Conference on Data Mining and Optimization (DMO'11), Putrajaya, Malaysia, 28–29 June 2011; pp. 171–177.
61. Bolaji, A.L.; Khader, A.T.; Al-Betar, M.A.; Awadallah, M.A. University course timetabling using hybridized artificial bee colony with hill climbing optimizer. *J. Comput. Sci.* **2014**, *5*, 809–818. [CrossRef]
62. Fong, C.W.; Asmuni, H.; McCollum, B.; McMullan, P.; Omatu, S. A new hybrid imperialist swarm-based optimization algorithm for university timetabling problems. *Inf. Sci.* **2014**, *283*, 1–21. [CrossRef]
63. Al-Betar, M.A.; Khader, A.T.; Zaman, M. University course timetabling using a hybrid harmony search metaheuristic algorithm. *IEEE Trans. Syst. Man Cybern. Part Appl. Rev.* **2012**, *42*, 664–681. [CrossRef]
64. Lohpetch, D.; Jaengchuea, S. A hybrid multi-objective genetic algorithm with a new local search approach for solving the post enrolment based course timetabling problem. In *Recent Advances in Information and Communication Technology 2016*; Springer: Cham, Switzerland, 2016; pp. 195–206.

65. Geiger, M.J. Applying the threshold accepting metaheuristic to curriculum based course timetabling. *Ann. Oper. Res.* **2012**, *194*, 189–202. [CrossRef]
66. De Cesco, F.; Di Gaspero, L.; Schaerf, A. Benchmarking Curriculum-Based Course Timetabling: Formulations, Data Formats, Instances, Validation, and Results. In Proceedings of the 7th international Conference on the Practice and Theory of Automated Timetabling, PATAT, Montréal, QC, Canada, 18–22 August 2008.
67. Lach, G.; Lübbecke, M. Curriculum based course timetabling: Optimal solutions to the udine benchmark instances. In Proceedings of the Seventh International Conference on the Practice and Theory of Automated Timetabling, Montréal, QC, Canada, 18–22 August 2008.
68. Abdullah, S.; Turabieh, H. On the use of multi neighbourhood structures within a Tabu-based memetic approach to university timetabling problems. *Inf. Sci.* **2012**, *191*, 146–168. [CrossRef]
69. Bellio, R.; Di Gaspero, L.; Schaerf, A. Design and statistical analysis of a hybrid local search algorithm for course timetabling. *J. Sched.* **2012**, *15*, 49–61. [CrossRef]
70. Bagger, N.C.F.; Kristiansen, S.; Sørensen, M.; Stidsen, T.R. Flow formulations for curriculum-based course timetabling. *Ann. Oper. Res.* **2019**, *280*, 121–150. [CrossRef]
71. Kiefer, A.; Hartl, R.F.; Schnell, A. Adaptive large neighborhood search for the curriculum-based course timetabling problem. *Ann. Oper. Res.* **2017**, *252*, 255–282. [CrossRef]
72. Gozali, A.A.; Kurniawan, B.; Weng, W.; Fujimura, S. Solving university course timetabling problem using localized island model genetic algorithm with dual dynamic migration policy. *IEEJ Trans. Electr. Electron. Eng.* **2020**, *15*, 389–400. [CrossRef]
73. Kazakovtsev, L.A.; Gudyma, M.N.; Antamoshkin, A.N. Genetic Algorithm with Greedy Heuristic for Capacity Planning. In Proceedings of the International Congress on Ultra Modern Telecommunications and Control Systems and Workshops, St. Petersburg, Russia, 6–8 October 2014; pp. 607–613.
74. Kazakovtsev, L.; Kovlovskaya, E.; Rozhnov, I.; Patsuk, O. A genetic algorithm with greedy crossover and elitism for capacity planning. *Facta Univ. Ser. Math. Inform.* **2023**, *37*, 993–1006.

Disclaimer/Publisher's Note: The statements, opinions and data contained in all publications are solely those of the individual author(s) and contributor(s) and not of MDPI and/or the editor(s). MDPI and/or the editor(s) disclaim responsibility for any injury to people or property resulting from any ideas, methods, instructions or products referred to in the content.

MDPI
St. Alban-Anlage 66
4052 Basel
Switzerland
www.mdpi.com

Axioms Editorial Office
E-mail: axioms@mdpi.com
www.mdpi.com/journal/axioms

Disclaimer/Publisher's Note: The statements, opinions and data contained in all publications are solely those of the individual author(s) and contributor(s) and not of MDPI and/or the editor(s). MDPI and/or the editor(s) disclaim responsibility for any injury to people or property resulting from any ideas, methods, instructions or products referred to in the content.

www.ingramcontent.com/pod-product-compliance
Lightning Source LLC
LaVergne TN
LVHW070719100526
838202LV00013B/1128